# WATER LAW

## IN A NUTSHELL®

SEVENTH EDITION

SANDRA B. ZELLMER
Professor of Law
University of Montana
Alexander Blewett III School of Law

ADELL L. AMOS
Clayton R. Hess Professor of Law
University of Oregon School of Law

MELISSA K. SCANLAN
Professor and Lynde B. Uihlein Endowed Chair
Director of the Center for Water Policy
School of Freshwater Sciences
University of Wisconsin, Milwaukee

WEST ACADEMIC

860 Blue Gentian Road, Suite 350
Eagan, MN 55121
1-877-888-1330



Published in the United States of America

**ISBN:** 979-8-89545-969-0

*This book is dedicated to*
*David Getches*
*Mentor, Leader, Scholar, and Inspiration*
*to generations of water lawyers*

# ACKNOWLEDGMENTS

The authors are deeply grateful to David Getches for his guidance and his monumental contribution to the field of water law.

Sandra Zellmer is indebted to her long-time mentor in water and natural resources law, John D. Leshy. She also thanks the University of Montana School of Law for its summer scholarship stipend.

Adell Amos would like to thank students at University of Oregon School of Law for their work on this edition—Abigail Dompier who served as our project manager, Alicia Davis, Charles Gearing, Jay Everett, and Max McCool.

Melissa Scanlan thanks School of Freshwater Sciences master student, Daniel McLennon, esq., for his project management and research; and Sea Grant UW Water Science-Policy Fellow, Emma Ehrlich, Esq., for her research assistance.

SANDRA ZELLMER
ADELL AMOS
MELISSA SCANLAN

# FOREWORD TO THE SEVENTH EDITION

It is somewhat unusual for an area of law to be defined by a particular resource, but water is unique in the diversity and importance of the needs it fills. Water quenches our thirst, gives life to essential food crops, furnishes habitat to fish and wildlife, produces power, and satisfies recreational and aesthetic needs. Although it is one of the most plentiful substances, it is considered precious because there is not always enough fresh water of the right quality in the right place at the right time. There is keen competition among water users. The same stream may be sought by a municipality for domestic use, a farmer for irrigation, a factory for carrying away waste, a power plant for cooling, boaters and fishers for recreation, and conservation interests for preservation of stream flows and the fish and wildlife species that rely on them.

A decision to use water for a particular purpose can have far-reaching impacts. For instance, transporting water from a rural area across a mountain range to a city may provide water to sustain the city's population, but it may also force a decline in agricultural productivity and the farming community built on it, facilitate more rapid growth in the importing city, prevent future development of the exporting rural area, curtail recreational opportunities, make sewage treatment more difficult as streamflows to dilute wastewater discharges are diminished, deprive the exporting area of groundwater recharge, and cause ecological changes in both areas. Balancing these conflicting interests and demands is made ever more complex, challenging, and essential in the face of chronic drought cycles intensified by climate change.

The role of law is particularly important when so many varied needs must be recognized. More and more lawyers will be called upon to recognize and to resolve water rights conflicts. Although law students are the primary audience of this Nutshell, the growing demand for and interest among lawyers addressing water-related legal issues has guided us in preparing this edition.

This book is designed to support water law courses based on the major casebooks in the field, including Thompson, Leshy, Abrams & Zellmer, *Legal Control of Water Resources* (6th ed. 2018); Benson, Griggs & Tarlock, *Water Resources Management* (8th ed. 2021); Weber, Harder, and Beardon, *Cases and Materials on Water Law* (10th ed. 2020); and Adler, Craig, and Hall, *Modern Water Law* (2d ed. 2018). Nearly every principal case in each of the casebooks is discussed or at least cited. Much of the organizational scheme of the fifth edition has been retained, but we have taken some liberties to clarify, streamline, and highlight important emerging issues, such as the public trust doctrine, climate change, environmental interests, environmental justice and equity, non-consumptive uses of water, federal reserved rights for tribal and public lands, conjunctive use and management of surface and groundwater resources, and interstate and international themes. Throughout the book, we have strived to remain true to the vision of Professor Getches. We are honored—and humbled—by the opportunity to follow in his footsteps, though of course we would never purport to fill his shoes.

SBZ
ALA
MKS

Missoula, Montana
Eugene, Oregon
Milwaukee, Wisconsin
October 2025

# OUTLINE

# TABLE OF CASES

**References are to Pages**

---

# WATER LAW
## IN A NUTSHELL®
SEVENTH EDITION

# CHAPTER ONE

# OVERVIEW AND INTRODUCTION TO WATER LAW

## I. THE STUDY OF WATER LAW

The study of water law is, at one level, the study of property concepts, though rights to use water are unique. The fact that water is a moving and shared resource necessarily limits traditional concepts of ownership. Although water laws differ widely among jurisdictions, substantial public rights in the resource is a major theme across allocation regimes and throughout history. One result is that lawmakers have superimposed administrative systems in an attempt to regulate private interests in the use of water and to advance the broader public interest. Accordingly, the study of water law in the modern era requires a deep understanding of state and federal administrative law.

The field of water law also includes a study of the legal process. In many areas, the law is well-developed and it changes slowly, but water law is a comparatively dynamic field. It illustrates how courts, legislatures, and agencies create and alter law according to physical and societal stimuli: one set of conditions drove the initial development of water law in the eastern United States, but different circumstances provoked changes in the West.

Three central questions arise in the study of water law: (1) how do the established legal systems for allocating rights to use water compare; (2) how well do these systems perform in equitably allocating this precious resource; and (3) what are appropriate solutions to the unresolved issues in water law. The law's success—in any field, but especially in water law—has to be evaluated in terms of what society needs from it.

We ask a great deal of water law. Since we depend on water for so much, it touches our deepest values. Besides its commercial importance, it is at the core of things we care the most about, such as health, sustenance, ecological integrity, recreation, and aesthetics. It even can provide community identity and spiritual satisfaction. Is it possible for any legal system to fulfill all these values and to provide stability and fairness? With so much at stake, water law presents unparalleled opportunities for analysis and creativity. It is an evolving field bristling with conflicts among our most cherished values.

## II. PUBLIC RIGHTS

Most water law casebooks and other texts are organized to address private interests in water first. The chapters of this Nutshell follow that pattern; however, this introductory chapter opens with a discussion of public rights associated with water use and management. Understanding the public nature of waterways, water resources, and water law and policy before diving into private interests and allocation provides a useful analytical framework.

Water is a public resource with shared and overlapping uses. Although private property rights can be perfected in the use of water, water remains essentially public; private rights are always incomplete and subject to the public's common needs. The earliest expression of these needs, still viable, involved navigation. Navigable waters remain subject to public access and use for boating, fishing, hunting, and, more recently, recreational and aesthetic interests. Private activity affecting the quantity and quality of water cannot lawfully interfere with the overriding public interest.

The special public rights that exist in the use of the surface of waterways, and the government's power and responsibility to recognize and maintain those rights, are addressed in Chapter Seven. Public rights often turn on the definition of navigability, which is also the point of reference for ownership of the beds of waterways. More recently, public rights in groundwater and non-navigable waters have also been recognized, often based on their capacity to support recreation and other public rights. Concerns about environmental quality, hydropower, and flood control are also covered in Chapter Seven.

When private interests are impacted by public rights, landowners and holders of water rights may assert claims for compensation under the Fifth Amendment takings clause of the U.S. Constitution or similar provisions of state constitutions. Takings claims are addressed in relevant sections of various chapters throughout this book, including Chapter Seven (Navigable Waters), as well as Chapters Three (Prior Appropriation), Four (Hybrid Systems), and Five (Groundwater).

## III. LEGAL SYSTEMS FOR SURFACE WATER ALLOCATION

American jurisdictions can be grouped roughly into three legal systems governing private rights to use surface water: riparian; prior appropriation; and hybrid states. This book treats the systems separately, so that readers may focus attention on issues within the system of particular interest. These systems, however, overlap and borrow from one another so it is useful to compare them. Moreover, in operation, nearly all states rely on some sort of permitting regime administered by a state agency, some of which share common attributes regardless of the particular doctrine followed in the state.

### A. RIPARIAN RIGHTS

Landowners bordering a waterway are considered riparians. Their location gives them certain appurtenant rights under the laws of most states. Historically, a riparian location had special advantages because it enabled the owner to operate water-driven mills, to consume reasonable quantities of water, and to access the water's surface for boating, hunting, and fishing. There is generally no right to use water on non-riparian land.

Theoretically, early American decisions subscribed to a "natural flow" rule that gave every riparian owner the right to have water flow past the land undiminished in quantity or quality. This restrictive rule appeared to bar all consumption. From some of the earliest cases, the courts tempered the doctrine with "reasonable use" principles. Besides making exceptions for domestic uses, the courts showed concern for existing users. Today, all riparian doctrine states (mostly located in the eastern United States) permit riparians to use water in a way that is "reasonable" relative to other users. If there is insufficient water to satisfy the reasonable needs of all riparians, all must reduce their usage in proportion to their rights.

Because riparian rights inhere in land ownership, they need not be exercised to be kept alive. Thus, a landowner may initiate new uses at any time and other users must adjust their uses accordingly. Flexibility is one of the advantages of a riparian system; however, uncertainty is a key disadvantage.

The riparian doctrine, which is covered in Chapter Two, still applies to some extent in most of the eastern states, and it has some viability in the hybrid states covered in Chapter Four. However, riparian rules have been altered extensively by statute and case law so that no modern riparian state is governed simply by common law. Typically, riparians must obtain permits from a state agency in order to use water. In some states, permits may also be available to non-riparians.

Regardless of the legal doctrine that any particular state has adopted for allocating rights to use water, riparian landowners in all states have special rights to make use of the surface of waters adjoining their property. However, as Chapter Seven explains, if the waterway is considered navigable, riparians must tolerate certain surface uses by the public.

## B. PRIOR APPROPRIATION

Two factors distinguish the legal system governing the use of surface water in the West. First, the West was settled on lands occupied by indigenous peoples and then owned by the federal government; private and state ownership of land arose *after* many uses of water had commenced. Moreover, water is much scarcer throughout the arid lands west of the one-hundredth meridian.

The early miners, notably in California, sought water for their placer mining operations on the public lands. Miners could not assert riparian rights because they did not own the land. So the miners simply followed the same rule they used in resolving disputes over the minerals on the public domain: "first in time, first in right." The earliest miner to put the water to work had a right to continue using it to the exclusion of others.

Early court decisions in the West recognized water rights based on the miners' customs. The system worked satisfactorily for farmers, too, and became entrenched in the laws of virtually every western state. Rights, then, belong to anyone who puts water to a "beneficial use" anywhere (on riparian or non-riparian land), with superiority over anyone who later begins using water. Unlike riparian law, appropriative water rights depend on usage and not on land ownership. Once a person puts water to a beneficial use and complies with any statutory requirements, a water right is perfected and remains valid so long as it continues to be used.

Given a choice between riparian and appropriation law, western states realized that riparian law, at least in its theoretical rigidity, did not fit local needs. Mines and farms needing water could not always be located on riparian lands in a region where waterways are few and far between. Development would have been frustrated if the fortunate landowners along streams could monopolize scarce water and hoard it, unused, until they felt like putting it to some use.

The prior appropriation doctrine governs surface water rights in about a dozen western states. As Chapter Three details, all "pure" appropriation states except Colorado require permits to appropriate water. An administrative agency issues permits based on requirements designed to protect other water users. Most state agencies also consider public interest concerns. Permits to transfer or change appropriative rights may be issued if the ability of others to exercise vested water rights is not impaired.

## C. HYBRID SYSTEMS

Several states originally recognized riparian rights, but later converted to a system of appropriation while preserving existing riparian rights. California is the leading hybrid state. Oklahoma, Texas, and several others maintain aspects of both prior appropriation and riparianism. Hybrid systems are addressed in Chapter Four. Hawaii's system is a unique combination of rights established under laws of the ancient Hawaiian Kingdom and recent statutes. Louisiana's water law is atypical as well, as it is adapted from the French Civil Code. It is excluded from coverage in this volume.

## IV. SPECIAL TYPES OF WATER

Most surface water available for use is subject to one of the three allocation schemes listed above, but certain waters fall outside those systems.

### A. GROUNDWATER

Groundwater law grapples with two dominant concerns: depletion of essentially nonrenewable stores of underground water and conflicts among competing well-owners. In addition, groundwater contamination problems and the impacts of groundwater pumping on hydrologically connected surface water resources are increasingly troubling.

Vast underground resources supply much of the nation's needs. The law was slow to develop systems for the allocation of rights to groundwater. Until recently, the dynamics of groundwater occurrence and movement were considered too uncertain, even too mysterious, to try to regulate. The failure of states to deal comprehensively with groundwater left overlying owners free to extract water from under their lands as they pleased.

Even when water beneath the surface of land was connected with a stream or lake, the law treated groundwater under a separate set of rules or no rules at all. More progressive approaches now integrate groundwater and surface water management. For example, if pumping from a well affects the rights of those using stream water, many states will administer the groundwater as a part of the surface water allocation system.

Special rules are needed for groundwater management because waters are often withdrawn at a faster rate than they are replenished. Moreover, new wells may endanger existing wells by pumping groundwater from the same portion of the aquifer, even when the aquifer as a whole is not being withdrawn in excess of recharge rates. Some systems for allocating rights in groundwater are analogous to riparian rights (*e.g.*, correlative interests in water underlying neighboring parcels), while others are more like prior appropriation (*e.g.*, older wells are protected against depletion by newer pumpers).

Surface water allocation schemes, however, do not fit the physical realities of groundwater because they do not prevent rapid draining of an aquifer or protect the interests of neighboring pumpers. For example, appropriation concepts, if strictly applied, would give such complete protection to the first pumper that almost any new use could cause harm and be subject to legal objections. Consequently, special groundwater rules have been developed to balance competing interests of new and old well users and overlying owners, and to fulfill the state's obligation to prolong the life of the resource while allowing efficient usage. Many jurisdictions base their rules of liability between pumpers, and their criteria for granting permits for new wells, on a reasonable use standard, requiring that the relative utility of uses and equities of the parties be weighed. Groundwater laws are covered in Chapter Five.

### B. DIFFUSED SURFACE WATER

Ordinarily, only waters in natural streams are subject to surface water allocation systems. Water that is on the surface of land as runoff from rainfall or snowmelt, and has not yet joined a distinct watercourse, is called diffused surface water; it is generally not subject to water allocation rules.

Nearly all states allow diffused surface waters to be captured and used by a landowner without state regulation or limitation. However, legal rules concerning diffused surface waters were developed to determine liability between landowners when one attempts to drain such waters away from their property, thereby causing flooding and other problems for neighboring landowners. A majority of states allow landowners to divert or channel floodwaters away from their land if it is reasonable under the circumstances. These matters are covered in Chapter Six.

## V. INTERGOVERNMENTAL PROBLEMS

Although the creation and regulation of rights to use water are primarily state affairs, there are important spheres of federal control. As noted above, federal navigational projects may affect the way state water laws operate; state and private interests may also be impacted by other exercises of congressional power, ranging from water development projects to environmental laws. In addition, the federal government has an interest in waters for use on public lands that have been reserved for special purposes, like parks, forests, and military bases, as well as lands held for federally recognized Indian reservations. The allocation of interstate water bodies is also governed by federal law.

## A. RESERVED RIGHTS

The doctrine of federal reserved rights traces back to early litigation over water for Indian reservations. The Supreme Court held that Indian tribes could not be deprived of sufficient water supplies to make the reservation a viable place to live and to farm. The reserved rights doctrine recognizes a right to sufficient water to fulfill the purposes of the reservation. The same principle was later applied to federal reservations of public lands.

Reserved water rights, which are covered in Chapter Eight, have a priority as of the date the reservation was established, whether or not water has ever been used. In a system in which water rights are based on prior use, reserved water rights can cause dislocations among those whose water rights have a priority date later than the establishment of the reservation. In response, some courts have narrowly construed the extent of rights reserved and Congress has allowed reserved rights to be quantified in state courts in general stream adjudications.

## B. FEDERAL ACTIONS AFFECTING STATE WATER RIGHTS

The United States is involved in activities that sometimes affect, and because of federal supremacy, preempt state water law. In the first sixty or seventy years of the twentieth century, the federal role in water resources involved giving technical and financial support to states and managing large water development projects for navigation, flood control, agriculture, power generation, and other uses. Since the 1970s, the federal government's involvement with water has turned away from development and become more focused on environmental regulation. Today, federal laws that protect endangered species, wetlands, and water quality are at least as important as state water laws in shaping water development and use. These laws are covered in Chapter 7.VI and in other locations throughout this book.

## C. INTERSTATE AND INTERNATIONAL ISSUES

Tensions frequently arise among states and countries that share access to rivers, lakes, and groundwater sources. Chapter Nine covers the various methods for resolving these tensions.

Allocations among states can be made by compact—a negotiated interstate agreement made with the consent of Congress—or by adjudication. In one instance, Congress passed legislation effectively allocating waters of the Colorado River among the abutting states, demonstrating a third means for interstate allocation.

In attempting to protect their water resources, states may not improperly inhibit interstate commerce by placing limits on exports. Water is considered an article of commerce and, as such, trade in it cannot be restricted by regulations that discriminate against interstate commerce.

In the international context, principles of territorial sovereignty and equitable apportionment generally govern the resolution of water disputes. Chapter Nine discusses notable treaties, conventions, and other forms of international dispute resolution.

## VI. WATER INSTITUTIONS AND EQUITY

Chapter Ten describes various types of organizations formed to develop and distribute water, ranging from public municipal water systems to private irrigation districts. These organizations come in many different forms and may be established under state or federal law. They are the operating entities that deliver most of the water in the country.

The approaches and priorities adopted by water management institutions raise important issues related to the inequities of distribution and access to sufficient supplies in the quantity and quality needed. These concerns are addressed in Chapter Ten. Chapter Ten also covers federal water management institutions, namely, the Bureau of Reclamation and the Army Corps of Engineers.

# CHAPTER TWO
# RIPARIAN RIGHTS

The term "riparian" is based on the Latin word for the bank of a stream (*ripa*). Thus, riparian rights to water exist for those who own land adjacent to a water source. In the eastern United States, primarily east of the one-hundredth meridian (a line running south through the middle of North Dakota into Texas), water rights are established based on principles of riparianism. Other states, primarily those west of or along the one-hundredth meridian, have a hybrid system based on some combination of riparian and prior appropriation doctrines. *See infra* Chapters 4–5.

Riparian law developed as a common law doctrine. In a riparian jurisdiction, the owner of land bordering a waterbody (*i.e.*, the riparian owner), may make reasonable use of the water on the riparian land if the use does not interfere with reasonable uses of other riparian owners. Today, many riparian states have codified at least some principles of the common law into various statutory provisions. Some states have adopted more comprehensive statutory provisions and are commonly referred to as "regulated riparian" jurisdictions—these jurisdictions typically authorize state agencies to play a significant role in allocating and enforcing water rights.

# I. HISTORY OF THE RIPARIAN DOCTRINE

## A. EUROPEAN PRECEDENTS

Prior to the eighteenth century, most U.S. water cases involved rights of navigation and fishing. The natural flow doctrine, which entitled each riparian owner to the enjoyment of the watercourse without interference from others, governed early notions of water rights. The dawn of the Industrial Revolution, and the consequent increase in water-driven mills, created a need for uniform principles of law that could be applied in the growing number of water disputes concerned with access to the flow of the stream and the quantity and quality of water available for particular uses. The riparian doctrine, with deep origins in the Institutes of Justinian from Roman law as well as English common law and the French civil code, soon emerged in American courts.

The Institutes of Justinian, published in 533–34 A.D., held that running water was a part of the "negative community" of things that could not be owned, similar to the air, seas, and wildlife. At the same time, Roman law recognized that such things could be used through so-called usufructuary rights, a legal principle of water law that survives today. "Usufruct" is the right to use the advantages of the resource without over-exploitation. Modern U.S. law refers to water rights as usufructuary rights—rights to use without altering the fundamental nature of the resource. The Institutes declared that the right to use water belonged only to those who had access to the water by virtue of their ownership of riparian land.

Others could not gain access without committing a trespass, unless the stream was on the public domain. France codified this doctrine in 1804 with the promulgation of the Napoleonic Code.

The early English law of water rights was a mix of "ancient" or "prior" use, infused with to concepts of prescription, and "natural flow". In one case, the court applied the "prior use" doctrine to rule that one riparian could not use or divert water if the effect would be to deprive a prior user of water. This principle protected earlier mills from interference by newer mills. *See, e.g.*, Bealey v. Shaw, 102 Eng. Rep. 1266 (Eng. 1805). Other decisions embraced a "natural flow" theory, under which every riparian landowner had an equal right to use water in the stream and a duty not to diminish the quantity of water otherwise flowing to proprietors lower on the stream. Wright v. Howard, 1 Sim. St. 190 (Eng. 1823).

While English law influenced the early U.S. states, later, English judges borrowed from the opinions of American Justices Story and Kent, and incorporated the "reasonable use" theory, in large part because "natural flow" unduly restricted important new industrial users. Mason v. Hill, 110 E.R. 692 (Eng. 1833). Reasonable use principles modified the natural flow theory by allowing each riparian user to make all reasonable uses of the waters so long as those uses did not interfere with the reasonable uses of other riparian users.

## B. DEVELOPMENT IN THE EASTERN UNITED STATES

After the Revolutionary War, each state began developing its own common law for water allocation. The sparse population of European settlers lived mostly on the eastern seaboard, a rainy area with abundant streams and rivers. Some states, including Connecticut and Massachusetts, had few restrictions on the use of streams and allowed diversions of water if the surplus was returned to the stream. Other states, such as New Jersey, adopted a type of natural flow rule that allowed a riparian landowner to make use of the stream in its natural state, but prohibited any diversion that might materially reduce the flow to another. Farrell v. Richards, 30 N.J. Eq. 511 (N.J.Ch. 1879); Martin v. Bigelow, 2 Aik. 184 16 Am. Dec. 696 (Vt. 1827).

As America grew in the nineteenth century, large mills required reservoirs for storage, and at the same time, irrigation and industry needed to use water in areas away from the stream banks. Consequently, the notion of preserving the natural flow of streams for each user conflicted with economic development. Against this backdrop, the famous case of Tyler v. Wilkinson, 24 F.Cas. 472 (C.C.R.I. 1827), was decided. The Tylers were riparian proprietors with mills near a small dam used to impound water so that it would flow faster past their mills once it was released. The Wilkinsons constructed a dam upstream and diverted water into a trench that began above the Tylers' mills. The Wilkinsons' water use thus deprived the downstream Tylers of the flow of water they otherwise would have stored behind their dam. Justice Story held that, while the Tylers had a right to the natural flow of the river, any rights to water for the dam and mills would have to be based on "actual appropriation and use." Justice Story stated that all riparian users had an equal right to use the balance of the water naturally flowing in the stream and, departing from the natural flow doctrine, held that each riparian was entitled to make a reasonable use of the waters.

Many courts in the United States followed suit and shifted from the natural flow theory to reasonable use principles. *See* Snow v. Parsons, 28 Vt. 459 (Vt. 1856) (holding that courts should determine reasonableness based on the facts of the case and remanding to determine whether an upstream tannery that released so much debris that the downstream mill could not function was a reasonable use). Over time, cases involving one riparian landowner suing another over the reasonableness of a particular use of water further developed and enforced riparian law. These common law rights to make reasonable use of water flowing past one's land were limited to using the water on the riparian lands.

As population and development increased, demand for limited supplies also increased, resulting in an increase in the number and frequency of disputes over water. Ultimately, these conflicts and the desire to be more proactive in water allocation, including allowing the use of water on non-riparian lands, led many eastern states to adopt statutory permit systems for some or all water uses. Legal scholarship now refers to these states as regulated riparian jurisdictions. The permit systems in these jurisdictions reflect many of the judicial factors for determining "reasonableness" from the common law. *See infra* Section III of this chapter.

## C. THE ROLE OF RIPARIAN LAW IN THE AMERICAN WEST

Many regions west of the one-hundredth meridian considered the riparian doctrine to be impractical. As European settlers moved west, they built their livelihood on mining or homesteading, both of which required access to water. The eastern riparian system, which limited water rights to the owners of land bordering on a watercourse, would have stifled development in a region where so few parcels were riparian. Further, the federal government owned most western land, so the early miners and homesteaders were often trespassers on the public domain, with no riparian rights. Since many of the most promising mineral deposits were far from any stream, many mines could not operate without transporting water to the site.

The arid landscape resulted in the early miners developing their own customary law that recognized the right of individuals to divert water to mines that were not riparian to the water source. Access to water became an issue of timeliness, rather than location. This developing western customary law allowed anyone to divert water on a "first come, first served" basis, if they did not deprive "prior appropriators" of the quantity of water they were already diverting for themselves. *See infra* Chapter Three. While some western states initially adopted riparian rights, many eventually phased them out. The few "hybrid" states that preserved pre-existing riparian rights still apply riparian law in certain situations. California is an example of such a state. Herminghaus v. Southern California Edison Co., 252 P. 607 (Cal. 1926) (applying the reasonable use doctrine between riparian users, but *not* between riparian and appropriative users.) In response to *Herminghaus*, in 1976 Californians amended the state constitution to apply the reasonable use doctrine to *all* water rights. Cal. Const. art. X, § 2. *See infra* Chapter Four.

## II. CONTOURS OF THE RIPARIAN DOCTRINE

Under the riparian doctrine, rights attach to riparian land (*i.e.,* land bordering on a natural stream or lake) by virtue of its location. The riparian landowner does not actually own the water or the watercourse but instead holds numerous usufructuary rights to it. These usufructuary rights include: the right to the flow of the stream; the right to make a reasonable use of the waterbody, provided reasonable uses of other riparian users are not injured; the right of access to the waterbody; the right to fish; the right to wharf out; the right to prevent erosion of the banks; the right to purity of the water; and the right to claim title to the beds of non-navigable lakes and streams.

However, principles of public ownership and state and federal regulation limit many of these usufructuary rights. Public rights to use the surface of certain waterways further limit riparian rights. At common law, all persons had the right to travel any navigable waterbody for fishing and commerce. Today, public rights also include recreation, ecological health and scenic beauty, and some states have extended public rights to non-navigable waters and groundwater. *See infra* Chapter Seven and Section II.D.8 of this chapter. Use of water in place for instream or non-consumptive uses has substantial modern importance and may be recognized judicially in pure riparian jurisdictions or by statute in regulated riparian jurisdictions.

The ownership of riparian land creates rights and duties. Each riparian landowner has a duty to refrain from interfering with the rights of fellow riparian users under the reasonable use doctrine.

## A. THE BASIS FOR RIPARIAN RIGHTS—RIPARIAN LAND

In a pure riparian jurisdiction, only the owner of riparian land acquires rights to make use of the adjacent watercourse. This section defines what constitutes riparian land, the types of water bodies to which the owner of adjacent land may hold rights, and how subdividing riparian land impacts water rights. While all parcels of land are part of a watershed and are directly or indirectly connected to surrounding bodies of water, not all land is riparian. The law distinguishes between riparian land and non-riparian land based on ownership. Only the owner of a parcel of land touching a watercourse—contiguous with the water's edge—has riparian rights. Restatement (Second) of Torts § 843. These riparian rights do not extend to any portion of a parcel that is outside the immediate watershed of the watercourse.

## 1. Defining Riparian Land

### *a. Watershed Limitation*

Riparian rights attach only to an owner's land within the watershed. Town of Gordonsville v. Zinn, 106 S.E. 508 (Va. 1921). Thus, neither a non-contiguous parcel of land owned by a riparian landowner nor a portion of a riparian tract that is in another watershed qualifies for riparian rights.

Most jurisdictions consider use outside the watershed of origin to be unreasonable per se, though many will not enjoin it unless another riparian is actually harmed. While some jurisdictions bar all use of water outside the watershed, others permit it, subject to the reasonable use restriction. *See, e.g.*, Rancho Santa Margarita v. Vail, 81 P.2d 533 (Cal. 1938) (riparian rights only attach to use in the watershed); Pyle v. Gilbert, 265 S.E.2d 584 (Ga. 1980) (one can acquire the right to reasonable use on non-riparian land) *overruled on other grounds*, Tunison v. Harper, 690 S.E.2d 819 (Ga. 2010). Long-standing non-watershed use may ripen into a prescriptive right. *See infra* Section II.E.3.

### b. Divisions of Riparian Land

A conveyance of riparian land carries with it all the appurtenant riparian rights unless those rights have been severed. The extent to which a grantor may reserve these rights or convey them to a grantee are discussed in Section II.E of this chapter. Riparian rights attach only to waterfront land. Consequently, when a riparian owner conveys a parcel of land that is not on the water, riparian rights no longer attach to the conveyed parcel. If the parcels are reunited under common ownership, the parcel of land that is not on the water may remain without riparian rights, depending on which of the following rules prevails in the jurisdiction.

#### *i. Unity of Title Rule*

Under the unity of title rule, an entire tract of land fronting on a waterway held by a single owner is entitled to riparian rights. It does not matter that a landowner had earlier divided the land into several parcels, some of which did not front on the waterway. Thus, all land contiguous to a riparian parcel that is held by the same riparian landowner has riparian rights regardless of when or from whom the contiguous lands were conveyed. For example, Jones severs riparian land, retains the non-riparian lot, and conveys the riparian plot to Smith. Only Smith has the riparian rights. Under the unity of title rule, if Smith later re-conveys the riparian plot back to Jones, the entire tract (both plots) would again have riparian rights. Most riparian states follow this rule.

### *ii. Source of Title Rule*

Under the source of title rule (also called the "smallest tract rule"), riparian rights attach only to the smallest subdivision of waterfront land in the chain of title leading to the present owner. Thus, even if the original riparian owner later reacquires the tract, only the smallest parcel with frontage on the waterway has riparian rights; any land severed from contact with the waterway by conveyance can never regain riparian rights. Under this rule, the amount of riparian land shrinks as conveyances sever waterfront lands from uplands. For example, Jones conveys a portion of a tract of riparian land—the part bordering the stream—to Smith. No riparian rights remain with non-riparian tract. Under the source of title rule, if Smith later re-conveys the riparian plot back to Jones, riparian rights will not reattach to the non-riparian plot.

While most riparian states follow the unity of title rule, many western states apply the source of title rule. In these states, the fact that the water rights may be acquired by appropriation for the severed parcels tempers the apparent harshness of reducing the amount of land subject to riparian rights. The rule furthers the policy, typical in hybrid jurisdictions, of minimizing the reach of riparian rights and building a reliable system based on prior appropriation.

## 2. Types of Watercourses

To have riparian rights, a landowner must own property adjacent to or abutting a source of water that fits the definition of a "watercourse." The term "watercourse" may include natural streams, lakes, ponds, springs, marshes, so-called underground streams, and other natural waterways, as well as artificial bodies of water made by humans. Each state has its own body of law that sets forth which waters are included within the definition of a watercourse.

In contrast, diffused surface water is not subject to riparian rights until it enters a watercourse. Diffused surface water is water that flows intermittently over the land without a defined channel and includes the runoff from rain or melted snow. Borgmann v. Florissant Dev. Co., 515 S.W.2d 189 (Mo. Ct. App. 1974). The rules applicable to diffused surface water are covered in Chapter Six.

### *a. Streams*

A natural stream is a watercourse that flows constantly or recurrently on the surface of the earth in a reasonably definite channel. A stream may originate or flow through a spring, lake, or marsh. An early Maine case described a stream as a water body that "flows in a particular direction; and by a regular channel, having a bed with banks and sides; and (usually) discharging itself into some other body or stream of water. . . It need not flow continuously; but it must have a well defined and substantial existence." Morrison v. Bucksport and Bangor R.R. Co., 67 Me. 353, 356 (Me. 1877). However, because streams are so varied in form, it is difficult to provide a more precise definition, and the determination of whether flowing water is or is not a stream is often highly fact intensive.

### *b. Lakes and Ponds*

Lakes and ponds are also watercourses subject to riparian rights. A lake is defined as a reasonably permanent body of water substantially at rest in a depression in the surface of the earth, if both the depression and the body of water are of natural origin or part of a watercourse. Libby, McNeil & Libby v. Roberts, 110 So. 2d 82 (Fla. Dist. Ct. App. 1959). A person who owns land bordering on a lake is sometimes referred to as a "littoral" landowner, Jowers v. S.C. Dep't of Health & Env't. Control, 815 S.E.2d 446, 452 n.7 (S.C. 2018), but can also be called a "riparian," 2000 Baum Family Trust v. Babel, 793 N.W.2d 633, 637 n.1 (Mich. 2010); Mayer v. Grueber, 138 N.W.2d 197 (Wis. 1965).

Similar, smaller bodies of water are sometimes called ponds, and may be natural or artificial. 93 C.J.S. Waters § 196 (2025). In some eastern states, bodies of water known as "great ponds" are considerably larger than many lakes. Hollenberg v. Town of Union, 918 A.2d 1214 (Me. 2007), citing Me. Rev. Stat. Ann. tit. 38, § 480—B(5) (2006).

### *c. Springs and Other Natural Water Bodies*

A spring is a concentrated flow of water from under ground that naturally occurs at the surface. Holliston v. Holliston Water Co., 27 N.E.2d 194 (Mass. 1940). Whether the owner of land with a spring on it has riparian rights depends upon the source of the spring. The riparian doctrine may apply to springs emanating from definite underground watercourses; if so, landowners are entitled only to make reasonable use of the waters from such springs. However, in the absence of evidence to the contrary, courts presume that percolating groundwater formed the spring and the law of groundwater covered in Chapter Five applies.

Common law will treat a spring as diffused surface water if its flow dissipates before reaching a watercourse or before crossing the boundary of the parcel on which it is located. *See infra* Chapter Six. The owner of the land owns such springs and may use all the water from them. However, these determinations are highly fact-specific, and courts sometimes treat springs as watercourses even if the water does not flow off the owner's land in a regular, well-defined channel. *See* Oklahoma Water Resources Board v. City of Lawton, 580 P.2d 510 (Okla. 1978) (holding that spring water was a stream rather than groundwater or diffused surface water).

### *d. Underground Watercourses*

Some courts have found that the owner of land above waters flowing underground has all the rights of a riparian landowner so long as the course and the channel of the so-called "stream" are ascertained. *See, e.g.*, Findley v. Teeter Stone, Inc., 248 A.2d 106 (Md. 1968). Evidence of an underground "stream" may include soil composition, the growth of vegetation in dry seasons, and evaluations of groundwater and surface water interactions over time. However, the notion that groundwater may flow in "streams" is more legal fiction than physical reality and most states presume that underground water is groundwater. *See infra* Chapter 5.I.A.

### e. Oceans and Bays

Principles of riparian law do not typically apply to lands associated with oceans or bays. Principles of navigability and property boundaries govern questions of access to tidal water by littoral owners. States typically establish boundaries at high tide, though bays and coves require more intricate treatment. Joyce v. Templeton, 468 A.2d 1369 (Md. Spec. 1984). Most of the thirteen original states established their common law boundaries along shorelines. Cooper v. United States, 779 F. Supp. 833 (E.D.N.C. 1991). In Texas, the property boundaries for land grants established under Spanish or Mexican law is the mean of the higher of the two daily tides. Luttes v. State, 324 S.W.2d 167 (Tex. 1958). However, salt water and brackish water are not typically the subject of water allocation doctrines.

### f. Out of Basin (Foreign) Waters

The phrase "foreign waters" describes water transported from one watershed into another by human effort. Use of water outside its watershed is often held to be unreasonable per se. But once water is exported, the exporter may obtain rights to it by prescription. Crane v. Stevinson, 54 P.2d 1100 (Cal. 1936). Ownership of land bordering on a stream or ditch carrying foreign waters does not usually give the landowner riparian rights to the foreign water. City of Virginia Beach v. Champion International Corp., Civ. 84–10–N. (D. Va. 1984).

### g. *Artificially Created Watercourses*

Sometimes people build a canal, re-channel a stream, or create a lake-like reservoir. The new artificial watercourse may be an important source of water for those adjoining it. However, generally riparian rights attach only to natural watercourses. Thus, the riparian doctrine does not usually control the rights of owners of land riparian to an artificial stream or reservoir.

However, courts may treat artificial watercourses that are maintained for a long period of time as natural watercourses, particularly if adjacent landowners have relied on the water's use. *See* Gannon v. Rumbaugh, 772 N.W.2d 258 (Iowa 2009); Contra Costa Cty. v. Pinole Point Properties, 186 Cal. Rptr. 3d 109 (Cal. Ct. App. 4th 2015). In Bollinger v. Henry, 375 S.W.2d 161 (Mo. 1964), the court stated that a century-old millrace (a channel conveying water to power a mill) could be treated as if it were a natural watercourse. Likewise, property owners adjacent to a dam-created reservoir may acquire certain rights over time. In the classic case of Kray v. Muggli, 86 N.W. 882 (Minn. 1901), where a dam owner wanted to remove the dam after forty years, the court held that the upland property owners had acquired a prescriptive right to have the artificial lake maintained, and the dam owner had acquired a reciprocal prescriptive duty to maintain the artificial water level. *See also* Greisinger v. Klinhardt, 9 S.W. 2d 978 (Mo. 1928) (holding that riparian landowners were entitled to maintain the lake level based on substantial improvements they made in reliance on the lake being permanent).

Some courts, however, have been less willing to find a prescriptive easement for property owners adjacent to an artificial lake. *See* Green v. City of Williamstown, 848 F. Supp. 102 (E.D. Ky. 1994) (landowners did not have a right to compel dam owner to maintain a consistent water level in an artificial lake, despite having made improvements on their property based on the presence of the lake); Alderson v. Fatlan, 898 N.E.2d 595 (Ill. 2008) (riparian landowners were not entitled to surface rights to a water-filled quarry because they had not used it without dispute for a lengthy period of time); Incline Village Board of Trustees v. Edler, 592 S.W. 3d 334 (Mo. 2019) (landowners whose property abutted an artificial lake did not have a prescriptive easement to build a dock).

## B. MEASURE OF RIPARIAN RIGHTS—REASONABLE USE

All riparian states follow some variant of the reasonable use doctrine, which allows riparian landowners to use adjacent waters if the use does not interfere with the reasonable uses of other riparians. Thus, reasonable use is determined by comparing the uses of all riparians, a very fact intensive process. Mason v. Hoyle, 14 A. 786 (Conn. 1888); Red River Roller Mills v. Wright, 15 N.W. 167 (Minn. 1883);

Botton v. State, 420 P.2d 352 (Wash. 1966). Some riparian states have adopted rules and/or statutory provisions to address specific problems; others have adopted more comprehensive water codes known as regulated riparian law. *See infra* Section III.

In those states without comprehensive water codes or specific statutory provisions, courts determine the reasonableness of uses. Some follow the Restatement (Second) of Torts, which incorporates the common law notion that reasonableness is relative. It contains two sections applicable to riparian disputes:

**§ 850. Harm by One Riparian Proprietor to Another**

A riparian proprietor is subject to liability for making an unreasonable use of the water of a watercourse or lake that causes harm to another riparian proprietor's reasonable use of the water or his land.

**§ 850A. Reasonableness of the Use of Water**

The determination of the reasonableness of a use of water depends upon a consideration of the interests of the riparian proprietor making the use, of any riparian proprietor harmed by it and of society as a whole. Factors that affect the determination include the following:

(a) the purpose of the use,

(b) the suitability of the use to the watercourse or lake,

(c) the economic value of the use,

(d) the social value of the use,

(e) the extent and amount of the harm it causes,

(f) the practicality of avoiding the harm by adjusting the use or method of use of one proprietor or the other,

(g) the practicality of adjusting the quantity of water used by each proprietor,

(h) the protection of existing values of water uses, land, investments and enterprises, and

(i) the justice of requiring the user causing harm to bear the loss.

In suits between riparian landowners, the reasonableness of both landowners' uses is at issue. To prove that rights have been infringed, the plaintiff's own use of the water must be shown to be reasonable. This usually calls for the application of factors (a)–(d). A dispute often involves riparian users who are each putting the water to good use by suitable means and producing socially and economically desirable results. Because the uses are inconsistent, however, the court must consider additional factors (e)–(i). Factor (e) requires, in effect, that insubstantial, or *de minimis*, harms be borne by the complaining party. Factors (f) and (g) require the court to determine if the dispute can be settled by making adjustments to the uses. For instance, a court might require that the parties use the stream at different times. Factors (h) and (i) generally are applied if the defendant's reasonable use causes serious harm that cannot be avoided by adjustments.

Factor (h) recognizes that, other things being equal, it is usually unreasonable for a new use to destroy an existing use. Factor (i) allows courts to address situations where the defendant's use is of greater utility, but nevertheless, fairness requires that the defendant pay for the harm he has caused.

State courts apply a wide variety of tests to determine reasonable use. Most courts draw on either § 850A factors or common law to evaluate the reasonableness of competing uses. *See* Bollinger v. Henry, 375 S.W. 2d 161 (Mo. 1964) (applying common law reasonableness factors to a dispute regarding millrace water); Ripka v. Wansing, 589 S.W.2d 333 (Mo. Ct. App. 1979) (evaluating the reasonableness of competing agricultural uses by applying § 850A); McCavit v. Lacher, 447 P.3d 726 (Alaska 2019) (adopting § 850A factors to determine if a landowner's construction of a dock interfered with a neighbor's riparian rights). In Harris v. Brooks, 283 S.W. 2d 129 (Ark. 1955), the Arkansas court applied the Restatement factors to enjoin a farmer from withdrawing irrigation water from a lake when the water fell below the "normal" level, as the farmer was unreasonably interfering with the use of the lake for commercial boating.

Other courts have created tests that combine elements of § 850A and common law to determine reasonable use. For example, the Michigan Court of Appeals established a case-specific "reasonable use balancing test" to apply to disputes between riparian and groundwater users. They emphasized three principles: 1) fair participation in the use of water for the greatest number of users; 2) protection of reasonable uses; and 3) limiting redress to unreasonable harms. Mich. Citizens for Water Conservation v. Nestle Waters N. Am., Inc., 709 N.W.2d 174 (Mich. App. 2005), *rev'd on other grounds*, 737 N.W.2d 447 (Mich. 2007). The court issued a partial injunction against a bottling company's excessive pumping of groundwater, which negatively affected interconnected surface waterbodies. While the Michigan Supreme Court later reversed other aspects of the case, it did not overturn the reasonable use balancing test.

## C. LIMITS ON RIPARIAN RIGHTS

### 1. Unreasonable Use

In a riparian system, each riparian user has equal rights against every other riparian user. The "reasonableness" or "unreasonableness" of a particular use represents the limitation that any riparian water rights holder faces. If a new riparian use emerges, a riparian user can lose an existing right or have it diminished because it is deemed unreasonable with respect to the other riparian rights in the system. 1 Water and Water Rights § 7.02(d)(1) (Amy L. Kelley, ed., 3rd ed. 2018). To determine whether a use should be curtailed, courts often consider whether the use substantially harms other riparian rights. *See* Harris v. Brooks, 283 S.W.2d 129 (Ark. 1955) (holding that a riparian use must be limited because it unreasonably interfered with another riparian use). Often, when resolving conflicts between two competing riparian uses, courts have turned to the principle of sharing shortage (sometimes called "just proportion") to determine which existing riparian use should be diminished. Evans v. Merriweather, 4 Ill. 492 (Ill. 1842). The Illinois Supreme Court, 180 years later, clarified that this principle applies to consumptive or diversionary uses by riparians on their land, and does not allow a riparian to use the surface of a nonnavigable stream (via kayak) to enter water over another riparian's streambed. Holm v. Kodat, 211 N.E.3d 310 (Ill. 2022)). *Cf.* Jones v. Oz-Ark-Val Poultry Co., 306 S.W.2d 111 (Ark. 1957); Cozy Lake v. Nyoda Girls' Camp, 131 A. 892 (N.J. 1926).

### 2. Prohibition of Use on Non-Riparian Lands and Its Exceptions

Common law rules restricted use of water to "riparian land." As explained in Section II.A, *supra,* riparian lands are only the portions of parcels that are adjacent to a watercourse and within the same watershed. Many pure riparian jurisdictions continue to hold that any non-riparian use that interferes in any way with a riparian use is *per se* unreasonable. Stratton v. Mount Hermon Boys' School, 103 N.E. 87 (Mass. 1913); Michigan Citizens for Water Conserv. v. Nestle Waters N. Am., Inc., 709 N.W.2d 174 (Mich. App. 2005), *rev'd on other grounds*, 737 N.W.2d 447 (Mich. 2007).

Strict application of the watershed limitation has been the subject of much criticism and was rejected in the Restatement (Second) of Torts § 855. The Restatement provides that the classification of the use as riparian or non-riparian does not control the reasonableness of a water use by a riparian proprietor. Thus, use on unconnected land or land outside the watershed may be reasonable. Expansion of the reasonable use approach to non-riparian uses recognizes that the best economic use of water may be for agriculture, mining, manufacturing, or other purposes on land further from the watercourse. Several riparian states have followed the Restatement rule and have evaluated the reasonableness of a non-riparian use against a riparian use. *See, e.g.*, Pyle v. Gilbert, 265 S.E.2d 584 (Ga. 1980); Baumler v. Town of Newstead, 247 A.D.2d 861 (N.Y. 1998).

States with permit systems, known as regulated riparianism, and hybrid states where the law combines riparian and prior appropriation rights, temper the harshness of the watershed limitation. Regulated riparian states may issue permits for water use outside the watershed of origin, such that the permittee need not be a riparian landowner. Hybrid states may establish by appropriation water rights for non-riparian lands if sufficient water is available and can be put to a beneficial use without waste.

## D. SCOPE OF RIPARIAN USES

### 1. Preference for "Natural" Uses

Riparian law distinguishes between "natural" uses and "artificial" uses. Natural uses include those that meet the domestic needs of the riparian landowner, such as drinking, washing, and watering small gardens or a few livestock. Historically, under the natural flow rule, a riparian user could use water for natural (*i.e.*, domestic) purposes even if it diminished the flow to the harm of lower riparian users.

The modern reasonable use doctrine also reflects a preference for natural uses and typically prioritizes domestic uses before all other uses. *See, e.g.*, Prather v. Hoberg, 150 P.2d 405 (Cal. 1944); Harris v. Brooks, 283 S.W.2d 129 (Ark. 1955); Tunison v. Harper, 690 S.E.2d 819 (Ga. 2010). In most jurisdictions today, a riparian user can make natural uses of the water regardless of consequences to lower riparian users, while artificial uses such as for irrigation and industrial purposes are subject to reasonableness restrictions. There are practical reasons for the preference for natural or domestic uses. First, such uses are unlikely to consume enough water to injure lower riparian users. Second, enforcement of any restriction on domestic uses is difficult. Finally, uses that are necessary to sustain life are bound to be "reasonable" as against uses that are not directly related to survival.

### 2. Irrigation, Industrial, and Mining Uses

Historically, at common law, any significant irrigation was an "artificial" use of water. Theoretically, under this principle, courts did not allow irrigation except for small household gardens. However, most common law riparian jurisdictions now recognize irrigation uses as reasonable. Some riparian states have even enacted laws that prefer agricultural uses. In Kentucky, for example, agricultural uses do not require the permits needed for other riparian uses. Louisville v. Tway, 180 S.W.2d 278 (Ky. 1944). Other states single out specific crops for preferential treatment. *See, e.g.*, State v. Zawistowski, 290 N.W.2d 303 (Wis. 1980) (construing Wisconsin's cranberry preference). Statutes may also give agriculture preferential treatment by exempting farm ponds from regulation.

Manufacturing and industrial uses of water, like agricultural uses, are artificial uses. Today, those uses are subject to the reasonable use rule. *See, e.g.*, Michigan Citizens for Water Conserv., 709 N.W.2d 174 (Mich. App. 2005), *rev'd on other grounds*, 737 N.W.2d 447 (Mich. 2007) (recognizing that industrial use of water is an artificial use subject to the reasonable use rule).

Mining often requires substantial amounts of water and is also considered an artificial use. Some states require a finding that a particular mining operation is in the public interest before a permit can be issued. *See, e.g.*, Minn. Stat. Ann. § 103G.297 Subd. 3(3). Other states have statutes giving miners a right of access to waterways, implying that they have a right to use those waters. *See, e.g.*, Ga. Code Ann. § 44–9–70; N.C. Gen. Stat. Ann. § 74–25.

Agricultural, industrial, and mining uses may come into conflict with downstream riparian users' right to pure water. The reasonable use rule requires a balancing test that may allow some pollution, similar to the approach used in actions for private or public nuisance cases. State and federal water pollution standards, such as the Clean Water Act, may also inform measures of reasonableness. In regulated riparian states, pollution is often an express factor to be weighed in issuing permits for water use.

### 3. Municipal Uses

When the United States was predominantly rural, local streams or individual wells provided most of the water needed for domestic uses. With urbanization came the growth of municipal water systems to supply domestic needs, to fight fires, and to water public parks. Since the 1990s, jurisdictions following riparian law have been required to confront the tension between requiring riparian land ownership and securing adequate public supplies for water.

Courts have split on the question of whether municipal water systems qualify as riparian users. In some cases, cities move water many miles from distant watersheds to satisfy their growing populations. *See, e.g.,* Catskill Mountains Chapter of Trout Unlimited, Inc. v. City of New York, 451 F.3d 77 (2d Cir. 2006); North Carolina v. Hudson, 731 F. Supp. 1261 (E.D.N.C. 1990). The prevailing view is that a public water system is only considered a riparian user with regard to parcels it owns along the watercourse. *See* Pernell v. Henderson, 16 S.E.2d 449 (N.C. 1941); Harrell v. City of Conway, 271 S.W.2d 924 (Ark. 1954). Other states treat municipalities as riparian users, even beyond riparian tracts. *See* City of Canton v. Shock, 63 N.E. 600 (Ohio 1902);

Hackensack Water Co. v. Village of Nyack, 289 F. Supp. 671 (S.D.N.Y. 1968).

Legislative action has typically resolved this tension. The charters incorporating most cities gave them powers to procure water supplies for purposes such as firefighting, watering public parks, supplying public buildings, and meeting the domestic needs of their residents. States have also passed special legislative acts giving such powers to particular cities. Some states have even chartered water corporations with the power to condemn water for public and domestic supply. *See* Adams v. Greenwich Water Co., 83 A.2d 177 (Conn. 1951). Today, states often grant such powers in general statutes applicable to all municipalities.

## 4. Storage Rights

Under the reasonable use rule, a riparian user can impound water so long as the reasonable uses of others are not impaired. Portage Cty. Bd. of Commrs. v. Akron, 846 N.E.2d 478 (Ohio 2006); Cent. Delta Water Agency v. State Water Res. Control Bd., 20 Cal. Rptr. 3d 898 (Cal. 2004); Heise v. Schulz, 204 P.2d 706 (Kan. 1949). Accordingly, a riparian user may not unreasonably alter the flow when releasing water from a storage facility. In addition, some riparian states give environmental agencies discretion to issue permits for water diversion and storage facilities upon consideration of the public necessity, instream flows, and other factors. *See, e.g.*, Hudson River Fisherman's Ass'n v. Williams, 531 N.Y.S.2d 379 (App. Div. 1988).

## 5. Waterpower

Harnessing the flow of a stream to generate power is one of the oldest uses of water. Waterpower uses range from the earliest waterwheels to large, modern hydroelectric dams.

### *a. Waterwheels and Mills*

Early in the nation's history, small waterwheels and mills adorned numerous streams, providing a cheap and accessible source of power. Eventually, larger mills were needed for manufacturing. As bigger waterwheels were needed, dams were often constructed upstream from the mills to create storage pools from which releases could be made to provide a stronger current. This could slow the flow elsewhere in the watercourse, thereby interfering with other uses. Some state legislatures enacted so-called "mill dam" acts to allow storage dams, provided they did not injure existing mills. This built an element of priority into the riparian system by assuring protection to the earliest uses that relied on the flow of the stream.

### *b. Hydroelectric Generation*

From the Industrial Revolution and through modern times, the generation of electrical power represents an important riparian use of water. Under the reasonable use rule, operators of a hydroelectric dam may not unreasonably store or release water to the detriment of other riparian users. Factors weighed to determine the reasonableness of dam operators' storage and release methods include the stream size, the state of technology, and uses of the stream by other riparians. Otwell v. Ala. Power Co., 944 F. Supp. 2d 1134 (N.D. Ala. 2013), *aff'd,* 747 F.3d 1275 (11th Cir. 2014); Hazard Powder Co. v. Somersville Mfg. Co., 61 A. 519 (Conn. 1905). Although the riparian doctrine generally limits water use to riparian land, electricity generated from dams may be transmitted to and used by owners of non-riparian land.

Hydroelectric dams also raise public concern because they can interfere with use of the surface of navigable rivers. Exercising its power under the Commerce Clause, Congress dictated in the Federal Power Act that no hydroelectric dam may be built on any navigable river unless first licensed by the Federal Energy Regulatory Commission (formerly the Federal Power Commission). Before it issues a license, the Commission must find that the "project be best adapted to a comprehensive plan for improving or developing the waterway." *See infra* Chapter 7.IV.

### 6. Recovery of Gravel

Some jurisdictions treat the removal of sand and gravel from a watercourse like any other riparian use and evaluate its reasonableness against other riparian uses on a case-by-case basis. Other jurisdictions treat the removal of sand and gravel as a lesser riparian use. In Joslin v. Marin Mun. Water Dist., 429 P.2d 889 (Cal. 1967), the Supreme Court of California put sand and gravel use on lower footing than an upstream storage dam for a water district.

The Court concluded that the dam, which interfered with gravel transport to a downstream sand and gravel business, was reasonable and served the public interest, while the sand and gravel business did not provide comparable benefits to the public.

Other jurisdictions seem to favor sand and gravel removal. In Arkansas, for example, a court held that while a statute only referenced the White River in permitting the removal of sand and gravel, the court could extend the authority to all navigable streams in the state based on legislative intent. White River Sand & Gravel Removal Com. v. Hayes Bros. Land & Timber Co., 532 S.W.2d 191 (Ark. 1976).

### 7. Discharge of Waste and the Protection of Water Quality

Historically, the riparian doctrine required landowners along the watercourse to prevent any deterioration in water quality. Over time, this requirement gave way to reasonable use principles. Almost every use of water alters the chemistry or temperature of a watercourse, either because it discharges some waste back into the stream or because the removal of water makes the stream less capable of diluting other contaminants. Consequently, whether the degree of change in water quality renders a water use unreasonable is a question of fact. *See* Borough of Westville v. Whitney Home Builders, Inc., 122 A.2d 233 (N.J. Super. Ct. App. Div. 1956) (balancing the uses of water and their harms); Snow v. Parsons, 28 Vt. 459 (Vt. 1856) (remanded to determine if a tannery's discharge of waste into a stream was a reasonable use).

A riparian user may also have a tort remedy for water pollution. Causes of action exist in trespass (for negligent or intentional interference with the possession of land to which riparian rights are appurtenant) and in nuisance (for interference with the use and enjoyment of land). To find nuisance under Restatement (Second) of Torts § 826, a court uses a balancing test to decide if the defendant's conduct was unreasonable by asking whether: "(a) the gravity of the harm outweighs the utility of the actor's conduct, or (b) the harm caused by the conduct is serious and the financial burden of compensating . . . would not make continuation of the conduct not feasible."

Today, state and federal statutes, most notably the Clean Water Act (CWA), govern nearly all discharges from point sources into waterways. Section 301 of the CWA prohibits discharges to waters of the U.S. except with a permit. 33 U.S.C. § 1311(a). *See infra* Chapter 7.VI. However, there are many non-point sources of pollution, including runoff from agricultural irrigation, that are exempt from the CWA. 33 U.S.C. § 1342(*l*)(1); 40 C.F.R. § 122.3. Despite these statutory schemes, state common law retains its relevance. *See, e.g.*, Anglers of AuSable v. Dept. of Env. Quality, 770 N.W. 2d 359 (Mich. App. 2009), *vacated on other grounds,* 796 N.W. 2d 240 (Mich. 2011).

### 8. Reciprocal Rights Among Riparian Users to Use the Entire Surface

The rights of riparian users whose lands border navigable waters co-exist with public rights in such waters. English common law allowed any person to navigate on navigable waters and to make uses incident to navigation, such as hunting and fishing. This rule is universally accepted in the United States, although the definition of "navigable waters" varies. *See infra* Chapter 7.I.

Some states recognize public rights in navigable waterways even when title to the bed has passed to the riparian owner. In Wisconsin, all riparians own the bed of a stream to the thread (geographic center of the stream) unless their ownership is limited by deed. Mayer v. Grueber, 138 N.W.2d 197 (Wis. 1965); Movrich v. Lobermeier, 905 N.W. 2d 807 (Wis. 2018). However, a riparian's ownership of navigable beds remains subject to the public right to use the surface. Muench v. Public Service Comm., 53 N.W.2d 514 (Wis. 1952). *See Movrich*, 905 N.W. 2d 807 (holding that although plaintiffs could not build a dock because defendants had private title to the bed of the artificial flowage, plaintiffs could access the water from their abutting property and had a public trust right to use the surface). A Minnesota statute declares certain waters that are managed or accessible for public purposes to be public waters. Minn. Stat. § 103G.201. Since colonial times in areas within Maine, Massachusetts, and New Hampshire, the common law has recognized that large, freshwater lakes known as "great ponds" (having a surface area over ten acres), though non-navigable, are subject to public use with limited rights of public access across private lands to reach the ponds.

Issues involving the use of a waterbody's surface also arise in the context of multiple riparian owners. States are divided on whether a riparian owner has a right to make reasonable use of an entire lake surface. Two disparate rules have emerged. Some states follow the "common law" rule, which supports a property owner's right to exclude others from the portion of the water surface overlying their property. *See, e.g.*, Orr v. Mortvedt, 735 N.W.2d 610 (Iowa 2007); Wehby v. Turpin, 710 So.2d 1243 (Ala. 1998); Ace Equip. Sales, Inc. v. Buccino, 869 A.2d 626 (Conn. 2005); Lanier v. Ocean Pond Fishing Club, Inc., 322 S.E.2d 494 (Ga. 1984); Duval v. Thomas, 114 So.2d 791 (Fla. 1959).

Other states follow the "civil" rule, which supports the right of every riparian to use the entire water surface for recreational purposes. *See, e.g.*, Duval v. Thomas, 114 So.2d 791 (Fla. 1959); Beacham v. Lake Zurich Prop. Owners Ass'n, 526 N.E.2d 154 (Ill. 1988). Under the civil rule, the right of other riparian owners to use the entire water surface for transportation, fishing, swimming, hunting, and other purposes tempers the rights of riparian users in waters overlying their privately owned beds. But multiple owners of the bed of a private, non-navigable lake can only use the surface water if they do not unduly interfere with the reasonable use of the waters by other owners and their licensees. *See, e.g.*, *Beacham*, 526 N.E.2d 157. *See also* Herr v. U.S.

Forest Service, 865 F.3d 351 (6th Cir. 2017) (holding that plaintiffs' valid existing rights included the reasonable use of entire surface of lake at reasonable speeds); Johnson v. Seifert, 100 N.W.2d 689 (Minn. 1960) (adopting a free access rule, but noting it would not apply to "[a] minor body of water which by its nature and character reasonably has no overall utility common to two or more abutting owners").

Waterbodies developed by private parties to promote recreational use present unique issues. In Anderson v. Bell, 433 So.2d 1202 (Fla. 1983), the court held that an owner of property that lies adjacent to an artificial, non-navigable reservoir is not entitled to use the surface of the entire waterbody by the sole virtue of the fact that he owns contiguous land. *See also* Incline Village Board of Trustees v. Edler, 592 S.W. 3d 334 (Mo. 2019) (landowners whose property abutted an artificial lake did not have riparian rights and could not build a dock on the lake); Movrich v. Lobermeier, 905 N.W. 2d 807 (Wis. 2018) (applying same limit to artificial navigable flowage, but allowing use under public trust doctrine); Holton v. Ward, 847 N.W.2d 1, 7 (Mich. 2014) ("no riparian rights arise from an artificial body of water").

In Thompson v. Enz, 154 N.W.2d 473 (Mich. 1967), a developer dredged a canal from a lake to subdivided parcels and granted easements to the property owners abutting the canal, allowing them to access the lake. The court held that, assuming riparian rights for recreational access may be established by easement, they must still meet a reasonableness test, and remanded for further findings.

## 9. Right to Wharf out

The right to "wharf out" allows a riparian to build a wharf or dock for private use if the structure does not impede navigation, although any obstruction that is a purpresture (an enclosure of what belongs to the public) is not allowed at common law. Williams v. Guthrie, 137 So. 682 (Fla. 1931). Also, if a wharf or dock injures the public right to navigation, the obstruction can be removed as a nuisance. Weems Steamboat Co. v. People's Steamboat Co., 214 U.S. 345 (U.S. 1909); Engs v. Peckham, 11 R.I. 210 (R.I. 1875). However, some courts have recognized that riparian landowners have a right to erect and maintain wharves and piers, which cannot be taken or damaged for public use without just compensation. 627 Smith St. Corp. v. Bureau of Waste Disposal, 289 A.D.2d 472 (N.Y. App. Div. 2001).

Although most Eastern and Midwestern states recognize a right to wharf out, Pacific Coast states generally do not, except by statute. *See, e.g.*, Port of Seattle v. Oregon & W. R. Co., 255 U.S. 56 (1921) (applying Washington law). In Alaska, the Department of Natural Resources may require a commercial property owner to enter into a lease with the state before constructing wharves into adjacent navigable waters. State v. Alaska Riverways, Inc., 232 P.3d 1203 (Alaska 2010).

To protect the states' interest in the beds of navigable waters and the rights of other riparian owners, many states have adopted regulatory provisions and permitting requirements that limit a riparian owner's right to wharf out.

## 10. Right to Maintain Water Levels

Dam installation or removal alters the elevation of the reservoir and the receiving stream. A riparian owner's right to have water levels maintained may depend on whether there is an express or negative easement, how long a dam has been in place, and whether it is a private or public dam.

Absent an easement or other enforceable agreement, an owner of land beneath or contiguous to an artificial lake has no right to use the entire lake based solely by virtue of land ownership. As a result, the landowner has no right to prevent the developer of the lake from draining it. Anderson v. Bell, 433 So. 2d 1202 (Fla. 1983) (citing Taylor v. Tampa Coal Co., 46 So.2d 392 (Fla. 1950)). *See* Lake Williams Beach Ass'n v. Gilman Bros. Co., 496 A.2d 182 (Conn. 1985) (rejecting claims by lakefront owners against dam owners following reduction in water levels in accordance with engineering recommendations for dam safety); Green v. City of Williamstown, 848 F. Supp. 102 (E.D. Ky. 1994) (owners of property adjacent to a lake created by a municipal dam did not have rights to a consistent water level even if they had improved their property in reliance on the lake).

Many states have adopted dam safety requirements and environmental provisions related to dam construction and operation. For example, Wisconsin law gives the Department of Natural

Resources power to regulate water levels "to promote safety and protect life, health and property. . ." Wis. Stat. Ann. § 31.02(1). In Michigan, the state Supreme Court affirmed the authority of a watershed management organization to manage the water level of a lake by use of a dam, but it ordered the adoption of the riparian owners' proposed management plan to protect downstream recreational and environmental interests. Glen Lake-Crystal River Watershed Riparians v. Glen Lake Ass'n, 695 N.W.2d 508 (Mich. 2004). Michigan has also upheld a partial injunction to protect riparian rights when excessive groundwater pumping resulted in a drop in the water level of a stream. Mich. Citizens for Water Conservation v. Nestle Waters N. Am., Inc., 709 N.W.2d 174 (Mich. App. 2005), *rev'd on other grounds*, 737 N.W.2d 447 (Mich. 2007).

### 11. Scenic Rights

Some courts have recognized a riparian's right to enjoy the scenic beauty of an adjoining waterway. In Collens v. New Canaan Water Co., 234 A.2d 825 (Conn. 1967), the court awarded plaintiffs compensatory damages and injunctive relief because the defendant's pumping of water for municipal purposes adversely affected "the recreational and scenic advantages of the plaintiffs' [river-front] properties." Moreover, the loss of scenic amenities may warrant compensation in an eminent domain action. In an action to condemn the rights of riparian owners surrounding Mono Lake so that the lake's tributaries could be drawn down for Los Angeles's water supply, the court awarded "substantial" damages based on injuries to scenic and recreational values. City of Los Angeles v. Aitken, 52 P.2d 585 (Cal. App. 1935).

With some degree of variation, courts in Florida, Mississippi, Georgia, and New Jersey recognize a riparian right to an unobstructed view of the water. In Florida, for example, riparian owners were compensated because the construction of a bridge by the county interfered with 80% of their view of a channel. Lee County v. Kiesel, 705 So. 2d 1013 (Fla. 1998). By contrast, an Indiana court declined to find that a riparian landowner had rights to an unobstructed view when the city installed a pedestrian bridge to connect a city park to an island. The court reasoned that the scope of a landowner's view was a policy decision "best left to the legislative branch generally and the local zoning authorities specifically." Ctr. Townhouse Corp. v. City of Mishaw, 882 N.E. 2d 762, 772 (Ind. App. 2008).

## E. TRANSFERS OF RIPARIAN RIGHTS

### 1. Granting Riparian Rights

Because riparian rights attach to those who own riparian land, riparian rights are often thought of as being a part of land ownership. Courts typically find that the parties intended to transfer water rights along with the land, such that a conveyance of riparian land carries with it all the riparian rights appurtenant to that land, even if not expressly conveyed by the deed. However, the presumption that a conveyance of riparian land conveys the appurtenant water rights is rebuttable. To avoid disputes, the parties should express their intent clearly in the deed. For example, in Everett's Lake Corporation v. Dye, 821 S.E.2d 637 (N.C. Ct. App. 2018), *review denied,* 824 S.E.2d 421 (N.C. 2019), the court held that a riparian could, by deed, transfer a riparian parcel but limit future owners' exercise of their riparian rights to non-commercial uses.

In rare cases, a subdivision of a riparian tract may grant riparian rights to the newly created parcel, even if that new parcel is non-riparian. In Modesto Irrigation District v. Tanaka, 262 Cal. Rptr. 3d 408 (Cal. App. 2020), an irrigation district challenged a farmer's ability to irrigate a non-riparian tract. The farmer's land had originally been part of a riparian tract that was later subdivided. The court held that the non-riparian parcel retained riparian rights because, at the time of the 130-year-old grant, the parties intended to ensure that the parcel could continue to be used for agriculture.

## 2. Reserving Riparian Rights

Although riparian rights attach only to riparian land, a riparian landowner may expressly reserve the right to use the water when conveying part of a riparian parcel to another. Such reservations of water rights are typically binding only as between the parties. Reservations typically arise in two settings.

In the first, a landowner divides a riparian parcel, and, assuming the divided parcel remains riparian, the grantor expressly reserves the water rights attached to the parcel. The grantor may later convey the retained portion of the riparian parcel to another person, granting along with it the riparian rights expressly reserved from the first conveyance. Any such reservation is only effective if recorded. 1 Waters and Water Rights § 7.04(a)(2). As a practical matter, the grantor who reserves water rights in such a situation will usually allow the grantee at least sufficient water to satisfy the grantee's domestic needs. *See* Steuart Transportation Co. v. Ashe, 304 A.2d 788 (Md. 1973); Legendary, Inc. v. Destin Yacht Club Owners Assoc., Inc., 724 So. 2d 623 (Fla. App. 1998).

In the second, a riparian landowner retains a portion of the original riparian tract that does not border on the waterbody and conveys the abutting riparian portion to another, reserving some or all riparian rights. Courts handle these cases similarly to situations where a riparian owner grants an easement that allows non-riparian owners use of the water. Because the common law disfavors non-riparian use, easement holders typically face a high burden to establish that the easement exists. *See* Little v. Kin, 664 N.W.2d 749 (Mich. 2003) (recognizing that courts will look first to the language of the easement, considering extrinsic evidence only if the text is ambiguous). *See also* Burkhart v. City of Fort Lauderdale, 168 So. 2d 65 (Fla. 1964); J-T Assoc. v. Hudson River-Black River Regulating Dist., 175 A.D.2d 438 (N.Y. 1991); Cooper v. Kolberg, 442 S.E.2d 639 (Va. 1994).

### 3. Acquiring Riparian Rights by Prescription

Property owners who would not normally be considered riparian may obtain riparian rights by prescription. 1 Water and Water Rights § 7.04(c) (inventorying state cases recognizing riparian rights established through prescription). Typical adverse possession laws provide that the open and notorious, hostile, exclusive, actual, and continuous possession of property for a prescribed number of years vests title in the adverse possessor. Obtaining a prescriptive riparian right depends on two factors: whether the person against whom the prescriptive right is sought is (1) a riparian or a non-riparian owner, and (2) upstream or downstream from the riparian plaintiff. Moreover, riparian states now incorporate some form of the reasonable use rule when considering whether a prescriptive right has been established.

When a prescription conflict occurs between two riparian owners—an upstream defendant and a downstream plaintiff—the rule is that an upper riparian owner's use is not adverse unless it unreasonably interferes with the rights of a lower riparian owner. Pabst v. Finmand, 211 P. 11 (Cal. 1922). *Cf.* Kirby v. Hook, 701 A.2d 397 (Md. 1997) (landowners' use of water from a spring on neighbors' property through an underground pipeline without written permission was "adverse" for purposes of establishing an easement by prescription).

Downstream users (riparian or non-riparian) generally cannot acquire prescriptive rights against upstream riparian users. The rule is sometimes stated as "prescription does not run upstream." Since it is difficult for a downstream use to adversely affect an upstream riparian use, the downstream use is not adverse. For two interesting exceptions, see Dontanello v. Gust, 150 P. 420 (Wash. 1915) (lower riparian acquired prescriptive right by building a diversion mechanism on upper riparian's land), and Sandford v. Town of Wolfeboro, 740 A.2d 1019 (N.H. 1999) (trespassory flowage established prescriptive right).

Generally, the rules governing prescription in riparian states also apply in the hybrid states, at least as between riparian landowners. Between a riparian and a non-riparian owner, the rules may differ because, under most hybrid systems, new (non-riparian) uses must be acquired by making an appropriation pursuant to statutory requirements. Prescription in hybrid states is discussed in *infra* Chapter 4.III.C.

## F. LOSS OF RIPARIAN RIGHTS

The general rule, in contrast to prior appropriation jurisdictions, is that riparian rights cannot be lost by non-use. However, prescription, avulsion, permit systems, or the exercise of eminent domain by a city or other governmental unit to secure a water supply can extinguish riparian rights. Additionally, in most states with hybrid systems, statutes limit the right of a riparian owner to initiate new uses and may even declare vested riparian rights to be forfeited by non-use over a statutorily prescribed period.

## 1. Effect of Non-Use

Ordinarily, riparian rights are not lost by non-use. Because riparian rights attach only to riparian land, it follows that the owner of a riparian parcel also has riparian rights in the adjacent watercourse whether those rights are exercised or not. As one court put it, "[u]se does not create the right, and disuse cannot destroy or suspend it." Lux v. Haggin, 391, 10 P. 674, 753 (Cal. 1886). *See* 1 Waters and Water Rights § 7.04(d).

By contrast, most hybrid states, in order to protect appropriators' rights, have forfeiture statutes that limit the ability of riparian landowners to initiate new riparian uses after a certain date.

## 2. Accretion, Reliction, Erosion, and Avulsion

Accretion and reliction occur when a stream changes course over a period of many years. Accretion is the gradual addition of sediment to one bank along the waterline. Reliction occurs when water gradually withdraws from one side of the stream. Erosion is a term used to describe the gradual wearing away of land. If accretion, reliction, or erosion occur, the property boundary line shifts with the waterline so that a riparian owner adjacent to added land will gain title to the new land, keeping riparian rights. 1 Waters and Water Rights § 6.03(c)(3). A riparian owner whose land is carried away loses title to that land but retains appurtenant riparian rights so long as the stream remains adjacent to the land. *See* Burkart v. City of Fort

Lauderdale, 168 So.2d 65 (Fla. 1964); Strom v. Sheldon, 527 P.2d 1382 (Wash. App. 1974).

In contrast, courts treat avulsion—which occurs when a stream suddenly changes its channel—quite differently. If avulsion moves a stream away from a landowner's property, the property boundary line remains where it was before the stream left its channel. *See* Cox v. F-S Prestress, Inc., 797 So.2d 839 (Miss. 2001); City of Long Branch v. Jui Yung Liu, 4 A.3d 542 (N.J. 2010). Avulsion can effectively transform riparian land into non-riparian, thereby depriving the unfortunate owner of riparian rights. Although the distinction between avulsion and accretion is murky, a change in stream course generally constitutes avulsion if it is considerable, violent, and abrupt. Courts consider the circumstances of the shift in the channel and the consequences to the parties in deciding which rule to apply. *See, e.g.,* Fly Fish Vt., Inc. v. Chapin Hill Estates, Inc., 996 A.2d 1167 (Vt. 2010). Thus, in one case, a court applied the accretion rule to a sudden shift in channel caused by the defendant's dredging that would have cut off the plaintiff entirely from stream access if the avulsion rule were applied. Strom v. Sheldon, 527 P.2d 1382 (Wash. App. 1974).

### 3. Legislation—Moving from a Common Law to Statutory Law System

States converting to statutory permit systems or to hybrid systems intended in part to remedy the uncertainty and insecurity of the riparian system. A riparian owner's ability to commence any reasonable use in the future, as well as to continue existing uses, allows great and unanticipated increases in water use. Forfeiture statutes are designed to limit riparian rights that have not been exercised within a certain period in an attempt to diminish this uncertainty. In the hybrid states of Kansas and Washington, a landowner can even lose vested riparian rights—those the riparian has historically exercised—by a period of non-use under statutory forfeiture provisions. In addition, as discussed in Section III below, the movement from common law to regulated riparian systems also attempts to address this uncertainty by requiring permits for riparian uses and, in some cases, by creating time-limited permits.

## III. PERMIT SYSTEMS—REGULATED RIPARIANISM

For many years, the common law system of reconciling water use conflicts through courts applying a reasonable use standard was an effective and efficient way to manage water resources in the eastern United States. In the last several decades, however, eastern states have seen more frequent water shortages, increased demand from urban and industrial growth, and excessive pollution. This dynamic led many riparian states to adopt statutory provisions, including permit requirements, to address competing water uses. These states are known as "regulated riparian" states.

"Regulated riparianism" encompasses the wide array of statutory provisions adopted in the eastern states that have moved away from judicially determined standards of reasonableness toward legislatively-enacted permit systems. Statutory schemes can range from relatively simple registration systems to comprehensive water codes. In an attempt to create a set of general provisions, the American Society of Civil Engineers developed the Regulated Riparian Model Water Code in 2003, available at https://ascelibrary.org/doi/book/10.1061/9780784414682. The Model Water Code serves as a useful tool for looking broadly at the basic structure and function of comprehensive regulated riparian codes, but each state has tailored its statutory provisions to its own particular needs.

About half of the eastern states (19 out of 31 states) developed permit systems to allocate rights to divert water. These states include Alabama, Arkansas, Connecticut, Delaware, Florida, Georgia, Iowa, Kentucky, Maryland, Massachusetts, Michigan, Minnesota, Mississippi, New Jersey, New York, North Carolina, South Carolina, Virginia, and Wisconsin. *See* 1 Waters and Water Rights § 9.01, footnote 37 (providing cites to state code provisions). Several also require permits for use of groundwater (*e.g.*, Illinois, Maryland, Kentucky, South Carolina). Thus, common-law riparianism for the most part has been replaced with varying degrees of "regulated riparianism." Iowa and Florida have implemented detailed permit systems, while other states have adopted less comprehensive systems of regulation.

Other eastern states have adopted some sort of administrative system to address water management for at least some portion of the water supply. *See*

Joseph W. Dellapenna, *Developing A Suitable Water Allocation Law for Pennsylvania,* 17 Vill. Envtl. L.J. 1, 46 (2006). States without permitting systems often require, at a minimum, that surface water users report the amount of water used to a central agency. *See* Me. Rev. Stat. §§ 470–A to 470–H (requiring a report of water withdrawals in Maine).

Statutory provisions vary by state but share some common themes and characteristics. First, states with comprehensive systems require a permit to divert water. Permits are granted based on riparian principles, and the reasonableness standard is the primary method for determining if a use is appropriate. Second, water use is often expressly allowed on non-riparian land. This represents one of the more dramatic substantive departures from the common law. Third, in many states, the permits are time-limited. Fourth, regulated riparianism often expressly recognizes public values, and in some instances, treats water as a form of public property that cannot be fully privatized by any individual. These code provisions are typically designed to protect the public's interest in sustaining a reliable supply of water, maintaining stream flows, and allowing states to make decisions about water uses and their impacts. Finally, competing uses are typically resolved through an administrative process rather than through the courts. *See, e.g.,* Dellapenna, *supra,* at 50;Fla. Stat. § 373.233; Green v. City of Williamstown, 848 F. Supp. 102 (E.D. Ky. 1994).

## A. REQUIRING A PERMIT TO DIVERT WATER

Among the most significant differences between pure riparian law and regulated riparianism is the requirement that a water user obtain a permit to divert water. States vary considerably with regard to when a permit is required. All state permit systems include some special exemptions or preferences for activities such as fire emergencies, or water for oil and gas recovery or steam power plants, often due to political compromises in the legislature.

Several states exempt withdrawals up to a certain amount from the permit requirement. Ala. Code § 9–10B–20(c); Conn. Gen. Stat. § 22a–377(a)(2); Del. Code Ann. Tit.7, § 6029(2); Mich. Comp. Laws § 324.32723; Wis. Stat. Ann. §§ 30.18(2)(b), 281.35(4)(b). Other states exempt domestic uses. Fla. Stat. §§ 373.019(6), 373.219(1); Ky. Rev. Stat. Ann. §§ 151.140, 151.210(1); Md. Env. Code § 5–502(b)(1); Minn. Stat. § 103G.271(1)(b)(1); Miss. Code Ann. §§ 51–3–3(c), 51–3–7(1). Agricultural irrigation is also exempt from permitting requirements in certain states. Ky. Rev. Stat. Ann. § 151.140; N.J. Stat. Ann. § 58: 1A–5.1; S.C. Code Ann. § 49–4–30(A)(3); Tenn. Code Ann. § 69–7–304(d). *See* Jowers v. S.C. Dep't of Health & Envtl. Control, 815 S.E.2d 446 (S.C. 2018) (rejecting riparians' claims that an exception for agricultural users violated due process and was an unconstitutional taking of private property). Some states specifically require a permit for agricultural use. Wis. Stat. § 30.18(2)(a)(2).

In general, regulated riparian permits specify the volume, rate of diversion, and the location and nature of the permitted use. Permit holders are often required to monitor and report on their diversions. Some states charge water users a set fee to obtain a permit or charge a fee based on the amount of water used. Many states authorize various enforcement mechanisms, such as injunctions and civil and criminal penalties.

## B. ALLOWING WATER USE ON NON-RIPARIAN LAND

The Regulated Riparian Model Water Code authorizes permits for water use on non-riparian lands. *See* American Soc'y of Civil Eng'rs, Regulated Riparian Model Water Code § 2R–1–02. However, many regulated riparian states have not expressly adopted this provision. Some regulated riparian states allow for use on non-riparian lands only when there is "excess" or "surplus" water. *See, e.g.,* Ark. Stat. Ann. § 15–22–304; Minn. Stat. § 103G.265; Wis. Stat. § 30.18(5)(a)(2). A few states permit water uses on non-riparian lands even if they are outside the watershed of origin. *See* N.C. Gen. Stat. § 143–215.22L (providing authority to approve transfers outside the watershed of origin if specified criteria are met); Fla. Stat. Ann. § 373.223(2) (authorizing permits to divert water outside the watershed if "consistent with the public interest").

## C. ISSUING TIME LIMITED PERMITS

In both riparian and prior appropriation jurisdictions, common law water rights are essentially permanent. In riparian states, one must retain ownership of the riparian lands to preserve a water right. In prior appropriation states, one must put the water to beneficial use to maintain a water right. As long as these conditions are met, the water right never expires or is forfeited.

Both riparian law and prior appropriation law have been critiqued for protecting early uses without a mechanism to re-evaluate as new needs for water arise. Regulated riparianism attempts to address this by limiting the duration of a water rights permit.

Of the regulated riparian states that have permit systems in place, few allow a water use permit to be issued in perpetuity. N.Y. Envtl. Conserv. Law §§ 15–1501, 15–1503; Most regulated riparian states with a permit system grant the water right for a fixed term of years. *See, e.g.*, Fla. Stat. § 373.236 (20 year permits for private entities, 50 year permits for public entities); Ga. Code Ann. § 12–5–97(a) (50 year permits); Miss. Code Ann. § 51–3–9(1) (10 year permits with unspecified longer period for public entities); Md. Env. Code § 5–511 (3 year review of most permits). When the permit expires, the state agency can re-evaluate the reasonableness of the water use as against other potential uses. Renewal of fixed term permits is not automatic in some states, while in other states, renewal applications are favored. *Compare* Fla. Stat. § 373.239(3) (renewal not favored); Iowa Code § 455B.265 (renewal favored).

## D. PROTECTING THE PUBLIC INTEREST IN A REGULATED RIPARIAN JURISDICTION

While both riparian law and prior appropriation law have mechanisms to protect the public's interest in water, each doctrine has limitations. In pure riparian jurisdictions, water rights are essentially an interest associated with land ownership. Often, the "public" does not qualify as a landowner that can assert the reasonableness of their use in a typical riparian case. In the modern era, all prior appropriation jurisdictions have provisions that allow water rights to be established for non-consumptive uses and have requirements that water rights applications be evaluated against public interest standards. However, given the first-in-time, first-in-right nature of appropriative rights, the public's interest is often established later in time in the priority system. Regulated riparian law seeks to remedy some of these challenges.

Regulated riparian statutes typically provide that water is a form of public property. The recognition of water as public property distinguishes regulated riparianism from pure riparian law, where water rights are essentially a form of common property, and prior appropriation law, where water rights may be characterized as private property. Regulated riparian codes also set forth criteria for evaluating water use and/or preferences for use that specifically recognize the public's interest in the water. These often include conserving water, protecting the public interest, establishing minimum stream flows, and protecting public water supplies. *See, e.g.*, Ala. Code

§ 9–10B–2; Ark. Code Ann. § 15–22–201; Conn. Gen. Stat. § 22a–380; Del. Code Ann. tit. 7, § 6001(c); Fla. Stat.§ 373.016(3); Haw. Rev. Stat. § 174C–2; Iowa Code § 455B.262; Ky. Rev. Stat. Ann. § 151.110(1); Md. Env. Code § 5–501; Mass. Gen. Laws ch. 21G, § 3; Mich. Comp. Laws § 324.32702(1); Minn. Stat. § 103G.101; Miss. Code Ann. § 51–3–1; N.Y. Envtl. Conserv. Law § 15–0105; N.C. Gen. Stat. § 143–215; Va. Code Ann. § 62.1–11. Georgia, Iowa, and Kentucky provide that permits may be modified to deal with shortages or otherwise to accommodate the public interest or property rights of others. Ga. Code Ann. § 12–5–31 (f), (*l*) (1982); Iowa Code Ann. § 455B.271(2)(d), (3) (1971); Ky. Rev. Stat. Ann. § 151.200(*l*) (1980). Some states, such as Georgia, North Carolina, and South Carolina, may revoke or cancel a permit if contrary to the public interest. Ga. Code Ann. § 12–5–96(c)(4) (Supp. 1982); N.C. Gen. Stat. § 143–215.15(c), (h) (1978); S.C. Code Ann. § 49–4–120 (1976).

Despite the movement toward protecting non-consumptive uses and the public interest, regulated riparian jurisdictions, like pure riparian and prior appropriative states, have complex dynamics regarding preferences and priorities for certain private uses of waters. Typically, states recognize human consumption as the highest use. After human consumption, an array of private uses may be preferred over recreational, aesthetic, or other non-consumptive uses, including agriculture, municipal, industrial, commercial, and hydropower, among others. *See, e.g.*, Ark. Code Ann. § 15–22–217; Minn.

Stat. § 103G.261(a); Iowa Code § 455B.266; Md. Env. Code § 5–502(d); Ala. Code § 9–10B–2(7).

## E. ALLOCATING WATER THROUGH AN ADMINISTRATIVE AGENCY

In most regulated riparian states, the state legislature gave an administrative agency the power to confer water rights. Florida and Arkansas represent exceptions to this general trend by delegating the permitting authority to regional conservation and water districts. Ark. Code Ann. §§ 15–22–202(4), 15–22–221; Fla. Stat. §§ 373.069 to 373.083. Officials charged with issuing permits must evaluate competing uses using factors that closely resemble the common law reasonableness factors set forth in pure riparian states. 1 Waters and Water Rights § 9.03(5)(A). Thus, the difference between pure riparian states and regulated riparian states is not the substantive decision of which rights are reasonable and which are not. Rather, the differences between the two systems are found in the decision maker and in the timing of the decision.

In terms of the decision maker, a court determines the reasonableness of a water use as against another water use in pure riparian jurisdictions. In a regulated riparian jurisdiction, an administrative agency determines the reasonableness of competing uses. In terms of timing, for a pure riparian jurisdiction, competing uses are not reconciled against one another unless there is a conflict that makes its way to court. In a regulated riparian jurisdiction, competing uses are reconciled during the permitting process in advance of the use commencing.

When determining the reasonableness of a water use in a regulated riparian jurisdiction, the agency determines the quantity one may divert and sets the terms and conditions. The administrative process typically provides for public hearings and notice to those impacted by a permit decision. Once the agency has issued the permit, the agency's decision is subject to judicial review pursuant to state administrative law mechanisms. *See, e.g.*, Marion County v. Greene, 5 So.3d 775 (Fla. Dist. Ct. App. 2009) (Judicial review of Water Management District's decision to adopt an Administrative Law Judge's order approving a consumptive use permit). In the end, regulated riparian law, in theory, transfers the decision-making power from private litigants in courts to executive branch agencies with expertise in water management. Joseph W. Dellapenna, *The Importance of Getting Names Right: The Myth of Markets for Water,* 25 Wm. & Mary Envtl. L. & Pol'y 317 (2000); Eric Freyfogle, *Water Rights and the Common Wealth*, 26 Envtl. L. 27 (1996).

# CHAPTER THREE
# PRIOR APPROPRIATION

## I. INTRODUCTION TO PRIOR APPROPRIATION

The prior appropriation doctrine was developed to serve the practical demands of nineteenth century water users in the western United States. It originated in the customs of miners who recognized superior rights of those who first used water. Later, prior appropriation was extended to ranchers, farmers, and other water users. Many western state legislatures have memorialized prior appropriation in their constitutions.

Prior appropriation rights are granted based on the time when a person applies a particular quantity of water to a beneficial use. Those rights continue so long as the beneficial use is maintained. The basic elements of a valid appropriation are:

- *Intent* to apply water to a beneficial use;
- An actual *diversion* of water from a natural source of surface water; and
- Application of the water to a *beneficial use* within a reasonable time.

The date of the appropriation determines the user's priority, with the earliest user having the superior right. If water is insufficient to meet all needs, those earliest in time of appropriation (senior appropriators) will typically obtain all of their allotted water; those who appropriated later (junior appropriators) may receive only some, or none, of the water to which they have rights, depending on the amount available. This "first in time, first in right" concept contrasts sharply with the riparian tradition of prorating the entitlement to water among all users during times of scarcity. However, a few states, most notably California, have "hybrid" systems that employ elements of the riparian doctrine as well as the appropriation doctrine.

A beneficial use that will support an appropriation must have a specific, stated purpose such as irrigation, domestic, industrial, firefighting, or livestock watering. The property where water is applied does not have to be adjacent to the source and does not even need to be within the same watershed. Most states allow the transfer of water away from the property to which the rights first attached if the rights of other appropriators are not harmed.

In general, water may be appropriated for any use the state deems beneficial. More economically or socially useful purposes that commenced later in time ordinarily will not be preferred over older, less valuable ones. Although some state statutes or constitutions express preferences for domestic and other critical uses, they do not alter the basic principle of priority based on first use.

Because the measure of an appropriative right is the quantity of water that is put to a beneficial use, an appropriator has no right to waste water. Diverting more water than is necessary is wasteful, deprives other users of water, and is not considered a beneficial use. If a determination of waste is made, the appropriator may lose that portion of the water right. Moreover, long term failure to use appropriated water can result in the loss of the right. If disuse is intentional, it may be construed as abandonment; unintended disuse results in forfeiture in some states.

Although the early reasons for creating private rights to use public waters—like mining on the public lands—were short-lived, and today's uses are far more diverse, the appropriation doctrine remains intact. It has, however, been tempered and modified. Although the underlying rights to most surface water in the West were established by prior appropriation, in most western states today, their use is governed, and new rights must be established, according to complex statutory schemes. Most require water users to have permits. In addition, in most states, statutes charge administrative agencies with assuring that new, transferred, or changed appropriations are in the public interest. States define public interest differently, sometimes necessitating choices among competing appropriators based on whether the public interest will be served and, in some cases, the public interest requires denials or conditions upon new appropriations, changes of use, or transfers. In addition, some courts have held that states have a "public trust" duty to examine appropriations to ensure that they are consistent with public purposes.

## II. DEVELOPMENT OF PRIOR APPROPRIATION DOCTRINE

The doctrine of prior appropriation can be traced to local customs developed during the nation's western expansion, particularly after the discovery of gold in California in 1848. Available water sources were limited, and mining (especially placer mining) demanded large quantities of water and it often took place on federal public lands, which meant that riparian reasonable use rules did not work well.

Rules were developed in the mining camps to allocate the available water peaceably. The rules were similar to those adopted for the establishment and protection of mining claims on public lands: first in time, first in right. Essentially, the first user of water from a specific source held a right that would be protected against the claims of others who came later. The same system was applied to agricultural lands as homesteaders moved west. It prevented farmers who took up land along the streams from monopolizing water that could be productively used on lands not touching any water source. This made sense in an arid region where much of the settled land and many homesteads were far from a stream.

The United States acquired western territory from foreign nations and Indian nations, and then disposed of its lands through a variety of public land laws, including the Homestead Act of 1862, the Mining Act of 1866, the Desert Land Act of 1877, and the Stock-Raising Homestead Act of 1916. Instead of conveying the land and (riparian) water rights together, the government acquiesced in the establishment of private water rights under local customs, including rights to divert water across public land to distant mining claims and irrigated tracts. Lands were then patented (granted by the government) separately from these water rights, but were subject to any rights that were previously established by others.

## A. FEDERAL STATUTES

### 1. 1866 and 1870 Mining Acts

Shortly after the Civil War, proposals were made in Congress to withdraw mines from the public domain and to operate or sell them to pay war debts. When western legislators voiced opposition, Congress passed the 1866 Mining Act. The Act reads in relevant part:

> Whenever, by priority of possession, rights to the use of water for mining, agricultural, manufacturing, or other purposes have vested and accrued, and the same are recognized and acknowledged by the local customs, laws and decisions of courts, the possessors and owners of such vested rights shall be maintained and protected in the same.

30 U.S.C. § 51. The Act expressly confirmed the rights of miners and appropriators. It formally sanctioned appropriations of water on the public lands made before or after passage of the Act, as well as rights of way for transporting the water across public lands. The Act failed to define any method of acquiring water rights from the federal government,

thus deferring to established local customs, state or territorial laws, and judicial rulings. Broder v. Natoma Water Co., 101 U.S. 274, 276 (1879).

Even after the 1866 Act, it was not clear whether riparian landowners who obtained grants of land from the United States held riparian water rights or were instead subject to claims of prior appropriators. The 1870 amendment to the Mining Act clarified that issue in favor of prior appropriators. It stipulated that anyone who acquired title to public lands through federal patents, homestead rights, or rights of preemption took title subject to water rights, easements for water rights, or rights of way acquired by others while lands were in public ownership. 30 U.S.C. § 52; 43 U.S.C. § 661. These rights are good against both the United States and its grantees.

## 2. 1877 Desert Land Act

The Desert Land Act provided that water from non-navigable sources on the public lands was available for appropriation for irrigation, mining, and manufacturing purposes subject to existing rights. 43 U.S.C. § 321. It applied specifically to arid lands within Arizona, California, Idaho, Montana, Nevada, New Mexico, North Dakota, Oregon, South Dakota, Utah, Washington, and Wyoming. 43 U.S.C. § 323. Colorado was added by amendment in 1891.

For several decades, western states were divided concerning whether the Desert Land Act applied only to desert lands. The Supreme Court ultimately decided that the Act applied to all public domain in the named states and territories. California Oregon

Power Co. v. Beaver Portland Cement Co., 295 U.S. 142 (1935). The Court also found that the Desert Land Act severed the water from public lands, so that only water rights established under local law passed with a patent to the land. *Id.* at 162. The Act states:

> [T]he right to the use of water by the person so conducting the same on or to any tract of desert land of 640 acres shall depend upon bona fide prior appropriation, and such right shall not exceed the amount of water actually appropriated and necessarily used for the purpose of irrigation and reclamation; *and all surplus water over and above such actual appropriation and use, together with the water of all lakes, rivers, and other sources of water supply on the public lands and not navigable, shall remain and be held free for the appropriation and use of the public for irrigation, mining, and manufacturing purposes, subject to existing rights.*

43 U.S.C. § 321 (emphasis added). Thus, all unappropriated waters of non-navigable sources were open to appropriation according to state law.

## B. DEVELOPMENT OF MODERN SYSTEMS

The appropriation system was an expedient means to encourage development of the arid West, where much of the arable land is distant from streams and water is limited. It rewarded those who first risked their effort and money.

The eight most arid states (Arizona, Colorado, Idaho, Montana, Nevada, New Mexico, Utah, and Wyoming) constitutionally or statutorily repudiated riparian rights and adopted prior appropriation as the sole method of acquiring rights to the use of water for beneficial purposes. *See, e.g.*, Ariz. Const. Art. 17 § 1 ("The common law doctrine of riparian water rights shall not obtain or be of any force or effect in the state"); Colo. Const. Art.16 § 6 ("Priority of appropriation shall give the better right as between those using the water for the same purpose"). In these states, statutory systems have evolved to provide for initiation of appropriations, establishment and enforcement of priorities, and water distribution.

Early in Alaska's development, some riparian uses for mining purposes were allowed, but in 1966, its legislature converted all riparian rights into appropriative rights. Alaska Stat. § 46.15.040. This conversion was more ambitious than the approach taken by several other western states, where existing riparian rights were preserved to some extent after adoption of the appropriation doctrine. *See, e.g.*, Mont. Const. Art. 9 § 3(1).

Some degree of riparian common law continues to exist side-by-side with the statutory provisions of prior appropriation in California, Kansas, Nebraska, North Dakota, Oklahoma, Oregon, South Dakota, Texas, and Washington. These states generally recognized riparian rights but limited their expansion and recognized new rights only by prior appropriation. *See e.g.,* Cal. Water Code § 101. Hybrid systems are discussed in Chapter Four, *infra.*

## III. ELEMENTS OF APPROPRIATION

Although the definitions and details vary from state to state, a valid appropriation generally turns on water being *diverted* with *intent* to *apply* it for *beneficial use.*

At first, the appropriation system was encumbered by few procedures and legal requirements. One who needed water had only to begin using it. But in order to perfect a legal right in the water, the user had to show that the use amounted to an appropriation. The three elements—diversion, intent, application to beneficial use—were designed to prevent fraud and to provide some order in an otherwise unstructured system. Additionally, states have a special interest in assuring that water, a public resource, is devoted to beneficial uses consistent with the public good.

Historically, it was necessary for an appropriator to be able to prove that all three elements were satisfied to perfect a water right. Since these elements have become incorporated into modern state statutes, their importance is largely theoretical. Permit systems and agencies that review applications for water rights impose a variety of requirements designed to achieve the purposes of the common law elements of appropriation.

## A. INTENT

An appropriation is not valid unless the appropriator intends to divert water and apply it to a beneficial use. Thus, one who diverts water away from its normal flow pattern in order to prevent flood damage is not an appropriator. But such a diverter who later finds a beneficial use for that water may become an appropriator as of the time the requisite intent is manifested.

Issues regarding intent arise most frequently when one seeks to secure a priority that predates the diversion. The "relation back" doctrine allows an appropriator to perfect a water right with a priority date as of the time an intent to appropriate was first formed. "[T]he appropriation is not deemed complete until the actual diversion or use of the water, still if such work be prosecuted with reasonable diligence, the right relates to the time when the first step was taken to secure it." Ophir Silver Min. Co. v. Carpenter, 4 Nev. 534 (1869). Evidence must be presented to prove that one had such intent and that work was proceeding toward an actual diversion of water (not just speculation) as of the priority date.

In states where a permit is required for a valid appropriation, application for a permit is objective evidence of intent. However, one may not apply for a water right and then seek a place to use it, as that would constitute speculation. Lemmon v. Hardy, 519 P.2d 1168 (Idaho 1974). Early statutory systems gave appropriators the option of diverting or applying for a permit to secure water rights. An applicant could choose to divert without a permit and still relate back the priority to the time that work on the diversion facilities began. Sand Point Water & Light Co. v. Panhandle Dev. Co., 83 P. 347 (Idaho 1905).

Where permits are not required for a valid appropriation, as in Colorado, proof of intent retains some importance and is decided on a case-by-case basis. To establish the priority of an appropriation, an applicant must make a clear decision to use water and an "open, physical demonstration of that intent." Harvey Land & Cattle Co. v. Southeastern Colo. Water Conservancy Dist., 631 P.2d 1111, 1113 (Colo. 1981). This requirement is a means of giving notice to others that one intends to appropriate water, though the actual diversion will be in the future. City of Thornton v. Bijou Irrigation Co., 926 P.2d 1 (Colo. 1996); Teton Cooperative Reservoir Company, 414 P.3d 1249 (Mont. 2018).

Courts may examine other relevant evidence besides the first open physical act to determine whether the requisite intent was present. City of Aspen v. Colorado River Water Conservation Dist., 696 P.2d 758 (Colo. 1985). However, surveys that are not accompanied by a clear decision to undertake the project may not be sufficient. Colorado River Water Conservation Dist. v. Rocky Mountain Power Co., 486 P.2d 438 (Colo. 1971). In *Harvey Land & Cattle Co.*, 631 P.2d at 1113, the court found that drilling wells with capacity greater than the existing right constituted a "physical act" necessary to perfect a new water right; however, the priority date related back only to the time, years after the wells were drilled, when the intent to use the wells for larger quantities was formed.

Colorado law provides for conditional decrees that recognize rights to a particular quantity of water for a specific future use. In order to get a conditional decree, one must demonstrate a present, non-speculative intent to put the water to a beneficial use and then must proceed with due diligence to divert the water. Colo. Rev. Stat. §§ 37–92–103(6), 37–92–305(1). *See* Pagosa Area Water and Sanitation Dist. v. Trout Unlimited, 219 P.3d 774 (2009) (a water supply agency may get a conditional decree for future use for the amount that is reasonably necessary for substantiated population projections for a reasonable planning period). The applicant must describe with particularity the construction plans and amount of water needed. Colo. Rev. Stat. § 37–92–302. Opponents to the decree may file objections, and the application is adjudicated with respect to the rights of all parties in the stream system.

A conditional decree may be lost if a city loses a contractual agreement to use a necessary diversion facility. City of Lafayette v. New Anderson Ditch Co., 962 P.2d 955 (Colo. 1998). The applicant must establish that there is a substantial probability that the facilities necessary for the appropriation "can and will" be completed and the water put to a beneficial use within a reasonable time. Colo. Rev. Stat. § 37–92–305. In determining whether water is available for the conditional decree, the court considers absolute decrees and conditional decrees under which diversions have taken place, but can disregard conditional decrees for which no diversions have been made. Board of County Commissioners of the County of Arapahoe v. United States, 891 P.2d 952 (Colo. 1995). Environmental factors need not be considered in issuing the conditional decree (and hence in granting water rights). *Id.* at 971. However, if an instream flow right has been recognized, it will be superior to subsequent appropriators. Colorado Water Conservation Bd. v. City of Cent., 125 P.3d 424, 439 (Colo. 2005). *See infra* Section III.D.3.

## B. DIVERSION

Historically, water had to be physically diverted from a surface water body in order to obtain a valid appropriation. The diversion requirement provided notice to present and prospective appropriators that water had been appropriated. Today, many western states recognize various uses that do not depend on structures or human acts, despite the lack of a diversion.

### 1. Types of Diversions

A diversion is an alteration of part or all of a stream's flow away from its natural course. A common method of diversion is to build a structure in a natural stream that directs water into a nearby canal or ditch. Water may be channeled farther into smaller ditches, each with a headgate that controls when and how much water is used in each of several parcels of land, often by several appropriators. Other methods of diverting water include reservoirs, flumes, pipes, pumps, and water wheels.

Traditionally, a diversion had to be a human-made method of physically removing water from the stream, but courts have forged numerous exceptions for various kinds of uses, as discussed below in Section III.B.3. States that continue to insist on physical diversions have sometimes approved of the creative use of low control structures that divert the stream back to its historic channel to maintain recreational or aesthetic stream qualities. City of Thornton By and Through Utilities Bd. v. City of Fort Collins, 830 P.2d 915 (Colo. 1992).

### 2. Due Diligence Requirement and Conditional Rights

In states that require a permit to appropriate water, the priority date may relate back to the date the application was filed. In order to keep that priority date and to perfect a water right, the appropriator must complete construction with due diligence and actually use the water within the time specified in the permit or statute.

Some state statutes set maximum time periods for construction of facilities and application of water to beneficial use, often five years, subject to extension for good cause (*e.g.*, Arizona, Idaho, Nevada, Oregon, Wyoming, and New Mexico allow four additional years after construction to use the water). A few require actual construction to begin within a certain time, ranging from six months to two years after approval of the application. Some states readily allow time extensions upon a showing that the applicant has proceeded with due diligence; others grant extensions only in narrowly defined circumstances. Idaho, for example, allows extensions after its five-year limit only if the applicant is prevented from continuing by delays in receiving necessary federal approvals or the completion of litigation, or if the project is extremely large. Idaho Code Ann. § 42–222.

In Colorado, which does not have a permit system, an appropriator's priority date is generally the date of an application for a conditional right. Colo. Rev. Stat § 37–92–306.1; City and County of Denver v. Sheriff, 96 P.2d 836 (Colo. 1939). The priority date, however, will relate back only to the point when the "first step" was taken to appropriate water from a specific stream and not the first step taken to commence a project involving several streams, unless the appropriator can demonstrate that the diversions are for "one over-all integral plan" from "tributaries of one stream and one water basin in one water district." Metro. Suburban Water Users Ass'n v. Colo. River Water Conservation Dist., 365 P.2d 273, 283 (Colo. 1961). Also, a conditional priority date will be lost unless the prospective appropriator completes construction with due diligence within a reasonable time. Purgatoire River Water Conservancy Dist. v. Witte, 859 P.2d 825 (Colo. 1993); City of Thornton v. Bijou Irrigation Co., 926 P.2d 1 (Colo. 1996).

Colorado's procedure for obtaining a conditional decree is discussed in the preceding subsection. If a conditional decree is granted, the prospective user must proceed with due diligence in constructing the waterworks or risk forfeiture of the conditional right. Colo. Rev. Stat. § 37–92–301. The decree holder must obtain a finding of due diligence by a water court referee every six years. Colo. Rev. Stat § 37–92–301(4)(a)(1). Failure to do so will result in cancellation of the conditional right. Town of De Beque v. Enewold, 606 P.2d 48 (Colo. 1980). However, a conditional right cannot be cancelled absent adequate notice. Double RL Co. v. Telluray Ranch Props., 54 P.3d 908 (Colo. 2002). Once the diversion takes place, an absolute decree can be obtained with a priority date relating back to the initiation of the conditional decree.

### 3. Exceptions to the Diversion Requirement

A few states no longer require actual diversion if intent to appropriate, notice to others, and application to a beneficial use are clearly established. *See e.g.,* Phelps Dodge Corp. v. Arizona Dep't of Water Resources, 118 P.3d 1110 (Ariz. App. 2005). In Montana, for example, a physical diversion is not required unless the beneficial use depends on it. In re Adjudication of Existing Rights to the Use of All the Water, 55 P.3d 396 (Mont. 2002). If land can be irrigated naturally with the help of existing channels and depressions, it may be considered a waste of resources to require the appropriator to construct artificial ditches. In re Water Rts. in Silvies River, 237 P. 322 (Or. 1925). In dicta, one court even hinted that mist from a waterfall that nourishes vegetation might constitute a valid appropriation. Empire Water & Power Co. v. Cascade Town Co., 205 F. 123 (8th Cir. 1913).

Some western states consider it to be a diversion when ranchers allow livestock to drink water from ponds, marshes, or streams. *See, e.g.*, Joyce Livestock Co. v. U.S., 156 P.3d 502 (Idaho 2007); Matter of Rts. to Use of Surface Waters of Yakima River Drainage Basin, 498 P.3d 911 (Wash. 2021). However, the New Mexico Supreme Court rejected a rancher's claim that grazing cattle on grass watered by intermittent runoff evidenced his intention to appropriate water. State ex rel. Reynolds v. Miranda, 493 P.2d 409 (N.M. 1972). The court held that a man-made diversion was necessary for a valid appropriation, and found that the rancher had made no attempt to actually divert any of the water. *Id.* at 411.

Several states have embraced a trend allowing instream (*in situ*) appropriations of water despite the lack of a diversion. *See* In re Application A-16642, 463 N.W.2d 591 (Neb. 1990) (upholding instream appropriations for a trout fishery); *Phelps Dodge Corp.*, 118 P.3d at 1115 (recognizing instream flow rights for fish, wildlife, and recreation). Alaska, California, Colorado, Hawaii, Idaho, Kansas, Montana, Nebraska, Oklahoma, Oregon, Utah, Washington, and Wyoming have enacted legislation allowing instream uses of water. An instream appropriation generally requires that a certain amount of water be allowed to flow through a stretch of stream in order to protect fish and wildlife, scenic beauty, or recreation. *See* State, Dept. of Parks v. Idaho Dept. of Water Administration, 530 P.2d 924 (Idaho 1974) (upholding a statute declaring preservation of flows in Malad Canyon for scenic and recreational purposes).

In most states, instream flows may be appropriated only by a state agency, although the agency may be able to act upon requests of private individuals, other state and local agencies, or the federal government. Colorado allows instream flows to be appropriated exclusively by the state Water Conservation Board upon a finding that it will "preserve the natural environment to a reasonable degree." Colo. Rev. Stat. § 37–92–102(3). *See* Application for Water Rights in the San Miguel River, 346 P.3d 52 (Colo. 2015) (upholding an environmental instream flow right).

Colorado cities were successful in convincing the state supreme court to uphold their rights to an appropriation for recreational uses by constructing facilities such as boat chutes and fish ladders to ostensibly control the stream without actually removing water. City of Thornton v. City of Fort Collins, 830 P.2d 915 (Colo. 1992). This type of so-called diversion was later regulated by legislation that allows courts to adjudicate rights for "recreational in-channel diversions" (RICDs) upon findings related to promoting full development of the state's water and the appropriateness of the use for the stream in question. Colo. Rev. Stat. § 37–92–102(5)–(6)(c).

Arizona, Nevada, and South Dakota have recognized instream appropriations without enabling legislation; instead, they allow instream appropriations as part of their general appropriation procedures. The New Mexico Attorney General determined that a traditional water right can be changed to an instream use under certain circumstances and that the state constitution does not require an actual diversion. Op.Atty.Gen.No. 98–01 (1998). *See* Carangelo v. Albuquerque-Bernalillo Cnty. Water Auth., 320 P.3d 492 (N.M.App. 2013) (city's proposed non-consumptive use of Rio Grande water was a beneficial use). The New Mexico legislature has also authorized its interstate stream commission to purchase or lease water to create a "strategic water reserve" in order to achieve compliance with the Endangered Species Act and to meet water delivery requirements under various interstate compacts. N.M. Stat. Ann. § 72–14–3.3.

## C. BENEFICIAL USE

The last and most important step in perfecting an appropriation is application of the water to beneficial use. "Beneficial use" is "the use of such water as may be necessary for some useful and beneficial purpose in connection with the land . . . requir[ing] actual use for some purpose that is socially accepted as beneficial." State ex rel. Office of State Eng'r v. United States, 296 P.3d 1217, 1222 (N.M. App. 2012), *cert. denied,* 299 P.3d 862 (2013).

All prior appropriation states consider domestic, municipal, agricultural, and industrial uses to be beneficial. Recognized types of beneficial uses may be defined more elaborately by statute or case law (see Table A). Just because a use is among the types listed, however, does not mean it will be deemed "beneficial" under the circumstances or for all time.

Yesterday's beneficial use may be unreasonable or wasteful, and thus impermissible, today.

Table A– *David Getches 2008*

**BENEFICIAL USES SPECIFIED BY STATE LAW**

| Use: | Domestic | Municipal | Irrigation or agricultural | Industrial | Stock-watering | Power | Mining | Recreation | Fish & wildlife | Other |
|---|---|---|---|---|---|---|---|---|---|---|
| Alaska | X | X | X | X | | X | X | X | X | manufacturing, navigation, transportation, water quality |
| Arizona | X | X | X | | X | X | X | X | X | groundwater recharge |
| California | X | X | X | X | X | X | X | X | X | water quality |
| Colorado | X | X | X | X | | | | X | X | |
| Idaho* | | | | | | | | | | |
| Kansas | X | X | X | X | | X | | X | | |
| Montana | X | X | X | X | X | X | X | X | X | |
| Nebraska* | | | | | | | | | | |
| Nevada* | | | X | | | | X | X | X | state conservation purposes |
| New Mexico** | | | | | | | | | | |
| North Dakota | X | X | X | X | X | | | X | X | |
| Oklahoma* | | X | X | X | | | | X | X | not limited to these |
| Oregon | X | X | X | X | | X | X | X | X | pollution abatement |
| South Dakota*** | | | | | | | | | | |
| Texas | X | X | X | X | X | X | X | X | X | parks, aquifer recharge, "any other beneficial use" |
| Utah* | | | X | | X | | | | | |
| Washington | X | | X | X | X | X | X | X | X | frost protection |
| Wyoming* | X | X | X | | | | | | | |

* No comprehensive definition furnished by statute or case law.

** Case law defines beneficial use as "the use of such water as may be necessary for some useful and beneficial purpose in connection with the land from which it is taken." Erickson v. McLean, 62 N.M. 264, 308 P.2d 983 (1957).

*** Statute defines beneficial use as "any use of water within or outside of the state, that is reasonable and useful and beneficial to the appropriator, and at the same time is consistent with the interests of the public...." S.D.Cod.Laws § 46-1-6 (3).

Domestic use generally includes household uses such as cooking, drinking, laundering, washing, and gardening. In rural areas, domestic use may also include water for raising animals on a small scale, such as keeping a few dairy cows or chickens. Municipal use includes domestic use by residents, water used in operating public buildings, and even irrigation of city parks.

Initially, the range of beneficial uses was very limited. A federal appeals court refused to consider recreation a beneficial use. Empire Water & Power Co. v. Cascade Town Co., 205 F. 123 (8th Cir. 1913). The court would not allow a resort town to assert a right to keep the town's major attraction, a waterfall, flowing merely to retain its scenic beauty. However, the court seemed willing to allow the waterfall to continue flowing if the town could assert an agricultural use, such as misting the vegetation growing on the banks of Cascade Falls. *Id.* at 129. Similarly, the Colorado Supreme Court has held that to "use" is to "put into action or service." St. Jude's v. Roaring Fork Club, L.L.C., 351 P.3d 442, 451 (Colo. 2015) (rejecting a golf club's diversion application on the grounds that aesthetic and fly fishing uses are "passive" and not within the scope of beneficial use).

Most states now have accepted recreation as a beneficial use. *See, e.g.,* Or. Rev. Stat. § 536.300(1); Mont. Code Ann. § 85–2–102(4)(a). Some statutory provisions specify that scenic or aesthetic uses are also beneficial. *See, e.g.,* Wash. Rev. Code § 90.54.020(3)(a); Hawaii Rev. Stat. § 174C–71(1)(C). By comparison, Colorado has taken a relatively narrow stance by recognizing recreational in-channel diversions (RICDs), which limit water rights to the minimum flow necessary for a reasonable recreational experience in and on the water. Colo. Rev. Stat § 37–92–103(10.3). *See* Pagosa Area Water & Sanitation District v. Trout Unlimited, 219 P.3d 774, 781 (Colo. 2009) (rejecting districts' attempt to appropriate water in order to obtain priority over a city's potential kayak course).

Once an appropriator puts water to a use considered beneficial by state law, the right is perfected. The right becomes absolute and its priority in times of shortage will not be defeated even by more socially important, more economically valuable, or more efficient uses by a junior appropriator. Thus, a senior user applying vast quantities of water to the unprofitable production of rice in the desert might prevent a city with a junior right from receiving desperately needed water for domestic purposes, or a highly profitable industry from taking the water that it requires. Janet C. Neuman, *Beneficial Use, Waste, and Forfeiture: The Inefficient Search for Efficiency in Western Water Use,* 28 Envtl. L. 919, 970 (1998). To temper the effects of this rule, some jurisdictions have enacted preference statutes that allow junior appropriators with certain preferred uses, such as domestic and agricultural uses, to condemn senior rights with a beneficial use in a lower preference category, such as industry. *See infra* Section IV.D.

## D. WATERS SUBJECT TO APPROPRIATION

Private rights to use water cannot be acquired in all types of water. State law provisions may describe waters of a "natural stream" as being "public property" subject to appropriation, while excluding certain types of waters (such as runoff or seasonal floods) from the reach of private water rights. State law may also recognize greater or lesser private rights in various types of water (*e.g.*, groundwater) and define the extent to which such waters are subject to public use.

### 1. Watercourses

Once water enters a watercourse, it becomes subject to state control. It then becomes available for private uses according to state appropriation law.

"Watercourses" could be defined to include not only rivers and lakes, but every tiny brook flowing into them, all the gullies through which water flows to the brooks, the snowpack and rainfall that feed them, and the evaporating or transpiring water in the process of forming clouds. But it would be an immense challenge to regulate these sources. Legal definitions are intended to delineate a point beyond which a state does not regulate water use. Usually that point is when water is not in a "natural stream." *See* Cal. Const., art. X § 2 ("The right to water . . . in or from any natural stream or water course in this State is and shall be limited to such water as shall be reasonably required for the beneficial use"); Chatfield East Well Co., Ltd. v. Chatfield East Property Owners Ass'n, 956 P.2d 1260, 1268 (Colo.

1998) (waters of a natural stream, including tributary ground water, are subject to appropriation).

Courts often define a stream or watercourse as a body of water flowing in a defined channel with a bed and banks. Generally, the waterbody must have some permanence. Montana, for instance, defines a watercourse as "any naturally occurring stream or river from which water is diverted for beneficial uses." Mont. Code Ann. § 85–2–102(30). The definition excludes "ditches, culverts, or other constructed waterways." *Id.*

In contrast to defined watercourses, diffused surface water ordinarily may be freely taken and used by landowners without regulation. Drainage Dist. No. 1 of Lincoln Cnty. v. Suburban Irr. Dist., 298 N.W. 131, 132 (Neb. 1941); State v. Hiber, 44 P.2d 1005, 1008 (Wyo. 1935). However, Alaska, Montana, Nevada, Oregon, Texas, and Utah claim broader control over various kinds of waters, and Utah and Colorado construe the state's authority as extending well beyond natural watercourses to virtually all surface water and even some groundwater, *see* Utah Code Ann. § 73–1–1(1); Colo. Const., Art. 16 § 5. For details on diffused surface water, *see* Chapter Six, *infra*.

### *a. Streams*

Although western states typically apply the prior appropriation doctrine to watercourses with a definite bed, bank, and channel, these requirements rarely resolve hard cases. For example, freshets (flows due to runoff from rainfall or melting snow) may appear to be streams at least part of the year, cutting draws or ravines as water flows toward rivers, but a court may also require that there be a continuous flow to be covered as a natural stream. Yet some indisputable "watercourses" flow only intermittently and are made up solely of snowmelt and rainwater. This is especially true in the high mountains of the West where streams dry up in summer. Further, some genuine streams simply do not run in great enough volume or speed to carve out banks or scour a bed. In flat areas, a river may spread out and avoid cutting a defined channel, or it may meander through different routes each season.

Besides considering the geographic characteristics discussed above, some courts resort to a functional test. In Texas, the courts have asked whether the volume and regularity make it practicable to use the stream for irrigation. Hoefs v. Short, 273 S.W. 785 (Tex. 1925). Arizona law subjects "subflow"—where groundwater pumping "appreciably diminishes the surface flow of a stream"—to prior appropriation. Gila River Indian Cmty. v. Schoubroek, 145 F.4th 1058, 1068 (9th Cir. 2025).

Other courts have rested their decisions on factual determinations that escape easy classification. In State v. Hiber, 44 P.2d 1005 (Wyo. 1935), the state sought to enjoin the defendant from impounding waters that flowed down a swale or draw behind a small dam because the impoundment allegedly interfered with the flow of a natural stream. The court reviewed decisions in various states that distinguished between watercourses and diffused surface water, and found some attributes of a watercourse present but others lacking. *Id.* at 1009–10. Concluding that it was not a watercourse, the court leaned heavily on the peculiar characteristics of the flow in question, stating "[j]udging from the testimony, no one would instantaneously perceive that it is a watercourse." *Id.* at 1011.

This perception test ("I know a stream when I see it") may seem unworkable, but in difficult cases, the outcome may be dictated by the practicality and utility of state regulation of the water. Presumably, the more arid the area, the more important a small flow will be and the greater the likelihood it will be found to be a watercourse.

### b. Lakes and Ponds

The water of natural lakes and ponds is subject to appropriation by state law. The right to appropriate water from such sources may be qualified by the littoral (lakeshore) landowners' rights to use the surface (as distinguished from rights to consume water), even in prior appropriation states. *See supra* Chapter 2.II.D. For instance, an appropriator may be precluded from drawing water from a lake if it would substantially lower water levels and interfere with littoral owners' rights to access the lake for fishing, recreation, or other lawful purposes. In re Martha Lake Water Co. No. 1, 277 P. 382 (Wash. 1929).

### c. Springs

The treatment of spring water varies by state, and also by the type of spring. Some states consider a spring subject to appropriation only if its flow forms a stream; otherwise, spring water is treated as groundwater. Okla. Water Res. Bd. v. City of Lawton, 580 P.2d 510, 513 (Okla. 1977). Others subject spring water to appropriation. Parker v. McIntyre, 56 P.2d 1337, 1340 (Ariz. 1936); Dalton v. Wadley, 355 P.2d 69, 88 (Utah 1960). Colorado subjects springs to appropriation if they are "tributary" (closely connected, hydrologically) to surface waters. SRJ I Venture v. Smith Cattle, Inc., 820 P.2d 341, 345 (Colo. 1991) (citing Colo. Rev. Stat. § 37–82–102).

### 2. Waters Made Available by Human Effort

Sometimes water ends up in a natural stream in ways other than those that would normally occur in nature. This may be because irrigation return flows delay the seasonal decline in natural streamflow, or it may be the result of massive diversions from one watershed to another. The general rule is that water that would never be available in the stream except for human efforts can be used without restriction by the person responsible for its being there, and it is not subject to appropriation unless that person abandons it. Ariz. Pub. Serv. Co. v. Long, 773 P.2d 988, 995 (Ariz. 1989). Courts draw distinctions, however, between foreign and developed water, and salvage water.

#### *a. Foreign or Developed Water*

Foreign or developed water is characterized as water that would not have been in a stream without human effort. It includes imported water brought to the stream from another watershed by tunnels, canals, pumps, and other facilities. It also includes groundwater pumped from an aquifer not hydrologically connected with the stream, as well as trapped water recovered from a mine. The rainfall from artificially induced precipitation, *i.e.*, "rain-making" by seeding clouds, is considered developed water in some states but not others. It may be sound policy to reward such private efforts, though it is virtually impossible to differentiate natural precipitation from the results of cloud seeding.

Imported or foreign water, *e.g.*, from transbasin diversions, is not part of the stream and thus not subject to appropriation by others. City and County of Denver v. Fulton Irrigating Ditch Co., 506 P.2d 144 (Colo. 1972). However, water diverted from an interstate stream through a headgate located just over the state line is still subject to regulation by authorities in the state of use. In State Eng'r of New Mexico v. Diamond K Bar Ranch, LLC, 385 P.3d 626, 631 (2016), the state sought to enjoin a ranch's illegal use of Animas River water to irrigate additional acreage for which the ranch had no permit. The court held that water diverted directly from the Animas should be characterized as unappropriated natural surface waters upon entry into New Mexico.

If the water is characterized as foreign, it will not be subject to restrictions on recapture and reuse. Water Supply and Storage Co. v. Curtis, 733 P.2d 680 (Colo. 1987); *see infra* Section V.C. Similarly, such water is not subject to the change of use restrictions discussed in Section VII.D.

Western irrigation practices involve repeated diversions, applications, and return flows of water as it moves downstream. Consequently, successive irrigators, often relying on return flows from upstream irrigators, depend on water being used in essentially the same manner year after year. If the water was not naturally present in the stream, the downstream irrigators may be cut off, despite their reliance on continued flows. Stevens v. Oakdale Irrig. Dist., 90 P.2d 58, 62 (Cal. 1939).

Thanks to importers, appropriators may have supplies available to them at times when they otherwise would have insufficient water. For instance, in a year of low natural flow, juniors below the point in a stream where a large importer ceases using water may, in effect, be using almost entirely return flows of imported water. Although such users may benefit incidentally, they can gain no appropriative right in the imported water. *Id.*; City of Thornton v. Bijou Irr. Co., 926 P.2d 1, 69 (Colo. 1996).

Just as an importer can stop importing water at any time, the importer can reuse the water, remove it from the stream at a different location, or sell it to others, without legal restraint. Thayer v. City of Rawlins, 594 P.2d 951, 956 (Wyo. 1979); Arizona Public Service Co. v. Long, 773 P.2d 988 (Ariz. 1989). Typically, imported water has been obtained from another watershed pursuant to a water right in that watershed. The right is, as to the original watershed, 100% consumptive. Streams in the new watershed are used only to transport the water and so it never becomes a part of the "natural stream." An exception arises if both the importing and exporting watersheds are part of the same larger watershed. In that case, the water remaining in the stream below the confluence of the two sub-watersheds would belong to the stream and again be subject to appropriation.

Once an importer ceases using imported water, the water is treated as abandoned and can be taken and used by others. Elgin v. Weatherstone, 212 P. 562 (Wash. 1923); Dodge v. Ellensburg Water Co., 729 P.2d 631 (Wash. App. 1986).

### b. *Salvaged Water*

In contrast to foreign or developed water, which would not naturally be in a stream but for human effort, salvaged water is recovered from existing uses or losses within the original watershed. City of Santa Maria v. Adam, 149 Cal.Rptr.3d 491, 522 (2012). For instance, if seepage or evaporative losses are prevented by human effort, fuller use could be made of the water. But it is not "new" to the stream in the same sense as imported water. Thus, salvaged water is considered subject to appropriation. It can be recaptured and reused according to rules discussed in Section V.C of this chapter, but it is subject to the priority system.

In Southeastern Colorado Water Conservancy Dist. v. Shelton Farms, Inc., 529 P.2d 1321, 1326 (Colo. 1974), applicants who had increased streamflow by removing water-consuming plants (phreatophytes) sought water rights free of all calls by others. The court held that water that had been freed from the plants was subject to the priority system and was therefore made available to other appropriators whose appropriations had not been fulfilled in the past. The court reached a similar result when an applicant proposed to pump water out of an aquifer in order to lower the water table, reduce the number of plants in the area, and reduce evapotranspiration rates. City of Aurora v. Colorado State Eng'r, 105 P.3d 595, 608 (Colo. 2005).

### 3. Withdrawals from Appropriation

Water in natural watercourses can be removed from availability for appropriation by state action or federal law for instream flows or to preserve it for future public use.

#### *a. Maintenance of Instream Flows*

Protection of streamflows and lake levels for fish and wildlife, recreation, water quality, and scenic beauty is accomplished in two ways. The waters can be "appropriated" for instream uses or they can be withdrawn from appropriation to preserve flows from depletion. The first approach initially conflicted with the fundamental requirements of the appropriation doctrine that water be diverted and put to a beneficial use; however, most states have relaxed their requirements and most consider recreation and wildlife protection to be beneficial uses. *See supra* Section III.B.3.

Withdrawing water from appropriation was one of the earliest methods for avoiding the obstacles that prevented appropriations for instream flows.

Statutes that remove waters from appropriation usually preserve all pre-existing, perfected appropriations as the date of enactment. Oregon and Idaho enacted statutes that removed certain rivers and lakes from appropriation and protected them from damage by state or private projects. The state engineer of North Dakota has power to reserve water for aquatic life, recreation, or other future beneficial uses. Other states, such as Alaska, Oklahoma, and California, identify particular rivers to be protected as "recreation rivers," "scenic river areas," "wild rivers," or "free-flowing rivers."

Utah allows its state engineer to deny appropriations if they would be detrimental to recreation or the natural stream environment. Utah Code Ann. § 73–3–8(1)(b). In Washington, the Department of Ecology has required maintenance of instream flows to protect endangered fish as a condition to a Clean Water Act water quality certification. PUD No. 1 of Pend Oreille v. Washington, 51 P.3d 744 (Wash. 2002); PUD No. 1 of Jefferson Cnty. v. Washington, 511 U.S. 700 (1994). Washington also allows administrative withdrawal of certain amounts of water from critical rivers or lakes, but only if withdrawal is in the public interest. Wash. Rev. Code. § 90.54.020(3)(a). Montana enacted the most sweeping law of this type when it gave state, municipal, and federal agencies the authority to apply for the reservation of waters for instream flows for fish and wildlife, recreation, and water quality. Such reservations may not exceed 50% of the average annual flow. Mont. Code Ann. § 85–2–316(6)(b).

Montana law also allows reservations of water for future uses, as discussed in the next subsection.

Instream flows may receive some protection under the federal Wild and Scenic Rivers Act, 16 U.S.C. §§ 1271–87. *See infra* Chapter 8.III.D.E. Congress, or state legislatures with the Secretary of Interior's approval, may designate certain river segments that contain "remarkable scenic, recreational, geologic, fish and wildlife, historic, cultural or other similar values." 16 U.S.C. § 1271. Once a river is designated, hydropower facilities and some other types of water development projects are restricted. 16 U.S.C. § 1278. If the United States wants to protect the flow from existing users, it may purchase water rights or exercise its power of eminent domain to acquire the rights of appropriators upon payment of compensation. 16 U.S.C. § 1284(b).

The doctrine of federal reserved water rights (*see infra* Chapter Eight) may also be applied to preserve instream flows on federal public lands or Indian lands. If the federal government reserves public land for particular uses that require maintenance of instream flows (*e.g.*, enough water to sustain aquatic life in a wildlife refuge, natural conditions in a park, or a fishery on an Indian reservation), the courts have recognized impliedly reserved rights to sufficient water to fulfill that purpose. Cappaert v. U.S., 426 U.S. 128, 138 (1976). Each reservation must be examined to determine whether reserved instream flows are essential to its purposes. *See* United States v. New Mexico, 438 U.S. 696 (1978) (water was not reserved for instream flows in a national forest because fish and wildlife maintenance was not a primary purpose of the forest).

#### *b. Reservations for Future Uses*

Many states provide by statute (Arizona, California, Idaho, Nevada, North Dakota, Oklahoma, Oregon, Washington) or by judicial decision (Wyoming), or both (Colorado), that municipalities may appropriate water for reasonably anticipated future needs. The Montana Water Use Act allows all levels of government to apply for water to be reserved for any future beneficial use (including municipal or irrigation). Mont. Code Ann. §§ 85–2–316, 85–2–102(24). In most states, the water need not be diverted and applied to a beneficial use in the meantime, in recognition of the complexities and logistics of developing large-scale municipal supplies. Colorado and California require that a beneficial use be made, but this can be satisfied by leasing the water for other purposes.

There are two caveats to this rule. First, speculation is prohibited. *See supra* Section III.A. Also, at some point, if the municipality fails to put the water to beneficial use, abandonment or forfeiture may be found. *See infra* Section VIII.A.

## IV. PRIORITY AND PREFERENCES

### A. PRIORITY

Priority is the bedrock feature of prior appropriation. A person whose appropriation is first in time has the highest priority and hence a right to make beneficial use of water superior to all others. An appropriator with an earlier priority date is known as the senior, while a later appropriator is the junior. All water rights holders are ranked according their appropriation dates. When there is not enough water for all appropriators, the doctrine of priority allows the full senior right to be exercised before the junior can use any water. The first user to be limited is the most junior on the list of priorities; juniors must abate their use until everyone senior to them has been served.

The priority date may relate back to an earlier date when one first formulated the intent to appropriate or received a permit or decree for a planned future use. Thus, the doctrine provides an incentive for water users to invest in expensive diversion works by giving them legal protection for their water supply as against juniors. But the doctrine as applied may have adverse economic consequences. First, appropriators may build diversion works prematurely or unnecessarily in order to protect their early priority. Second, the doctrine often frustrates transfers of water to higher economic uses. For example, a senior may hold a reliable water right to irrigate crops of comparatively low value. If a municipal or industrial user wishes to use that water in a higher-value use, it may "buy out" the senior's water right. In practice, however, the transfer of water rights may be legally prohibited or at least inhibited by transaction costs and the "no harm" rule. *See infra* Section VII.

## B. QUALIFICATIONS OF THE SENIOR'S RIGHT

No appropriator has a right to waste water. Water in a stream belongs to the public, and private rights are allowed only to the extent that appropriators can use water beneficially. *See* Nebraska Const. Art. XV, § 5. As a practical matter, however, one who holds a right to a specific quantity of water is rarely restricted from diverting the full quantity recognized in the permit, although states are beginning to be more rigorous in imposing restrictions on wasteful or inefficient uses. *See infra* Section V.B.

A senior cannot change an established use to the detriment of a junior. Seniors may be obligated to ensure juniors the same stream conditions that existed at the time the juniors began using water. Farmers Highline Canal & Reservoir Co. v. City of Golden, 272 P.2d 629 (Colo. 1954); Okanogan Wilderness League, Inc. v. Town of Twisp, 947 P.2d 732 (Wash. 1997). For example, a senior cannot change the place water is taken out of the stream ("point of diversion") if it adversely affects a junior. *Farmers Highline,* 272 P.2d at 632. The same rule applies to a change of purpose or time of use. If an appropriator has only used water during a particular growing season, a transferee's use of the right ordinarily will be limited to that season. Thorne v. McKinley Bros., 56 P.2d 204, 207 (Cal. 1936); Farmers Reservoir & Irrigation Co. v. City of Golden, 44 P.3d 241, 254 (Colo. 2002). For details on changes and transfers, see *infra* Section VII.

## C. ENFORCEMENT OF PRIORITIES

Junior appropriators may not interfere with a senior's water right. Any interference with the quantity, time, place, or quality of water necessary to support the seniors' use is subject to legal recourse. To enforce a right against a junior, a senior may make a "call on the river," which the state will enforce against juniors by curtailing their usage until the senior's right is fulfilled. Courts can impose fines, monetary damages, and injunctive relief against users who divert out of priority. Typically, the state engineer enforces priority on water users in a given basin; however, if curtailing junior users will not *actually* deliver water to the senior, then it is considered a "futile call" and will not be enforced. *Compare* Hill v. Ellinghouse, 553 P.3d 365, 375 (Mont. 2024) (stating that a senior stockwater user could not call junior irrigation users without first showing that curtailment would result in water reaching the senior's place of use in amounts that could be put to beneficial use), *with* S. Valley Ground Water Dist. v. Idaho Dep't of Water Res., 548 P.3d 734, 764 (Id. 2024), as amended (Jan. 12, 2024) (finding that curtailment of groundwater pumping by juniors would not be futile because curtailment would "help minimize [senior] surface water users' crop and revenue losses").

Strict enforcement of priorities can cause waste, as illustrated by State ex rel. Cary v. Cochran, 292 N.W. 239, 247 (Neb. 1940), where senior appropriators downstream on the Platte River sued to compel the state engineer to prevent upstream juniors from interfering with their rights. Because of seepage and evaporation losses along the lengthy stretch between the juniors and seniors, the juniors had to let 700 c.f.s. of water pass by in order for the 162 c.f.s. needed to satisfy the seniors' rights to reach them. The court enforced the seniors' right to shut off the juniors, but only so long as usable quantities would reach the seniors. Requiring some water to be deliverable prevented a futile call. Yet the juniors were prevented from taking a substantial amount of water to allow small quantities to pass to the seniors.

## D. PREFERENCES

Many states have statutes or constitutional provisions that express a preference for certain types of water use over others. Typically, they rank uses according to the view of the relative importance of various uses that prevailed at the time the preferences were established. Almost all place the highest preference on domestic purposes. Although there are many variations, most put irrigation second and industrial uses (such as mining or hydropower) third. *See, e.g.,* Colo. Const. art. 16 § 6; Neb. Const. art. 15 § 6; Wy. St. § 41–3–102; Cal.Water Code § 106.

Some state statutes or constitutional provisions require condemnation and compensation as the means of effectuating preferred uses, thereby requiring the preferred users to condemn the rights of senior users with lower preferences. *See, e.g.,* Idaho Const. art. XV, § 3; Neb. Rev. Stat. §§ 70–669, 76–711; In re 2007 Administration of Appropriations of the Niobrara River, 768 N.W.2d 420 (Neb. 2009). A few preference laws are interpreted as mandates for agencies to give preference to applicants for higher water uses over those whose applications for less preferred uses are simultaneously pending. *See, e.g.*, East Bay Municipal Utility Dist. v. Dept. of Public Works, 35 P.2d 1027 (Cal. 1934).

## V. EXTENT OF THE APPROPRIATIVE RIGHT

An appropriator is entitled to the amount of water continuously taken and beneficially used. The quantities stated in many old permits or decrees, however, are much larger than the amounts actually used by the appropriator. This is because old paper rights often were based only on declarations of the appropriators or the capacity of the diversion works. Overstating rights is less widespread today, largely because state appropriation systems are administered by professional engineers who verify claims before rights are granted.

All modern appropriation systems provide that persons may object to the recognition of a new right by an administrative agency or court on the ground that the right is excessive for the purposes claimed. In addition, junior appropriators may challenge a senior's rights, claiming that some portion of them has been abandoned by non-use. East Twin Lakes Ditches and Water Works, Inc. v. Bd. of County Com'rs of Lake County, 76 P.3d 918 (Colo. 2003).

Appropriative rights also entail a sufficient quality of water to allow a continuation of beneficial uses.

However, this principle has been invoked only rarely to prevent another appropriator from polluting. Early cases prevented upstream miners from polluting water to the detriment of downstream seniors. Arizona Copper Co. v. Gillespie, 100 P. 465 (Ariz. Terr. 1909). Most states now have dual systems under which one agency or court deals with water allocation and a separate agency deals with pollution. In Colorado, a Water Quality Control Commission regulates water quality and is prohibited by statute from interfering with the exercise of certain agricultural water rights. Colo. Rev. Stat. § 25–8–205(5). The water court deals exclusively with water rights, but when approving an exchange where water is substituted into the stream to satisfy the rights of another appropriator, it considers whether the water is of comparable quality. In re Application for Plan for Augmentation of City and County of Denver ex rel. Bd. of Water Com'rs, 44 P.3d 1019, 1032 (2002).

A depletion in flow that results in stricter limitations on a discharger's effluent does not constitute a legally cognizable injury to a party under the prior appropriation doctrine as long as the party is still able to divert the full amount of the water right. City of Thornton v. Bijou Irr. Co., 926 P.2d 1 (Colo. 1996). To hold otherwise would effectively create a private instream flow right for the purpose of waste assimilation, which is not allowed. *Id.* at 93.

## A. MEASURE OF THE RIGHT: BENEFICIAL USE

Beneficial use is said to be the basis, the measure, and the limit of an appropriator's right to use water. Before development of modern administrative systems, the primary limit on an appropriator's right to use a certain quantity of water was the capacity of the diversion facilities. *See, e.g.*, Fort Morgan Land & Canal Co. v. South Platte Ditch Co., 30 P. 1032 (Colo. 1892). This was based on the assumption that one would not go to the expense of building ditches with a capacity far greater than was necessary, but in fact most appropriators built oversized ditches to ensure that they had sufficient capacity. Further, they did not use the ditches during every irrigation season, though they sometimes claimed rights to do so.

Challenges to an appropriator's claims were rare, and the aggregate claims on a stream sometimes amounted to many times its total flow. Only in extreme cases did a court find that an appropriator's right exceeded beneficial use. *See, e.g.*, State ex rel. Erickson v. McLean, 308 P.2d 983 (N.M. 1957). Some courts are now taking a stricter view of beneficial use, even under old rights. For example, in State ex rel. Martinez v. City of Las Vegas, 89 P.3d 47 (N.M. 2004), the court found that the pueblo water rights doctrine, which allows the pueblos to use as much water as is necessary, including expansion of the right to meet future needs, was inconsistent with the requirement that water be put to a beneficial use.

The statutory systems of all western states include administrative mechanisms for verifying amounts of water that are to be put to a beneficial use before rights are embodied in a permit or decree. In addition, adjudications of all existing rights throughout large watersheds have been undertaken in many states, including Arizona, California, Idaho, Montana, and Washington. *See infra* Section VI.B. Such adjudications typically require holders of existing rights to prove that their existing uses are beneficial. Competing users may object to appropriations of excessive quantities of water.

A water right, once manifested in a permit or decree, is rarely disturbed. Change of place, purpose of use, or point of diversion requires permission by an agency or court. No change may be made if it results in harm to other appropriators.

In assessing harm, the agency or court may deny the application if the change will result in an increase in the amount of water that has historically been put to a beneficial use. Historical use may be limited to the amount of water actually required for beneficial uses of the kind made. Thus, the quantity that can be applied to the changed use may be reduced to less than the amount of the original appropriation. The same process is followed when one appropriator seeks to transfer a water right to another.

The historical use approach may be equally useful in showing that one has abandoned the unused portion of a water right. Washington, for example, requires partial relinquishment of rights after five years of using less than the full permitted amount. Wash. Rev. Code § 90.14.140; Dept. of Ecology v. Acquavella, 935 P.2d 595 (Wash. 1997). However, it is rare to find partial abandonment, even in states like Washington.

## B. BENEFICIAL USE AS A LIMIT

Appropriative rights extend only to beneficial use, and therefore there is no right to use water wastefully. State laws and court decisions interpret "beneficial use" as requiring that water use be "reasonable" or "reasonably efficient." *See, e.g.*, McNaughton v. Eaton, 242 P.2d 570, 575 (Utah 1952). Standards for reasonableness change as the demand for scarce resources grows and conservation technology improves, leading to stricter regulation.

Because there is no vested right to waste water, state regulation of water use can restrict the amount of water used to amounts less than a permit or decree provides and to means of diversion and manner of application other than were used historically. As described below, administrators and courts may consider the "duty of water" in determining whether waste is occurring. They may also consider whether the amount being used is "unreasonable." When the California Water Resources Control Board found that hundreds of thousands of acre-feet of water were being lost by inefficient delivery and distribution systems in the Imperial Irrigation District, it required major conservation efforts, substantially changing the district's use of water. Imperial Irr. Dist. v. State Water Resources Control Board, 275 Cal.Rptr. 250 (Ct. App. 1990).

In addition, basin-wide general stream adjudications represent an opportunity for examining the quantity and manner of water use. Besides providing evidence that they have actually diverted a quantity of water, existing users must prove that their uses continue to be beneficial. *See* Washington Dept. of Ecology v. Grimes, 852 P.2d 1044 (Wash. 1993) (reducing an appropriation to half of the amount historically diverted because the delivery system was highly inefficient).

### 1. "Duty of Water" Limitations

Irrigation uses account for around 90% of all water withdrawals in the West. Water is sometimes applied to land far in excess of what crops can use. One means of limiting waste is to limit the volume or rate of water use based on a presumption of the maximum quantity required in the area. This limit is called the "duty of water." Water duties are indicative of whether the water is being beneficially used, and such duties may be presented as evidence of partial forfeiture through waste. Delta Canal Co. v. Frank Vincent Family Ranch, 420 P.3d 1052 (Utah 2013).

Rates or volumes are determined according to informed judgments of the amount of water needed for agriculture in the area and the maximum rate at which it could be applied without waste, considering soil conditions, climate, crops, and other relevant factors. State engineers and courts consider the duty of water when they review applications for new appropriations, changes in use, and transfers.

In South Dakota, Wyoming, and Nebraska, appropriators may apply water at a rate of no more than one cubic foot per second (c.f.s.) for every seventy acres irrigated. In addition, Nebraska law specifies that no more than three acre-feet of water may be used per year per acre of land. Neb. Rev. St. § 46–231. South Dakota allows no more than two acre-feet of water per year for each acre of land and California allows no more than two and one half acre-feet per acre on uncultivated areas. S.D. Codified Laws § 46–5–6; Cal. Water Code § 1004. In Kansas, "reasonable quantities" for irrigation range from one to two acre-feet per acre of land, depending on the area's geography. Kan. Admin. Regs. § 5–3–19. New Mexico, by contrast, requires the amount of water for irrigation to be consistent with "good agricultural practices." N.M. Stat. Ann. § 72–5–18(A).

Some states authorize exceptions from the water duty if irrigation methods, time constraints on diversions, or types of soil so require. *See, e.g.*, S.D. Codified Laws § 46–5–6. Moreover, if a water duty unreasonably limits the ability of the appropriator to make the beneficial use that is the basis of the right, the law may constitute an impermissible interference with vested water rights. In Enterprise Irrigation Dist. v. Willis, 284 N.W. 326 (Neb. 1939), the Nebraska Supreme Court enjoined enforcement of a provision limiting appropriations to three acre-feet per acre per year against an irrigator who had perfected greater rights (3.5 acre-feet per acre) before passage of the act. Although the opinion broadly disapproved of applying a statutory limitation enacted after a water right had been perfected, it can be read as limited to the facts of the case because there was evidence that the crops required more water than the duty of water allowed. *Id.* at 329–30.

Other courts have found that reductions based on statutory requirements for "reasonable use" were necessary to prevent waste and were not unconstitutional takings. *See, e.g.,* Washington Dept. of Ecology v. Grimes, 852 P.2d 1044, 1055 (Wash. 1993); Imperial Irr. Dist. v. Water Resources Control Board, 275 Cal.Rptr. 250, 265 (Ct. App. 1990).

## 2. Reasonably Efficient Means of Diversion

Some of the earliest cases invoking the beneficial use doctrine to prevent waste involved inefficient diversion and conveyance facilities. Facilities for diversion and transportation of water must be reasonably efficient to avoid waste. In an early case, the Supreme Court refused relief to a party whose waterwheel, used to remove water from the Snake River to irrigate 429 acres, was inundated by the defendant's downstream dam, which was part of a project to irrigate some 300,000 acres. Schodde v. Twin Falls Land & Water Co., 224 U.S. 107 (1912). One of the Court's alternate holdings was that an unreasonable and inefficient means of diversion (the waterwheel) could not interfere with the reasonable use of water by others. *Id.* at 125. Similarly, where 5/6ths of the water diverted by an appropriator was lost to evaporation and seepage in a two and one half mile open ditch, a California court found impermissible waste. Erickson v. Queen Valley Ranch Co., 99 Cal.Rptr. 446, 450 (Ct. App. 1971). Although the *Erickson* court found excessive waste, it refused to order the senior appropriator to line his ditch, imposing a "physical solution" instead where juniors could pay to line it if they wished. Seniors are rarely ordered to line leaky ditches. *See, e.g.*, United States v. Gila Valley Irrigation Dist., 31 F.3d 1428 (9th Cir. 1994); Middelkamp v. Bessemer Irrigating Ditch Co., 103 P. 280 (Colo. 1909).

Whether a senior appropriator has a reasonably efficient means of diversion is typically judged by standards applicable when the diversion works were built. In State ex rel. Crowley v. District Court, 88 P.2d 23 (Mont. 1939), the court upheld the right of a downstream senior to insist that upstream juniors leave sufficient water in the stream to reach the senior's rudimentary, turn-of-the-century wing dam. Streamflows would have been adequate for all users if the senior had modified its diversion dam, but the court refused to require modifications. *Id.* at 24.

On a related note, appropriators' arguments that they were entitled to a certain silt content in their water were rejected in A-B Cattle Co. v. United States, 589 P.2d 57 (Colo. 1978). The presence of silt in the water served to seal unlined earthen ditches and prevented seepage losses. When the federal government constructed a dam on the river, the silt settled out. The clear water released from the dam seeped from the ditches more readily, resulting in less water being delivered to the appropriators. But the court found that they had no right to maintain earthen ditches. It noted that, "while the time may not yet have arrived when all ditches can be required to be lined or placed in pipes," the notion of beneficial use may eventually require such measures. *Id.* at 61. *See also* In re Willow Creek, 144 P. 505, 647 (Or. 1914) (suggesting that diversion facilities efficient enough to support a water right at the time they were built may have to be made more efficient as conditions and technology change).

Economic theory indicates that water use will become efficient whether the burden of efficiency is placed on the senior or junior. Under both *Crowley*, in Montana, and *Erickson,* in California, if greater efficiency by the senior would benefit the junior appropriators, the juniors would pay the senior to make the needed improvements or buy out the senior's rights. If instead, the Oregon *Willow Creek* rule applied and the senior had to bear the burden of upgrading the diversion facilities to modern standards, the senior would either make the expenditure or buy out the juniors. If it were not to the senior's advantage to do so, the senior would sell to the juniors.

In practice, transaction costs and other factors, such as devotion to a lifestyle or a location, disparity in size of use, and relative wealth of the parties, may be barriers to moving water to efficient use. Thus, legislatures and courts may seek to impose rules that maximize efficiency. In Alamosa-La Jara Water Users Protection Ass'n v. Gould, 674 P.2d 914 (Colo. 1983), the court indicated that the state engineer should require optimum utilization of water pursuant to regulations requiring consideration of "all significant factors, including environmental and economic concerns." The court held that seniors could be required to construct wells rather than preventing juniors from taking water from the stream to protect the seniors' diversions. *Id.* at 935. Similarly, the

Idaho court upheld rules requiring senior surface water users to employ reasonable diversion and conveyance efficiency and conservation practices before calling a junior well owner who was allegedly interfering with the senior's use. American Falls Reservoir Dist. No. 2 v. Idaho Dept. of Water Resources, 154 P.3d 433 (Idaho 2007).

### 3. The Evolving Concept of Beneficial Use and the Public Trust Doctrine

Water is a public resource, but rights to use it may be appropriated by private parties so long as the use is "beneficial." The public now recognizes a wider array of non-economic uses (beauty and spiritual fulfillment) and economic uses (recreation) of water. The beneficial use doctrine can provide a means to account for changing values. In addition, greater understanding of the physical environment and the value of functioning ecosystems may influence decisions about water allocation and uses.

Some modern cases recognize the dynamic nature of beneficial use. As water supplies become more scarce and as demands increase, the negative consequences of allowing less socially valuable uses come into question, and what once was deemed beneficial may no longer be seen as such. In Environmental Defense Fund, Inc. v. East Bay Municipal Utility Dist., 125 Cal.Rptr. 601 (Ct. App. 1975), *vacated on other grounds,* 605 P.2d 1 (Cal. 1980), an environmental group successfully argued that the applicant failed to make reasonable and beneficial use of water because the applicant was not reclaiming its *existing* water supply.

Although allocation systems seek to establish reliable rights to use water and, in some contexts, recognize such rights as "vested property interests," the law in most states also maintains that water is a public trust resource that may not be capable of full privatization. *See* Mineral County v. Lyon County, 473 P.3d 418 (Nev. 2020) (finding that the public trust doctrine, which applies to all waters of the state, informs but does not reallocate valid existing appropriation rights).

Because the public trust doctrine is "a matter of state law," PPL Montana, LLC v. Montana, 565 U.S. 576 (2012), the reach of the doctrine varies considerably. In some jurisdictions, it has been interpreted narrowly. *See, e.g.,* Idaho Code §§ 58–1201 to 58–1203 (declaring that the public trust doctrine shall not apply to the appropriation or use of water). Other states take a more expansive view, and in some cases the concept of "beneficial use" has been qualified by the public trust doctrine. In *Mineral County,* 473 P.2d at 426, the Nevada Supreme Court found that the state's statutory factors for assessing beneficial use were "consistent with the public trust doctrine." However, in light of the "significance of finality in water rights," it held that the legislature had prohibited courts from "reallocating adjudicated water rights that have not been otherwise abandoned or forfeited in accordance with the state's water statutes." *Id.* at 429.

A few states have imposed the public trust doctrine as a limitation on private appropriations. *See, e.g.*, National Audubon Society v. Superior Court (Mono Lake), 33 Cal.3d 419, 658 P.2d 709 (1983); In re Water Use Permit Applications, 93 P.3d 643, 650, 657 (Haw. 2004). With its now-famous *Mono Lake* decision, the California Supreme Court limited private appropriative rights in a non-navigable tributary to Mono Lake in order to protect the public's interest in maintaining lake levels. *National Audubon Society (Mono Lake)*, 33 Cal.3d at 448. In applying the public trust doctrine, the court noted the potential conflict with the appropriative rights system, but acknowledged that the doctrine reflects the state's power as a sovereign to exercise continuous supervision and control over the waters of the state. The court described the public trust as "an affirmation of the duty of the state to protect the people's common heritage of streams, lakes, marshlands, and tidelands, surrendering that right of protection only in rare cases when the abandonment of that right is consistent with the purposes of the trust." *Id*. at 441.

There may be limited circumstances in which a state can restrict the public's rights under the public trust doctrine, *i.e.*, where limiting the trust furthers a value within the scope of the trust or where developing trust lands or waters does not substantially impair public use. *See* Illinois Central R.R. v. Illinois, 146 U.S. 387, 452 (1892) (observing that the state could sell small parcels of trust land so long as it could be done without impairing the public interest in the remaining submerged land and water); Phillips Petroleum Co. v. Mississippi, 484 U.S. 469, 475 (1988) (holding that states are empowered to "define the limits of the lands held in public trust and to recognize private rights in such lands as they see fit"). However, in San Carlos Apache Tribe v. Superior Court ex rel. Cnty. of Maricopa, 972 P.2d 179, 215 (Ariz. 1999), the Arizona Supreme Court held that a state statute declaring the public trust doctrine inapplicable to water rights adjudications violated separation of powers and a constitutional limit on legislative authority to give away trust resources.

For details on the doctrine's implications for permitting decisions and for public access and use, see *infra* Section VI.A.5 and Chapter 7.II.C (Navigability), respectively.

### C. RECAPTURE AND REUSE

Water is "reused" multiple times. Agricultural water is diverted, spread on fields, and then some is returned through tail ditches or by seepage to a stream. Municipal water is usually returned as treated (or untreated) sewage to a waterway, where others may divert and use it. These return flows become supplies for other water users. A question arises, however, when an appropriator seeks to recapture and reuse water without initiating a new appropriation.

Waters originating within the watershed generally can be recaptured and reused by an appropriator if: (1) the total used does not exceed rights under a permit or decree; and (2) the recapture and reuse occur within the land for which the appropriation was made. No such limits are imposed on reuse of foreign waters imported by an appropriator. *See* Stevens v. Oakdale Irrig. Dist., 90 P.2d 58 (Cal. 1939); Water Supply and Storage Co. v. Curtis, 733 P.2d 680 (Colo. 1987). *But see* Coors Brewing Co. v. City of Golden, 420 P.3d 977, 986 (Colo. 2018) (holding that water diverted from a creek pursuant to an augmentation plan constituted native tributary water rather than "foreign or developed" water, and thus Coors had no right to make successive uses of it and any unconsumed water had to be returned to the creek for appropriation by others).

Recapture and reuse of water encourages conservation and maximum utilization of water. Much of the water diverted for irrigation is not actually consumed by crops. Most unconsumed water seeps into the ground or goes back to the stream as return flow and is appropriated and put to use by others. Such water is not truly "wasted" in the sense that it cannot be used by anyone. Still, significant amounts of water used in irrigation become unusable by being "trapped" in marshy areas or as unrecoverable groundwater. Much is lost by evaporation from open canals or transpiration (evapotranspiration) through unwanted (non-crop) plants that draw water out of the earth. Because millions of acre-feet of water are "lost" annually, states are seeking ways to encourage greater efficiency through reuse and other methods.

## 1. Total Use Must Not Exceed Water Right

Typically, one uses only a portion of the total water diverted and returns the rest to the stream. Water rights are usually expressed as a maximum amount or rate of flow to be diverted for a certain time period and use on specific land. A right may also be limited by the amount to be consumed. Within these limits, consumption may be increased by reuse so long as there is no "change of use"—a change in the place, purpose, or time of use, or the means or point of diversion. Thus, an appropriator ordinarily may "recycle" irrigation return flows or capture seepage and use it within limits imposed by state law.

The upstream appropriator's increased efficiency or reuse of water on the original land can potentially reduce the downstream appropriator's supply. Downstream appropriators often are dependent on the upstream appropriator's "waste" as a source of supply. If the increased consumption came about by a change in use, it would not be allowed to harm other appropriators. But when it is the result of recapture and reuse or conservation measures on the same land, it will be permitted without regard to harm caused to others so long as the amount diverted (and the amount consumed, if it has been quantified) does not exceed one's "paper right" (*i.e.,* the amount specified in a permit or court decree). The applicable principle is that a junior appropriator who depends on a senior's waste as a source of supply is subject to the waste being curtailed. Montana v. Wyoming, 563 U.S. 368 (2011); Thayer v. City of Rawlins, 594 P.2d 951 (Wyo. 1979). *See also* Binning v. Miller, 102 P.2d

54 (Wyo. 1940) (noting that "[t]he lower landowner using such water merely takes his chances as to future supplies"); Rocky Ford Irrigation Co. v. Kents Lake Reservoir Co., 469 P.3d 1003 (Utah 2020) (rejecting the downstream user's claim to water generated by the upper user's efficiency gains from using sprinklers instead of flood irrigation, as the downstream user had no right to return flows produced by less efficient irrigation in the past).

This rule also applies to groundwater that is discharged into a stream. The discharge may be stopped even to the detriment of the downstream user as long as the upstream user can identify the water that is not subject to appropriation. Arizona Public Service Co. v. Long, 773 P.2d 988 (Ariz. 1989). The Arizona court also ruled that cities may sell sewage effluent to the detriment of water users downstream of the former sewage return. *Id.* at 998.

In contrast to recapturing return flows for reuse, one may not enlarge a decreed right by means of water salvage techniques. In Colorado, a landowner removed streamside phreatophytes (plants that consume large amounts of water) and filled in marshy areas. Southeastern Colorado Water Conservancy Dist. v. Shelton Farms, Inc., 529 P.2d 1321 (Colo. 1974). The growth of phreatophytes over the years had gradually deprived many junior users of the water to which they were entitled. Since the saved water was originally in the stream and had been appropriated by juniors, the court held that it was error to create a new and senior right in it. *Id.* at 1327. Similarly, in R.J.A., Inc. v. Water Users Ass'n of Dist. No. 6, 690 P.2d 823 (Colo. 1984), the court denied an expansion of a senior right to include water saved by draining a 3000 year-old peat bog. The water belonged to the stream and could not be used to enlarge an existing right, because to hold otherwise would encourage "altercations of long existing physical characteristics of the land" with potentially adverse effects. *Id.* at 828. Presumably the court would have recognized rights to the water in each case if its original source had been the senior's diversion (not from natural circumstances which trapped water on the seniors' land) and the total amount of the senior's right was not enlarged beyond the decree. The senior also could have applied for a junior appropriation of the salvaged water added to the stream.

### 2. Reuse Limited to Original Land

Generally, one may recapture and reuse seepage and "waste-water" so long as it is within the original land and for the original purpose of the right. Cleaver v. Judd, 393 P.2d 193 (Or. 1964) (citing Stevens v. Oakdale Irr. Dist., 90 P.2d 58 (Cal. 1939)); Estate of Steed v. New Escalante Irrig. Co., 846 P.2d 1223 (Utah 1992). Recaptured water may be used on the same land to increase crop yield. However, it cannot be reused on an adjoining parcel. Salt River Valley Water Users' Ass'n v. Kovacovich, 411 P.2d 201 (Ariz.App. 1966). Of course, if the diversion point, means of diversion, or place, time, or purpose of use is changed, a reuse will be allowed only if no harm occurs to other appropriators. *See infra* Section VII.

Once the water leaves the appropriator's land and is destined for or has reached a natural stream, it may be subject to appropriation by others. Fuss v. Franks, 610 P.2d 17 (Wyo. 1980). Some states qualify this rule, requiring that the appropriator must have intended to recapture the water when it was appropriated and must actually recapture it within a reasonable time or else the water will be considered abandoned to the stream. Jones v. Warmsprings Irr. Dist., 91 P.2d 542 (Or. 1939). Other states hold that after water is commingled, appropriators who attempt to recapture the water must be able to identify their portion. Arizona Public Service Co. v. Long, 773 P.2d 988 (Ariz. 1989). A minority of jurisdictions hold that water that enters a stream or seeps into the ground, even while on the original land, is not subject to recapture and reuse. *See* Fort Morgan Reservoir & Irr. Co. v. McCune, 206 P. 393 (Colo. 1922) (seepage from dam on owner's land was destined for stream and could not be recaptured).

The rule allowing recapture and reuse of reclaimed water on the original land can result in more efficiency, but it can also result in more water being consumed. For instance, if a water user is consuming less than the permitted amount of water and plants a more water-intensive crop or puts in a more efficient irrigation system, most or all of the water that had previously been returned to the stream might be consumed. This can deprive other appropriators of water on which they depend, but it is allowed since it is technically within the terms of the original appropriation. Montana v. Wyoming, 563 U.S. 368, 380 (2011). Being able to recapture and reuse water on the land benefited by the original use provides a big advantage for large irrigation districts and federal reclamation projects. *See id.;* Dept. of Ecology v. U.S. Bureau of Reclamation, 827 P.2d 275 (Wash. 1992) (federal project in the Columbia River basin retained the right to recapture seepage and return flow throughout the project area). To encourage more efficient water use, a few states (*e.g.*, California, Montana, New Mexico, and Oregon) have passed laws facilitating the use of reclaimed and even salvaged water on other land or for new purposes.

Any person, including the original appropriator, who intercepts seepage water that has left their land is considered a junior appropriator subject to the rights of all prior appropriators. A seepage appropriator is at the mercy of the person whose activity makes the seepage available. The original appropriator may cause the seepage to stop by making more efficient use of it, by lining, relocating, or abandoning a canal or reservoir, or by ceasing the appropriation, without liability to the seepage appropriator. Bower v. Big Horn Canal Ass'n, 307 P.2d 593 (Wyo. 1957); *Montana,* 563 U.S. at 384.

## VI. PROCEDURES FOR PERFECTING AND ADMINISTERING RIGHTS

Appropriation of water began several years before statehood in most western states. Miners developed relatively uniform customs for appropriations, and these were incorporated into the common law of water rights by the early territorial and state court systems. A miner's right to get water depended upon two acts: posting notice at the point of diversion and diverting the water to apply it to a beneficial use.

The quaint system of appropriation that spread throughout the West reflected the independence of the miners who conceived it. There was no administration required, no central authority, and no records. But there were conflicts. Courts were called upon to resolve disputes between appropriators competing for priority to water and between appropriators and riparian landowners. *See* Power v. People, 28 P. 1121 (Colo. 1892) (rejecting a justifiable homicide defense raised by a riparian who shot an appropriator). Litigation, however, was reactive, rather than proactive, and was determinative only of the rights of the parties, not of all users of the same water sources. Realizing the inefficiency of a common law water administration system, some states enacted statutory procedures.

In 1873, California became the first state to enact a statutory appropriation procedure. Since then, all western states have followed suit, primarily with administrative permit systems.

## A. PERMIT SYSTEMS

### 1. Purpose

All western states have statutory systems to allocate and administer rights to use water. In addition, every state but Colorado has vested authority in an administrative agency. *See infra* Section VI.D.

The chief purpose of administrative procedures is to provide an orderly method for appropriating water and regulating water rights. Some states allow appropriators the option of applying for a permit or perfecting a common law appropriation by posting notice and diverting water. More typically, state law requires a permit as the exclusive means of making a valid appropriation. Wyoming Hereford Ranch v. Hammond Packing Co., 236 P. 764 (Wyo. 1925).

## 2. Constitutionality

The authority to adopt and enforce permit systems to govern the use of water stems from the broad police power of the state. Ormsby County v. Kearney, 142 P. 803, 806 (Nev. 1914). Water is subject to public control by state statutes or constitutions. *See, e.g.*, Cal. Const. Art. 10, § 5; Neb. Const. Art. XV § 5. Although the state's interest may be expressed in property-like terms, it is not one of ownership but of sovereignty. Sporhase v. Nebraska ex rel. Douglas, 458 U.S. 941, 956 (1982).

Most state water administration systems include an adjudication process that casts an administrative body or official in a quasi-judicial role. Water users have challenged the mixed executive (regulatory) and judicial role of agencies; however, courts have upheld the delegation of administrative powers to an agency, official, or board. Farm Investment Co. v. Carpenter, 61 P. 258, 267 (Wyo. 1900). Oregon, for example, has a mixed judicial and administrative system in which permit determinations are made by the state engineer and filed in a court that presides over appeals, makes modifications, and grants final approvals. The Oregon Supreme Court found the engineer's duties to be "quasi-judicial in their character," and the findings only "*prima facie* final and binding." In re Willow Creek, 74 Ore. 592, 610 (Or. 1914). The U.S. Supreme Court agreed "that the state, consistently with due process of law, may thus commit the preliminary proceedings to the board and the final hearing and adjudication to the court." Pacific Live Stock Co. v. Lewis, 241 U.S. 440, 451 (1916). *See* United States v. Oregon, 44 F.3d 758 (9th Cir. 1994).

The Texas Supreme Court invalidated a 1917 water rights statute, similar to one in Wyoming, noting that the Wyoming constitution provided ample authority for such a system, but that Texas had no similar constitutional provision. Board of Water Engineers v. McKnight, 229 S.W. 301 (Tex. 1921). Texas later amended its constitution and adopted a system similar to Oregon's, Tex. Const. art. XVI, § 59; Tex. Water Code Ann. §§ 11.301, 11.320–11.321 (West 1977), and the court found that it did not violate the separation of powers or constitute a taking. In re Adjudication of Water Rights of Upper Guadalupe Segment of Guadalupe River Basin, 642 S.W.2d 438, 442 (Tex. 1982).

### 3. Permitting Procedures

All appropriation states except Colorado have statutes requiring permits to appropriate water. Wyoming adopted the first permit system in 1890. It divided the state into four water divisions and established the office of state engineer to collect stream records, make surveys, and provide staff support to the Board of Control, which adjudicates all claims and administers the permit system. *See* Wyo. Const. art. 8 § 2; Wyo. Stat. Ann. § 41–3–501.

Under most permitting systems, approval is granted when an applicant follows prescribed procedures and the state engineer finds that there is unappropriated water and that the appropriation is not detrimental to public welfare.

### *a. Filing*

In all permit states, a formal written application to take unappropriated water must be made to the state engineer or an administrative body, such as the Department of Natural Resources or Water Resources Control Board. This is almost always the exclusive way to obtain a water right and must be done before creating a physical diversion. The time of filing becomes the priority date if all later requirements are met.

Typical of most states, Montana law requires applications to include the name of the claimant and watercourse, quantity of water, time of use, legal description of the point of diversion, purpose of use, date of application to beneficial use, and any applicable support such as a map, plat, or aerial photograph. Mont. Code Ann. § 85–2–361.

### *b. Notice*

Applicants for new appropriations must give notice. The notice must be published, and efforts must be made to contact all affected appropriators. *See, e.g.*, Mont. Code Ann. § 85–2–307–308; *see also* Western Water, LLC v. Olds, 184 P.3d 578, 585 (Utah 2008); Pete's Mountain Homeowners Ass'n v. Oregon Water Resources Dept., 238 P.3d 395, 399 (2010). In Colorado, a monthly list of all applications is compiled, then the water clerk publishes it in the local newspapers of general circulation and mails it to potentially affected parties. Colo. Rev. Stat. § 37–92–302(3); SL Group LLC v. Go West Industries, 42 P.3d 637, 641 (Colo. 2002). However, personal service is not required. S. Ute Indian Tribe v. King Consol. Ditch Co., 250 P.3d 1226, 1236 (Colo. 2011). Absent sufficient notice, new appropriations may not be perfected. *Id.*; City of Thornton v. Bijou Irr. Co., 926 P.2d 1, 24 (Colo. 1996).

### *c. Hearing*

Opponents to a permit application have a fixed time to file objections, but most states recognize exceptions for cause. *See* In re Adjudication of the Existing Rights to the Use of All the Water, 55 P.3d 396, 398 (Mont. 2002) (allowing an objection by the Department of Fish, Wildlife, and Parks outside of the 10-day objection period). Objections are typically based on allegations that the statutory criteria for permit issuance are either legally or factually lacking. Water right holders who may be adversely affected by a new permit generally have standing to object. *See, e.g.*, Idaho Code § 42–203A ("any person, firm, association or corporation concerned in . . . such application" may object); Wash. Rev. Code § 90.03.200 ("any interested party" may object). Whether non-appropriators have standing to object varies from state to state. *Compare* Texas Rivers Protection Ass'n v. Texas Natural Resource Conservation Com'n, 910 S.W.2d 147, 151–52 (Tex. App. 1995) (riparians have standing to challenge an application on the ground that it may damage aesthetic, recreational, and business interests), *and* City of Bozeman v. Montana Dep't of Nat. Re. & Conservation, 471 P.3d 46, 50 (Mont. 2020) (city did not have a "protectable interest" to support its challenge to a change application) *with* In re Application A-19594, 995 N.W. 2d 655 (Neb. 2023) (water districts opposing an interbasin transfer application lacked standing).

The administrative agency holds public hearings on properly filed objections, serving notice of the hearing on the applicant and objector. *See, e.g.*, Mont. Code Ann. § 85–2–309. The state engineer or equivalent official investigates factual data and reports to the agency on whether the statutory criteria were satisfied. Based on the findings, the agency then approves, disapproves, or approves with modification, the permit application. The applicant also has a right to present any pertinent evidence to support the application. The agency's findings may be appealed to the courts. *See, e.g.*, *id.* § 85–2–235.

### *d. Issuance of Permit*

The next stage of the process is issuance of a permit. A permit is not a water right but will ripen into one if all conditions of the permit are met. During a stipulated time period, the permittee is required to construct a physical diversion, divert water, and apply water to a beneficial use. The permit ripens into a water right once the water is applied to a beneficial use. If the permittee exercised "due diligence" throughout the process, priority will relate back to the date of filing. Colville Confederated Tribes v. Walton, 752 F.2d 397, 402 (9th Cir. 1985).

Most administrative agencies impose permit conditions that dictate how the water right is to be exercised. California, for instance, authorizes the State Water Resources Control Board to permit the appropriation for beneficial purposes under "such terms and conditions as in its judgment will best develop, conserve, and utilize in the public interest, the water sought to be appropriated." Cal. Water Code § 1253. The Board has considerable discretion to fashion conditions, which will be set aside only if a court finds them to be unreasonable or not based on substantial evidence. East Bay Mun. Utility Dist. v. Dept. of Public Works, 35 P.2d 1027 (Cal. 1934).

In addition to regular permits, some states issue temporary and seasonal permits. In California, such permits may be issued if there is unappropriated water available and no harm to downstream users or unreasonable harm to the environment. Cal. Water Code §§ 1425, 1430.

In most states, the final document issued in the permit process is called a "license," "certificate," "certificate of appropriation," or "water right certificate." The certificate may be recorded like a deed to real property.

## 4. Statutory Criteria

The permit procedures discussed above determine whether the criteria set forth in the statute are satisfied. In most states, this requires evidence of:

a. a beneficial use;

b. availability of unappropriated water;

c. no harm to prior appropriators;

d. adequate diversion facilities; and

e. a possessory interest in the property where water is to be put to beneficial use.

*See, e.g.,* Mont. Code Ann. § 85–2–311; N.M. Stat. Ann. § 72–5–6; Or. Rev. Stat. Ann. § 537.153; Utah Code Ann. § 73–3–8.

On many streams, the "paper rights" to divert water far exceed the quantity of water actually flowing in the stream. This is a result of two phenomena: (a) many users may depend on the same water, as downstream users divert water previously diverted and returned by upstream users; and (b) the most junior rights may be exercisable only in years of heavy flow or low senior usage. Thus, many streams in the West are "over appropriated."

The requirement that an applicant show that unappropriated water is available has become a more significant consideration in recent years. *See, e.g.*, Confederated Salish & Kootenai Tribes v. Clinch, 992 P.2d 244, 250 (Mont. 1999) (stating that, for water to be "legally available," there must be water supplies that, among other things, have not been federally reserved for Indian tribes); Flathead Lakers Inc. v. Montana Dep't of Nat. Res. & Conservation, 530 P.3d 769 (Mont. 2023) (invalidating a bottling scheme for failure to adequately analyze availability of affected surface waters). Still, it is relatively rare for a permitting agency to deny a new appropriation, transfer, or change in use for lack of available water. *See* Clark Fork Coal. v. Dep't of Nat. Res. & Cons., 481 P.3d 198 (Mont. 2021) (holding that "legally available" water does not incorporate restrictions imposed by water quality standards); Silver v. Pueblo Del Sol Water Co., 423 P.3d 348 (Ariz. 2018) (finding available supply although an increase in pumping would diminish streamflow and conflict with federal reserved water rights); Dovel v. Dobson, 831 P.2d 527 (Idaho 1992) (finding available supply where the evidence indicated that during normal years there was enough water to fill existing rights plus those granted by a new permit); HEAL Utah v. Kane Cnty. Water Conservancy Dist., 378 P.3d 1246 (Utah 2016) (finding available supply where Utah had issued permits in excess of its share under the Upper Colorado Basin Compact because many of the previously approved appropriations had not yet been applied to beneficial use).

### 5. Public Interest Considerations and the Public Trust

The laws of most states authorize the state agency or engineer to reject or place conditions on applications that are inconsistent with the public interest. In an early case, the New Mexico territorial engineer denied an application for a proposed irrigation project that seemed too large for the available supply and thus might result in high costs and uncertain supplies for those who bought land and accompanying water rights. Young & Norton v. Hinderlider, 110 P. 1045, 1050 (N.M. 1910). The court rejected the applicant's contention that "public welfare" concerns should only include matters that are a "menace to public health and safety," and upheld the engineer's use of broad policy considerations to deny the application. *Id.* The court subsequently held that the state engineer could not deny a transfer on the basis of general "public interest" considerations, Application of Sleeper, 760 P.2d 787, 791 (1988), but the legislature later adopted a public welfare requirement for water transfers in N.M. Stat. Ann. § 72–5–23. *See* Montgomery v. N.M. State Engineer, 114 P.3d 339, *affirmed in relevant part*, 150 P.3d 971 (2006).

Utah requires the state engineer to determine whether proposed appropriations would interfere with a "more beneficial use" or "prove detrimental to the public welfare." Utah Code Ann. § 73–3–8. The Utah Supreme Court upheld a decision to reject an early application (a private power plant) in favor of a later one (a federal water project) because the later appropriation was more beneficial to the public interest. Tanner v. Bacon, 136 P.2d 957 (Utah 1943).

Alaska has enacted one of the most detailed state statutes on public interest considerations. It delineates an array of public interest factors, including: (1) benefit to the applicant; (2) effect of resulting economic activity; (3) effect on fish and game and recreation; (4) public health effects; (5) loss of future alternative uses; (6) harm to others; (7) intent and ability of applicant; (8) effect on access to navigable or public waters. Alaska Stat. Ann. § 46.15.080.

In states with less explicit public interest provisions, courts have directed water administrators to consider a wide variety of factors. For example, Idaho's express statutory requirements are limited, mandating only that the Director of Water Resources reject or modify a permit application if the appropriation "will conflict with the local public interest." Idaho Code Ann. § 42–203A. Local public interest is defined as "the interests that the people in the area directly affected by a proposed water use have in the effects of such use on the public water resource." *Id.* § 42–202B. The statute further provides that the Director must consider whether the proposed use "will adversely affect the local economy of the watershed or local area within which the source of water for the proposed use originates, in the case where the place of use is outside of the watershed or local area where the source of water originates." *Id.* § 42–203A. The Idaho Supreme Court held that public interest elements also include those reflected in Idaho laws dealing with instream flows, water quality, water waste, and conservation. Shokal v. Dunn, 707 P.2d 441 (Idaho 1985). In addition, the court found that the factors specified in Alaska and other state statutes made "common sense" when evaluating the public interest. *Id.* at 449. In contrast, the Nevada Supreme Court upheld the state engineer's administrative definition of the public interest based on reference to Nevada water statutes, but found the laws of other states unpersuasive. Pyramid Lake Paiute Tribe of Indians v. Washoe Cnty, 918 P.2d 697 (Nev. 1996). As such, the preservation of wildlife "is part of the public interest" in Nevada. Sullivan v. Lincoln County Water Dist., 542 P.3d 411, 424 (Nev. 2024).

Opponents to appropriation permits argue that the state agency not only has the authority—but the affirmative duty—to reject applications for permits that may be contrary to the public interest. *See* Stempel v. Dep't of Water Res., 508 P.2d 166, 171 (Wash. 1973) (holding that the department must examine the effects of pollution resulting from the issuance of an appropriation permit). A Washington statute authorizes withdrawals of water that conflict with minimum flow requirements "only in those situations where it is clear that overriding considerations of the public interest will be served." Wash. Rev. Code Ann. § 90.54.020(3). *See* Foster v. Washington State Dep't of Ecology, 362 P.3d 959, 963 (Wash. 2015) (concluding that the department may not grant a permit to a municipality if permanent impairment to minimum streamflows would result).

In addition to statutory public interest or welfare requirements, the common law public trust doctrine may influence permitting decisions. One court applied the public trust doctrine to require "at a minimum, a determination of the potential effect of the allocation of water [to major energy projects] on the present water supply and future water needs of this State." United Plainsmen Ass'n v. North Dakota State Water Conservation Comm'n, 247 N.W.2d 457, 462 (N.D. 1976). The ruling implies that comprehensive planning or some other cost-benefit analysis is required for the allocation of water. North Dakota recognized several interests served by the public trust doctrine, including "bathing, swimming, recreation, and fishing, as well as irrigation, industrial, and other water supplies." Sorum v. State, 947 N.W. 2d 382, 397 (N.D. 2020).

National Audubon Soc'y v. Superior Court (Mono Lake), 33 Cal. 3d 419, 658 P.2d 709 (1983), represents the most extensive application of the public trust doctrine to limit a state's authority over appropriation permits. There, the court found that Los Angeles' 1940 permit to use water from tributaries that feed into Mono Lake had been granted without consideration of public trust factors, including fish, wildlife, and recreation, and that such factors provided grounds for later permit challenges. *Id.* at 729. Thus, the city's established appropriations could be qualified by subsequent restrictions to protect the public trust uses dependent on an inflow of fresh water to the lake. *Id.* This decision is remarkable in that it signifies that permits can be subsequently conditioned if public uses were not adequately considered at issuance.

A later case held that the California State Water Resources Control Board, which has authority over surface water allocation and water quality, has a public trust duty to condition water permits to accomplish water quality goals. United States v. State Water Res. Control Bd., 227 Cal. Rptr. 161 (Ct. App. 1986). The Board may also regulate another agency's actions if the actions affect water quality. Pac. Lumber Co. v. State Water Res. Control Bd., 126 P.3d 1040 (Cal. 2006). The public trust doctrine operates "simultaneously" with the state's water rights regime "with neither completely yielding to the other." Bring Back the Kern v. City of Bakersfield, 110 Cal. App. 5th 332, 345 (Ct. App. 2025).

States vary as to the geographic scope of the doctrine. California applies the public trust doctrine to all state waters, Santa Teresa Citizen Action Grp. v. City of San Jose, 7 Cal. Rptr. 3d 868, 884 (Cal. App. 4th 2003), including groundwater hydrologically connected to navigable waters. Envtl. Law Found. v. State Water Res. Control Bd., 237 Cal. Rptr. 3d 393, 403–405 (Cal. App. 5th 2018).

Hawaii applies the doctrine to "all water resources without exception," including groundwater. In re Water Use Permit Applications, 9 P.3d 409, 453 (Haw. 2000). *See* Kauai Springs, Inc. v. Plan. Comm'n of Kauai, 324 P.3d 951, 985 (Haw. 2014) (finding that the planning commission properly denied a bottling company's application to extract water from an underground spring).

The Colorado Supreme Court rejected public trust concerns as a basis for reviewing water rights filings. Bd. of Cnty. Comm'rs of Arapahoe v. United States, 891 P.2d 952, 972 (Colo. 1995). However, "[m]aximum utilization does not mean that every ounce of Colorado's natural stream water ought to be appropriated; optimum use can be achieved only through proper regard for all significant factors, including environmental and economic concerns." Pagosa Area Water and Sanitation Dist. v. Trout Unlimited, 170 P.3d 307, 314 (Colo. 2007).

## B. ADJUDICATION

There are three types of adjudicative procedures affecting water rights: general stream adjudications; appeals of agency permit decisions; and resolution of conflicts among individual appropriators.

### 1. General Stream Adjudications (GSAs)

Many states have adopted procedures for adjudicating the competing rights of all water users in a particular basin. All persons, tribes, or organizations claiming water rights in the system typically must be joined as parties. In some states, judicial proceedings may be initiated by the users, in others by a state agency, and in others by either users or an agency.

State-initiated adjudications proceed according to rules set by state legislatures. They typically require all water rights claimants to prove their water rights relative to all other appropriators. Legislatures are motivated to pass GSA laws, not only to achieve more certainty in quantifying and setting the relative priorities of existing water rights in major watersheds, but also to utilize the McCarran Amendment, a federal statute that requires the United States to adjudicate its water rights if it is joined in a GSA. 43 U.S.C. § 666. Significant GSAs have been undertaken pursuant to legislation in Arizona (Ariz. Rev. Stat. Ann. § 45–252 (1992)) (Gila River), Idaho (Idaho Code Ann. § 42–1405 (1994)) (Snake River), Oregon (Or. Rev. Stat. § 539.005 (1989)) (Klamath River Basin), and Utah (Utah Code Ann. § 73–4–1 (2013)) (Great Salt Lake and Colorado River Basins). Washington began the Yakama River Basin GSA in 1997 with Wash. Rev. Code § 90.03.105 and completed it in 2021. Matter of Rts. to Use of Surface Waters of Yakima River Drainage Basin, 498 P.3d 911 (Wash. 2021). Montana authorized a statewide GSA process in 1979 pursuant to Mont. Code Ann. §§ 85–2–212, –228 with the adjudication of over 240,000 claims to be completed in 2028. *See, e.g.*, Rights to the Use of All the Water, 55 P.3d 396 (Mont. 2002); Montana Judicial Branch, Water Court, https://courts.mt.gov/courts/water/ (visited July 25, 2025).

In a GSA, a state agency or special master often serves as a fact-finder, gathering information, conducting surveys, and compiling claims. The initial hearings and decisions are typically made by an administrative body. The administrative determination of rights is filed in a court, which will embody the determination in a final decree, except to the extent findings may be altered in response to appeals from interested parties. The GSA legislation or decree may provide a process for integrating new permits that are issued after a GSA is commenced.

## 2. Review of Agency Permit Decisions

Once an official or agency makes a decision on an appropriation permit, it is final unless it is appealed. Appeals may go to another administrative level before proceeding to court, depending on the jurisdiction. In some states, the court engages in a trial de novo, but most appeals are based on the administrative record, and administrative decisions will only be overturned if they are arbitrary and capricious or lack substantial evidence. Revert v. Ray, 603 P.2d 262 (Nev. 1979). However, on questions of law, including the meaning of statutes, courts will reach their own conclusions independent of the administrative body's legal conclusions. In re 2007 Admin. of Appropriations of Waters of Niobrara River, 851 N.W.2d 640, 645 (Neb. 2014).

Courts may overturn an administrative decision to approve an application for a water right if the official failed to consider the "public interest" or other statutory criteria. In re: Howard Sleeper, No. RA 84–53(C), *on appeal,* In re: Application of Sleeper, 760 P.2d 787 (N.M. App. 1988). *See* N. Snake Ground Water Dist. v. Idaho Dep't of Water Res., 376 P.3d 722, 728 (Idaho 2016) (setting aside the Director's conclusion that an application was not in the local public interest where neither of the Director's rationales were authorized by the statute).

### 3. Conflicts Among Water Users

In some states, administrative bodies may have authority to resolve conflicts between individual water users, whereas other states require resolution in court. Court decisions generally bind only those who are parties to the suit. Decisions of an administrative body are subject to judicial review either on appeal or as a required step in the permitting process.

## C. REGULATION OF WATER DISTRIBUTION

An administrative agency usually enforces established rights based on the relative priorities of appropriators. Wyoming's system is illustrative. The state engineer has overall supervision, with division superintendents located in each of the four water divisions. Wyo. Stat. Ann. § 41–3–501. Each superintendent oversees several water commissioners who regulate physical distribution of the water. *Id.* § 41–3–503. The commissioner's job is to ensure the water of each stream is distributed in proper quantities at the right times to authorized appropriators. *Id.* § 41–3–603.

The commissioner regulates headgates in accordance with a list of all appropriators in order of priority and operates as a streamside policeman with power to make arrests if necessary. *Id.* § 41–3–605. As streamflow wanes in late summer, the commissioner closes headgates, starting with the lowest priority (*i.e.,* latest in time), to ensure that senior appropriators have access to their entitled quantity of water. *Id.* § 41–3–604. If streamflow increases, the commissioner may open gates and give juniors the benefit of the increase. Regulation of headgates requires no notice or hearing because it is purely a ministerial duty. Hamp v. State, 118 P. 653, 661 (Wyo. 1911). Commissioners report streamflow measurements and water usage to the division superintendents. Wyo. Stat. Ann. § 41–3–608. Appeals from a commissioner's decisions are taken to the superintendent, then to the state engineer, and finally to the district court. *Id.* § 41–3–603.

## D. THE COLORADO SYSTEM

Unlike the other western states, Colorado did not create an agency with permitting and regulatory authority. Instead, it retained a judicial system and charged it with administrative functions.

The Water Rights Determination and Administration Act of 1969, C.R.S. §§ 37–92–101 through 37–92–602, divides the state into seven divisions that correspond to the seven major drainage basins. Colo. Rev. Stat. Ann. § 37–92–201. A division engineer is appointed for each division. *Id.* § 37–92–202. "Water judges" are selected from among district court judges in each division. *Id.* § 27–92–203.

Applications for determinations of water rights are made to the clerk of the water court. *Id.* § 37–92–302. The clerk prepares a monthly docket of applications that are sent to any potential objecting party and published in local newspapers and other media. After an opportunity for statements of opposition to be filed, a referee conducts fact-finding. The state engineer and subordinate officials provide the clerk with a list of decreed and conditional water rights. The referee then approves, disapproves, or approves in part the application. *Id.* § 37–92–303. In some difficult cases, the referee refers the matter back to the water judge for a decision.

Interested parties then have an opportunity to protest the ruling to the water judge. *Id.* § 37–92–302. Rulings not protested are confirmed unless the water judge finds them to be contrary to law. Protested rulings may be confirmed, modified, reversed, or reversed and remanded. Once confirmed, the water right has a priority as of the date of filing the application. *Id.* § 37–92–306.1. Appellate review of the decree from the water judge is available in the Colorado Supreme Court. *Id.* § 37–92–304.

The state and division engineers regulate the distribution of water according to priorities and quantities decreed by the courts. *Id.* § 37–92–501. Division engineers compile and maintain tabulations of all water rights in a division. The tabulations are available to the public and are subject to protests, which the water judge resolves. Colo. Rev. Stat. Ann. § 37–92–401.

The functions of Colorado's water courts are similar to the permitting agencies in other states. One key distinction in the Colorado system is that appropriators may begin using water before asking the court for a water right. This reflects Colorado's interpretation of its constitutional provision declaring that "the right to divert the unappropriated waters of any natural stream to beneficial uses shall never be denied." Colo. Const. Art. 16, § 6. However, the ability to exercise the constitutional right to divert water has little importance because it remains subordinate to, and subject to the call of, all senior users with adjudicated rights. Kobobel v. State, 249 P.3d 1127, 1134 (Colo. 2011).

## VII. TRANSFERS AND CHANGES OF WATER RIGHTS

The increasing urbanization of the West has driven demand to transfer water from agriculture to uses that generate higher economic returns. Because agriculture consumes far more water than municipal or industrial uses, acquiring irrigation rights can provide a substantial supply for these growing sectors. Due to the "first in time, first in right" principle, irrigation rights with early priority are especially valuable. *See supra* Chapter 3.IV.A.

The transfer of a water right along with land is generally routine. In most states, water rights pass with the land upon conveyance unless the deed provides otherwise. When land is divided, a pro rata share of the water right may accompany each parcel. Stephens v. Burton, 546 P.2d 240 (Utah 1976).

Water rights may also be granted separately from the land or reserved by the grantor upon conveyance of the land. Transfers involving different locations, purposes, timing, or changes in the point of diversion or return are more complex, as they must comply with the "no harm" rule. *See infra* Section VII.D.1.

## A. TRANSFERS GENERALLY

Water rights may be transferred by sale, lease, or exchange. However, applications for water rights are not assignable as they are not vested rights until approved. In re Application of Catherland Reclamation Dist., 433 N.W.2d 161 (Neb. 1988).

A transfer may not exceed the quantity of rights held by the transferor. Rocky Ford Irr. Co. v. Kents Lake Reservoir Co., 135 P.2d 108, 114 (Utah 1943). A transfer may or may not be accompanied by a change of use (*e.g.*, a different place or purpose of use). State permission may not be required if land is conveyed along with appurtenant water rights and there is no change in the purpose, time, place of use, or point of diversion or return.

When water rights are conveyed separately or a different use is contemplated, any or all of the above use characteristics may change, thus affecting the rights of other appropriators. This triggers procedures for determining whether harm to other appropriators would result, as described below.

## B. RESTRICTIONS ON TRANSFERS APART FROM THE LAND

Some states have historically restricted transfers for uses away from the land (*e.g.*, Montana, Oklahoma, Nebraska, Nevada, South Dakota, Wyoming). A likely motive was to prevent appropriators from making speculative claims to water in amounts well beyond the quantity of beneficial use and then selling the early priority right to others for use elsewhere.

Some remnants of historic restrictions remain on the books. Wyoming's 1909 "no-change" statute provides that no severance of water rights from land may be made without loss of priority, Wyo. Stat. Ann. § 41–3–101, but this rule is riddled with exceptions for domestic uses, steam power, industry, and other activities. Wyo. Stat. Ann. §§ 41–3–104–112. Nebraska's Irrigation District Act of 1895 makes irrigation water rights appurtenant to land. Neb. Rev. Stat. § 46–122(1); State ex rel. Blome v. Bridgeport Irr. Dist., 286 N.W.2d 426, 432 (1979). However, because the statute applies prospectively, pre-1895 rights (very desirable due to their seniority) can be sold, and modern statutory amendments allow a variety of other transfers. Similarly, in Idaho, the fact that a right has been decreed for the irrigation of appurtenant lands does not prevent a substitution or exchange of water. Bd. of Dirs. of Wilder Irr. Dist. v. Jorgensen, 136 P.2d 461 (Idaho 1943).

In Nevada, Oklahoma, and South Dakota, water rights are ordinarily appurtenant, but may be severed if their use on the originally benefited land becomes economically infeasible. Nev. Rev. Stat. § 533.040; Okla. Stat. tit. 82, § 105.22; S.D. Codified Laws §§ 46–5–33, –34. The Nevada statute limits only the transfer of irrigation rights; others are freely transferable. However, the state engineer may allow water rights to be transferred even if the original land can be irrigated. United States v. Alpine Land and Reservoir Co., 878 F.2d 1217 (9th Cir. 1989). In

Arizona, transfers of irrigation rights apart from the land are subject to approval by the Director of Water Resources; transfers outside the boundaries of irrigation districts also require the consent of the district. Ariz. Rev. Stat. Ann. § 45–172.

In addition to statutory restrictions, some mutual ditch companies and irrigation districts impose restrictions on private stock transfers. *See infra* Chapter 10.III.C. These restrictions may appear on the face of stock or be included in the company's by-laws or articles of incorporation.

### C. TRANSBASIN DIVERSIONS

The prior appropriation doctrine generally permits the removal of water from one watershed for use in another, known as transbasin diversions or interbasin transfers. The seminal case of Coffin v. Left Hand Ditch Co., 6 Colo. 443 (1882), involved a diversion of water out of the basin of its origin. The court recognized that the appropriation doctrine is fundamentally different from riparian rights in that it allows such diversions. *Id.* at 449.

Transbasin diversions are sought when population growth and economic expansion arise in areas where water supplies are inadequate. Bringing water to demanding watersheds requires significant investments in diversion facilities. But imported water allowed arid regions like Southern California and Colorado's eastern slope to flourish. If rights are purchased from appropriators in the area of origin, the no harm rule applicable to changes in use provides some protection for existing appropriators.

But the no harm rule does not consider harm to the economy, ecology, lifestyle, or potential future growth of the area where the water originates. Because these effects tend to be severe and lasting when there are massive exports of water out of a watershed, some states have enacted restrictions to protect the interests of areas of origin.

Area of origin legislation often attempts to safeguard present conditions, including established water rights and streamflows for fish and wildlife. Some laws attempt to provide for development in the area of origin, but in practice, it is difficult to quantify future needs. California allows transbasin diversions subject to the right of the area of origin to appropriate the water when it is needed, with an absolute priority over the exporter. California also protects the county of origin's ability to develop water that may be necessary in the future. *See, e.g.,* Watershed Protection Act, Water Code §§ 11460–11465; County of Origin Protection Act, Water Code § 10505; Delta Protection Act, Water Code §§ 12201–12205; and Protected Area Act, Water Code §§ 1215–1222.

The largest transbasin diversions in Colorado are from the Colorado River Basin west of the Continental Divide to Denver and other heavily populated areas in the east. The legislature enacted a statute to protect the western slope's "present appropriations of water and, in addition thereto, prospective uses of water for irrigation and other beneficial consumptive use purposes." Colo. Rev. Stat. Ann. § 37–45–118(1)(b)(II). Those who divert water from the western slope must show that future water supplies for the western slope "will not be impaired nor increased in cost." *Id.* This can be satisfied by providing "compensatory storage" to help meet future needs in the area of origin. Colorado River Water Conservation Dist. v. Mun. Subdistrict, N. Colorado Conserv. Dist., 610 P.2d 81 (Colo. 1979).

Texas law allows interbasin transfers if the water diverted is surplus to the reasonably foreseeable needs of the basin of origin for the next fifty years. Tex. Water Code § 11.085. Oklahoma requires that sufficient reserves be established to meet present and future needs. Okla. Stat. tit. 82, § 1085.20.

A Nebraska provision that allowed interbasin transfers of 75% of the flow of major rivers in the state was interpreted to authorize the denial of transfers that are "contrary to the public interest." Little Blue Natural Res. Dist. v. Lower Platte N. Natural Res. Dist., 294 N.W.2d 598 (Neb. 1980). Subsequently, the statute was amended to outline specific factors that the Director of Natural Resources must consider when deciding whether an interbasin transfer is in the public interest. Neb. Rev. Stat. § 46–289.

## D. CHANGES IN USE

### 1. No Harm Rule

Whenever one seeks to change the point of diversion, place, purpose, or timing of a water right, special protections against harm to other appropriators apply. An appropriator who seeks to change a use or transfer a right to another for a changed use must apply to the appropriate administrative body or court for approval.

Changes in use may affect stream conditions upon which other appropriators depend for their beneficial uses. While a junior appropriator may not impair a senior appropriator's prior rights to water, juniors are also protected from changes made by seniors. The prior appropriation doctrine recognizes that junior appropriators have a right to "the continuation of stream conditions as they existed at the time of their respective appropriations." Farmers Highline Canal & Reservoir Co. v. City of Golden, 272 P.2d 629 (Colo. 1954). *See* Okanogan Wilderness League, Inc. v. Town of Twisp, 947 P.2d 732 (Wash. 1997).

Irrigation practices typically result in at least half of all diverted water returning to the stream. Only a portion of irrigated water is actually consumed by evaporation or taken up by plants to be retained or transpired into the atmosphere. The rest either flows or seeps back into the stream or is caught in sumps, ponds, groundwater aquifers, and the like. The amount that returns to the stream—"return flow"—becomes available at certain times and places for others to divert. Changes in the point of diversion or the place, time, or purpose of use must not cause material harm to the uses of other appropriators.

However, not all actions that injure juniors are subject to the no harm rule. The no harm rule does not cover reuse or more intensive consumptive use of the water on the same land for the same general purposes (*e.g.*, irrigation), changes in use of imported water, and, in some jurisdictions, certain changes in the point of return. Moreover, a change in the use of relatively small quantities of water may be allowed where the change meets certain minimal criteria. *See* Mont. Code. Ann. § 85–2–402 (imposing more stringent requirements on changes over 5.5 c.f.s. or 4,000 acre-feet per year).

### 2. Procedures

An appropriator must seek permission to change the use of a water right or to transfer it to another who will use it differently. In permit jurisdictions, the decision of whether to allow a change in use rests with a state agency or state engineer. Such administrative decisions are subject to review by state courts. In Colorado, a change of use must be approved through a statutorily established court proceeding and evidenced by a court decree. Colo. Rev. Stat. §§ 37–92–302 to –505; Santa Fe Trail Ranches Prop. Owners Ass'n. v. Simpson, 990 P.2d 46, 53 (Colo. 1999). Notice must be provided to persons who may be affected. Colo. Rev. Stat. § 37–92–302(3). *See* Sheek v. Brooks, 440 P.3d 1145, 1149 (Colo. 2019) (holding that a misidentified ditch headgate location in a change application notice did not render the notice deficient where it adequately alerted the affected water rights owner of the proposed change's nature, scope, and impact).

In general, the primary substantive issue in a change of use proceeding is whether the change violates the no harm/injury rule. In most states, the person seeking the new use has the burden of proving that no harm will result. In some states, once a prima facie case has been made, the burden is on objectors to refute the evidence and prove harm. *See* Montana Env't. Info. Ctr. v. Westmoreland Rosebud Mining, LLC, 545 P.3d 623 (Mont. 2023) (the burden of proof is placed on the party challenging the initial permitting decision).

Some states impose additional requirements. Under Wyoming's change in use statute, the Board of Control may consider economic loss to the locality and the state. Wyo. Stat. Ann. § 41–3–104. Nevada allows the state engineer to consider the economic consequences to the state for changes to uses "involving the industrial purpose of generating electricity to be exported." Nev. Rev. Stat. § 533.372.

Changes may also be denied on "public interest" grounds. The Utah Supreme Court held that it would be unreasonable to allow the state's interest in protecting public recreation, natural environment, or public welfare at the time of an appropriation be defeated upon a change of use. Bonham v. Morgan, 788 P.2d 497 (Utah 1989). In a New Mexico case, a change of water rights from agricultural to a proposed ski resort was found contrary to the public welfare. In re: Application of Sleeper, 760 P.2d 787 (N.M. App. 1988). The decision was reversed on appeal because, at the time, the public welfare statute only applied to new appropriations, not changes. *Id.* at 791. The statute was subsequently extended to changes and transfers of water rights. N.M. Stat. Ann. §§ 72–5–23 –24.

## 3. Types of Changes

A change in use may take several forms. Changes may be made to the point of diversion or point of return; to the place of use or place of storage; to the purpose of use (*e.g.*, irrigation or municipal); or to the time of use (*e.g.*, seasonal, intermittent, or continuous). Harm may occur either from depriving an appropriator of the quantity or quality of water that was available before the change or by increasing an appropriator's obligations to seniors.

### *a. Change in Point of Diversion*

One of the most common types of changes is a change in the point of diversion. An irrigator may want to divert through a new ditch or use a surface diversion instead of a well drawing from the same water source. The proposed change must not harm other appropriators. Langenegger v. Irr. Dist., 483 P.2d 297 (N.M. 1971). In addition, a decree permitting a change in point of diversion cannot enlarge the recipient's right; the right is limited to the amount of water historically used, even if that amount was less than the decreed right. Orr v. Arapahoe Water and Sanitation Dist., 753 P.2d 1217 (Colo. 1988).

### *b. Change in Place of Use*

Changes in place of use often change the place or timing of return flows from irrigation. A change in place of use must not increase consumptive use, even if the amount diverted remains the same. Enlarged Southside Irrigation Ditch Co. v. John's Flood Ditch

Co., 210 P.2d 982 (Colo. 1949). Changing to an out-of-basin use eliminates return flows, making the new use 100% consumptive and thereby interfering with downstream rights.

A change in the place of storage, such as an alternative reservoir site, is a type of change in the place of use. Increased seepage and evaporation loss could harm juniors; however, a change may be permitted, for instance, if the new reservoir is at a higher elevation with lower losses than the original site. Lindsey v. McClure, 136 F.2d 65 (10th Cir. 1943). Uses that involve a change from direct use to storage may affect both the timing and amount of consumptive use.

Exchange statutes in several western states authorize agreements between water users to furnish water at one point in the stream and withdraw at another. *See, e.g.*, Utah Code Ann. § 73–3–3; Colo. Rev. Stat. § 37–83–101; Idaho Code Ann. § 42–240. Exchanges are subject to the no harm rule. Almo Water Co. v. Darrington, 501 P.2d 700 (Idaho 1972).

### c. *Change in Purpose of Use*

A change in purpose of use typically involves a change from irrigation use to municipal or industrial use. Municipal uses are usually more consumptive than agricultural uses because returns (usually sewage effluent) are a small percentage of the quantity diverted, while irrigation return flows are more substantial. By contrast, hydroelectric power generation and cooling are less consumptive than irrigation. Thus, changes from irrigation to municipal use (Farmers Reservoir & Irrigation Co. v. City of Golden, 44 P.3d 241 (Colo. 2002); City of Westminster v. Church, 445 P.2d 52 (Colo. 1968)) or from power generation to irrigation use (Hutchinson v. Stricklin, 28 P.2d 225 (Or. 1933), *overruled on other grounds*, Rencken v. Young, 711 P.2d 954 (1985)), may be limited to prevent increased consumption.

Planting crops that consume more water or changing irrigation methods (*e.g.*, from flood irrigation to sprinklers) are not typically considered changes in purpose, even though the manner of use differs. However, such changes can harm other appropriators by reducing seepage or eliminating return flows due to reduced application or increased consumption. Montana v. Wyoming, 563 U.S. 368 (2011). This apparent loophole in the no harm rule is rooted in traditional assumptions held by water users, especially irrigators, that they can plant any crop they want and irrigate as necessary, as long as their total use does not exceed the amount allowed by their permit or decree. The prevailing rule remains: changes in the purpose of use that necessitate permission of an administrative agency or court, and invocation of the no harm rule, occur only when water is put to a different type of beneficial use.

### *d. Change in Time of Use*

A change in the timing of use can harm others. For example, irrigation rights are seasonal (used only during the growing season), while municipal and industrial uses are typically year-round. Similarly, a storage right may permit constant diversion into the reservoir, even though withdrawals are intermittent, since a direct flow right occurs only when actual uses are present. A change in the timing of return flows is also a possible source of harm. The slow-moving character of seepage returning to the stream provides a form of "transient storage" that may furnish late-season return flows to juniors, thus extending their irrigation season.

### *e. Change in Point of Return*

A change in the point of return can also cause harm to others. Ordinarily, such a change accompanies other changes in use. Although cases involving only a change in point of return are rare, one would expect the no harm rule to apply. But in Metropolitan Denver Sewage Disposal Dist. No. 1 v. Farmers Reservoir & Irrigation Co., 499 P.2d 1190 (Colo. 1972), the court held that irrigators who depended on discharges of Denver's sewage effluent suffered no legal harm from Denver's change in the point of return when a new sewage plant was constructed. *See also* Arizona Pub. Serv. Co. v. Long, 773 P.2d 988 (Ariz. 1989) (cities did not have to continue to discharge effluent to satisfy needs of downstream users).

In a later case, the Colorado Supreme Court in dicta reiterated the proposition that a change in the point of return is not subject to the no harm rule. City of Boulder v. Boulder & Left Hand Ditch Co., 557 P.2d 1182 (Colo. 1976). The case was distinguishable from *Metro Denver* because a change in place of use was also involved. However, the court moderated the *Metro Denver* rule, saying it only applies to "wastewater." Thus, there is no protectable right to the continued flow of "wastewater" (water returning to a stream in surface ditches), but there is a right against changes in "return flow" (water seeping back to the stream), at least when triggered by a change in the place of use.

### 4. Limits on Changed Use

A change in use will be granted if conditions can be imposed that sufficiently protect junior appropriators from harm. For example, a seasonal direct-flow irrigation right may be transferred to a continuous storage use, provided diversions are restricted to the irrigation season, Brighton Ditch Co. v. City of Englewood, 237 P.2d 116 (Colo. 1951), and are made under the same conditions as the original diversions, Colorado Milling & Elevator Co. v. Larimer & Weld Irrigation Co., 56 P. 185 (Colo. 1899).

The amount diverted for the changed use can never exceed the diversion right stated in the permit or decree. Schuh v. State Dept. of Ecology, 667 P.2d 64, 68 (Wash. 1983); Santa Fe Trail Ranches Property Owners Ass'n v. Simpson, 990 P.2d 46 (Colo. 1999). Additionally, it is common to limit new uses to the necessary historical consumptive use. Neb. Rev. St. § 46–294(1)(e); Okanogan Wilderness League, Inc. v. Town of Twisp, 947 P.2d 732 (Wash. 1997). For example, if a decreed right of 200 c.f.s. has the historical consumptive use of 100 c.f.s. (50% consumptive), the new user is entitled to 100 c.f.s.

But if the new use is only 40% consumptive, the new user would have to divert 250 c.f.s. to consume 100 c.f.s. Since the changed use is limited to the original decreed right of 200 c.f.s., the new user can only use 80 c.f.s. (200 c.f.s. × 40% consumption).

Actual historical use can be shown by records of the amount of water diverted and the amount of water returned. However, expert testimony is usually necessary. Records may not exist, and they are rarely adequate to demonstrate the amount of water that has been diverted and returned. Further, actual use may exceed the amount necessary for the beneficial use of the appropriated water's purpose. Thus, estimating historical use may depend on evidence of the amount of water required for the purposes to which it was devoted. Evidence includes soil conditions, proximity to the stream, crop water requirements minus average rainfall, and irrigation efficiency. Green v. Chaffee Ditch Co., 371 P.2d 775 (Colo. 1962). *See* CF & I Steel Corp. v. Rooks, 495 P.2d 1134 (Colo. 1972) (objectors lost for failure to refute applicant's expert testimony); Concerning the Application of Water Rights of Boulder County v. Boulder and Weld County Ditch Co., 367 P.3d 1179, 1193 (Colo. 2016) (applicant failed to show the actual amount of water historically used on specific acres as required to support its application for a change of use from irrigation to augmentation of ponds).

Statutes, case law, and regulations restricting transfers to historical consumptive use are intended to prevent harm to others. The rules have been applied to restrict a change even if the impact on the stream from the new use would be lower. In Basin Electric Power Coop. v. State Board of Control, 578 P.2d 557 (Wyo. 1978), water had been taken to another watershed for irrigation, making the old use 100% consumptive in the watershed of origin. The new use, however, was entirely within the watershed of origin. One might expect the change to be approved for the full amount historically used—all the water diverted. But the court limited the right transferred to the quantity of water consumed in the destination watershed (diversion less returns), although none of the returns had actually reached the basin of origin.

Changes may also be denied or restricted if they diminish the quality of water supplied to other appropriators. *See* Heine v. Reynolds, 367 P.2d 708 (N.M. 1962) (denying an application for a change where stream salinity would be increased). An increasingly common condition requires bypasses or releases of water to maintain streamflows or water quality. *See* City of Thornton v. City & County of Denver ex rel. Bd. of Water Comm'rs, 44 P.3d 1019 (Colo. 2002) (finding that the water court had jurisdiction to decide whether decreased water quality made it unsuitable for the city's use). Other water quality-related barriers to changes of use exist, such as federal and state environmental pollution laws, minimum and maximum streamflow requirements, and land use restrictions.

## VIII. LOSS OF WATER RIGHTS

Water rights acquired by prior appropriation may be lost if they are not used. Nonuse for a long time, coupled with intent to relinquish, constitutes abandonment. Statutory forfeiture for nonuse may occur despite the appropriator's contrary intent. However, a water user cannot generally acquire an appropriative right by prescription because any unused water by appropriators belongs to the stream, to fulfill the rights of existing appropriators, and for new appropriation permits. *See infra* Section VIII.C.

## A. ABANDONMENT

Prior appropriation water rights are abandoned and lost if they are not used for an extended time. Mere nonuse is not enough, however, as one must intend to abandon the rights. Beaver Park Water, Inc. v. City of Victor, 649 P.2d 300 (Colo. 1982). The burden of proving intent lies with the person attempting to establish abandonment, but an unreasonable period of nonuse may create a rebuttable presumption of intent to abandon. Haystack Ranch, LLC v. Fazzio, 997 P.2d 548, 553 (Colo. 2000); Twin Creeks Farm & Ranch, LLC v. Petrolia Irrigation Dist., 461 P.3d 91 (Mont. 2020); State ex rel. Off. of State Eng'r v. Intrepid Potash, Inc., No. S-1-SC-40182, 2025 WL 1821806, *11 (N.M. July 2, 2025). The period giving rise to the presumption is found in statute or case law. In Colorado, the state engineer publishes a list of abandoned water rights based on the statutory presumption arising from ten years of nonuse. Colo. Rev. Stat. § 37–92–401(4).

In some states, "growing cities" may avoid the presumption of abandonment despite long periods of nonuse. Such exceptions allow cities to retain water for foreseeable future needs. *See, e.g.,* MCA § 85–2–227(4). *See also* Waterwatch of Oregon, Inc. v. Water Res. Comm'n, 88 P.3d 327, 341 (Or. App. 2004), *vacated,* 119 P.3d 221 (Or. 2005) (noting that the "legislature does not favor the forfeiture of a water right implicating municipal purposes"). However, abandonment may still be shown if the amount of water claimed by a city "is more than the amount needed to satisfy the current use plus normal increases in population over a reasonable period." U.S. Dep't of Army Corps of Engineers, 445 P.3d 828, 833 (Mont. 2019). If its population and its water use have been declining from historical levels, the city may lose its water right. *Id.; See also,* City of Helena v. Cmty. of Rimini, 397 P.3d 1 (Mont. 2017) (applying the presumption of non-abandonment when the city proved its intent to use the water by constructing a conveyance with sufficient capacity).

Once a presumption of abandonment arises, the burden of proof lies with the right holder to rebut it. Broad unsupported generalities and "expressions of desire or hope or intent" (*i.e.,* speculation) are insufficient to overcome the presumption. *Intrepid Potash, supra,* at *11; Musselshell River Drainage Area, 840 P.2d 577 (Mont. 1992); Beaver Park Water, Inc. v. City of Victor, 649 P.2d 300, 302 (Colo. 1982). Likewise, the right holder's "self-serving declarations of intent are insufficient to overcome this presumption." McKenna v. Witte (In re McKenna), 346 P. 3d 35, 43 (Colo. 2015).

Natural disasters and economic, financial, or legal obstacles that frustrated attempts to use water may negate the intent to abandon. *Compare* Hallenbeck v. Granby Ditch & Reservoir Co., 420 P.2d 419 (Colo. 1966) ("financial difficulties . . . during the depression prevented Granby's ability to keep reservoirs in peak operating condition"); Twin Creeks Farm & Ranch, LLC v. Petrolia Irrigation Dist., 399 Mont. 431, 461 P.3d 91 (2020) (obstacles arising from the appropriator's remote and flood-prone place of use did not excuse nonuse). However, economic infeasibility of the project is not enough to overcome the presumption. CF & I Steel Corp. v. Purgatoire River Water Conservancy Dist., 515 P.2d 456 (Colo. 1973). The distinction appears to be that in the former case, genuine economic constraints impeded water use, and in the latter, it was delayed due to strategic business reasons. However, the Colorado court allowed an appropriator to rebut the presumption of abandonment with evidence that it was trying to sell the water right for which it apparently had no use. People ex rel. Danielson v. City of Thornton, 775 P.2d 11 (Colo. 1989).

## B. FORFEITURE

Forfeiture, unlike abandonment, does not require proof that the appropriator intended to abandon water rights by nonuse. Involuntary loss of all or a portion of one's rights is triggered simply by nonuse for a statutory period. The burden of proving nonuse is on the state (or other party) asserting forfeiture. Rencken v. Young, 711 P.2d 954 (Or. 1985).

Courts may declare a right "forfeited" where the evidence is insufficient to prove intent to abandon. Jenkins v. State, Dept. of Water Resources, 647 P.2d 1256 (Idaho 1982). Non-use may result in forfeiture, even if the appropriator allowed the water to be used by others during the statutory period, unless the others' use is in accordance with a lease or other agreement. Salt Lake City Corp. v. Haik, 438 P.3d 913 (citing Utah Code Ann. § 73–1–4(2)(a)), *aff'd on other grounds*, 466 P.3d 178 (Utah 2019).

Forfeiture statutes typically provide for notice by a state agency or official that rights will be forfeited if nonuse is not cured within a specified grace period. New Mexico provided for automatic forfeiture after four years of nonuse, State ex rel. Reynolds v. South Springs Co., 452 P.2d 478 (N.M. 1969), but the statute was amended to allow a one-year period during which the appropriator can recommence use or show why it was impossible to put the water to a beneficial use. N.M. Stat. § 72–12–8. Other states recognize exceptions for "reasonable" or "sufficient" cause such as physical events beyond the appropriator's control (such as drought) or service in the armed forces. *See, e.g.,* Utah Code § 73–1–4(4); Ariz. Rev. Stat. Ann. § 45–189(E); Neb. Rev. Stat. § 46–229.04(4)(d)).

Some courts have held that once the right is lost, it cannot be revived. *See* Baugh v. Criddle, 431 P.2d 790 (Utah 1967) (following a fire that destroyed a mill, the party who failed to provide notice that the use had been resumed lost his right to use water); Wheatland Irr. Dist. v. Laramie Rivers Co., 659 P.2d

561, 567 (Wyo. 1983) ("Only the use of the water will prevent a forfeiture."). The Idaho Supreme Court held that resuming use to defend a forfeiture claim is ineffective if a junior appropriator applied the water to a beneficial use *after* non-use reached the statutory period. Sagewillow, Inc. v. Idaho Dept. of Water Resources, 70 P.3d 669 (Idaho 2003). *See* Millview County Water Dist. v. State Water Resources Control Bd., 229 Ca. App. 4th 879 (Cal. App. 1st Dist. 2014) (discussing the resumption of use doctrine established in *Sagewillow*).

Forfeiture statutes may provide exceptions for certain uses. Municipal users are sometimes given preferential treatment. *See, e.g.*, Or. Rev. Stat. Ann. § 540.610(2). Washington law protects rights claimed for municipal water supply purposes, Wash. Rev. Code Ann. § 90.14.140(2)(d), but water delivered to an industrial park did not qualify even though the holder provided water to 5,000 to 6,000 hotel workers and guests, because the water was not being used in a residential setting. Crown W. Realty, LLC v. Pollution Control Hearings Bd., 435 P.3d 288 (Wash. App.), *review denied,* 447 P.3d 165 (2019).

To encourage efficient use or conservation of water, some states have provided that a right is not subject to forfeiture when appropriators use less water to carry out the same beneficial use so long as they are still capable of using the entire amount. Or. Rev. Stat. § 540.610(3); Cal. Water. Code. § 1011(1); Wash. Rev. Code Ann. § 90.14.140(1)(i).

## C. ADVERSE POSSESSION AND PRESCRIPTIVE RIGHTS

One may obtain another's rights in real property by taking actual, open, notorious, continuous, and hostile exclusive possession of the property. A few courts have ruled that, in certain circumstances, a junior appropriator could adversely possess a senior's water right. *See, e.g.,* Sears v. Berryman, 623 P.2d 455 (Idaho 1981); Head v. Merrick, 203 P.2d 608 (Idaho 1949). Although Utah was once among these states, Smith v. North Canyon Water Co., 52 P. 283, 286 (Utah 1898), the Utah legislature abolished prescriptive rights in Utah Code Ann. § 73–3–1.

In the majority of states, water rights held by prior appropriation cannot be lost to others by adverse possession. First, private individuals can obtain water rights only by complying with statutory procedures. Montana's statute explicitly states that an appropriation right cannot be acquired by any method not statutorily provided, including by adverse possession, estoppel, or prescription. Mont. Code Ann. § 85–2–301(3). Second, one's use of water cannot be adverse to others because of the assumed right that any water use occurred within the priority system. Coryell v. Robinson, 194 P.2d 342 (Colo. 1948). This is especially true if the would-be adverse possessor holds some rights on the watercourse. Third, some courts have reasoned that rights to use a public resource, like water, cannot be adversely possessed. *See* Mountain Meadow Ditch & Irrigation Co. v. Park Ditch & Reservoir Co., 277 P.2d 527 (Colo. 1954) (unappropriated stream water was public property and could not be adversely possessed). Others disallow adverse possession against the state but recognize it between private parties. *See* People v. Shirokow, 605 P.2d 859 (Cal. 1980) (Water Code's comprehensive scheme for granting of appropriative rights precluded acquisition of prescriptive rights against the state); Brewer v. Murphy, 74 Cal. Rptr. 3d 436 (2008) (claimants had developed a right to prescriptive easement in a spring).

## IX. PHYSICAL ACCESS TO SOURCE AND TRANSPORTATION OF WATER

Irrigated land, particularly in the western United States, does not often border a stream. Therefore, rights-of-way for ditches, canals, and pipelines are critically important to water users. Water users often need to build facilities on the land of one or more intervening property owners to bring water to their property. Even when land is adjacent to a stream, use of another's land may be necessary to use a gravity flow pipe or a ditch that follows the contours of the terrain. Federal and state laws govern the acquisition of rights-of-way by water rights holders.

### A. ACROSS FEDERAL PUBLIC LANDS

As water law began to develop during the western expansion of the United States, much of the land in the West was public, owned, and controlled by the federal government. Congress provided for ditch and canal rights-of-way across public lands in the 1866 Mining Act. In addition to recognizing the right of trespassers to establish water rights by prior appropriation on federal lands, the Act stated, "the right-of-way for the construction of ditches and canals for the purposes herein specified is acknowledged and confirmed." 30 U.S.C. § 51. The 1870 amendment to the Mining Act made all patents of public lands and all homesteads "subject to any vested and accrued water rights, or rights to ditches and reservoirs used in connection with such water rights." 43 U.S.C. § 661. These laws opened the way for the construction of necessary facilities without fear of later dispossession or interruption by the government or its patentees. *See supra* Section II.A.

Today, rights-of-way across public land are obtained by special permission from the federal agency that manages the area. For BLM and Forest Service lands, the Federal Land Policy and Management Act of 1976 (FLPMA), 43 U.S.C. § 1761, authorizes the Secretary of the Interior and the Secretary of Agriculture to grant, issue, or renew rights-of-way across public lands for water storage and distribution facilities (*e.g.*, ditches, pipelines, and tunnels). Permits are granted for a fixed term and subject to annual rentals and conditions on use deemed necessary to comply with mandates in public land laws, such as requirements for protecting fish and wildlife, recreational uses, biodiversity, and other environmental values. 43 U.S.C. § 1765; 43 C.F.R. § 2805.12. For rights-of-way across lands managed by agencies other than the Forest Service or the Bureau of Land Management, water rights holders must secure a permit from the relevant agency. *See, e.g.*, 43 U.S.C. § 959, 36 C.F.R. pt. 14

(National Park Service); 16 U.S.C. § 668dd(d), 50 C.F.R. pt. 29 (National Wildlife Refuge).

In 1890, Congress created a right-of-way for ditches and canals constructed by the authority of the United States on all public lands patented to private ownership west of the 100th meridian. 43 U.S.C. § 945. A 1964 amendment to this act required the government to pay compensation for any such lands that were used for rights-of-way to access water. 43 U.S.C. § 945a. Thus, many lands in the West are impressed with rights-of-way for private uses. New appropriators whose water uses began after the land was privately patented, even if formerly part of the public domain, generally seek rights-of-way under state law from private landowners. In some instances, if the federal government denies formerly available right-of-way access across public land, the landowners may seek compensation under the Fifth Amendment's Takings Clause. *See* Estate of Hage v. United States, 687 F.3d 1281, 1290 (Fed. Cir. 2012) (holding that the Forest Service could reasonably regulate the use of ditches but could not deny access to vested water rights without providing compensation). The law remains somewhat unresolved in terms of determining what will trigger a viable takings claim in these circumstances. *See, e.g., id.*; Joyce Livestock Co. v. United States (In re SRBA Case No. 39576), 156 P.3d 502 (Idaho 2007).

## B. ACROSS PRIVATE LANDS UNDER STATE LAW

### 1. Status of Trespassing Appropriators

Several state laws and cases address whether appropriators may transport water across the lands of others. Some state courts (*e.g.*, Idaho and Oregon) invalidated the appropriation of one who trespasses on another's land to create a diversion. Allen v. Magill, 189 P. 986, 989 (Or. 1920). More typically, trespassing appropriators may be subject to a trespass claim, but this does not void their water right. For instance, in Colorado, trespass will not prevent perfection of a water right, but the trespasser must compensate the owner for the fair market value of using the land and any resulting damages. Bubb v. Christensen, 610 P.2d 1343, 1346 (Colo. 1980). This is tantamount to a right of private condemnation.

While appropriators who transport surface water across the land of another may be subject to a trespass claim, storing or transporting water in an aquifer under another party's property does not constitute a trespass. Board of County Comm'rs v. Park County Sportsmen's Ranch, LLP, 45 P.3d 693, 713–14 (Colo. 2002); South West Sand & Gravel, Inc. v. Cent. Ariz. Water Conservation Dist., 212 P.3d 1, 10 (Ariz. 2009), *cert. denied*, 559 U.S. 1008 (2010). Moreover, a state's approval of an application for an incidental aquifer storage right is not an unconstitutional taking of private property. In re Application U-2, 413 N.W.2d 290, 299 (Neb. 1987).

If a trespasser enters the land of another and constructs pipelines, ditches, or other facilities without the landowner's permission, and the facilities remain for an established time period, the use could ripen into a prescriptive right. Pabst v. Finmand, 211 P.11 (Cal. 1922); Pedersen v. Dep't of Transp., 717 P.2d 773 (Wash. Ct. App. 1986); Graveley Simmental Ranch Co. v. Quigley, 65 P.3d 225 (Mont. 2003): *see also* Chester v. Wild Idaho Adventures RV Park, LLC, 519 P.3d 1152 (Idaho 2022) (overspray from landowners' irrigation pivot onto neighbor's adjoining property was an "adverse use" that could give rise to a prescriptive easement).

## 2. Purchase of Rights-of-Way

The most common way to obtain a right-of-way to convey water across private land is by purchase. Often, water delivery facilities can serve the property owner, and the parties can reach a mutually beneficial arrangement. The right-of-way for a canal, ditch, or pipeline typically includes a secondary easement for necessary maintenance and repairs. Ass'n of Apt. Owners of Wailea Elua v. Wailea Resort Co., 58 P.3d 608, 626 (Ha. 2002); Newmyer v. Roush, 120 P. 464 (1912).

Grants of easements or rights-of-way, like other interests in land, usually must be in writing and conform to other property conveyance formalities. *See, e.g.*, Or. Rev. Stat. § 93.020. Yet some state courts have held that a landowner's oral permission or informal letter to construct a ditch is valid as a license, and the landowner is estopped from contesting the license. Shaw v. Proffitt, 109 P. 584 (Or. 1910). To become irrevocable and transferable, courts require licensees to show reliance through a substantial amount of money and labor invested in the project. In McReynolds v. Harrigfeld, 140 P. 1096 (Idaho 1914), the court refused to quiet title to an irrigation ditch because the ditch builder could not show that he made an investment dependent upon the landowner's permission. But when a water user can prove a substantial investment, licenses are essentially treated as easements. However, not all courts treat licenses the same. For example, the court in Rhoades v. Barnes, 102 P. 884 (Wash. 1909), stated that the licensor may revoke the license at any time, regardless of the acts performed or amount of money spent in reliance on the license.

### 3. Condemnation of Rights-of-Way

Some western states enacted statutes authorizing appropriators to condemn rights-of-way to transport water across private lands. *See, e.g.*, Wash. Rev. Code § 90.03.040. Water rights holders can utilize these statutes, where they exist, to gain access to water when the owner is unwilling or unavailable to grant permission. In New Mexico, for example, an irrigation company was granted the right to enter onto private property to install a canal that diverts water from the Rio Grande River. Albuquerque Land & Irrigation Co. v. Gutierrez, 61 P. 357 (N.M. 1900).

Challengers to these private condemnation statutes argue they do not further a public use. The U.S. Supreme Court upheld Utah's grant of eminent domain power against a challenge that the law offended the Due Process Clause of the Fourteenth Amendment. The Court recognized the importance of water development under conditions prevailing in the West. Clark v. Nash, 198 U.S. 361 (1905). *See* O'Neill v. Leamer, 239 U.S. 244 (1915); California Oregon Power Co. v. Beaver Portland Cement Co., 295 U.S. 142 (1935). Western state courts have upheld similar statutes. In Kaiser Steel Corp. v. W.S. Ranch Co., 467 P.2d 986, 992 (N.M. 1970), the Supreme Court of New Mexico held that any beneficial use pursuant to state law (coal mining in that case) would suffice to support a valid "public use." Further, a landowner's only remedy against an appropriator who enters without permission is an inverse condemnation action. *Id.* at 993.

### C. APPURTENANCY OF DITCH RIGHTS TO WATER RIGHTS

The right-of-way for a ditch and a water right are usually considered appurtenant to one another—conveyance of one carries the other with it; unless reserved in the conveyance, the right-of-way passes by the deed. Ruhnke v. Aubert, 113 P. 38 (Or. 1911). This does not prevent one from being sold apart from the other if the parties express that intention. Fitzstephens v. Watson, 344 P.2d 221 (Or. 1959).

## X. STORAGE

In nearly all areas of the western United States, storage rights are an essential piece of the water allocation system. Water can be stored underground in an aquifer or above ground in a reservoir, tank, or channel. Without storage, beneficial use of water would be limited to short runoff periods, and the maximum use of scarce water resources would be defeated. Storage water rights function differently from direct appropriations because they do not require the immediate diversion and use of water.

On-channel storage means the facility is physically part of the appropriated stream. Most dams, which often function to retain natural flow during peak periods, are examples of on-channel storage. This on-channel storage allows water not needed for senior downstream appropriators to be stored for later use. Off-channel storage requires diversion and transportation works to get water to a storage location away from the stream channel.

As a legal matter, there is no distinction between off-stream and on-stream storage rights. In general, for purposes of the diversion requirement, artificially retaining water in the streambed qualifies as a "diversion" for purposes of perfecting a water right. A&B Irrigation Dist. v. State (In re SRBA), 336 P.3d 792, 796 (Idaho 2014); City of Lafayette v. New Anderson Ditch Co., 962 P.2d 955 (Colo. 1998).

Many states recognize an exception to the diversion and storage requirements for the protection of established minimum instream flows. *See, e.g.*, Swinomish Indian Tribal Cmty. v. Dep't of Ecology, 311 P.3d 6 (Wash. 2012); California v. Federal Power Com., 345 F.2d 917 (9th Cir. 1965).

## A. ACQUISITION OF STORAGE RIGHTS

State and federal law treat permission to divert and store water as distinct from permission to construct and maintain the physical works. To maintain a storage reservoir, a person or organization must secure a storage water right under state law, in addition to the relevant state or federal permits and permissions to construct and maintain the dam, depending on the facility's size and location.

### 1. Storage Water Rights

The same general principles of appropriation for immediate use (direct flow water rights) govern appropriations for subsequent uses (storage water rights), although some states make a statutory distinction between the two. Users obtain a permit or decree for a storage water right from the same agency or court that determines direct flow water rights. Storage rights are usually only valid if the stored water will eventually satisfy a recognized beneficial use; storage itself is not considered a beneficial use. People ex. rel. Simpson v. Highland Irrigation Co., 917 P.2d 1242, 1251 (Colo. 1996). A Washington court held that for a water right to vest, actual application of the water to a beneficial use must be made. Lummi Indian Nation v. State, 241 P.3d 1220 (Wash. 2010): *see also* Bridge Creek Ranch, LLC v. Oregon Water Res. Dep't, 541 P.3d 920 (Or. Ct. App. 2023) (an applicant for a permit to store water obtains a primary water right; however, a secondary permit is needed for use of the water from the reservoir, and the final certificate of appropriation issues only after the beneficial use has been completed and perfected. A storage appropriation should not be granted if it would injure any prior appropriator on the stream. Whitcomb v. Helena Water Works Co., 444 P.2d 301, 303 (Mont. 1968); Colo. Rev. Stat. § 37–87–101 ("No water storage facility may be operated in such a manner as to cause material injury to the senior appropriative rights of others.").

A right to use water directly from the stream does not entitle the user to store water, and a right to store water does not mean that water can be used directly from the stream. Handy Ditch Co. v. Greeley & Loveland Irrigation Co., 86 Colo. 197, 280 P. 481 (1929). In other words, the right to divert water does not automatically confer the right to store water. Central and West Basin Water Replenishment Dist. v. Southern Calif. Water Co., 135 Cal. Rptr. 2d 486, 505 (Cal. App. 4th 2003).

Some states require separate permits for storage and for application to a beneficial use. *See e.g.*, Ariz. Rev. Stat. § 45–161; Nev. Rev. Stat. § 533.440; Wyo. Stat. § 41–3–302; Neb. Rev. St. § 46–242. This approach recognizes that the entity diverting and storing the water (*e.g.*, a reservoir company) is often distinct from the entity or persons putting water to beneficial use (*e.g.*, irrigators). Some states consider the two to be joint appropriators. Others require the ultimate user to obtain a separate appropriation permit by showing a valid agreement with the reservoir owner. *See, e.g.*, Wyo. Stat. § 41–3–302.

## 2. Permission to Construct Storage Facilities

Besides perfecting a right to store water, one seeking to impound it in a reservoir must have permission to build the facility. Federal law applies if the facility is to be built on a navigable waterway and generates a sufficient level of hydropower as defined in the Federal Power Act (FPA). *See infra* Chapter 7.IV.A. Additionally, the federal government may own and operate its own dams as part of flood control or irrigation projects. *See infra* Chapter 10.VI. Federal law provides for the construction of these facilities, but often the authorizing legislation requires the federal agency to secure water rights under state law. *See* 16 U.S.C. § 802(a)(2).

Outside of these federal authorizations to construct facilities, state law applies to facilities on non-navigable waterways, with some exceptions. *See e.g.*, Or. Rev. Stat. §§ 537.400–409; Wash. Admin. Code § 173–175–100. In most states, the same agency that determines water rights approves plans for the construction of dams and reservoirs. Often, the agency or official may consider factors related to the public interest, such as safety, impacts on fish and wildlife, and aesthetics. A party proposing to use the stored water must also file an application for a permit to apply the water to a beneficial use, known as a secondary permit. Or. Rev. Stat. § 537.400. Arizona only requires a single permit when the same person constructs the reservoir and puts water to beneficial use. Ariz. Rev. Stat. § 45–161(D).

Most states exempt small storage facilities, such as stock watering ponds, from permit requirements. For example, in Washington, a permit is required to construct and maintain any dam capable of storing 10 acre-feet or more, while dams with a capacity less than 10 acre-feet are exempt. Wash. Admin. Code § 173–175–020. For similar exemptions, *see, e.g.*, Or. Rev. Stat. 537.405(1); Neb. Rev. Stat. § 46–241(2).

## B. USE OF STORAGE RIGHTS

The holder of a storage water right can use stored water for any beneficial purpose. Basey v. Gallagher, 87 U.S. 670 (1874); California Oregon Power Co. v. Beaver Portland Cement Co., 295 U.S. 142 (1935). Appropriative rights on a stream, whether for storage or direct flow, are governed by the same rules of priority. Donich v. Johnson, 250 P. 963 (Mont. 1926). Storage and direct flow water rights are integrated in that neither is given preference over the other. People ex. rel. Park Reservoir Co. v. Hinderlider, 57 P.2d 894, 899 (Colo. 1936).

Some states allow exchanges between appropriators. For instance, water stored downstream may be exchanged for direct flow diversions upstream. Exchanges among rights holders maximize the beneficial use of water, allowing junior appropriators (with storage rights and available capacity) to share storage with seniors (with no storage rights) who have rights to direct flow beyond their needs. The seniors' water is stored in the juniors' reservoir, and its use is later shared, provided that others are not harmed. Colorado Water Conservancy Dist. v. Fort Lyon Canal Co., 720 P.2d 133, 145 (Colo. 1986). Exchanges are permitted in most states upon compliance with conditions imposed by an agency. Moreover, stored water may also be used under a contract, lease, or other arrangement. Kearney Lake, Land & Reservoir Co. v. Lake DeSmet Reservoir Co., 475 P.2d 548 (Wyo. 1970).

## C. LIMITS ON STORAGE

A widely applied limitation on holders of storage water rights is the "one-fill rule." Under this rule, an appropriator may fill a reservoir only once annually and may not store a cumulative volume exceeding the reservoir's full capacity over the course of the year. City of Grand Junction v. City & Cnty. of Denver by & Through Board of Water Comm'rs, 960 P.2d 675 (Colo. 1998); Burlington Ditch Reservoir & Land Co. v. Metro Wastewater Reclamation Dist., 256 P.3d 645 (Colo. 2011); Wheatland Irrigation Dist. v. Pioneer Canal Co., 464 P.2d 533 (Wyo. 1970).

The purpose of the one-fill limitation was the ease of regulation, but its application can be complex. A series of several fillings and drawdowns may be necessary to even out flows throughout the year. A small regulating dam can release many times its capacity during a year, but this pattern of fill and release is prohibited when strictly applying the one-fill rule. Moreover, if the purpose of the dam is hydropower generation as opposed to irrigation storage, the one-fill rule greatly reduces the dam's utility. In fact, most of the case law concerns irrigation reservoirs. *See, e.g.,* Burlington Ditch Reservoir & Land Co. v. Metro Wastewater Reclamation Dist., 256 P.3d 645 (Colo. 2011).

Storage rights are also limited by their priority date, meaning downstream senior appropriators must have their rights fulfilled before junior storage rights can be fulfilled. Granite Cty. Bd. of Comm'rs v. McDonald, 383 P.3d 740 (Mont. 2016), provides a helpful assessment of the relationship between storage rights and downstream appropriators. The court explained:

> [D]ownstream appropriators of irrigation rights with senior priority dates are entitled to the natural flow of a stream as it existed at the time of appropriation but they cannot demand release of water from storage when natural flows are unavailable. . . At the same time, the law on storage does not require release of lawfully impounded storage water when natural flows drop below the amounts needed by downstream irrigators.

*Id.* at 744. Storage rights are designed to ensure that water not consumed by the storage right is returned to the stream, and not diverted elsewhere, *id.*, which is consistent with the concept of return flows mentioned previously in this chapter.

Water diverted to a reservoir but not immediately used may be retained for future use by the appropriator. *See e.g.*, American Falls Reservoir Dist. No. 2 v. Idaho Dept. of Water Res., 154 P.3d 433 (Idaho 2007). This is known as "carryover storage," and has developed as a practice to help reservoir operators balance water supply over wet and dry years. *See* Pagosa Area Water & Sanitation Dist. v. Trout Unlimited, 219 P.3d 774 (Colo. 2009) (carryover storage may be necessary to meet reasonably anticipated water needs). Some states do not allow the appropriator to use the amount of carryover storage plus the reservoir's full capacity of new water the following year; the limit of one filling still applies, with the amount carried over debited against the single filling. *See, e.g.*, Wyo. Stat. Ann. § 41–3–325; Lake De Smet Reservoir Co. v. Kaufmann, 292 P.2d 482, 487 (Wyo. 1956).

# CHAPTER FOUR

# HYBRID SYSTEMS AND OTHER VARIATIONS

Not all states fit neatly into the categories of prior appropriation or riparian law. However, the principles of riparian and appropriative rights form the foundation in states where different systems have emerged. Ten states employ a mixture of riparian and appropriation doctrine in their water laws. They include the four West Coast states (California, Oregon, Washington, and Alaska) and the six states that straddle the 100th meridian—the dividing line between the arid West and the relatively wet East (Texas, Oklahoma, Kansas, Nebraska, South Dakota, and North Dakota). Mississippi also had a hybrid system based on riparian law but later modified it with a statutory code that closely resembles prior appropriation.

Hybrid states are sometimes said to follow the "California doctrine" because California addressed the relationship between the two systems when the state adopted the appropriation doctrine. Other states adopted their appropriative codes and addressed riparian rights later, often creating a system to phase out riparian rights. Oregon was the first state to adopt a process for simultaneously addressing vested riparian rights and extinguishing new riparian rights. In practice, each hybrid state has its own approach for reconciling early riparian rights with appropriative rights. Today, California, Nebraska, and Oklahoma are notable because riparians can still originate new uses superior to prior appropriators.

Unlike the hybrid states, eight intermountain west states (Colorado, Arizona, Utah, Nevada, Idaho, Wyoming, New Mexico, and Montana), abolished all prior riparian rights. In these so-called "Colorado doctrine" states, riparian law is not relevant because all riparian rights were abolished either at the enactment of the state's comprehensive water code or relatively soon after through common law. The only mechanism for securing a water right in Colorado Doctrine states is through the prior appropriation system.

This chapter also examines several special water allocation schemes in the United States, including the unique features of Louisiana and Hawaii, as well as pueblo water rights recognized by California and New Mexico.

## I. DEVELOPMENT OF HYBRID SYSTEMS

### A. CALIFORNIA'S EARLY RECOGNITION OF BOTH RIPARIAN RIGHTS AND APPROPRIATIVE RIGHTS

In Irwin v. Phillips, 5 Cal. 140 (1855), the court was faced with a water rights dispute among miners on the public domain. One group used water on land adjacent to a stream, but they were not riparian *landowners*, as they operated on federal public land. The other group had previously diverted water from the same stream through a canal for use on non-adjacent federal public lands. Thus, neither could assert riparian rights to prevent others from interfering with their use. The court concluded that, among trespassers on the public domain, the rule of prior appropriation was so customary among the early miners that it had become entrenched and had "the force and effect of res judicata." *Id.* at 145. As a result, the miners who first diverted water through their canal prevailed. In reaching this conclusion, the court noted that the state legislature had recognized mining canals as taxable property, thereby implicitly approving the use of water by prior appropriation. *Id.* at 146. *See* Maynard v. Watkins, 173 P. 551 (Mont. 1918) (holding that a completed ditch and application of water to a beneficial use constituted a valid appropriation).

Shortly after the decision in *Irwin*, the California Supreme Court acknowledged the continuing viability of the riparian doctrine as between bona fide settlers and appropriators subsequent to settlement. In Crandall v. Woods, 8 Cal. 136 (1857), as in *Irwin*, the parties were all on the public domain. The defendant, however, had settled on a tract contiguous to a stream under the public land laws, so he was not a trespasser on public land. The defendant began using water after the downstream plaintiff had appropriated water to supply a nearby town. When the defendant started diverting water, the downstream user sued, claiming it had priority. The court held that the defendant had settled under federal laws and was the absolute owner as against all but the United States. Thus, the defendant was entitled to riparian rights, subject only to the rights of appropriators who diverted water before he claimed his land. From these two cases, the California rule emerged: between appropriators on public land, the prior appropriator holds the superior right, but a settler with legal title to land who has not yet diverted water cannot be defeated by an appropriator whose use began after the settler's claim.

The California Supreme Court later affirmed the common law of riparian rights as between riparian landowners. Lux v. Haggin, 10 P. 674 (Cal. 1886). The court, however, suggested in dictum that the rights of riparians whose land was conveyed to them by the United States after Congress passed the Mining Act of July 26, 1866, and an 1870 amendment (declaring that prior appropriation would determine water rights on the public lands) might be defeated by post-enactment appropriations. The Mining Act is discussed in the next Part.

## B. FEDERAL RECOGNITION OF APPROPRIATIVE RIGHTS

As discussed above, the California courts assumed that water on federal land belonged to the federal government and passed with the land to settlers. However, courts in the Colorado Doctrine states held that water law was entirely a state matter and that a federal patent carried no riparian rights. Coffin v. Left Hand Ditch Co., 6 Colo. 443 (1882). These two distinct approaches created a question of whether Colorado doctrine states were depriving landowners of riparian rights that the federal government intended to convey with the underlying land. Several federal land statutes helped clarify the situation.

In the 1866 Mining Act, codified at 30 U.S.C. § 51 and 43 U.S.C. § 661, Congress recognized the validity of rights established under the appropriation doctrine that many western states and territories were applying on the public domain. *See supra* Chapter 3.II.1. The statute should have made clear that a patentee of riparian land could not defeat the rights of an appropriator on the public domain. To eliminate any doubt, the Placer Act of 1870 (amending the 1866 Act) clarified that future patentees of riparian land would take subject to the vested rights of appropriators.

In addition to the Mining Act, the Desert Land Act of 1877, 43 U.S.C. § 321, intended as an incentive program in which the federal government gave desert lands to persons who would establish agriculture. *See supra* Chapter 3.II.2. States differed on the impact of the Act's language on existing riparian rights. *See* Hough v. Porter, 95 P. 732 (Or. 1908) (holding that the Desert Lands Act removed all riparian rights from federal land patents); Cook v. Evans, 185 N.W. 262 (S.D. 1921) (following the Oregon rule); *cf.* Platt v. Rapid City, 291 N.W. 600 (S.D. 1940) (holding Desert Lands Act did not remove riparian rights from patents); Still v. Palouse Irrigation & Power Co., 117 P. 466 (Wash. 1911) (interpreting the Desert Lands Act as removing riparian rights on the narrow set of lands patented under that particular provision, but not other federal lands patented under other statutes); San Joaquin and Kings River Canal &

Irrigation Co. v. Worswick, 203 P. 999 (Cal. 1922) (holding that riparian land patents had riparian rights that trumped the rights of appropriators).

The Supreme Court addressed the issue of whether the Desert Lands Act extinguished all riparian rights on federal lands patented after March 3, 1877, in California Oregon Power Co. v. Beaver Portland Cement Co., 295 U.S. 142 (1935). A riparian landowner in Oregon claimed riparian rights based on an 1885 land patent, predating Oregon's statute subjecting all water in the state to appropriation. The Court said that federal land laws recognize that each state has "the right . . . to determine for itself to what extent the rule of appropriation or the common law rule in respect to riparian rights should obtain." 295 U.S. at 164. Therefore, the Court announced that Congress "effected a severance of all waters upon the public domain . . . from the land itself," but that state law could establish water rights for these lands. *Id.* at 158. Notably, the Court recognized two specific situations where the federal government retains an interest in water. First, the federal government retains an interest in water on federal lands where water is necessary for established purposes. *See infra* Chapter 8.I. Second, the federal government retains an interest in water to satisfy navigational interests. *See infra* Chapter 7.III.

## II. MODIFICATIONS OF RIPARIAN RIGHTS IN HYBRID SYSTEMS

All hybrid states limited the extent to which present riparian rights could be exercised and future riparian rights asserted. The ability of riparians to insist on the continued flow of a watercourse and to begin and cease using water as they pleased was incompatible with the successful operation of an appropriation system.

## A. REASONABLE USE LIMITATIONS

In an early case, the California Supreme Court upheld the right of riparians to enjoin diversions by subsequent appropriators even in the absence of actual harm. Lux v. Haggin, 10 P. 674 (Cal. 1886). The rule's practical inefficiency was that riparians could lock up water and prevent other beneficial uses. *See* Herminghaus v. Southern California Edison Co., 252 P. 607 (Cal. 1926) (riparians who relied on heavy spring flows to flood their lands successfully enjoined construction of an upstream hydroelectric plant that would have deprived them of natural irrigation). As a result, all hybrid states now follow some form of the reasonable use rule. Thus, a riparian cannot defeat an appropriator unless undue interference with the riparian's reasonable use of the water is proved. *See, e.g.,* Tulare Irr. Dist. v. Lindsay-Strathmore Irr. Dist., 45 P.2d 972 (Cal. 1935); City of Barstow v. Mojave Water Agency, 5 P.3d 853 (Cal. 2000); Brown v. Chase, 217 P. 23 (Wash. 1923).

## B. EXTINGUISHMENT OF UNUSED RIPARIAN RIGHTS

Riparian and appropriation systems conflict at an essential level, namely because riparian rights—being appurtenant to riparian land—do not depend on use. In contrast, appropriation rights require putting water to beneficial use. This dynamic failed to give appropriators assurance that their rights would be protected when formerly inactive riparians suddenly decided to exercise their rights. The uncertainty provided little incentive for appropriators to undertake expensive water projects. As a result, all of the hybrid states have attempted to curtail unused riparian rights by statute.

State legislatures in hybrid states adopted provisions for recognizing early or "vested" riparian rights. These statutory provisions typically created a time period during which those who claimed a prior riparian right had to assert it to gain recognition in the appropriative system. Some provisions required the riparian landowner to establish the amount of water they actually put to use. *See, e.g.,* Or. Rev. Stat. § 539.010 (effective Feb. 24, 1909); Wash. Rev. Code § 90.03.010 (effective 1917, although fifteen years of "reasonable notice" was allowed under In re Deadman Creek, 694 P.2d 1071 (1985)); Okla. Stat. tit. 82, § 105.2 (effective June 10, 1963); Kan. Stat. Ann. § 82a–703 (effective June 28, 1945); Neb. Rev. Stat. § 46–204 (effective April 4, 1895); S.D. Codified Laws § 46–1–9(1) (effective March 2, 1955); N.D. Cent. Code § 61–04–01.2 (effective July 1, 1963).

## C. CONSTITUTIONAL CHALLENGES

Legislation limiting or extinguishing riparian rights has been upheld when challenged as a taking of property without just compensation in all but three California doctrine states. As a result, riparian rights are only still at issue today in California, Nebraska, and Oklahoma, where the courts have blocked efforts to extinguish unexercised riparian rights. Tulare Irr. Dist. v. Lindsay-Strathmore Irr. Dist., 45 P.2d 972 (Cal. 1935); Franco-American Charolaise v. Oklahoma Water Res. Bd., 855 P.2d 568 (Okla. 1990); Wasserburger v. Coffee, 141 N.W.2d 738 (Neb. 1966).

By contrast, Oregon, Washington, Alaska, Texas, Kansas, South Dakota, and North Dakota have all taken action to address prior riparian rights. Each state approached it a bit differently, and several examples are provided below.

Kansas adopted a statute stating that: "[s]ubject to vested rights, all waters within the state may be appropriated for beneficial use as herein provided. . . ." Kan. Stat. Ann. § 82a–703. The statute also required riparians to obtain permits to preserve their vested rights, which were limited to water beneficially used at or within three years of the law's 1945 enactment. The statutory scheme was tested when the United States refused to proceed with a major irrigation project that depended on appropriative rights unless the law was found constitutional. The Kansas Supreme Court upheld the legislation. State ex rel. Emery v. Knapp, 207 P.2d 440 (Kan. 1949). The Kansas scheme is typical of others that limited "vested rights" to those applied to a beneficial use some time prior to passage of the statute or, in the case of works under construction at the time of enactment, within a reasonable time afterwards. Such laws have generally been upheld, and compensation denied for the extinguishment of unused rights. *See, e.g.*, Hough v. Porter, 95 P. 732 (Or. 1908); In re Hood River, 227 P. 1065 (Or. 1924), *appeal dismissed,* 273 U.S. 647 (1926).

A few state courts faced difficulties with laws limiting riparian rights in favor of a new appropriation system. In 1913, South Dakota's 1907 appropriation law was declared unconstitutional for taking riparian property without just compensation. St. Germain Irr. Co. v. Hawthorne Ditch Co., 143 N.W. 124 (S.D. 1913). A subsequently enacted appropriation system in South Dakota was upheld in light of several intervening U.S. Supreme Court decisions, which distinguished police power regulation from takings. Knight v. Grimes, 127 N.W.2d 708 (S.D. 1964). More recently, the South Dakota Supreme Court reiterated that legislative control of water rights—even where it divests formerly vested rights—is a legitimate exercise of the state's police power. Parks v. Cooper, 676 N.W.2d 823 (S.D. 2004).

Although California still nominally recognizes unused riparian rights, a 1979 decision held that a legislatively authorized water rights adjudication of all users in an entire river system can limit riparian users to the amount of water currently being applied to a beneficial use, plus a quantified future right. In re Waters of Long Valley Creek Stream System, 599 P.2d 656 (Cal. 1979).

Language in the Nebraska Constitution resembles language construed in other states to cut off future riparian claims, but Nebraska courts declared that riparian rights on lands patented before the 1895 Act have not been abolished and that riparian uses can still be claimed for these lands. Wasserburger v. Coffee, 141 N.W.2d 738 (Neb. 1966). Riparians are limited to a quantity that is reasonable for their purposes, relative to the purposes of uses by appropriators.

The Oklahoma Supreme Court followed a similar path in holding that a thirty-year-old prior appropriation law was unconstitutional insofar as it purported to extinguish unexercised riparian rights. In Franco-American Charolaise, Ltd. v. Oklahoma Water Res. Bd., 855 P.2d 568 (Okla. 1990), the court held that a riparian owner has a vested property right to initiate or change reasonable uses of water at any time. Since the statute failed to protect those rights (except for future domestic uses), it violated the takings clause of the Oklahoma Constitution. Thus, the rights of riparians to make future uses continues, limited only by the requirement of reasonableness. In 1993, the legislature acted to clarify its intent to extinguish future riparian claims, an effort that overcame the portion of *Franco-American* that said rights could not be extinguished by implication. But it could not overcome the portion of the decision that said such an extinguishment was subject to takings claims. A trial court held that the 1993 Act is either unconstitutional or does not apply to pre-1993 riparian claims. Thus, Oklahoma was effectively converted back to the hybrid system that the legislature tried to curtail in 1963.

## III. ADMINISTRATION OF HYBRID SYSTEMS

Because of the substantial differences between riparian and appropriation systems, courts have struggled to give effect to rights under both systems. Issues typically arise in times of shortage where riparians must all share the shortage based on reasonableness, but appropriators exercise the full measure of their right based on priority.

### A. RESOLVING DISPUTES AMONG WATER USERS

In hybrid states, where permits for riparian rights specify quantity, these rights can be treated as part of the hierarchy of appropriative water rights. If no fixed quantity is set, it may be necessary to quantify unused riparian rights (discussed in the next subsection). The priority date of riparian rights is ordinarily ahead of many appropriators, since most states created appropriative rights to replace the riparian system. These old riparian rights continue to complicate the use and allocation of water today. *See, e.g.*, Modesto Irrigation Dist. v. Tanaka, 262 Cal. Rptr. 3d 408 (Cal. App.), *review denied* (2020) (finding that a 130-year-old deed conveyed riparian rights for a subdivided parcel of farmland that had been part of a larger riparian tract but was no longer contiguous to the river).

As noted above, California limits the circumstances in which an appropriator on public land can defeat a riparian. Thus, in California, a riparian will prevail over an appropriator except in cases in which water rights were appropriated *after* the 1866 Mining Act and *before* the riparian's patent. Lux v. Haggin, 10 P. 674 (Cal. 1886).

In Oklahoma and Nebraska, competing rights of riparians and appropriators are determined based on their relative reasonableness. However, in Nebraska, the issue arises only as to riparian lands patented before the 1895 Nebraska Irrigation Act; prior appropriation prevails as to later patented lands. Wasserburger v. Coffee, 141 N.W.2d 738 (Neb. 1966).

In Alaska, the legislature provided for the conversion of riparian rights in 1966. Alaska Stat. § 46.15.060. In effect, both used and unused riparian rights were converted to appropriative rights if the riparian had put water to beneficial use or established a beneficial use within five years of the statute's effective date. Pre-1966 rights must have been filed to be recognized. *Id.* § 46.15.065. By integrating the two systems, Alaska created an exclusive appropriative rights-based system.

## B. ADJUDICATION OF UNUSED RIPARIAN RIGHTS

Most hybrid states have procedures for adjudicating water rights among users. In hybrid states, riparians must be made parties to general adjudications to have their rights reflected in a final determination of all rights on a stream system. Riparian rights may be quantified based on past usage, and unused rights may be extinguished.

Some hybrid states have extinguished unused riparian rights, but created exceptions allowing riparians to claim water rights for future "domestic" purposes that are superior to all appropriative rights. Tex. Water Code § 11.303 (2013); Kan. Stat. Ann. § 42–311 (2013); S.D. Codified Laws § 46–1–5 (2014). In Oklahoma, riparians can claim water for "de minimis" household purposes such as lawn watering. Okla. Stat. tit. 82, § 1020.1(2) (2013); Heldermon v. Wright, 152 P.3d 855 (Okla. 2006); Franco-American Charolaise, Ltd. v. Okla. Water Res. Bd., 855 P.2d 568 (Okla. 1990). The quantities involved are small, so the uncertainties about unquantified, unused rights are minimal.

Although California nominally allows the future exercise of unused riparian rights, the right can be substantially limited by administrative decisions. The California Supreme Court held that when a riparian uses only a small fraction of its available water, the riparian's right could be limited in "scope, nature and priority" to assure that uses are reasonable and beneficial (in accordance with the 1928 constitutional amendment). *See* In re Waters of Long Valley Creek Stream System, 599 P.2d 656 (Cal. 1979) (a riparian owned several thousand acres, but was irrigating only eighty-nine). Thus, unused riparian rights may be put to any reasonable, beneficial use in the future, but may be presently quantified by the State Water Resources Control Board and granted a priority lower than all appropriations prior to the time riparian uses actually commence.

### C. PRESCRIPTION

Appropriation is the sole method of acquiring water rights in prior appropriation states; acquisition of a water right by adverse possession is generally not allowed. *See supra* Chapter 3.VIII.C. In riparian states, upper riparians can gain prescriptive rights against lower riparians if the lower owner is aware of the prescriptive claim or suffers harm. The opposite is not true because a lower riparian using any amount of water left unused by the upper riparian cannot be adverse; the upper riparian could physically divert the water at any time. An upstream non-riparian may also acquire a prescriptive right against a downstream riparian, as any use by a user without riparian rights is considered adverse. *See id.* and *supra* Chapter 2.II.F; *see also* Pabst v. Finmand, 211 P. 11 (Cal. 1922).

## IV. OTHER WATER LAW VARIATIONS

Some water law systems are not easily characterized as prior appropriation, riparian, or hybrid. These systems include Hawaii's ancient system, remnants of civil law in Louisiana, and pueblo rights applicable in some parts of the Southwest.

### A. WATER LAW IN LOUISIANA

Although Louisiana is often considered a riparian state, its system of water law is based on a civil code with French and Spanish origins; it is the only state in the Union that has a civil code system. The relevant rules for settling water disputes are found within the code. The courts are not bound by the principle of *stare decisis* but may refer to common law precedents if they are on point.

The code establishes basic principles like those of a riparian system, such as:

> Article 657: The owner of an estate bordering on running water may use it as it runs for the purpose of watering his estate or for other purposes.
>
> Article 658: The owner of an estate through which water runs, whether it originates there or passes from lands above, may make use of it while it runs over his lands. He cannot stop it or give it another direction and is bound to return it to its ordinary channel where it leaves his estate.

Article 657 is a nearly verbatim adoption of the French Civil Code. It is not clear whether the provision expresses the natural flow rule or the reasonable use rule. The early case of Long v. Louisiana Creosoting Co., 69 So. 281, 282 (La. 1915), applied a reasonable use rule in a water pollution context:

> [W]hether a use that pollutes a water course is a reasonable or an unreasonable use is for the judge or jury to determine from all of the circumstances of a case, including the nature of the water course, its adaptability for particular purposes, the extent of injury caused to the riparian owner, etc.

By statute, Louisiana has various types of water districts that supply water to customers. Municipalities also have statutory authority to maintain their own waterworks systems. *See* La. Stat. Ann. § 33:3815.

Historically, groundwater in Louisiana was almost totally unregulated. Article 490 of the Civil Code states:

> Unless otherwise provided by law, the ownership of a tract of land carries with it the ownership of everything that is directly above or under it. The owner may make works on, above or below the land as he pleases, and draw all the advantages that accrue from them, unless he is restrained by law or by rights of others.

In Adams v. Grigsby, 152 So.2d 619 (La. App. 1963), the court held that water under a person's land is not owned until it is reduced to possession by pumping. This "rule of capture" undermines any incentive to conserve water. In response, the legislature authorized the Department of Public Works to regulate wells pumping over 50,000 gallons per day and to designate "Areas of Ground Water Concern." La. Stat. Ann. §§ 38:3091–94. However, small wells remain governed by the *Adams* rule.

Those injured by groundwater pumping may find some relief in Article 10 of the Mineral Code: "A person with rights in a common reservoir or deposit of minerals may not make works, operate, or otherwise use his right so as to deprive another intentionally or negligently of the liberty of enjoying his rights, or that may intentionally or negligently cause damage to him." La. Stat. Ann. § 31:10. If the injury involves groundwater contamination, complainants are directed to provide notice to the Department of Environmental Quality. La. Stat. Ann. § 30:2015.1.

## B. HAWAIIAN WATER LAW

Water law in Hawaii is governed by public trust principles. Hawaiian law is rooted in an ancient system of land tenure. During Hawaii's territorial period, courts treated water as an individual property right, but they later revived Hawaii's ancient notions of water as a public resource. Modern Hawaii follows a State Water Code, which is limited in scope by public trust provisions in the Hawaii Constitution, Article XI, Sections 1 and 7.

Historically, water was commonly used by islanders to cultivate taro, a dietary staple, and for this purpose was considered a part of the land. *Konohiki* (chiefs of land divisions and fishing rights) acted as trustees and dictated the quantity and location of water used among commoners. The *konohiki* in charge of each subdivision of land (or *ahupua'a*, typically triangularly shaped with an apex at mountains and widening towards the sea) allocated any surplus waters remaining after basic needs were satisfied. Water distribution was based on recognition of the mutual dependence of the *konohiki* and those who produced the crops. Judicial decisions under Hawaii's various governments (the Kingdom of Hawaii became a republic, then a United

States territory, and eventually a state) announced principles of water law that now govern the creation of individual, privately held water rights. The decisions dealt with "appurtenant" and "surplus" waters.

Appurtenant rights are based on the amount of water used for taro cultivation. Early cases responded to the water demands of sugar plantations and allowed transfers of appurtenant rights, but only after the party seeking transfer demonstrated that the change would not harm others. Kahookiekie v. Keanini, 8 Haw. 310 (1891). Thus, courts scrutinized changes in the place of use, Peck v. Bailey, 8 Haw. 658 (1867), type of use, and point of diversion, Carter v. Territory, 24 Haw. 47 (1917). Appurtenant rights also could be obtained by prescription following adverse use for the statutory period. Lonoaea v. Wailuku Sugar Co., 9 Haw. 651 (1895).

"Surplus" waters generally include all waters not needed to satisfy appurtenant water rights. Early courts disagreed about whether the rights to surplus waters belonged to the proprietor (*konohiki* or a successor in interest) of the land subdivision (*ahupua'a*) where the water originated or to the *konohikis* of all the *ahupua'as* through which the water passed. In 1973, the Hawaii Supreme Court applied riparian principles to hold that surplus water rights could not be used on any land except the riparian parcel and that appurtenant rights, by their nature, could not be used on other lands. McBryde Sugar Co. v. Robinson, 504 P.2d 1330, *on rehearing,* 517 P.2d 26 (Haw. 1973), *cert. denied,* 417 U.S. 976

(1974). The court accepted the "natural flow" doctrine, finding that it best fit the language of an 1895 statute vesting rights to free-flowing streams in "the people." *Id.* Shortly after, the court changed its view, holding that the modern reasonable use test and requirement of actual harm applied to riparian rights. Hawaii. Reppun v. Bd. of Water Supply, 656 P.2d 57 (Haw. 1982).

*McBryde* also held that an 1850 statute could not allow uses of surplus water away from the original land because the water did not belong to the landowner. Rather, it had been "reserved for the people of Hawaii for their common good in all of the land grants." 504 P.2d at 1338. Prescriptive rights were defeated because prescription is void against the state, which holds water in trust for all the people. *Id.*

The effect of the *McBryde* decision prohibited parties with extensive water rights from exercising those rights on lands outside of the watershed. After nearly twenty years of litigation, the Ninth Circuit decided that ownership of surplus water was a "settled question in Hawaii law" under *McBryde's* announcement of riparian principles. Robinson v. Ariyoshi, 753 F.2d 1468 (9th Cir. 1985), *vacated on other grounds,* 887 F.2d 215 (9th Cir. 1989). Diverging from the existing riparian system used in other states, the *Robinson* court characterized Hawaiian law as rooted in ancient Hawaiian custom, giving the state, as the trustee for the public, much greater authority to allocate riparian rights.

The court explained that, as successor to the monarchs and chiefs who formerly held all the lands, the state is obligated to ensure a fair distribution of waters among all the people who put it to productive use. *Id.* at 1474. At the *Mahele*, lands had passed to private parties subject to a reservation of rights in the monarch (now the state) to allocate water among all those needing it. The waters are held in a public trust for common usage of the citizenry, including diversion and use. This is analogous to the public trust doctrine, which obligates states to protect waterways for public uses such as navigation, recreation, wildlife, and fish. The Hawaii Supreme Court expanded the doctrine by applying it to instream flows for ecosystem restoration. In re Water Use Permit Applications for the Waiāhole Ditch, 9 P.3d 409 (2000). Thus, the Court explained that the state has an "affirmative duty under the public trust to protect and promote instream uses." In re Surface Water Use Permit Applications, 550 P.3d 1167, 1198 (Haw. 2024). To meet its duty, the state must "designate instream flow standards as early as possible, during the process of comprehensive planning, and particularly before it authorizes offstream diversions potentially detrimental to public instream uses and values." *Id.* at 1199.

The Hawaii Supreme Court also described Hawaiian rights as more akin to federally reserved water rights for Indian reservations (*see infra* Chapter Eight) than to true riparian rights. Reppun v. Bd. of Water Supply, 656 P.2d 57 (Haw. 1982).

During the pendency of the *Robinson* litigation, Hawaii amended its constitution to recognize the state's trust obligation to assure water for the public benefit and to establish a water resources agency to regulate use and conservation. Haw. Const. art. XI, § 7. In 1987, Hawaii adopted its State Water Code, providing for a comprehensive state water plan, the designation of water management areas, and the protection of instream uses. HRS §§ 174C–1 *et seq.* While the State Water Code allows water to be used outside of its original watershed, the public trust provisions of the Hawaiian constitution require greater scrutiny to do so. Under the State Water Code, existing and new water users must have permits, and the common law is largely supplanted once an area is designated as a water management area, triggering the statutory requirements.

The public trust nature of Hawaiian water rights puts affirmative burdens on the state agency charged with water allocation. One application of the public trust doctrine required surface and groundwater users to release water into a stream to promote more natural stream conditions. In re Water Use Permit Applications, 9 P.3d 409, 448 (Haw. 2000). Moreover, the "reasonable-beneficial use" standard and the obligation that water be used "consistent with the public interest," requires the state to examine both proposed and established uses relative to other public and private uses of water from the same source. *Id.* at 472–74 (citing HRS § 174C–49(a)). Thus, Hawaiian law requires that there are "absolute priorities" between uses of public trust resources, and the state must "weigh competing public and private uses on a case-by-case basis." Surface Water Use Permit Applications, 340 P.3d 1167, 1198 (Haw. 2024). As a result, out-of-stream diversions may be curtailed to protect instream uses.

## C. PUEBLO WATER RIGHTS

Two types of pueblo water rights are discussed in this section—municipal water rights and Pueblo Indian Tribes' water rights.

With respect to municipal rights, in a few places in the Southwest, communities and cities may assert pueblo water rights arising from land grants and principles applied by predecessor Spanish or Mexican governments. Like the ancient Hawaiian system, pueblo law characterizes water as communal property. Pueblo communities employ a waterseer to protect water rights. In California, the waterseer is called a zanjero and is typically appointed by a government official. In New Mexico, the position is called a majordomo and is typically elected.

Spain ruled portions of the Southwest before 1821, followed by the Republic of Mexico until 1848. In that year, the territory was ceded to the United States by the Treaty of Guadalupe Hidalgo. The treaty confirmed then-existing property rights, including water rights.

Under Spanish law, municipalities held water rights as common property for the benefit of their inhabitants. Grants of pueblo lands were intended to encourage settlement by facilitating the growth of villages and agricultural production. In some cases, land grants also defined the areas outside of pueblo territory available for settlement by others.

Generally, pueblo water rights recognized that municipalities could use all the naturally occurring ground and surface water within their boundaries that was needed for their residents, and residents could use water in common with neighboring pueblos. The quantity of water available under a pueblo water right could increase with population growth, the annexation of new land, or new uses.

The existence of pueblo water rights has been acknowledged in cases arising in California (Vernon Irrigation Co. v. City of Los Angeles, 39 P. 762 (Cal. 1895) (overruled in part)) and New Mexico (Cartwright v. Public Service Co., 343 P.2d 654 (N.M. 1958) (overruled in part)).

The municipal pueblo right retains special importance for some California cities. Under pueblo law, actual use of water is not required to keep a city's right alive; a successor city may displace long-established uses even if it has not historically used the water. The policy reason behind California's pueblo right is to limit "waste by leaving water accessible to others until such time as the city needs it." City of Los Angeles v. City of Glendale, 142 P.2d 289, 293 (Cal. 1943). Thus, Los Angeles, as the successor to a pueblo right, was able to assert rights to groundwater supplies to satisfy its municipal needs and those of its inhabitants. City of Los Angeles v. Pomeroy, 57 P. 585 (Cal. 1899). The California Supreme Court also held that the city's rights were superior to the established rights of other appropriators (including other cities). City of Los Angeles v. City of San Fernando, 537 P.2d 1250 (Cal. 1975), *overruled in part*, City of Barstow v. Mojave Water Agency, 5 P.3d 853 (Cal. 2000). *City of Barstow* limited the reach of pueblo rights by stating that overlying landowners' rights to use groundwater must also be honored "to the extent those priorities do not lead to unreasonable use." 5 P.3d at 853, 868.

The New Mexico Supreme Court departed from California by stating that municipal pueblo water rights are antithetical to the prior appropriation doctrine's requirement of beneficial use, and by requiring pueblo rights to be based on actual beneficial use rather than future needs. New Mexico v. City of Las Vegas, 89 P.3d 47 (N.M. 2004) (overruling Cartwright v. Public Service Co., 343 P.2d 654 (N.M. 1958)).

The rights of Pueblo Indians in New Mexico have been central to several decades-long general stream adjudications. *See* New Mexico v. Aamodt, 537 F.2d 1102 (10th Cir. 1976) (involving the Nambe-Pojoaque River System); United States v. Abouselman, 976 F.3d 1146 (10th Cir. 2020) (involving the Jemez River Basin). Unlike the federal reserved rights discussed in Chapter 8.II, Pueblo Indians hold grant lands with established laws predating the authority of the federal government. The *Aamodt* court held that the Pueblos' water rights are prior to all non-Indians whose land ownership was recognized by the federal government under the 1924 and 1933 Pueblo Lands Acts. 537 F.2d at 1113. In *Abouselman*, the court held that the Pueblos' aboriginal rights to water had not been extinguished by Spain. 976 F.3d at 1160.

The quantification of Pueblo Indian water rights remains unsettled. The *Abouselman* court declined to reach the "important question" of quantifying the Pueblos' water rights. *Id.* at 1153. The United States and the Pueblos argue that the Pueblos are entitled to the quantity of water necessary to fulfill not only their historic and present needs, but also their future needs. On remand, the district court held that the Pueblos had a right to pre-existing uses of water under United States v. Winans, 198 U.S. 371 (1905) that neither Spain nor Mexico had extinguished those aboriginal rights, and that the Pueblos' existing rights were recognized by statute and treaty. United States v. Abousleman, 695 F. Supp. 3d 1277 (D.N.M. 2023). But in *Aamodt,* a federal district court took a more restrictive stance by referencing "historically irrigable acreage" based on the Pueblo's irrigation practices between the 1848 Treaty of Guadalupe Hidalgo and the 1924 Pueblo Lands Act. State of N.M. ex rel. Reynolds v. Aamodt, 618 F. Supp. 993, 1010 (D.N.M. 1985). This issue was not resolved on appeal, however, as the *Aamodt* case was ultimately settled, along with another long-running case involving Rio Pueblo de Taos and the Rio Hondo. The settlement quantified the Pueblos' senior water rights and provided funds for the development of infrastructure to deliver water to the Pueblos. Claims Resolution Act of 2010, Pub. L. No. 111–291 Titles V–VI, 124 Stat. 3064. For discussion, see Richard W. Hughes, *Pueblo Indian Water Rights: Charting the Unknown,* 57 Nat. Resources J. 219 (2017).

# CHAPTER FIVE
# GROUNDWATER

Though unseen on the surface of Earth, groundwater is a crucial water source, whether it be found in small local sources or vast, multistate systems, such as the Ogallala (High Plains) and Floridan Aquifers. An estimated 30% of the world's freshwater is groundwater (compared to surface water, which only makes up 1.2% of the world's freshwater—the remainder is found in glaciers and ice caps). U.S.G.S., *Where is Earth's Water* (2020), *available at* https://www.usgs.gov/special-topic/water-science-school/science/where-earths-water?qt-science_center_objects=0#qt-science_center_objects. The United States heavily relies on groundwater for agriculture, drinking water, and mining. The resource is especially critical in areas where surface water is scarce, notably in the Southwest. A broad mix of state-based approaches exist for groundwater. In summary, overlying land ownership, prior appropriation, or rules of liability for interfering with neighboring wells or surface waters influence groundwater use rights. Conservation and pollution control statutes also impact groundwater use.

The first section of this chapter focuses on basic hydrology of groundwater formations. The second section turns to the mechanisms for allocating groundwater. The third focuses on groundwater that is hydrologically connected and used conjunctively with surface water sources. The final two sections concern groundwater storage and mechanisms for controlling contamination.

# I. BASIC HYDROLOGY

## A. HOW GROUNDWATER OCCURS

### 1. Permeability of Rock Formations

Geological conditions and the laws of physics govern the occurrence and movement of groundwater. Although it can occur in relatively defined underground formations, most groundwater is *percolating* water stored in the pores, or interstices, of rock formations. The size of these interstices varies with the size of the rock particles; a bed of gravel has interstices visible to the naked eye, but clay has minute particles and interstices. Geological processes created interstices at the time the rock was formed, and later cracking and erosion can create interstices.

*Porosity* is the measure of the amount of open space within rock. It is defined as the percentage of the rock's total volume occupied by pore space. Other factors being equal, the greater the porosity, the more freely water can move through the rock and the more water that can be stored within.

The force of gravity can cause water to move "downhill" through rock formations. Slowing this movement are the forces of *molecular attraction*. Molecular attraction is inversely proportional to the surface area of the rock particles, which increases as their size decreases. To illustrate, compare the movement of water through gravel to its movement through sand. The gravel is made up of large particles, so the surface area of all the particles is cumulatively smaller than the surface area of all the particles of sand. Thus, molecular attraction slows the movement of water through minute interstices found in substances such as sand. The porosity of a volume of sand may equal that of gravel, but the *permeability* of the sand (its ability to transmit water) is lower.

Although permeability varies across a spectrum, rock formations are grouped into broad categories, described as "permeable" or "impermeable." Whether water percolates through rock, and the speed at which it does so, are functions of the force of gravity and the permeability of the formation. Groundwater is often in permeable formations that are bounded and contained by impermeable (confined) formations, as depicted in Figure 1, below.

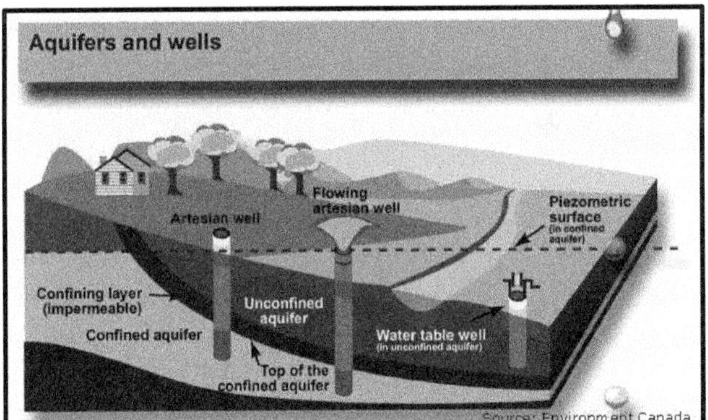


*Figure 1: Water Movement in Aquifers, from U.S.G.S., Aquifers (2014), http://water.usgs.gov/edu/earthgwaquifer.html.*

## 2. Zones of Groundwater Occurrence

Almost all usable groundwater occurs within two miles of the earth's surface and is commonly within a half mile. Groundwater is found in strata that may be defined as the *zone of aeration* and the *zone of saturation*. In the zone of aeration, which is nearest the surface, moisture is present in the soil and accessible to the root systems of plants. Because it is held by molecular attraction, however, it cannot be captured readily by pumping.

Below the zone of aeration is the *piezometric surface*, or *water table*. Underneath the piezometric surface is the zone of saturation, in which groundwater saturates the interstices completely. In this zone, water flows in response to gravity and can be withdrawn by pumping. Underlying the zone of saturation is a layer of impermeable *bedrock*, which has a very low porosity.

## 3. Aquifers

Aquifers are sometimes thought of as underground reservoirs. They are permeable rock formations that yield water in significant quantities. Aquifers may be confined or unconfined. Most are *unconfined*, where the water exists under normal atmospheric pressure. Unconfined aquifers must be pumped to withdraw the water. *Confined* or *artesian aquifers*, by contrast, are under a pressure greater than that of the atmosphere. This pressure is generated when the aquifer is squeezed between overlying and underlying impermeable strata. If the pressure between the strata is great enough, the water in a well may rise to the surface without pumping, but any pressure sufficient to raise the water above the water table can make the aquifer artesian. *See* Figure 1. This often occurs when a portion of the aquifer lies above the point where the well (or spring) is located, in which case the pressure is caused by gravity.

A *perched aquifer* is an unconfined aquifer underlain by an impermeable stratum that is perched above another aquifer. Perched aquifers are often hydrologically unaffected by withdrawals from the zone of saturation. Where perched aquifers outcrop on hillsides, springs may result. The term *spring*, however, applies to any concentrated discharge of groundwater that appears on the surface as flowing water.

Geological processes occurring when the rock was created may initially fill aquifers, or subsequent sources such as rainfall may fill them over time. Typically, precipitation falling or flowing where an aquifer outcrops on the surface recharges the aquifer, but hydrologically connected streams may also recharge the aquifer. The rate of recharge, like the rate of water movement, varies greatly and is a function of geologic conditions. Some aquifers get no recharge; others recharge so slowly that it takes millions of years to fill them.

Geologists call the amount of water an aquifer will yield without becoming depleted the "*safe yield.*" City of Los Angeles v. City of San Fernando, 537 P.2d 1250, 1308 (Cal. 1975). Economists, courts, and legislatures have also used the term to describe rates of depletion that may be in excess of recharge, but still considered reasonable in light of current demands for the water. California's modern approach favors the term "sustainable yield" instead of "safe." Cal. Water Code § 10721(w). When withdrawals from any aquifer exceed its recharge, an overdraft or *mining* condition is said to exist. Some harmful effects of chronic overdraft are discussed in the next section.

Aquifers may be isolated from other aquifers and from surface streams. If aquifers are hydraulically interconnected, however, the term *groundwater basin* is used to describe the physiographic unit usually consisting of a large aquifer and one or more smaller aquifers.

If an aquifer is hydraulically connected to a stream so that groundwater withdrawals affect stream flow, the groundwater may be considered *tributary* to the stream. *See* Simpson v. Bijou Irr. Co., 69 P.3d 50, 59 n. 7 (Colo. 2003) (en banc). Whether groundwater is tributary may have important legal consequences; sound management dictates that tributary groundwater and the stream be managed as a single system. Thus, a court in a prior appropriation state may enjoin pumping from a tributary aquifer to prevent injury to senior appropriators on the stream. Conjunctive management of groundwater and surface water uses is discussed in Section III of this chapter.

## 4. Underground Streams Distinguished

Courts and legislatures have occasionally characterized waters that flow underground within "reasonably ascertainable boundaries" and as "a constant stream in a known and well-defined natural channel" as underground streams. Hayes v. Adams, 218 P. 933, 935 (Or. 1923). An underground stream, like percolating waters, is in fact groundwater, but some states subject it to the law of surface streams rather than groundwater law. *See, e.g.,* Riordan v. Westwood, 203 P.2d 922 (Utah 1949). *See also* N. Gualala Water Co. v. State Water Res. Control Bd., 43 Cal. Rptr. 3d 821, 831 (Cal. Ct. App. 2006) (noting that "classification disputes in this field quickly take on an Alice-in-Wonderland quality because the legal categories . . . are drawn from antiquated case law and bear little or no relationship to hydrological realities"). *Cf.* In Matter of Water Rights, 361 P.3d 392, 399 (Colo. 2015) (determining that storm runoff should be designated as groundwater and subjected to the priority system).

In determining whether groundwater is stream-like or percolating, courts may consider circumstantial evidence, such as vegetation growing on the surface, indicating the course of the alleged stream. *Riordan,* 203 P.2d at 929 (Utah 1949). Drilling and hydrologic modeling are also used.

## B. GROUNDWATER PUMPING

### 1. Drilling and Pumping

As drilling and pumping technologies developed and grew more sophisticated, the character of groundwater use changed. The invention and use of the windmill hastened the spread of irrigated agriculture, especially in the Great Plains and the western United States. Confronted with unreliable surface flows and scant precipitation, irrigators tapped into shallow aquifers. The centrifugal pump and the delivery of electricity to rural America ushered in a new era of intensive groundwater use by making deeper aquifers accessible. WILLIAM ASHWORTH, OGALLALA BLUE: WATER AND LIFE ON THE HIGH PLAINS 140–41 (W.W. Norton 2006). In some cases, junior appropriators with deeper wells and more powerful pumps drew down water tables beyond the reach of the seniors pumping from the same aquifer, causing them substantially increased pumping costs. *See, e.g.,* Prather v. Eisenmann, 261 N.W.2d 766 (Neb. 1978).

### 2. Effects of Well Use

#### *a. Cone of Influence*

Once a well begins operating, water from the surrounding aquifer begins percolating through the formation to replace the water being withdrawn. As shown in Figure 2 below, this creates a *cone of influence* (sometimes referred to as a "*cone of depression*"), a cone-shaped depression in the water table from which water has temporarily been removed. The cone is inverted—its tip is at the point of withdrawal and its base is the surface of the water table. As the cone of influence broadens, it may affect the wells of neighboring users, forcing them to deepen or move their wells to avoid losing their supply.

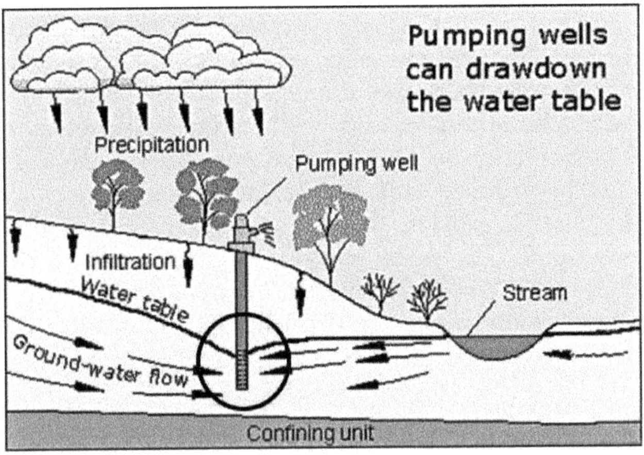


*Figure 2: Effects of pumping. Note the cone of influence formed at the source of the well as water is withdrawn. Source: USGS, Aquifers (Mar. 2014), http://water.usgs.gov/edu/earthgwaquifer.html.*

### b. Effects of Depletion

In addition to the localized cone of influence effect, the rate and extent of pumping also may affect the quality of the groundwater and the aquifer's capacity to produce water. Salt water can contaminate groundwater when water from the ocean or underground deposits intrudes to replace the water withdrawn from an aquifer. Depletion of a finite supply of groundwater may also cause *subsidence*, where the surface of the land overlying an aquifer sinks. Subsidence occurs when certain formations (*e.g.*, compressible, low-permeability clays) are unable to support the weight of overlying strata unless they are saturated with water. As the support provided by *hydrostatic pressure* is removed, the formation collapses. The resultant sinking of the overlying surface may damage buildings, highways, railroads, ditches, and wells. Natural geological features may be harmed, aquifer storage capacity may be reduced, and cracks in the earth's surface may lead to erosion. Coastal areas may be flooded as they sink. The most severe subsidence within the United States has occurred in areas experiencing heavy groundwater overdraft in Arizona, California, Florida, and Texas.

Subsidence, like other consequences of groundwater overdraft, tends to be an economic externality of the pumper; that is, the cost of damage to others is not assessed to the individual pumper. Some jurisdictions provide legal remedies to help internalize the costs of subsidence. Theories of liability include negligence, nuisance, and the obligation for subjacent support. Alabama has applied nuisance law where no liability would have attached under the state's common law of groundwater, which allows landowners to make any use of underlying water for which there is a "reasonable need." Henderson v. Wade Sand & Gravel Co., Inc., 388 So.2d 900 (Ala. 1980). Texas has imposed liability for negligent pumping.

Friendswood Dev. Co. v. Smith-Southwest Indus., Inc., 576 S.W.2d 21 (Tex. 1978). Texas also confers power to control subsidence on groundwater conservation districts. Tex. Water Code Ann. § 36.101.

### 3. Common Pool Resource Management

A declining water table imposes significant economic burdens on pumpers. Groundwater creates common-pool resource management dynamics. A person who owns the land overlying an entire aquifer might want to reduce current consumption to save part of the groundwater for future uses, obtaining the maximum economic benefit over time. If other users have access, however, little incentive exists to conserve for the future. The individual who forgoes present uses takes the risk that others will consume any water saved; each individual is induced to pump as much water from the common pool as can be used for any purpose, even a wasteful or marginal use, before other pumpers use up the supply. This disincentive to conserve results in a "race for the bottom" of the aquifer, preventing optimal economic utilization of the resource. Noh v. Stoner, 26 P.2d 1112, 1114 (Idaho 1933). Garrett Hardin called the phenomenon the "tragedy of the commons."

As water tables fall, progressively deeper wells are required, resulting in increased drilling and pumping costs. Entities such as municipalities and large farms may enjoy economies of scale, enabling them to pump from great depths. In contrast, small irrigators are caught between high pumping costs and comparatively low economic return per unit of water applied. For an irrigator, the cost of pumping an acre-foot of water may be close to the benefit from an acre-foot of water applied to crops. Slight increases in cost can render further pumping uneconomical.

The state's groundwater law determines the obligation of the new pumper to the existing well owner. Depending on which legal system is followed (*see infra* Section II), the newcomer may have to cease pumping, pay the senior's well-deepening and increased pumping costs, or furnish the senior with water from the junior's well.

## II. ALLOCATING AND MANAGING RIGHTS IN GROUNDWATER

### A. NATURE OF RIGHTS

Legal rights and obligations pertaining to the use of groundwater may be based on overlying land ownership, established uses, or the notion that water is a shared public resource. However, rules adopted by a state's common law and legislation usually reflect more than a single theory of rights in groundwater. Jurisdictions that claim to follow one theory invariably incorporate elements of others. Thus, a state may proclaim to recognize "ownership" of groundwater by an overlying landowner but limit the owner to reasonable uses, provide protection for earlier users against subsequent pumpers, and protect the public interest by prohibiting contamination of aquifers.

States with relatively plentiful water resources paid relatively little attention to the allocation of legal rights in groundwater in the past, but pollution problems have caused even those areas to focus on groundwater rights. Generally, one having a right to extract groundwater has a right to protect it from pollution by others and to seek remedies when pollution occurs. *See, e.g.,* In re Methyl Tertiary Butyl Ether (MTBE) Products, 457 F. Supp. 2d 455 (S.D.N.Y. 2006); Exxon Corp. v. Yarema, 516 A.2d 990 (Md. Ct. Spec. App. 1986). Although an integrated approach may be desirable, statutory protections and administrative agencies dealing with pollution problems are usually separate from the mechanisms for allocating rights to use groundwater.

## 1. Rights Based on Land Ownership

### *a. Absolute Ownership Doctrine*

Under the absolute ownership doctrine, landowners have an unlimited right to withdraw any water found beneath their land. Also known as the "English Rule," the doctrine was set forth in Acton v. Blundell, 152 E.R. 1223 (Eng. 1843). The *Acton* court viewed groundwater as part of the soil and based its holding upon the ancient right of a landowner to the airspace above and the soil beneath the land. Another reason for the holding, however, seems to have been the mysterious character of groundwater. The primitive state of hydrology at the time made it difficult to establish a causal connection between withdrawals by a defendant and harm to a plaintiff.

*See, e.g.*, Roath v. Driscoll, 20 Conn. 533 (1850); Frazier v. Brown, 12 Ohio St. 294, 311 (1861).

The absolute ownership doctrine was widely adopted in the United States during the 1850s. It is still the law in Indiana, Louisiana, Maine, Rhode Island, and Texas.

The majority of states updated their legal doctrine, starting as early as 1862, to reflect a fuller scientific understanding of groundwater hydrology. The absolute ownership doctrine was rejected in a series of cases beginning with Bassett v. Salisbury Mfg. Co., 43 N.H. 569 (1862). The reasoning behind rejecting it grew as technology advanced to access and extract groundwater through high-capacity wells. Courts found "absolute ownership" in groundwater harsh and impractical because it leads to premature depletion of the resource and leaves groundwater users at the mercy of nearby high-capacity pumpers. Even malicious withdrawal of water for the purpose of injuring a neighbor was not actionable under strict application of the absolute ownership rule. Friendswood Dev. Co. v. Smith-Southwest Indus., Inc., 576 S.W.2d 21 (Tex. 1978). Today, most states following the absolute ownership doctrine allow remedies for willful injury, and some impose liability for land subsidence caused by negligent pumping and/or subject groundwater use to regulation under some of the rules discussed below.

In Texas and possibly other "absolute ownership" states, disputes between a surface landowner and a groundwater owner in a "split estate" situation are resolved much like disputes between surface owners and mineral owners. In Coyote Lake Ranch, LLC v. City of Lubbock, 498 S.W.3d 53 (Tex. 2016), the court held that the City of Lubbock, which owned a severable groundwater estate underlying the plaintiff's surface estate, could proceed with its plan to extract groundwater, but that it must accommodate the surface owner's interest. Groundwater pumping would be enjoined if "(1) the groundwater owner's use of the surface completely precludes or substantially impairs the existing use, (2) the surface owner has no available, reasonable alternative to continue the existing use, and (3) given the particular circumstances, the groundwater owner has available reasonable, customary, and industry-accepted methods to access and produce the water and allow continuation of the surface owner's existing use." *Id.* at 64–65.

The reasonable use "American Rule" doctrine is similar to the absolute ownership rule, but restricts landowners by requiring them to use the groundwater on the overlying land. *See infra* Section II.B.3.

### *b. Correlative Rights*

Under the correlative rights doctrine, land ownership determines rights to groundwater. However, owners of land overlying a single aquifer are each limited to a reasonable share of the total supply of groundwater. The correlative rights doctrine was applied in Katz v. Walkinshaw, 74 P. 766, 772 (Cal. 1903), where the court ruled that, in times of shortage, each overlying owner must limit withdrawals to a "fair and just proportion" of the supply—a proportion based on the ratio of each landowner's acreage overlying the aquifer.

California allows surplus groundwater (*i.e.*, groundwater available in excess of a landowner's needs) to be used on lands that do not overlie the aquifer. Santa Maria v. Adam, 149 Cal. Rptr. 3d 491 (Cal. Ct. App. 2012). Rights to export water are based on prior appropriation. As between two exporters, the doctrine of prior appropriation applies. In conflicts between overlying owners and exporters, an overlying owner is entitled to a reasonable share regardless of priority relative to the exporter, but any surplus is allocated according to priority. *Katz*, 74 P. 766. Other jurisdictions adopting correlative rights have not embraced this aspect of the *Katz* allocation scheme, but have accepted the generalized notion of pro rata reductions based on land ownership or other factors.

California has introduced another appropriation concept, as well as incorporating a measure of public interest, into the law of correlative rights. In a case involving a basin subject to serious overdrafts caused by pumping for both overlying and export uses, the court held that all pumpers had used water contrary to the rights of one another. Consequently, the continuous adverse uses had resulted in "mutual prescription," and the users' rights were allocated in proportion to their actual historical use. City of Pasadena v. City of Alhambra, 207 P.2d 17, 30 (Cal. 1949). The mutual prescription approach was developed to avoid the hardship of completely cutting off some users such as municipalities and public utilities. But it provoked a scramble to pump large amounts of groundwater to establish or prevent loss of prescriptive rights.

The mutual prescription doctrine was significantly qualified in City of Los Angeles v. City of San Fernando, 537 P.2d 1250 (Cal. 1975). There, the court held that municipalities were exempt from prescription and required that owners be put on notice of the adversity caused by commencement of the overdraft. The court also altered the correlative rights allocation formula. Under the new formula, prescriptive rights against private owners are determined and a correlative rights allocation made; prescriptive rights are then subtracted from each private owner's allocation. Any remaining surplus is allocated by priority of appropriation. *Id.* at 1280–81.

While *City of Los Angeles* limited the doctrine of mutual prescription, it left open the possibility that equitable apportionment methods could be used in future groundwater adjudications. However, the California Supreme Court subsequently held that any equitable solutions must respect the existing rights and priorities of overlying landowners. City of Barstow v. Mojave Water Agency, 5 P.3d 853, 868 (Cal. 2000).

Although it took over a decade to adopt comprehensive groundwater legislation after the *Barstow* decision, severe drought and "chronic" groundwater mining eventually motivated the California legislature to enact the Sustainable

Groundwater Management Act (SGMA), which took effect in 2015. Melissa K. Scanlan, *Droughts, Floods, and Scarcity on a Climate-Disrupted Planet: Understanding the Legal Challenges and Opportunities for Groundwater Sustainability,* 37 Va. Envtl. L.J. 52, 83 (2019). SGMA requires local Groundwater Sustainability Agencies to collect information, prepare a management plan, regulate pumping, and enforce limits to maintain sustainability. Cal. Water Code §§ 10720–10737.8. Groundwater transfers are allowed in some cases. *See, e.g.,* Cal. Water Code §§ 10726.2(d), 10726.4.

### 2. Rights by Prior Appropriation

Under the prior appropriation doctrine, the person who first begins using water has the best legal rights. This doctrine protects investments in wells, irrigation equipment, land, and businesses that are based on an expectation of a water supply. Farmers Inv. Co. v. Bettwy, 558 P.2d 14, 21 (Ariz. 1976).

Allocation of rights in groundwater strictly based on prior use is not practical; a senior groundwater appropriator theoretically could demand that no pumping be allowed because virtually any new pumping causes some effect on existing wells. The appropriation doctrine also ignores the equities of individual uses. It may be unfair to deny rights in groundwater to a junior pumper who owns overlying land and has no other readily available source. Thus, appropriation states must determine the extent to which new uses will be allowed to interfere with established uses. Appropriators also may be limited in the uses they may make of groundwater to prevent an aquifer from being overused. This may mean that no more than the average annual recharge can be pumped. Where there is little or no natural recharge, the state must decide whether the resource can be "mined" and, if so, at what rate and for what purposes. *See infra* Section II.D.2 of this chapter.

Laws allowing the first users to monopolize rights in groundwater also run contrary to the public interest and the state's obligation to protect and regulate use of a limited or nonrenewable public resource. In short, a strict application of prior appropriation could deprive other users—and society—of the ability to make full beneficial use of the resource. Many appropriation states have adopted statutes that modify the doctrine in order to set reasonable pumping levels for all or parts of the state (*e.g.*, Alaska, Colorado, Idaho, Kansas, Montana, Nevada, New Mexico, North Dakota, Oregon, South Dakota, Utah, Washington, and Wyoming). The objective is to balance the interests in protecting senior users, optimizing new economic uses, and assuring a sustained supply.

### 3. Groundwater as a Public Resource

Most states consider groundwater to be subject to management as public property. *See, e.g.*, Cal. Water Code § 102; Kan. Stat. Ann. § 82a–702; Ariz. Rev. Stat. § 45–401(B). Rights to use groundwater are typically created under permits granted by the state, usually with some recognition for the interests of overlying owners and established uses. An administrative agency or official allocates rights. The Colorado Supreme Court held that non-tributary groundwater is neither subject to the constitutional right of all citizens to appropriate water nor owned by the overlying owner. Thus the legislature is free to decide how to manage the resource. State Dep't of Natural Res. v. Sw. Colorado Water Conservation Dist., 671 P.2d 1294 (Colo. 1983) (en banc).

States may exercise their police power in order to protect competing users and allocate the groundwater resource in the public interest. The police power is extensive enough to justify permit systems and strict regulatory schemes so long as vested property rights are respected. Williams v. City of Wichita, 374 P.2d 578 (Kan. 1962). Changes in the law ordinarily do not result in a taking if they deprive landowners or former users of the right to use a portion of the groundwater. In re Water Use Permit Applications, 9 P.3d 409 (Haw. 2000); Town of Chino Valley v. City of Prescott, 638 P.2d 1324 (Ariz. 1981); Bamford v. Upper Republican Natural Res. Dist., 512 N.W.2d 642 (Neb. 1994). However, courts have reached varying results when pumping by a governmental unit causes private wells to go dry. *Compare* Bingham v. Roosevelt City Corp., 235 P.3d 730 (Utah 2010) (rejecting a takings claim because land ownership did not create private property interests in water in the soil), *with* McNamara v. Rittman, 838 N.E.2d 640 (Ohio 2005) (finding that landowners have a sufficient property interest in groundwater to support a takings claim when a city interferes with that interest). For more on takings, *see infra* Section II.D.4.

## B. RULES OF LIABILITY

Most groundwater disputes arise when an existing user alleges that new or increased pumping by another is causing harm. The principal rules of liability are influenced by, and in turn reflect, the various property law theories defining the source of rights in the particular jurisdiction, detailed above in the preceding subsection.

### 1. No Liability Rule

Absolute ownership states that recognize property rights to groundwater in overlying landowners allow pumping without liability to other users. Theoretically, every landowner has a right to take whatever water may be pumped from the land by paying only those costs directly incurred (*e.g.*, drilling, equipment, and electricity); no obligation is incurred for harm or expenses caused to others. *See, e.g.*, Sipriano v. Great Spring Waters of America, Inc., 1 S.W.3d 75 (Tex. 1999). Very few states continue to follow this rule. *See* Maddocks v. Giles, 728 A.2d 150, 154 (Me. 1999) (refusing to overturn Maine's absolute ownership rule, stating that a more enlightened understanding of groundwater science "does not mean that the rule itself has interfered with water use or has caused the development of unwise water policy").

### 2. Prior Appropriation—"Junior-Liable" Rule

States that adhere strictly to the prior appropriation doctrine impose liability on new pumpers for harm caused to existing pumpers with vested senior rights. *See, e.g.*, Yeo v. Tweedy, 286 P. 970 (N.M. 1929); Utah in Current Creek Irr. Co. v. Andrews, 344 P.2d 528 (Utah 1959); Garetson Bros. v. Am. Warrior, Inc., 435 P.3d 1153 (Kan. App. 2019). In effect, seniors with shallow wells can block juniors with larger or deeper wells from withdrawing water.

To avoid locking up groundwater supplies from future uses, some states have modified appropriation law to limit protection of seniors to reasonable pumping levels. Seniors may be required to show that they have taken steps to maximize their usage through reasonable methods of diversion and application. A & B Irr. Dist. v. Idaho Dep't of Water Res., 284 P.3d 225 (Idaho 2012). Some states review an array of factors in order to balance protecting seniors with maximizing the beneficial use of water. Arave v. Pineview West Water Company, 477 P.3d 1239 (Utah 2020); Parker v. Wallentine, 650 P.2d 648 (Idaho 1982). The Utah Supreme Court clarified that courts should consider the total situation and, in order for a senior to prevail on a claim of well interference, they must establish that their methods and means of diversion are reasonable and that despite reasonable efforts they are unable to obtain the quantity or quality of water to which they have a right. *Arave*, 477 P.3d at 1248.

### 3. Reasonable Use Doctrine

So many American jurisdictions adopted the reasonable use doctrine that it became known as the "American Rule." Adams v. Lang, 553 So.2d 89 (Ala. 1989). The doctrine favors users on overlying land.

Traditionally, any beneficial use on the overlying land (short of actual waste) was considered reasonable and any use off the land was considered unreasonable. *See, e.g.*, Brady v. Abbot Laboratories, 433 F.3d 679 (9th Cir. 2005) (applying Arizona law); Martin v. City of Linden, 667 So.2d 732 (Ala. 1995); Higday v. Nickolaus, 469 S.W.2d 859 (Mo. Ct. App. 1971); Finley v. Teeter Stone, Inc., 248 A.2d 106 (Md. 1968); Willis v. City of Perry, 60 N.W. 727 (Iowa 1894). In this sense, the American Rule is another form of the rule of capture, with the limitation that the water must be used on the overlying land.

Some states have modified the American Rule by adding a layer of correlative rights, in recognition that, absent some constraints, a well owner's use of water on overlying land could deplete an aquifer to the point that uses by others become difficult or impossible. The correlative rights doctrine accommodates all overlying owners when the water supply is insufficient to meet the reasonable needs of all. All users must ratably reduce their use of water so that each landowner gets a fair and just proportion of the supply; pumpers making excessive use of the groundwater may be held liable to those who are harmed. *See* Olson v. City of Wahoo, 248 N.W. 304, 308 (Neb. 1933) (adding a "correlative" twist to the American "reasonable use" rule such that, in the event of insufficient supply, each overlying user is entitled to a reasonable proportion).

Although the common law does not allow water to be transferred off overlying land, a legislature may recognize exceptions. *See, e.g.*, Estermann v. Bose,

892 N.W.2d 857 (Neb. 2017) (rejecting a challenge to an augmentation project designed to increase the amount of water available in the Republican River Basin, some of which would be used in Kansas, and holding that the project proponent did not need to obtain a groundwater transfer permit) (citing Neb. Rev. Stat. § 46–613.01); Neb. Rev. Stat. Ann. § 46–691 (allowing transfer off the overlying land for "agricultural purposes, or for any purpose pursuant to a ground water remediation plan"). If transfers are generally allowed, a legislative attempt to prevent interstate transfers may violate the dormant Commerce Clause. *See* Sporhase v. Nebraska ex rel. Douglas, 458 U.S. 941 (1982) (invalidating a Nebraska statute that prohibited groundwater exports to states that did not provide reciprocal privileges).

### 4. Restatement (Second) of Torts § 858

The Restatement (Second) of Torts Section 858 attempts to balance equities and hardships among competing users. It imposes liability only for withdrawals that unreasonably affect other users. The Restatement approach differs from the American Rule by inquiring into the nature of the competing uses and the relative burdens imposed upon each user. It is distinct from the correlative rights approach in that it attaches no special significance to use of the water on overlying land.

Section 858 is phrased as a rule of non-liability. It states that a well owner is not liable for withdrawal of groundwater unless the withdrawal:

a. unreasonably causes harm to a neighbor by lowering the water table or reducing artesian pressure;

b. exceeds the owner's reasonable share of the total annual supply or total store of groundwater; or

c. has a direct and substantial effect on a watercourse or lake and unreasonably causes harm to a person entitled to the use of its water.

The first limitation uses a balancing test to determine "unreasonableness." It seems to require that a plaintiff's well be reasonably efficient considering the type of use. A court may inquire into such issues as relative wealth of the parties (*e.g.*, municipalities vs. small farmers), relative ability to obtain financing, and relative value of the uses. The second limitation in § 858 incorporates a "correlative rights" notion as an additional basis of liability. The last limitation contemplates administration of groundwater use in conjunction with surface appropriation systems.

Although most courts in reasonable use jurisdictions apply some of the Restatement considerations, only a few specifically purport to follow it. In Prather v. Eisenmann, 261 N.W.2d 766 (Neb. 1978), the court looked to the nature of the use in determining reasonableness, and held a high-capacity irrigation user liable for lowering the artesian pressure of a domestic well. The court invoked the state preference statute (rather than the Restatement) to say that causing harm to preferred domestic users may be *per se* "unreasonable." *Id.* at 770. A subsequent Nebraska decision, Spear T Ranch v. Knaub, 691 N.W.2d 116 (Neb. 2005), applied § 858 in a case where groundwater pumping interfered with surface water uses. In *Spear T*, a senior surface water irrigator sued junior groundwater irrigators pumping from hundreds of wells that had reduced streamflow. The court found that § 858(c) applied, but denied the claim because *Spear T* had failed to show that the pumpers had "unreasonably caused harm." *Id.* at 132.

Courts in several Great Lakes states have also followed the Restatement approach. Maerz v. United States Steel Corp., 323 N.W.2d 524 (Mich. Ct. App. 1982); Cline v. American Aggregates Corp., 474 N.E.2d 324 (Ohio 1984); State v. Michels Pipeline Constr., Inc., 217 N.W.2d 339 (Wis. 1974) (adopting Tentative Draft No. 17, § 858 (1971)). But *see* Michigan Citizens for Water Conservation v. Nestlé Waters North America, Inc., 709 N.W.2d 174 (Mich. Ct. App. 2005) (applying a reasonable use balancing test informed by Restatement 850A factors rather than § 858 to a dispute between riparians and groundwater users), *reversed in part on other grounds,* 737 N.W.2d 447 (Mich. 2007). By contrast, Indiana and Maine have specifically rejected Restatement § 858. Wiggins v. Brazil Coal & Clay, 452 N.E.2d 958 (Ind. 1983); Maddocks v. Giles, 728 A.2d 150 (Me. 1999).

## 5. "Economic Reach" Rule

The economic reach approach is somewhat similar to the Restatement in attempting to strike a balance between junior and senior rights. The leading case exemplifying this approach is City of Colorado Springs v. Bender, 366 P.2d 552 (Colo. 1961) (en banc). Colorado applies prior appropriation to hydrologically connected "tributary" groundwater. In *Bender*, a senior groundwater user sought to enjoin a junior pumper who interfered with the senior's shallow well. The court looked to the law of surface streams, which does not protect a senior's means of surface diversion against diversions by juniors unless it is reasonably adequate (a suggestion made by the Supreme Court in Schodde v. Twin Falls Land & Water Co., 224 U.S. 107 (1912)). *Bender* held that a senior well must be reasonably adequate in light of economics and historical use. This implies that an established domestic well need not be as deep as an irrigation well.

The *Bender* rule, like the Restatement, invites inquiry into issues such as the relative wealth of parties and values of competing uses. The court observed that, while seniors "cannot reasonably command the whole source of supply merely to facilitate the taking by them of the fraction," they "cannot be required to improve their extraction facilities beyond their economic reach, upon a consideration of all the factors involved." *Id.* at 556. This approach was followed in Baker v. Ore-Ida Foods, Inc., 513 P.2d 627 (Idaho 1973), and Wayman v. Murray City Corp., 458 P.2d 861 (Utah 1969).

Section B.2 above discusses how these prior appropriation states have continued to refine their approach to groundwater use.

## C. PERMITS

Many states have enacted groundwater permit systems to replace piecemeal litigation between water users with a unified administrative scheme that establishes and protects rights to use groundwater consistent with other state goals. Most permit requirements include criteria designed to prevent overdraft and protect existing wells. Rights embodied in permits can be based to some degree on land ownership, prior use, and the public interest. Thus, permit systems largely supplant use of common law and tort remedies. The objective of permit systems is to regulate development and use of groundwater so that it is used beneficially for society. Such systems also provide for public involvement and community control of pumping activity.

Although the permit systems adopted by a few states are comprehensive (in particular, Florida and Minnesota), most states apply separate requirements to different types of groundwater and different types or quantities of use. Many distinguish groundwater connected with (*i.e.*, "tributary" to) surface streams and lakes. Most western states require a permit for groundwater withdrawals, but exempt small domestic and stock watering wells. Texas requires no permits for groundwater withdrawals (except from the Edwards Aquifer), but provides for voluntary formation of local management districts by landowner petition. Tex. Water Code Ann. § 36.013. Other states have designated "critical areas" where permit requirements and other regulations apply.

There are two types of permits: well permits and permits evidencing a water right. Both may be required.

## 1. Well Permits

Permits are often a prerequisite to well drilling. Applications for well permits typically must specify the type of use and amount of water to be withdrawn, legal descriptions of well location and land on which the water is to be used, type of well, and description of geologic strata through which it is to be drilled.

Most states have laws specifying requirements for well construction, and some also govern proximity of wells to one another. Construction provisions may require that all wells be cased or sealed as they pass through other water-bearing formations to prevent migration of pollutants into or from another aquifer and accidental tapping of other aquifers. Well drillers must also be licensed and report information on geological structures, locations, and depths of aquifers for all wells drilled.

## 2. Pumping Permits

In addition to a well-drilling permit, an applicant may need a separate permit to use groundwater. Permit statutes often require public notice and provide procedures for interested parties to file objections. Many authorize administrative appeals and judicial review of decisions to grant or deny permits.

In evaluating applications for groundwater rights, administrators are primarily concerned with whether additional permits will impair existing pumpers' rights. Determination of "impairment" is based in part upon hydrologic data on aquifer recharge and on the extent of existing uses.

In states that incorporate appropriation concepts into their permit systems, the user must proceed with reasonable diligence to drill the well and apply the water to a beneficial use once the well and water use permits are issued. The right vests when the water is put to use, and a certificate is usually issued evidencing the right. Permits are subject to loss by abandonment, forfeiture, or violation of conditions.

## D. LIMITS ON PUMPING

Typically, state statutes provide some protection for existing uses. Many states also statutorily limit the rate or volume of groundwater pumping to allow for future as well as existing uses. State statutes often address groundwater mining and overdraft. Several states have enacted laws to deal with areas having special groundwater pumping problems.

### 1. Protection of Existing Rights

States that have replaced common law rights based on appropriation or land ownership with statutory permit systems sometimes "grandfather" pre-existing wells to exclude them in whole or in part from the permit requirements. New wells must receive a permit from a state administrative body and comply with state statutory criteria for allocating groundwater. Harloff v. City of Sarasota, 575 So.2d 1324 (Fla. Dist. Ct. App. 1991).

Most statutory groundwater systems include some measures to protect existing wells. The goal is not absolute protection, because any new well potentially interferes with existing wells in the same aquifer, but rather to prevent "unreasonable" interference.

Prior appropriation states have taken additional steps to protect senior groundwater users. The 1965 Colorado Groundwater Management Act seeks to reconcile protection of vested appropriative rights with full economic utilization of groundwater. The statute employs a "modified" appropriation doctrine to govern administration of designated basins. In contrast to the pure appropriation doctrine under which a new use would be denied if any harm resulted to seniors, the statute requires refusal of a permit only if unreasonable harm to senior rights or unreasonable waste would result. Unreasonable harm is defined as "the unreasonable lowering of the water level, or the unreasonable deterioration of water quality, beyond reasonable economic limits of withdrawal or use." Colo. Rev. Stat. § 37–90–107(5). Criteria for determining unreasonable harm or waste include geologic conditions, average annual yield and recharge rate of the supply, priority and quantity of existing claims to the water, proposed method of use, and other appropriate factors. *Id.* The Colorado Groundwater Commission has adopted complex regulations to implement this rather vague statutory mandate. *See* Fundingsland v. Colorado Ground Water Comm'n, 468 P.2d 835 (Colo. 1970) (en banc) (upholding rule denying new permits that would result in 40% depletion of aquifer by all wells within 3-mile radius in 25 years).

In New Mexico, if a proposed new use will not impair existing water rights, the state engineer is authorized to grant a permit so long as the new use is not contrary to water conservation objectives and is not detrimental to the public welfare. N.M. Stat. Ann. § 72–12–3 (West). In Mathers v. Texaco, Inc., 421 P.2d 771 (N.M. 1966), the court rejected the argument that any pumping whatsoever by juniors in a closed basin constitutes *per se* impairment just because pumping would lower the water table. However, according to the court, "it does not follow that the lowering of the water table may never in itself constitute an impairment of existing rights." City of Roswell v. Reynolds, 522 P.2d 796, 800 (N.M. 1974). A determination of impairment to existing water rights depends on the facts of each case. *See id.* (upholding conditions imposed by the state engineer to protect seniors).

## 2. Forfeiture

Many prior appropriation states provide for forfeiture of groundwater rights upon a showing of non-use. *See, e.g.,* State ex rel. Office of State Eng'r v. Romero, 455 P.3d 860 (N.M. App.), *cert. granted* (2019) (finding that a portion of former railroad water rights held by a landowner were not beneficially used for the statutory four-year period, and thus were subject to forfeiture). However, appropriators tend to maintain groundwater rights during periods of time when an aquifer fails to yield sufficient water to satisfy the water right, as in a sustained drought, so long as the appropriator beneficially uses material amounts of available water. Delta Canal Co. v. Frank Vincent Family Ranch, 420 P.3d 1052 (Utah 2013) (citing Utah Code 73–1–4(3)(f)(i)).

### 3. Legislative Schedules for Groundwater Mining

Several states have provided for controlled mining of aquifers so that depletion occurs over a predictable number of years. The term "safe yield," in its strictest sense, means a level of withdrawals that does not exceed recharge. In the case of aquifers that are not rechargeable or that take many years to recharge appreciably, the concept has been modified so that "safe yield" refers to a level of withdrawals that will allow depletion of an aquifer over a period thought to be socially optimal.

In some states, administrators also make value judgments as to the permissible rate of aquifer depletion, usually guided by statutory criteria. Such criteria reflect policy choices made by the legislature in reconciling priority of use rights with rights of overlying owners, economic efficiency, and other social goals. *See* A. Dan Tarlock, L. of Water Rights and Resources § 6:15 (noting that Colorado, New Mexico, and Arizona control the rate of groundwater mining).

The choice of time period is a policy judgment. A long depletion period preserves groundwater for future uses, but requires greater limitations on present withdrawals; thus, it imposes a hardship on well owners who must invest large sums in well drilling and irrigation equipment. By contrast, a shorter period allows larger withdrawals for the benefit of current users, but may allow depletion to occur so rapidly that an established irrigation economy can fail suddenly as pumping costs exceed economic returns from the water. Usually, legislatures reach a compromise under which investors have time to recover their equipment costs and aquifer life is also prolonged. Oklahoma's Groundwater Management Act allows a comparatively rapid 100% depletion within 20 years. Okla. Stat. tit. 82, § 1020.5(b). By contrast, pumping in non-tributary aquifers outside designated basins in Colorado must provide for a 100-year aquifer life. Colo. Rev. Stat. § 37–90–137(4)(b)(I). The Nebraska legislature has expressed a state-wide goal of extending aquifer life "to the greatest extent practicable consistent with reasonable and beneficial use of the ground water and best management practices." Neb. Rev. Stat. § 46–702. However, Nebraska law authorizes local districts to establish their own depletion timetables unless the basin in question is designated as fully or over-appropriated, at which point an integrated management plan must be adopted in order "to achieve and sustain a balance between water uses and water supplies for the long term." Neb. Rev. Stat. § 46–715(1).

## 4. Critical Area Legislation and Designations

Even where there are no statewide problems of groundwater overdraft, there may be localized overdrafts that demand strict management. Many western states statutorily provide for identification and management of "critical areas" in which new well drilling and pumping may be severely curtailed or prohibited. These states include Arizona, California, Colorado, Hawaii, Idaho, Kansas, Nebraska, Montana, Nevada, New Mexico, Oklahoma, Oregon, Texas, Washington, and Wyoming. The state engineer's office or an equivalent administrative body commonly regulates critical areas, which tend to be geographically defined by the boundaries of an aquifer or basin.

Requirements for critical area status vary. Montana and Oregon, for example, may designate a critical area if withdrawals from the basin exceed recharge (the definition of "overdraft"). Mont. Code. Ann. § 85–2–506(5)(a); Or. Rev. Stat. Ann. § 537.730(1)(e). Wyoming may designate a "control area" as soon as withdrawals approach the recharge rate. Wyo. Stat. Ann. § 41–3–912(a)(i). Colorado does not need to find an overdraft condition to establish an area as a "designated groundwater basin" if the basin is non-tributary or located in an area where groundwater has been the principal water source for fifteen years prior to the application for designation. Colo. Rev. Stat. § 37–90–106.

Critical area legislation also varies in the remedy applied to correct the overdraft. Under the Idaho Groundwater Management Act, Idaho Code Ann.

§§ 42–226 *et seq.*, the Department of Water Resources will deny groundwater permits when further withdrawals would affect present or future use of any groundwater right, or cause overall withdrawals to exceed recharge. Courts have construed this provision to prohibit junior pumping if it would cause groundwater mining to the detriment of seniors. Baker v. Ore-Ida Foods, Inc., 513 P.2d 627 (Idaho 1973). Senior pumpers are not absolutely protected in either their historic water levels or their historic means of diversion; rather, seniors may have to accept some modifications in order to achieve the state's goal of full economic development of water resources. If the senior users are maintaining reasonable pumping levels, however, the Department of Water Resources may place a call upon juniors to protect the seniors. Clear Springs Foods, Inc. v. Spackman, 252 P.3d 71 (Idaho 2011).

Colorado, Nevada, and Washington statutes also provide for pumping reductions, but reductions are made on the basis of priority; senior appropriators may continue to pump while juniors are shut down. Colo. Rev. Stat. § 37–92–102(2)(d); Nev. Rev. Stat. § 534.110(7)(b); Wash. Rev. Code § 90.44.130.

In Arizona, years of unregulated pumping led to severe overdrafts, particularly in the metropolitan areas of Phoenix and Tucson. Accordingly, Arizona's 1980 Groundwater Management Act contains some of the strictest controls of any state statute. It provides for establishing "active management areas" or AMAs that now encompass eighty percent of the state's population, but only thirteen percent of the land mass. Ariz. Rev. Stat. Ann. § 45–411. The state Director of Water Resources may designate an AMA if overdraft exists, withdrawals threaten to create subsidence, or groundwater quality is threatened by saltwater intrusion. *Id.* § 45–412. The management goal is to achieve safe yield (withdrawals not in excess of recharge) by 2025. *Id.* § 45–562. To reach this goal, the state Director of Water Resources is required to formulate a management plan that includes mandatory conservation by "reasonable reductions" in per capita use, pump taxes with revenues earmarked for expenses of administration and augmentation plans, retirement of irrigated lands, and a requirement that new subdivisions demonstrate an assured water supply for 100 years or have a contract for Central Arizona Project (Colorado River) water. *Id.* §§ 45–564 through 45–568. The Act does not, however, mandate a moratorium on development in the absence of "absolute certainty" of a future water supply. Silver v. Pueblo Del Sol Water Co., 423 P.3d 348 (Ariz. 2018).

As Arizona approached the 2025 deadline for AMAs to meet a safe yield, most of the AMAs were not meeting their management goals. Arizona Department of Water Resources, Overdraft, Safe-Yield, and the Management Goals of Arizona's Active Management Areas (2022), https://www.azwater.gov/sites/default/files/2022-07/2022_SYReport_0.pdf. To protect aquifers and promote lower water use development in two of the AMAs not meeting their goals, Phoenix and Pinal, enacted the "Ag-to-Urban" Groundwater Conservation Program. S.B. 1611, 57th

Leg., 1st Reg. Sess. (Az. 2025). This program allows water users with high-use irrigation grandfathered rights to retire these rights in exchange for Groundwater Savings Credits that can be used for lower water use development for housing. Ariz. Rev. Stat. Ann. § 45–465.05. This program could potentially apply to 384,000 acres used for high water use irrigation in the Phoenix and Pinal AMAs, which account for over 1 million acre-feet of water being used every year. Arizona Department of Water Resources, Governor's Water Policy Council Meeting (Dec. 2, 2024), https://www.azwater.gov/gwpc/meetings.

Kansas authorizes residents to petition for the formation of groundwater districts to manage scarce resources. Management plans are subject to approval by the Chief Engineer of the Department of Water Resources. Each local district has permitting authority and may apply its own standards for safe yield. Kan. Stat. Ann. § 82a–1022; F. Arthur Stone & Sons v. Gibson, 630 P.2d 1164 (Kan. 1981).

Nebraska has created 23 natural resource districts with the authority to establish groundwater "management" or "control" areas. The state requires the districts, in coordination with the Nebraska Department of Natural Resources (DNR), to adopt integrated management plans that "balance" long-term demands and supplies in fully and over-appropriated basins. Neb. Rev. Stat. §§ 46–702 through 45–705; Christina Hoffman & Sandra Zellmer, *Assessing Institutional Ability to Support*

*Adaptive, Integrated Water Resources Management,* 91 Neb. L. Rev. 805, 817–21 (2013).

### 5. Takings

In some states, groundwater restrictions may amount to an unconstitutional taking for which the landowners must be compensated. Actions by a city or other government body that destroy water quality or cause shortages for overlying landowners may also constitute a taking. *See, e.g.,* McNamara v. Rittman, 838 N.E.2d 640 (Ohio 2005).

The Texas Supreme Court found that, under the absolute ownership doctrine, landowners possessed separate, distinct, and exclusive ownership of groundwater found on their land. Edwards Aquifer Authority v. Day, 369 S.W.3d 814 (Tex. 2012). Applying rules that had originated with doctrines concerning the ownership of oil and gas, the court found that a landowner's interest in groundwater required compensation when regulatory restrictions prevented pumping. *Id. See* Stratta v. Roe, 961 F.3d 340 (5th Cir. 2020) (holding that a Texas landowner's property includes the ownership of groundwater beneath his acreage, subject to takings and due process claims). In Edwards Aquifer Authority v. Bragg, 421 S.W.3d 118 (Tex. App. 2013), *review denied,* (2015), the Texas Court of Appeals found that the Aquifer Authority's decision to deny a permit application amounted to a regulatory taking of desiccated pecan orchards where the lack of water affected both the yield of the existing crop and the quality and size of future crops.

Nebraska and several other states have refused to recognize takings claims brought by groundwater pumpers against a state or local agency. For example, in Prokop v. Lower Loup Nat. Res. Dist., 921 N.W.2d 375 (Neb. 2019), the court held that a natural resources district's issuance of a cease and desist order suspending a landowner's access to groundwater due to his failure to submit an annual report was an appropriate exercise of the police power and did not amount to a taking. *See also* Kobobel v. State, Dep't of Nat. Res., 249 P.3d 1127 (Colo. 2011); In re General Adjudication of All Rights to Use Water in the Gila River System and Source, 9 P.3d 1069 (Ariz. 2000); In re Water Use Permit Applications, 9 P.3d 409 (Ha. 2000); Peterson v. Dep't of Ecology, 596 P.2d 285 (Wash. 1979).

Another variation on takings claims is seen in Hill v. State, 894 N.W.2d 208 (Neb. 2017), where the court held the DNR did not have authority to regulate groundwater users in order to protect surface water appropriators; thus, the DNR's failure to curtail pumping that depleted surface waters was not a taking of the surface appropriators' water rights.

## III. CONJUNCTIVE USE AND MANAGEMENT

The term "conjunctive use" refers to the joint management of hydrologically connected groundwater and surface water sources. The term can also refer to the use of two unconnected sources to maximize available supplies. Although "conjunctive management" of connected sources is the only logical way to deal with what is in fact a single resource, most states manage water use from wells and streams separately. In recent years, however, more states are working toward integrated management of interconnected groundwater and surface resources. One promising approach is to create an agency with powers over conjunctive use, but there is often political resistance to giving agencies substantial new powers to tax, incur bonded indebtedness, take legal action, and exercise broad administrative powers over water management.

## A. REGULATION OF GROUNDWATER CONNECTED WITH SURFACE SOURCES

### 1. Interaction of Groundwater and Surface Water

Groundwater is often hydrologically connected to surface streams. For example, seepage from a stream may charge an underlying aquifer. The surface flow of a stream may "ride piggyback" upon the groundwater contained in the aquifer beneath the stream. Or, as noted in Section I.A of this chapter, seepage from aquifers may feed a stream. In these situations, stream use may diminish water in the aquifer and, in turn, groundwater withdrawals may diminish surface flow.

Although the scientific community has long recognized the interconnection of groundwater and surface water, the law has been slow to catch up. Although a few early cases enforced rights based on this truth, *see, e.g.*, Smith v. City of Brooklyn, 54 N.E. 787 (N.Y. 1899) (riparian entitled to prevent interference with streamflow from use of groundwater), the laws of many states are still founded on the misconception that the two types of water exist in isolation from one another; thus, they apply separate regulatory systems for groundwater and surface water. *See* Spear T Ranch v. Knaub, 691 N.W.2d 116 (Neb. 2005), *supra* Section II.B.4.

To varying degrees, several states, including California, Colorado, New Mexico, Utah, and Washington, administer groundwater sources affected by or affecting surface flow as part of the surface appropriation system. Cal. Water Code § 1200; Colo. Rev. Stat § 37–92–102(1)(a); Templeton v. Pecos Val. Artesian Conservancy Dist., 332 P.2d 465 (N.M. 1958); Utah Code Ann. §§ 73–1–1, 73–3–1; Wash. Rev. Code § 90.03.010. *See also* Whatcom Cty. v. Hirst, 381 P.3d 1 (Wash. 2016) (holding that a permit to appropriate groundwater must be denied where withdrawals would impair existing surface water rights, including minimum flow rights); Bassett v. Dep't of Ecology, 438 P.3d 563 (Wash. App. 2019) (stating that a decision to issue a permit for the appropriation of groundwater must consider the interrelationship with surface waters to determine whether surface water rights would be impaired by withdrawals); Envtl. Law Fnd. v. State Water Res. Control Bd., 237 Cal. Rptr. 3d 393, 409 (2018) (imposing a public trust responsibility on permitting decisions for hydrologically connected groundwater); Justesen v. Olsen, 40 P.2d 802, 809 (Utah 1935) ("An appropriation . . . follows the water to its original source whether through surface or subterranean streams or through percolation").

Some states do not treat tributary groundwater as part of the surface system *per se*, but empower regulatory agencies to impose special conditions on groundwater withdrawals that interfere with surface rights. *See, e.g.*, Oregon, Or. Rev. Stat. § 537.525. The Arizona Supreme Court, however, has ruled that courts should treat tributary groundwater as part of the groundwater system unless it is "subflow," the extraction of which will "diminish appreciably and directly the flow of the surface stream." Maricopa Cnty. Municipal Water Conservation Dist. No. 1 v. Sw. Cotton Co., 4 P.2d 369, 380 (Ariz. 1931). It defined subflow as "waters which slowly find their way through the sand and gravel constituting the bed of the stream, or the lands under or immediately adjacent to the stream, and are themselves a part of the surface stream." *Id.* at 380. If groundwater is not subflow, it is subject only to reasonable use limitations and is not treated as part of the surface water regime. Arizona has since adopted an administrative test limiting subflow to the saturated floodplain of the stream. In re General Adjudication of All Rights to Use Water in the Gila River System and Source, 9 P.3d 1069 (Ariz. 2000).

Because groundwater may percolate very slowly through aquifers, there is often a delay between groundwater withdrawals from a connected aquifer and their effect on the surface stream. In addition, the effect on the stream may be less in amount than the groundwater withdrawal. The timing and magnitude of the effect of well pumping on streamflows are expressed by the U.S. Geological Survey as the "stream depletion factor," defined as a percentage of the streamflow (not of the amount withdrawn). For example, a thirty-day, five percent stream depletion factor means that pumping will diminish the streamflow by five percent within thirty days. To calculate the depletion factor, the U.S. Geological Survey uses computer models, stream depletion contour maps, and hydrological data.

The length of the delayed effect of well pumping on streamflow helps define which waters have a sufficient hydrologic connection to be conjunctively managed. In addition, in states that do engage in conjunctive management, the length of delay determines when junior well-owners must be shut down to protect senior surface rights holders. It also determines when juniors will be allowed to pump even though a senior surface user may be deprived of water under the "futile call" doctrine (see *supra* Chapter 3.V).

### 2. Definition of Hydrologically Connected ("Tributary") Groundwater

The word "tributary" refers to groundwater that has a hydrologic connection with a surface stream that is sufficiently direct to warrant legal attention. Proving that groundwater is tributary to a stream can be difficult and expensive, but it has important legal consequences.

To simplify fact-finding, Colorado courts have adopted a "presumption of tributariness." Safranek v. Limon, 228 P.2d 975 (Colo. 1951) (en banc). Where pumping would affect a stream within 40 years, the water is presumed to be tributary; conversely, where pumping would not affect a stream for more than 100 years, courts have ruled that the water is non-tributary. Dist. 10 Water Users Ass'n v. Barnett, 599 P.2d 894 (Colo. 1979) (en banc). A Colorado statute now defines non-tributary water as water, "the withdrawal of which will not, within one hundred years, deplete the flow of any natural stream at an annual rate greater than one-tenth of one percent of the annual rate of withdrawal." Colo. Rev. Stat. § 37–90–103(10.5). As a practical matter, the presumption operates in favor of surface water appropriators since the burden of proof is borne by groundwater users. *See* Kobobel v. State, Dep't of Natural Res., 249 P.3d 1127, 1136 (Colo. 2011) (well owners were subject to the presumption that pumping caused material injury to senior appropriators).

Conversely, Colorado presumes that groundwater in a designated groundwater basin has "no more than a de minimis impact on any surface stream." Gallegos Family Properties, LLC v. Colorado Groundwater Comm'n, 398 P.3d 599, 606 (Colo. 2017). The Colorado Groundwater Commission has the authority to de-designate or "alter the boundaries or description" of such a basin where pumping within the basin is causing injury to surface water rights. *Id.* at 607 (citing § 37–90–106(1)(a)).

### 3. Conjunctive Use Management

Interrelation of ground and surface supplies gives flexibility to users with access to both. Conjunctive use can take advantage of the delayed stream effects of pumping that may allow months between the time of withdrawals and the time a surface user feels the effects. In states with flexible administrative policies, the junior may continue to pump so long as the senior is provided with sufficient supplemental water to prevent harm to appropriative rights.

Not only may withdrawals from the tributary aquifer have a delayed impact on the stream, but the magnitude of the measurable stream effects may be less than the amount withdrawn from the tributary aquifer. For example, if the withdrawal of five acre-feet from an aquifer underlying a stream reduces streamflow by only two acre-feet, other sources of water can make up the difference, at least in the short-run or in the immediate vicinity. In this situation, a pumper may furnish seniors on the surface stream with a substitute supply of sufficient quantity and quality, thereby making a much larger supply of groundwater available. In the example given, the pumper might withdraw five acre-feet while bypassing two acre-feet directly into the stream to avoid stream depletion effects on surface water users—a technique known as "bypass pumping." The physical recharge to the aquifer and possible effects on adjacent wells limits the effectiveness of bypass pumping. Pumpers may use stored or imported surface water to satisfy surface priorities, thus allowing greater amounts of groundwater to be pumped without adverse effects on senior rights in the connected stream.

States have taken varying approaches to conjunctive use management. In New Mexico, a senior stream appropriator may be able to "follow the source" to get a more reliable supply by sinking a well to tap water flowing under the stream. In Templeton v. Pecos Valley Artesian Conservancy Dist., 332 P.2d 465 (N.M. 1958), a senior water right holder who was unable to divert sufficient surface water because groundwater pumping had diminished surface flows sought to drill a well in the alluvial aquifer supporting the stream. The court held that the supplemental well used the same water from a deeper source, so it had the original surface priority rather than a more recent priority as of the time the well was drilled. *Id.* at 471. Later, the same court held that the "follow-the-source" rule allowed surface appropriators to tap a deep aquifer that partially fed a shallower aquifer connected with the river. Langenegger v. Carlsbad Irrigation Dist., 483 P.2d 297 (N.M. 1971). The factual question is whether the same, hydrologically continuous aquifer that feeds base flow to the source of the senior's surface appropriation provides water to the juniors' wells. Herrington v. State of New Mexico, ex rel. Office of State Engineer, 133 P.3d 258 (N.M. 2006). Remarkably, New Mexico law allows the senior and the junior to pump their full rights, even in times of shortage. However, the state engineer may deny a groundwater permit if pumping would interfere with vested surface rights. City of Albuquerque v. Reynolds, 379 P.2d 73 (N.M. 1962).

In Idaho, when confrontations between established surface users and more recent groundwater pumpers arise, the priority system applies and administrative officials have a duty to enforce those priorities. Musser v. Higginson, 871 P.2d 809 (Idaho 1994).

However, by regulation, before allowing a senior surface water user to "call" a junior well owner, the Director of Water Resources must consider whether the senior user's "water right could be met with the user's existing facilities and water supplies by employment of reasonable diversion and conveyance efficiency and conservation practices." American Falls Reservoir Dist. No. 2 v. Idaho Dep't of Water Res., 154 P.3d 433, 449 (Idaho 2007).

The Nevada Supreme Court found that the State Engineer had implied statutory authority to conjunctively manage both surface and groundwater and to jointly administer across multiple basins after finding the basins were all interconnected water. Sullivan v. Lincoln County Water District, 542 P.3d 411 (Nev. 2024); Nev. Rev. Stat. Ann. § 533.085.

The Colorado 1969 Water Rights Determination & Administration Act provides for conjunctive use management by means of "augmentation plans" in order to encourage "maximum beneficial utilization of the waters of the state." Colo. Rev. Stat. § 37–92–501.5. Junior appropriators may satisfy senior rights by use of a comprehensive plan that protects senior priorities. These plans commonly provide for replacement of the seniors' water with groundwater. Other augmentation methods include development of new diversion and storage facilities, alternative points of diversion, water exchange projects, substitute supplies, and development of new sources of water. The plans are subject to terms and conditions designed to protect senior appropriators and must be approved by the State Engineer.

Typically, junior appropriators threatened with curtailment will enter into augmentation plans and share costs. A central water manager, who relies on hydrologic studies and computer models to formulate a basin-wide water budget, will administer some augmentation plans. Although there is some risk to seniors that their rights will not be satisfied because hydrologic data may be in error or the plan will fail for other reasons, the validity of augmentation plans was upheld in Cache LaPoudre Water Users Ass'n v. Glacier View Meadows, 550 P.2d 288 (Colo. 1976) (en banc).

In addition, Colorado law allows wells as alternate points of diversion for hydrologically connected surface sources. Colo. Rev. Stat. §§ 37–92–301(3)(b)-(c). Colorado law even requires seniors who have wells and surface diversions from the same source to use their wells as alternate points of diversion before they "call the river" (require upstream juniors to shut down). It is not clear how much expense courts will require seniors to bear in operating or deepening a well as an alternate point of diversion. It is likely that the Colorado courts will follow the same approach they use in well interference cases: require the senior's well to have a reasonable economic reach before a junior will be shut down. *See supra* Section II.B.5.

### 4. Regulation of Tributary Groundwater: The Colorado Example

As noted above in Section III.A.2, the Colorado State Engineer administers tributary groundwater as part of the system of surface priorities. Junior well owners are subject to shutdowns in the event of a senior call, but the Colorado Supreme Court has mandated that the State Engineer's power to protect senior rights be used judiciously in order to maximize economic use of water. In Fellhauer v. People, 447 P.2d 986 (Colo. 1968) (en banc), the court set aside an order shutting down junior wells because it was not shown that seniors would benefit. This is the tributary groundwater equivalent of the "futile call" doctrine (Chapter 3.IV, *supra*). For example, if a junior's pumping does not affect streamflow within twenty days, and if a senior's use would end within the twenty days (*e.g.*, at the end of the irrigation season), the junior is allowed to continue pumping. *Fellhauer,* 447 P.2d at 994.

The Colorado legislature reaffirmed *Fellhauer*'s mandate of maximum use and acceptance of the futile call doctrine for groundwater in the 1969 Water Rights Determination and Administration Act. The Act recognized vested water rights of well owners, but effectively required appropriators to have a reasonably efficient means of diversion. Colo. Rev. Stat. § 37–92–102(2). No one is permitted "to command the whole or a substantial flow of the stream merely to facilitate his taking [of a] fraction . . . ." City of Colorado Springs v. Bender, 366 P.2d 552, 555 (Colo. 1961) (en banc), citing Schodde v. Twin Falls Land & Water Co., 224 U.S. 107 (1912).

### 5. The Public Trust Doctrine and Groundwater

Several states, including Hawaii, Vermont, and Alaska, subject groundwater permits to the public trust doctrine even if groundwater pumping does not affect surface waters. The Supreme Court of Hawaii has held that the state's public trust doctrine "applies to all water resources without exception or distinction." In re Water Use Permit Applications, 9 P.3d 409, 445 (Haw. 2000). The court reasoned that all water is vital to the public welfare, whether it is found below or above ground, and that the public trust should be extended to groundwater because the doctrine "does not remain fixed for all time, but must conform to changing needs and circumstances." *Id.* at 447. Accordingly, groundwater permit decisions must "embod[y] a dual mandate of protection and maximum reasonable and beneficial use." *Id.* at 451. In a subsequent case, the court clarified the sweep of the doctrine, stating that, just as private trustees are judicially accountable to their beneficiaries for dispositions of the res, the legislative and executive branches are also accountable for dispositions of the public trust. In re Waiola O Molokai, Inc., 83 P.3d 664 (Haw. 2004). Although courts cannot supplant their judgment for that of the legislature or agency, courts must take a "close look" to determine if the decision in question complies with the public trust doctrine. *Id.* at 685. The court remanded the agency's determination that a private ranch's proposed water use would not interfere with public trust purposes for further fact finding.

In 2008, Vermont enacted legislation explicitly stating that the groundwater resources of the state are held in trust for the benefit of the public. Vt. Stat. Ann. tit. 10, § 1390. The Supreme Court of Vermont interpreted the statute and held that no taking occurred when a private property owner was deprived of groundwater, in part because groundwater is a public trust resource. In re DJK, LLC WW & WS Permit, 323 A.3d 911 (Vt. 2024).

Moreover, the Supreme Court of Alaska held that the public trust doctrine applies beyond navigable water, to "all other water, whether inland or coastal, fresh or salt, that is reasonably suitable for public use and utility." Williams Alaska Petroleum, Inc. v. State, 529 P.3d 1160, 1187 (Alaska 2023), citing Alaska Stat. Ann. § 38.05.965(21). As such, the court held that groundwater is a public trust resource. *Id.*

Other states, notably Wisconsin and California, apply the public trust doctrine when the groundwater is hydrologically connected to navigable waters. *See, e.g.,* Clean Wis., Inc. v. State Dep't of Nat. Res., 961 N.W.2d 621 (Wis. 2021); Lake Beulah Mgmt. Dist. v. State Dep't of Nat. Res., 799 N.W.2d 73, 76 (Wis. 2011) (holding "the DNR has the authority and a general duty to consider whether a proposed high capacity well may harm waters of the state"); Carlin Lake Ass'n, Inc. v. Carlin Club Properties, LLC, 929 N.W.2d 228 (Wis. App. 2019) (finding riparians were entitled to a permanent injunction against a lodge owner who attempted to transport groundwater for off-site commercial sale in violation of shoreland zoning).

In Envtl. Law Fnd. v. State Water Res. Control Bd., No. 34–2010–80000583, 2014 WL 8843074 (Cal. Super. July 15, 2014), *aff'd,* 237 Cal. Rptr. 3d 393 (Cal. App. 2018), the court held that the state must take the public trust into consideration when granting groundwater permits. *Id.* at 6 (*citing* National Audubon Society v. Superior Court, 658 P.2d 709, 728 (1983)). Within the last twenty years, the Scott River, a major tributary to the Klamath River, had experienced phases of "dewatering" due to increased groundwater pumping, most commonly during the summer months. Dewatering had reduced the river to a series of pools, negatively impacting both fish populations and recreation. The court concluded that the public trust doctrine "protects navigable waters from harms caused by the extraction of groundwater, where the groundwater is so connected to the navigable water that its extraction adversely affects public trust uses." *Id.* at 7. Effectively, the public trust protects hydrologically connected groundwater "if extraction of groundwater adversely impacts a navigable waterway to which the public trust doctrine does apply." *Id.* The court also found that the public trust doctrine co-existed with California's new Sustainable Groundwater Management Act. *Id.* at 9 (citing Cal. Water Code §§ 10720–10737.8).

## B. IMPORTED SUPPLIES AND INTENSIVE MANAGEMENT: THE CALIFORNIA EXAMPLE

Southern California's rapid population growth long ago created demands exceeding the capacity of water supplies. Persistent droughts are not uncommon in this semi-arid region, and 2020 through 2022 was California's driest three-year period on record. Public Policy Inst. of California, *Policy Brief: Drought and Groundwater Sustainability in California's Farming Regions* (June 2024). Large aquifers have been overdrafted and threatened with saltwater intrusion and subsidence. Meanwhile, building new aboveground storage reservoirs has become increasingly impractical due to excessive costs and environmental impacts. Local water users responded by implementing a unique system to increase the physical supply through actively recharged groundwater banking and management for conjunctive use.

The state legislature formed the Metropolitan Water District (MWD) in 1969 to meet the supplemental needs of its public agency members—several southern California municipalities and municipal water districts. Metropolitan Water District Act, Cal. Water Code Ann. §§ 109–1 through 109–551. MWD imports water from northern California and the Colorado River and wholesales it to MWD members, who then distribute it to local users and water companies. MWD uses some imported water to recharge aquifers, through spreading basins or injection wells, and the district later withdraws the water from storage by pumping. *See infra* Section IV (Groundwater Recharge and Storage).

To manage and distribute imported water and to integrate its use with naturally occurring groundwater, southern California has engaged in a two-step process. First, all groundwater rights in a particular basin must be adjudicated. Once basins have been adjudicated, metropolitan water districts may be formed to manage basin-wide development and use of water. Cal. Water Code Ann. § 109–25. The water district makes pumping allocations among users consistent with adjudicated rights, and levies pumping assessments to purchase imported water to fulfill the needs that cannot be met by local supplies. *Id.* § 109–315.

Some districts use market mechanisms to adjust uses of groundwater and imported water. The Orange County Water District buys imported water from MWD and then allocates imported water and groundwater by pricing incentives, attempting to achieve an economic solution to conjunctive use problems. The district sets a basin-wide goal for the proportional use of groundwater and imported MWD water. Users who pump more groundwater than the indicated proportion of their total entitlements are subject to a special pump tax equal to the difference between the cost of pumping an acre-foot of groundwater and the cost of buying an acre-foot of MWD water. Thus, everyone effectively pays the same for an acre-foot of water, whether groundwater or MWD water.

## IV. GROUNDWATER RECHARGE AND STORAGE

Storage capacity greatly enhances flexibility in water planning decisions. If erratic seasonal surface flows are collected and stored underground, they can be pumped and used as needed throughout the year. Aquifer storage avoids many of the high costs, environmental effects, evaporation losses, and pollution problems of surface reservoirs. As explained above in Section III.B, southern California uses underground storage in conjunction with its importation of waters from the Colorado River and northern California rivers. Similarly, Arizona has adopted a program to enable it to store Central Arizona Project water underground and pump it as needed.

There are several ways to augment the natural recharge of aquifers with imported surface water. Water can be placed directly into the aquifer through injection wells, or it can be spread on the overlying lands so that it percolates down in to the aquifer.

Despite its advantages over surface storage, underground storage may be infeasible unless the importer has legal rights in the stored supply. Public agencies and private investors are reluctant to undertake an expensive importation scheme without the right to recapture and to exclude others from taking waters it has captured or imported and stored. Absent comprehensive statewide programs to determine who has rights to use underground storage space, conjunctive use and underground water storage projects have been slow to gain momentum. Yet the cases support the existence of three types of storage rights: (1) the right of a public agency to import and store water without obligation to overlying landowners; (2) the right to protect the stored water against use by others; and (3) the right to recapture the stored water.

Commingling stored and naturally occurring groundwater does not cause the stored water to lose its separate identity. *See, e.g.*, Jensen v. Dep't of Ecology, 685 P.2d 1068 (Wash. 1984) (en banc). In California, underground storage constitutes a beneficial use, Cal. Water Code § 1242, and a public importer and storer has a right in the stored supply as long as its use does not harm existing groundwater rights. In City of Los Angeles v. City of San Fernando, 537 P.2d 1250 (Cal. 1975), the court held that Los Angeles had the exclusive right to recapture imported water it stored in an groundwater basin. In Niles Sand & Gravel Co. v. Alameda Cnty. Water Dist., 112 Cal. Rptr. 846 (Ct. App. 1974), a water district was engaged in a groundwater storage program. Niles pumped water out of its sand and gravel pit, which was hydrologically connected to the storage aquifer. The dewatering operation drew down the level of the stored water in the aquifer while the water district was attempting to recharge it to prevent salt-water intrusion. The court enjoined pumping, ruling that the storage plan was within the police power of the water district and that the district had a "public duty" to maintain the water level. Consequently, the gravel company's use was burdened with a "public servitude" in favor of storage; thus, there was no compensable taking. *Id.* at 854.

Similarly, the Nebraska Supreme Court held that a state law recognizing rights to store and recover water in the aquifers under the lands of others did not violate the property rights of overlying landowners. *See* In re Application U-2, 413 N.W.2d 290 (Neb. 1987) (approving an application for recognition of incidental aquifer storage); Neb. Rev. Stat. § 46–295 (recognizing that "rights to water intentionally or incidentally stored underground and rights to withdrawal of such water should be formally recognized and quantified").

The New Mexico legislature has encouraged conjunctive use through the Ground Water Storage and Recovery Act, which creates a permit procedure for storage and recovery projects. N.M. Stat. Ann. §§ 72–5A–1 through 72–5A–17. Prior to issuing a permit, the State Engineer must establish a storage account for each project and must limit well withdrawals to the "recoverable amount"—the amount that has reached the aquifer, remains in storage, and can be withdrawn without impairing vested rights. *Id.* § 72–5A–9. Absent compliance with this permit scheme, under New Mexico case law, once imported water percolates into an aquifer, it becomes public water subject to appropriation. Kelley v. Carlsbad Irrigation Dist., 415 P.2d 849 (N.M. 1966).

Statutes in several other states facilitate storage by authorizing permits or other types of regulatory programs. *See, e.g.,* Ariz. Rev. Stat. Ann. § 45–801.01 (encouraging a "flexible and effective regulatory program for the underground storage, savings and replenishment of water"); Utah Code Ann. § 73–3b–202 (authorizing underground storage permits if the project is hydrologically feasible, will not cause unreasonable harm to land, will not impair existing water rights, and will not adversely affect water quality); Wash. Rev. Code. Ann. § 90.44.460 (authorizing issuance of reservoir permits that enable artificial storage and recovery of water in underground formations).

## V. CONTROLLING GROUNDWATER CONTAMINATION

Some states have statutes that regulate pumping and/or regulate pollution to prevent groundwater contamination. Federal laws limit, mostly indirectly, the discharge or use of materials that may cause pollutants to enter groundwater. Common law remedies are also available to redress those who are harmed by aquifer pollution.

### A. REGULATION OF GROUNDWATER PUMPING

Groundwater extraction can cause pollutants to migrate from a contaminated aquifer into a relatively pure one. Improperly constructed wells and wells that draw out water in large quantities or at high rates can attract contaminated water into the aquifer. Sources of contamination include seawater intrusion, other saline or otherwise naturally contaminated waters, land disposal of pollutants, waste injection wells, and runoff from agriculture, city streets, and industry. The use of extracted groundwater can also cause pollution. If groundwater is already contaminated, its application to land or other uses can affect other aquifers or surface sources. A related problem is the "produced water" pumped incidentally as part of oil or gas extraction. Disposal of polluted produced water has become a major problem. *See, e.g.*, EQT Prod. Co. v. Dep't of Envtl. Prot., 193 A.3d 1137 (Pa. Comm. Ct. 2018) (affirming a penalty against a gas company that released wastewater from an impoundment); Starrh & Starrh Cotton Growers v. Aera Energy LLC, 63 Cal. Rptr. 3d 165 (Cal. Ct. App. 2007), *aff'd in part*, 2012 WL 210452 (Cal. Ct. App. 2012) (awarding a farmer $8.5 million against a company that contaminated well water by dumping millions of gallons of produced water). Concerns have mounted with the growth of hydraulic fracturing ("fracking") in recent years, prompting the U.S. Environmental Protection Agency to launch a Study of Hydraulic Fracturing for Oil and Gas and Its Potential Impact on Drinking Water Resources (2016), www.epa.gov/hfstudy.

A few states deny or condition well permits to prevent groundwater contamination by, for instance, controlling the rate and extent of extraction. In Arizona and Colorado, criteria for imposing permit conditions in certain districts or critical areas include prevention of groundwater contamination. Ariz. Rev. Stat. Ann. § 45–596(I); Colo. Rev. Stat. § 37–91–110. However, states rarely designate critical areas specifically to deal with contamination problems. For an exception, see Mont. Code Ann. § 85–2–506(5) (authorizing the designation of a controlled groundwater area if withdrawals adversely affect water quality or induce contaminant migration).

State permitting agencies may examine the effects of an application for a new well or for a change in well location to see if it will draw saline or other lower quality water into parts of an aquifer used by existing pumpers. *See* Texas Water Code § 36.001(8) (defining "waste" as "withdrawal of groundwater . . . at a rate and in an amount that causes or threatens to cause intrusion . . . of water unsuitable for agricultural, gardening, domestic, or stock raising purposes . . . [or] pollution or harmful alteration . . . by saltwater"); Fl. Admin. Code 40E–2.301 ("In order to obtain a permit, . . . an applicant must give reasonable assurances that the proposed water use . . . will not cause harmful saline water intrusion"). If serious degradation is likely, the agency may deny the permit, but the agency may consider minimal increases in the rate of intrusion or concentrations of pollution to be reasonable and grant the permit in the interest of allowing full development of water resources. Stokes v. Morgan, 680 P.2d 335 (N.M. 1984).

Virtually no jurisdictions deny the right to use groundwater because the use, as opposed to the extraction, of water will cause contamination. The Oklahoma Supreme Court has ruled, however, that an agency decision to allow withdrawal of groundwater for use in a waterflood operation (spreading water in old oil fields to help produce secondary recovery of oil) required a finding that it would not cause "waste" by either pollution or depletion. Oklahoma Water Res. Bd. v. Texas Cnty. Irr. and Water Res. Ass'n, 711 P.2d 38 (Okla. 1984).

## B. REGULATION OF POLLUTING ACTIVITIES

### 1. State Regulation

To prevent pollution, groundwater quality laws should regulate land use and other activities, in addition to well construction and use, because land-based activities are the major sources of aquifer contamination. Some laws classify aquifers according to the uses that can be made of them and limit pollution to protect those actual or anticipated uses. States that have enacted relatively comprehensive groundwater protection laws include Arizona, Florida, and Wisconsin. Ariz. Rev. Stat. Ann. § 45–401; Fla. Stat. § 403.061; Wis. Stat § 160.001.

Reporting requirements can assist a state in preventing or mitigating groundwater pollution. In Prokop v. Lower Loup Nat. Res. Dist., 921 N.W.2d 375 (Neb. 2019), the court upheld penalties assessed against a landowner who failed to submit the requisite annual report to a groundwater district. Reporting requirements were a proper exercise of the police power, as they were intended to address water quality and pollution control goals and, by failing to comply, the landowner prevented the district from collecting necessary data. Penalizing the landowner by issuing a cease and desist order against groundwater pumping did not amount to a taking without just compensation. *Id.* at 397 (citing Bamford v. Upper Republican Natural Res. Dist., 512 N.W.2d 642 (Neb. 1994)).

It is rare for the same agency that regulates groundwater allocation to regulate polluting activities. This fragmentation can cause a regulatory vacuum as well as interagency conflicts. *See, e.g.*, Matador Pipelines, Inc. v. Oklahoma Water Res. Bd., 742 P.2d 15 (Okla. 1987) (Water Board did not have jurisdiction to order remediation after a break in an oil pipeline because a different commission had exclusive authority over pollution).

The Keystone XL oil pipeline is a prominent example of instances where statutes other than water-related provisions may impact groundwater. The original proposed pipeline route from Alberta, Canada, crossed over large portions of the Ogallala (High Plains) Aquifer. Concerns about groundwater contamination sparked controversy and prompted a special session of the Nebraska legislature in 2011. Nebraska ultimately enacted legislation that gave the governor the power to approve the pipeline route. Neb. Rev. Stat. § 57–1503(4). However, the pipeline remained in legal limbo for years. Litigation in state court concerned whether the governor or the Public Service Commission had the power to regulate the route under the Nebraska Constitution. *See, e.g.*, In re Application No. OP-0003, 932 N.W.2d 653 (Neb. 2019). At the federal level, four Presidential administrations have attempted to stop or fast track the pipeline: President Obama vetoed, President Trump approved, President Biden revoked the permit, and President Trump rescinded the revocation. Veto Message to the Senate: S. 1, Keystone XL Pipeline Approval Act (Feb. 24, 2015); U.S. Army Corps of Engineers et al. v. Northern Plains Resource Council et al., 141 S. Ct. 190 (2020); Indigenous Envtl. Network v. Trump, 428 F. Supp.

3d 296 (D. Mont. 2019) (holding up construction with NEPA and other challenges to Trump approvals); Biden Exec. Order No. 13,990, 86 FR 7037 (Jan. 25, 2021); Trump Exec. Order No. 14,148, 90 FR 8237 (Jan. 28, 2025).

## 2. Federal Regulation

The Clean Water Act (CWA), described in Chapter 7.VI, *infra,* controls discharges of pollutants from point sources. 33 U.S.C. §§ 1251 *et seq.* Although the CWA does not apply to groundwater directly, it does regulate industrial and other point sources of pollutants into surface waters, thereby indirectly controlling some discharges into groundwater. *See* Cty. of Maui v. Hawaii Wildlife Fund, 590 U.S. 165 (2020) (finding a violation where pollutants injected into wastewater injection wells migrated through groundwater to navigable waters).

Non-point source pollution can seep into aquifers and run down wells from irrigation return flows and runoff from farming, construction, city streets, and mine sites. The CWA requires states to develop plans to control these sources, but there are no significant sanctions for failing to implement effective programs. 33 U.S.C. § 1329. However, in Nw. Envtl. Advocates v. U.S. Dep't of Commerce, 283 F. Supp. 3d 982 (W.D. Wash. 2017), the court allowed a challenge to the EPA's decision to give Assistance Grants to a state that allegedly lacked sufficient nonpoint pollution control practices.

The Safe Drinking Water Act, 42 U.S.C. § 300h, has a wellhead protection program that provides for designation and protection of wells and well fields used to extract drinking water. The Act's underground injection control program requires permits and adherence to certain standards. It also regulates disposal of liquid waste, including some hazardous waste that is injected into deep wells. To promote energy production, Congress explicitly exempted hydraulic fracking from the Act's definition of "underground injection." 42 U.S.C. § 300h(d)(1)(B)(ii).

Controlling landfills and cleaning up old dump sites are important means of preventing groundwater contamination. The Solid Waste Act, also known as the Resources Conservation and Recovery Act (RCRA), 42 U.S.C. §§ 6901–6991i, controls every aspect of hazardous waste generation, transportation, storage, treatment, and disposal. It also sets guidelines for state regulation of nonhazardous wastes. In addition, RCRA regulates underground storage tanks (such as gasoline tanks) to prevent leaking. 42 U.S.C. § 6991. States may seek authority for this program, and RCRA allows states to impose more stringent regulations and liabilities. *Id.* § 6991c, 6991g. *See* Mays v. City of Flint, Mich., 871 F.3d 437 (6th Cir. 2017) (addressing Flint residents' tort claims that the city and the state breached duties to them by violating SDWA standards for lead and copper in drinking water systems), *cert. denied*, 584 U.S. 932 (2018).

The Comprehensive Environmental Response, Compensation, and Liability Act (CERCLA), 42 U.S.C. §§ 9601 *et seq.*, also known as "Superfund," establishes a federal program to clean up releases of hazardous substances. CERCLA creates a cause of action against almost anyone connected with past disposal activities, not only for cleanup costs but also for damages to natural resources. The resource most frequently harmed is groundwater. *See* Utah v. Kennecott Corp., 801 F. Supp. 553 (D. Utah 1992) (setting aside CERCLA consent decree as giving inadequate protection to groundwater), *appeal dismissed,* 14 F.3d 1489 (10th Cir.), *cert. denied,* 513 U.S. 872 (1994); New Mexico v. Gen. Elec. Co., 335 F. Supp. 2d 1185, 1231 (D.N.M. 2004) (demanding $1.2 billion dollars for contamination of an aquifer that served the City of Albuquerque).

The Surface Mining Control and Reclamation Act (SMCRA), 30 U.S.C. §§ 1201–1328, aims to prevent water pollution by regulating coal-mining activities and reclaiming disturbed mine sites. SMCRA also requires that surface mine operators replace the water supply of any owner whose supply has been damaged by contamination. 30 U.S.C. § 1307(b).

Finally, legislation controlling the production and use of toxic substances provides indirect protection of groundwater. The Federal Insecticide, Fungicide, and Rodenticide Act (FIFRA), 7 U.S.C. §§ 136–136y, requires registration of pesticides and other chemicals regularly applied in farming. It also allows the U.S. EPA to limit the distribution, sale, or use of pesticides to protect the environment. The screening and reporting requirements of the Toxic Substances Control Act, 15 U.S.C. §§ 2601–2692, may also play a role in groundwater protection. *See, e.g.,* In re Methyl

Tertiary Butyl Ether (MTBE) Products Liability Litigation, 559 F. Supp. 2d 424 (S.D.N.Y. 2008).

## C. JUDICIAL REMEDIES

Most state courts entertain liability suits by well owners against persons, including other well owners, whose activities cause groundwater pollution. Common law claims for groundwater contamination include nuisance, trespass, negligence, and strict liability. *See, e.g.,* Mowrer v. Ashland Oil & Refining Co., 518 F.2d 659 (7th Cir. 1975); Benoit v. Saint-Gobain Performance Plastics Corp., 959 F.3d 491 (2d Cir. 2020). Some state laws, like Oklahoma's Oil Well Pollution Act, create special rights of action. Okla. Stat. tit. 52, § 296. *See also* EQT Prod. Co. v. Dep't of Envtl. Prot., 193 A.3d 1137 (Pa. Comm. Ct. 2018) (affirming a penalty of more than $1 million for violating the state's Clean Streams Law by releasing wastewater from a hydrofracking impoundment).

Groundwater contamination cases sometimes turn on whether federal statutes expressly or implicitly preempt state programs and actions. The outcome depends on the relevant federal provision. Congress preempts state law when it explicitly states its intent to displace state programs and causes of action, when Congress occupied the field, or when the state law is an obstacle to the accomplishment of federal objectives. *See, e.g.,* Atl. Richfield Co. v. Christian, 590 U.S. 1 (2020) (CERCLA did not preempt landowners' common law claims for restoration damages against the owner of a copper smelter that released pollutants into air, soil, and water); In re

Methyl Tertiary Butyl Ether (MTBE) Products Liab. Litig., 457 F. Supp. 2d 324 (S.D.N.Y. 2006) (the Clean Air Act did not preempt state tort claims), *aff'd,* 725 F.3d 65 (2d Cir. 2013).

Remedies for groundwater contamination may include injunctive relief and compensation for personal injuries and property damages. *See Benoit*, 959 F.3d at 509 (allowing claims for personal injuries and diminution of property value to proceed against a manufacturer whose perfluorooctanoic acid contaminated plaintiffs' drinking water); BSK Enterprises, Inc. v. Beroth Oil Co., 783 S.E.2d 236 (N.C. App. 2016) (holding that diminution in property value was the appropriate measure of damages for nuisance, trespass, and violation of statute based on groundwater contamination from a gas station's underground storage tanks); In re Methyl Tertiary Butyl Ether (MTBE) Prod. Liab. Litig., 67 F. Supp. 3d 619 (S.D.N.Y. 2014), *on reconsideration sub nom.* Orange Cty. Water Dist. V. Unocal Corp., No. SACV0301742CJCANX, 2018 WL 6133718 (C.D. Cal. 2018) (allowing certain remediation-related claims to proceed against gasoline stations for contamination of groundwater by methyl tertiary butyl ether (MTBE)). *Cf.* In re Lipsky, 460 S.W.3d 579 (Tex. 2015) (dismissing drilling company's counterclaims for defamation, business disparagement, and civil conspiracy against landowners who sued the company for contaminating their well). Recently, a federal judge approved a $10 billion settlement between 3M and numerous public water utilities to settle lawsuits stemming from the contamination of drinking water, including groundwater, with per- and polyfluoroalkyl substances (PFAS) from products manufactured by the company. In re Aqueous Film-Forming Foams Prods. Liab. Litig., No. 2:18-MN-2873-RMG, 2024 WL 1341122 (D.S.C. 2024).

Government regulators may also assess penalties against polluters. *See* Cty. of Maui v. Hawaii Wildlife Fund, 590 U.S. 165 (2020) (holding that the Clean Water Act authorizes penalties against a county that injected pollutants into wastewater injection wells when the pollutants migrated through groundwater to navigable waters).

# CHAPTER SIX
# DIFFUSED SURFACE WATERS

Much of water law deals with the use and allocation of water between users under riparian law, prior appropriation, and other legal systems. These systems address water that has entered a waterbody regulated by the state allocation system. Diffused surface waters, such as runoff from rainfall or snowmelt, are waters that have not yet joined a distinct watercourse. The law treats diffused surface water separately from surface water in watercourses.

When dealing with diffused surface waters, the law is often focused on how to channel, control, or drain the water to make the land more valuable. For example, landowners may direct surface flow toward another's land to keep water from collecting and saturating or flooding their property. In wetter climates, most litigation involves conflicts around channeling and drainage, while in more arid climates, conflicts arise around whether a landowner may take and use surface flows unrestrained by state laws concerning appropriation of water.

## I. DIFFUSED SURFACE WATERS DISTINGUISHED FROM WATERCOURSES

### A. DIFFUSED SURFACE WATERS

Surface water not in or connected with a watercourse is considered "diffused surface water." The Restatement (Second) of Torts § 846 defines this as "water from rain, melting snow, springs or seepage, or detached from subsiding floods, that lies or flows on the surface of the earth but does not form a part of a watercourse or lake." Diffused surface water usually includes water flowing in draws, swales, gullies, ravines, and hollows. It may also include water in puddles, depressions, marshes, and small ponds. State law may treat a spring as a watercourse rather than diffused surface water if the spring runs directly into a stream or has a large enough flow to constitute a stream. Martiny v. Wells, 419 P.2d 470 (Id. 1966). Generally, if water flows with some frequency and historical regularity, and carves a recognizable channel or reaches a lake or pond having some permanency, it is considered to be in a watercourse. Watts v. State, 140 S.W.3d 860, 870 fn. 6 (Tex. App. 2004); Happy v. Kenton, 247 S.W.2d 698, 701 (Mo. 1952); Hoyt v. City of Hudson, 27 Wis. 656, 661, 9 Am.Rep. 473 (1871). Some states, like California, distinguish floodwaters from diffused surface waters when they lose their connection with a stream by wildly overflowing the banks. Mogle v. Moore, 16 Cal. 2d 1, 104 P.2d 785 (1940); 6 Thompson on Real Property, Thomas Editions § 50.02(*o*) (2025).

## B. WATERCOURSES

State law defines which waters are within the definition of a "watercourse" for purposes of the allocation system in the states. In general, states exert authority over "natural watercourses." States usually define a natural watercourse as a body of water flowing in a defined channel with a bed and banks. *See, e.g.,* Locklin v. City of Lafayette, 7 Cal. 4th 327, 345, 867 P.2d 724, 734 (1994); State v. Hiber,

44 P.2d 1005 (Wyo. 1935). In both Texas and Kansas, a watercourse exists when there is a defined bed and bank, a current or flow of water, and a source of supply sufficient for irrigation use. Edwards Aquifer Authority v. Day, 274 S.W.3d 742, 752 (Tex. App. 2008), *aff'd*, 369 S.W.3d 814 (Tex. 2012); Johnson v. Board of County Com'rs of Pratt County, 913 P.2d 119, 127 (Kan. 1996). Indiana does not define a watercourse by whether there are beds and banks, but rather by whether there is a substantial existence, unity, regularity, and dependability of the water's presence or movement on a distinguishable course. Town of Avon v. West Central Conservancy Dist., 957 N.E.2d 598, 602 (Ind. 2011) (including flowing rivers as well as "self-contained" lakes and hydrologically connected aquifers). Most states require water to be present for a substantial portion of the year to qualify, but some states consider dry streams or lakebeds to be "natural watercourses." *See, e.g.,* Bilo v. El Dorado Broadcasting Co., 275 S.W.3d 660, 663–64 (Ark. App. 2008); Maddocks v. Giles, 728 A.2d 150, 152–53 (Me. 1999); Mogle v. Moore, 16 Cal. 2d 1, 8, 104 P.2d 785, 788 (1940). Water flowing in a surface depression as the result of rainfall or snowmelt is usually not considered to be in a watercourse (see *supra* Chapter 3.III.D).

Theoretically, the definition of a "watercourse" may include almost all waters. Most rivers have tributaries which in turn include not only small streams but also the gullies and washes that channel rainwater and snowmelt throughout the watershed. A watercourse may also include underground water that is hydrologically connected with surface water.

But there are limits to the confidence with which science can trace water destined for streams and lakes, and to the state's practical and political ability to impose controls on water use. Thus, each state adopts criteria for defining "watercourses" that come under state regulation.

## C. OTHER WATERS

Property owners may have to drain water, other than diffused surface waters, from their lands. For instance, a person using water diverted from a stream or lake (*e.g.*, for irrigation or to power a mill) may need to dispose of the unconsumed water, often referred to as "tail water." Tail water is not diffused surface water and it can only be drained across the land of another within a natural stream channel in a manner that does not increase a lower landowner's burden. Loosli v. Heseman, 162 P.2d 393 (Id. 1945).

Special rules apply to impounded water, such as in a reservoir. A landowner may sue for trespass or nuisance when their land is flooded by a neighboring landowner who builds a dam or otherwise backs up water (whether or not it is diffused surface water). Kowalski v. TOA PA V, 206 A.3d 1148 (Pa. 2019); Bobo v. Young, 61 So. 2d 814, 815 (Ala. 1952). Other theories of liability include negligence, Stott By & Through Dougall v. Finney, 950 P.2d 709 (Id. 1997), and strict liability for abnormally dangerous activities, Covey v. Brishka, 445 P.3d 785 (Mont. 2019); Cities Serv. Co. v. State, 312 So. 2d 799, 803 (Fla. App. 1975). However, if the flooding is continuous and satisfies the relevant statute of limitations, the landowner may gain a prescriptive right to flood the land. Stewart v. Shook Hill Rd. Prop. Owners' Ass'n, 726 So. 2d 694, 696 (Ala. App. 1998).

Sovereign immunity may shield government entities from common law tort claims when their structures flood another's property, but it does not shield the government from constitutional takings claims. Arkansas Fish and Game Comm'n v. United States, 568 U.S. 23 (2012); Akins v. State, 71 Cal. Rptr. 2d 314, 341 (1998), *as modified on denial of reh'g* (1998). In some states, water saturation and pooling caused by a government stormwater detention pond is not a compensable taking (even when applying the *Arkansas Game and Fish* multi-factor test). Kaltenberg v. County of Dane, 683 F. Supp.3d 875 (Wis. 2023). Also, property owners may be barred from a takings claim if the government opened the flood gates in an emergency. Orr v. United States, 166 Fed. Cl. 1 (2023).

## II. PROTECTION FROM DAMAGE BY SURFACE FLOWS

There are often disputes when diffused surface waters cannot be diverted directly into a watercourse without causing harm to others. For example, an upper landowner may augment natural drainage to make marshy land useful, divert floodwaters to protect land or buildings, or fill, build on, or pave land as part of developing it. In each case, the upper landowner is altering drainage patterns, which affects lower landowners. Lower landowners may construct dikes, buildings, or other obstructions to the flow of surface waters that back water up onto the lands of upper landowners. Historically, states split between two rather extreme and opposite rules to resolve such disputes: the "common enemy doctrine" and the "civil law doctrine." Today, most jurisdictions have integrated, if not entirely adopted, a torts-based reasonable use approach.

## A. COMMON ENEMY RULE

The common enemy rule, with its roots in English common law, provides that landowners may take any action necessary to avoid diffused surface waters without liability for resulting damage to one's neighbor. Such actions include building a barrier to water flowing down from adjoining land, such as a dike along one's upper boundary, or altering natural drainage patterns by a system of berms, ditches, or pumps to keep it out of a basement or away from a field. The doctrine may also allow development of drainage systems to augment natural drainage. Excavations may be made for drains and channels to collect and divert flows or accumulations of water. The only limitation is that one may not store surface water (as in a dam or reservoir) and then "cast it" upon another. Argyelan v. Haviland, 435 N.E.2d 973, 977 (Ind. 1982).

The common enemy rule is sometimes called the "Massachusetts rule," even though the namesake state has since rejected the rule. Graziano v. Riley, 983 N.E. 2d 249 (Mass. App. 2013); Tucker v. Badoian, 384 N.E.2d 1195 (Mass. 1978) (embracing a reasonable use rule). Although Indiana still follows the common enemy rule, *see, e.g.*, N.G. Hatton Trust v. Young, 97 N.E. 3d 282 (Ind. App. 2018), nearly all states that once followed that rule have modified it with the familiar tort concept of reasonableness. Deflection or other activity causing surface water to flow onto the lands of another must be in good faith, not be negligent, and not cause substantial harm. The modified rule still allows landowners to divert the flow of diffused surface waters, so long as not done maliciously, unreasonably, or negligently. Millard Farms, Inc. v. Sprock, 829 S.W.2d 1, 2 (Mo. Ct. App. 1991); McCauley v. Phillips, 219 S.E.2d 854, 858 (Va. 1975). Some states, Washington for example, have modified the rule so extensively that they effectively apply the reasonable use rule. Currens v. Sleek, 983 P.2d 626 (Wash. 1999).

## B. CIVIL LAW RULE: NATURAL FLOW THEORY

The civil law rule, traceable to the Code Napoleon, entitles every landowner to have the natural drainage maintained. Each owner has a reciprocal duty to refrain from adversely affecting others by damming, channeling, or diverting diffused surface waters that would change or increase drainage. The rule effectively places a servitude upon adjoining lands for natural drainage. The upper owner cannot modify the natural system of drainage so as to increase the burden on the lower owner, and the lower owner must accept the surface water that naturally drains onto his land. If a person interferes with the natural flow of surface waters and that interference results in hindering another's interest in the use and enjoyment of his land, that person is liable to the other. *See* Roberts v. Jensen, 477 P.3d 892 (Id. 2020) (stating that the upper landowner has a natural servitude of drainage across lower land, but cannot artificially accumulate the water and release it upon the lower landowner in an unnatural concentration).

The civil law rule is unsuited to settled areas because it prevents most development, inhibiting improvement of land. For example, construction of a building or paving a parking area displaces natural runoff. In rural areas, cultivation for agricultural use often depends on altering the natural drainage pattern. States adhering to a literal application of this doctrine would not permit these activities.

As with the common enemy doctrine, time has modified the civil law rule to fit societal needs. Several states have incorporated notions of reasonableness into the civil law doctrine to allow for some alteration of drainage patterns. Colorado and Iowa allow deviations that do not change the quantity or manner of flows. Hankins v. Borland, 431 P.2d 1007, 1010 (Colo. 1967); Ditch v. Hess, 212 N.W.2d 442, 448 (Iowa 1973). Maryland insists that its "reasonableness of use" test is merely a qualification of the civil law, though the outcomes are hard to distinguish from a reasonable use rule. Whitman v. Forney, 31 A.2d 630 (Md. 1943); Kidwell v. Bay Shore Dev. Corp., 194 A.2d 809 (Md. 1963). Some states, including Alabama, Florida, Pennsylvania, and South Dakota, have made "reasonable use" exceptions to the civil law rule to accommodate development in urban areas where lots are typically small and close together. *See, e.g.*, Matter of Drainage Permit 11-81, 922 N.W. 2d 263 (S.D. 2019) (application of civil rule, modified by reasonable use).

Additionally, some states have incorporated elements of the common enemy rule for flood waters. For instance, Arizona and California have held that while one may not interrupt the flow of diffused surface waters, one has the right to obstruct waters that have escaped from a natural watercourse, even if that sends water onto another's land. Southern Pac. Co. v. Proebstel, 150 P.2d 81 (Ariz. 1944); Mogle v. Moore, 16 Cal. 2d 1, 104 P.2d 785 (1940).

## C. REASONABLE USE DOCTRINE

Allowing landowners reciprocal rights to make reasonable alterations in the natural drainage of their property leads to increased uses of property and enhanced land values. Thus, courts and legislatures have crafted numerous exceptions to temper the effects of the common enemy and civil law rules. Most have adopted some form of the reasonable use doctrine as embodied in the Restatement (Second) of Torts §§ 822–831, 833.

New Hampshire was the first state to invoke the reasonable use doctrine to resolve disputes over diffused surface waters. Bassett v. Salisbury Mfg. Co., 43 N.H. 569 (1862). Other states have gradually come to embrace it. *See, e.g.*, McGlashan v. Spade Rockledge Terrace Condo Development Corp., 62

Ohio St. 2d 55 (1980). In the last several decades nearly two dozen states have modified their rules to apply principles of reasonable use. *See e.g.*, Sanford v. University of Utah, 488 P.2d 741 (Utah 1971); Tucker v. Badoian, 384 N.E.2d 1195 (Mass. 1978); State v. Deetz, 224 N.W.2d 407 (Wis. 1974).

The reasonable use doctrine takes either of two forms: nuisance or negligence. In jurisdictions that apply a nuisance-like theory, courts generally balance the gravity of harm against the utility of the conduct. To determine the gravity of harm, a court may consider the extent and character of the injury, the social value of the activity harmed, the suitability of the harmed use to the location, and the difficulty that the injured party would have had avoiding the harm. In evaluating the utility of the conduct, courts may consider the social value of the activity for the location, the impact on the activity if compensation for harm were required, and the difficulty to the person harmed of avoiding injury. McGlashan v. Spade Rockledge Terrace Condo Development Corp., 402 N.E.2d 1196 (Oh. 1980). These factors allow the courts to be flexible and steer away from the harsh results produced by the traditional doctrines.

Several other jurisdictions resolve drainage disputes with a negligence-like standard. Landowners who drain property in an unreasonable manner that proximately causes harm to a neighboring landowner are subject to liability claims. Hall v. Wood, 443 So. 2d 834 (Miss. 1983).

Regardless of the approach taken, the cases involving diffused surface water tend to be very fact specific. Often "reasonableness" criteria will not point clearly to a particular result. Several jurisdictions refer to the common enemy or civil law rule in deciding what is "reasonable." For example, California considers the reasonable use doctrine to be a modification of the civil law rule. The California Supreme Court, in deciding disputes over diffused surface waters, noted that judicial determinations of reasonableness depend on a case-by-case judgment. Keys v. Romley, 412 P.2d 529 (Cal. 1966). If the conduct and uses of both parties are reasonable and necessary, the burden of harm will fall on the landowner who changes the natural drainage system, a result that is consistent with the civil law rule.

## D. PUBLIC CONTROL OF SURFACE DRAINAGE

### 1. Public Drainage Projects

In the United States, there are numerous special districts that administer drainage projects. Drainage districts are typically formed under state law after a local election or petition showing consent of a majority of affected landowners. The public usually finances these projects, and the districts make assessments against all property benefited, whether all individual landowners have consented. Tex. Water Code Ann. § 56.011; La. Rev. Stat. Ann. § 38:1580; Kan. Stat. Ann. § 24–401; Mo. Ann. Stat. § 242.020. Local law may modify the rules of liability discussed above as applied to drainage districts to support the overall goals of the districts.

Projects undertaken by drainage districts can increase the agricultural capacity of drained lands and provide "new" land for buildings and other improvements. Indeed, these drainage district projects have reclaimed many thousands of acres of marshes and swamplands for development and use. Drainage or flood control districts may also construct and maintain levees to foster and protect development in floodplains.

In the mid to late 1990s, constructing concrete-lined channels to divert stormwater runoff away from developed areas was a common practice. More recently, the combination of aging infrastructure and climate change have overwhelmed these flood control measures. Many cities have added green infrastructure to drain, capture, store, infiltrate, and reduce the flow into sewer systems. Melissa Keeley, Althea Koburger, David P. Dolowitz, Dale Medearis, Darla Nickel & William Shuster, *Perspectives on the Use of Green Infrastructure for Stormwater Management in Cleveland and Milwaukee,* 51 Env't Mgmt. 1093, 1093–1108 (2013); Emma Knapik, Luigia Brandimarte & Mark Usher, *Maintenance in Sustainable Stormwater Management: Issues, Barriers and Challenges*, J. Env't Plan. & Mgmt. 1, 1–27 (2024). Some cities have begun to explore opportunities to use stormwater runoff for aquifer recharge and treatment. *See, e.g.,* Cal. Water Code § 10561.7 (allowing public entities to use stormwater captured from urban areas to augment water supplies). Floodplain managers have also begun to integrate wetland restoration into their plans. Christine A. Klein & Sandra B. Zellmer, *Mississippi*

*River Stories: Lessons from A Century of Unnatural Disasters,* 60 SMU L. Rev. 1471, 1520 (2007).

## 2. Public Restrictions on Draining Wetlands

A wetland is an "ecosystem that depends on constant or recurrent, shallow inundation or saturation at or near the surface of the substrate." National Research Council, *Wetlands: Characteristics and Boundaries* 3 (1995). Prospective developers may view wetlands as obstacles, but wetlands provide important habitat for migratory waterfowl and other birds, fish, and wildlife. Drainage has an adverse effect on habitat and may also diminish recreational opportunities, increase fluctuations in streamflows, create flooding problems, and lower groundwater levels. Consequently, the federal government, states and tribes have passed laws regulating activities that would impair the desirable qualities of swamps, marshes, and other wetlands. *See, e.g.*, R.I. Gen. Laws Ann. § 2–1–21 (prohibiting drainage of freshwater wetlands without approval of the state); Minn. Stat. Ann. § 103G.221 (prohibiting drainage of "public waters wetlands" unless they are replaced by wetlands with equal or greater value); Bad River Reservation Wetland And Watercourse Protection Ordinance, Bad River Band of the Lake Superior Chippewa Indians Tribal Code § 3.11.020 (2009) (finding preserving wetlands necessary to maintain hydrologic, economic, recreational, subsistence, cultural, spiritual, and aesthetic assets for current and future residents of the Bad River Reservation).

The federal Clean Water Act (CWA) regulates pollution of "navigable waters," which it defines as "the waters of the United States ["WOTUS"], including the territorial seas." CWA § 502(7), 33 U.S.C. § 1362(7). *See supra* Chapter 7.VI. Whether WOTUS includes adjacent wetlands has been heavily contested since the 1980s.

In U.S. v. Riverside Bayview Homes, Inc., 474 U.S. 121, 133 (1985), the U.S. Supreme Court upheld CWA jurisdiction over non-navigable tributaries and adjacent wetlands. However, in Solid Waste Agency of Northern Cook County v. Corps of Engineers, 531 U.S. 159 (2001) (SWANCC), the Court concluded that the U.S. Corps of Engineers' (Corps') Migratory Bird Rule, which asserted jurisdiction over isolated, non-navigable wetlands that provide bird habitats, exceeded the Corps' statutory authority. The Court emphasized Congress' express use of the term "navigable" in the CWA, and found that clear congressional intent is required "[w]here an administrative interpretation of a statute invokes the outer limits of Congress' power," especially where it encroaches on a traditional state power like land use planning. *Id.* at 171.

Then in Rapanos v. United States, 547 U.S. 715 (2006), Justice Kennedy's concurring opinion stated that federal jurisdiction rests on a "significant nexus" between the wetlands or other waterbodies in question and actually navigable waters. If wetlands significantly affect the chemical, physical, and biological integrity of navigable waters, the Corps has jurisdiction over such waters. *Id.* at 779–80.

Kennedy's concurrence controlled in many courts, and in 2015 the Corps and the Environmental Protection Agency (EPA) released a rule with a definition of WOTUS that relied primarily on the significant nexus test. 80 Fed. Reg. 37054 (2015). *See, e.g.*, National Ass'n of Mfrs. v. Dep't of Defense, 583 U.S. 109, 116–117 (2018) (providing history of the 2015 WOTUS rule). The Trump Administration reversed course in 2020 by promulgating a much narrower definition that excluded many wetlands, some tributaries, and ephemeral streams and pools, but a district court quickly vacated this rule after determining that it violated the Administrative Procedure Act and raised the possibility of serious environmental harm. *See* 85 Fed. Reg. 22250; Pascua Yaqui Tribe v. United States Env't Prot. Agency, 557 F. Supp. 3d 949, 956 (D. Ariz. 2021).

In 2023, the Supreme Court in *Sackett v. EPA* rejected the significant nexus test and upended decades of EPA and Corps policy by announcing that, in order to be covered by the CWA, wetlands must have a "continuous surface connection" to traditional WOTUS such that it is "difficult to determine where the 'water' ends and where the 'wetland' begins." Sackett v. Env't Prot. Agency, 598 U.S. 651, 678–79 (2023). Following this decision, the EPA and the Corps issued a new rule that redefined "adjacent" waters to mean "having a continuous surface connection" to WOTUS, removed the term "significant nexus" wherever it appeared, removed "insterstate wetlands" from the defined list of WOTUS categories, and removed wetlands and streams from the WOTUS category of "additional waters". 88 Fed. Reg. 3004, amended by 88 Fed. Reg. 61964 (codified at 33 C.F.R. 328) (the "Amended 2023 Rule"). Due to ongoing litigation, the Amended 2023 Rule is not operative in all states. As of October 2025 the EPA and the Corps are still refining their approach post-*Sackett*. See 90 Fed. Reg. 13428.

For those wetlands still covered by the CWA, anyone who attempts to fill, dredge, drain, or otherwise modify them must obtain a 404 permit from the Corps. 33 U.S.C. § 1344(a). The EPA is authorized to veto a 404 permit if the discharge of fill material would have "unacceptable adverse effect on municipal water supplies, shellfish beds and fishery areas (including spawning and breeding areas), wildlife, or recreational areas." *Id.* § 1344(c). *See* Mingo Logan Coal Co. v. U.S. EPA, 829 F.3d 710 (D.C. Cir. 2016) (upholding EPA's veto of a coal mine's 404 permit). States and tribes may also use a 401 water quality certification to impact a Corp-issued 404 permit that fails to comply with water quality standards, and may define regulated wetlands more expansively to include isolated wetlands. Rajpreet K. Grewal & Melissa K. Scanlan, *Navigating Rough Waters After Sackett v. EPA: Federal, Tribal, and State Strategies*, 50 Colum. J. Env'l. L. 61 (2025).

## III. USE OF DIFFUSED SURFACE WATERS

The regulation of surface water often depends on a state's definition of water subject to state control and management. States vary as to whether they include diffused surface water within their water law allocation systems. *See* Section I.B, *supra*. The approaches are described below, followed by a discussion of rainwater harvesting.

## A. USE OF DIFFUSED SURFACE WATERS

Most states recognize an absolute right of landowners to use diffused surface waters on their lands, including waters from ravines and gullies, rainfall, snowmelt, and any standing water. This entitles them to dam, store, use, or sell the water and, consequently, to prevent it from flowing to adjoining lands. However, the application of this rule varies among states, particularly regarding which waters evade regulation. As noted above in Section I, most states limit regulatory control to "natural streams" or "watercourses" as opposed to diffused surface waters. For example, Indiana and South Dakota allow landowners to capture diffused surface waters. Gene B. Glick Co. v. Marion Const. Corp., 331 N.E.2d 26, 31 (Ind. 1975); Terry v. Heppner, 239 N.W. 759, 759 (S.D. 1931). North Dakota achieves the same result by excluding diffused waters from state control. Burlington N. & Santa Fe Ry. Co. v. Benson Cnty. Water Res. Dist., 618 N.W.2d 155, 160 (N.D. 2000). Similarly, in Arizona and New Mexico, the omission of diffused waters from the definition of waters subject to appropriation effectively excludes them from state control. Espil Sheep Co. v. Black Bill & Doney Parks Water Users Ass'n, 492 P.2d 450, 452 (Ariz. App. 1972); N.M. Stat. Ann. § 72–1–1.

Some riparian states exercise control over diffused surface waters by subjecting them to the reasonable use doctrine. *See, e.g.,* Dudley v. Beckey, 567 A.2d 573, 574 (N.H. 1989); Enderson v. Kelehan, 32 N.W.2d 286, 289 (Minn. 1948). Iowa affirms the right of a landowner to use diffused surface waters, but the right is conditioned on a continuation of minimum flows necessary to protect the rights of lower water users. Iowa Code Ann. § 455B.270.

States seeking broad control of waters are likely to define diffused surface waters narrowly, since watercourses are subject to state regulation. A few western states, including Nevada and Oregon, claim regulatory control over all waters. In re Manse Spring, Nye Cnty., 108 P.2d 311, 314 (Nev. 1940); O.R.S. § 537.110. A Texas statute explicitly exerts state control over all "storm water, floodwater, and rainwater of every river, natural stream, canyon, ravine, depression, and watershed in the state" by making it the "property of the state." Tex. Water Code Ann. § 11.021. The Texas Supreme Court limited the effect of this statute by holding that it cannot apply to lands granted prior to the effective date of the law because the right to such water had vested in the landowners. Turner v. Big Lake Oil Co., 96 S.W.2d 221, 228 (Tex. 1936). The provision was further qualified by a decision holding that "[d]iffuse surface water belongs to the owner of the land on which it gathers, so long as it remains on that land prior to its passage into a natural watercourse." City of San Marcos v. Texas Comm'n on Envtl. Quality, 128 S.W.3d 264, 272 (Tex. App. 2004).

Utah and Colorado also extend state control to diffused surface waters. Utah asserts jurisdiction over all waters in the state, thereby prohibiting the use of diffused surface waters outside the state regulatory scheme. Stubbs v. Ercanbrack, 368 P.2d 461, 463 (Utah 1962); *see* Richlands Irrigation Co. v. Westview Irrigation Co., 80 P.2d 458 (Utah 1938) (holding that all water destined for a stream is effectively part of the stream). Similarly, Colorado's Constitution provides that "natural streams" are within the state's power. Colo. Const. Art. 16, § 5. The Colorado courts have construed this provision as reaching diffused surface water, so that a landowner may not capture and use runoff destined for a stream outside of the appropriation system. Empire Lodge Homeowners' Ass'n v. Moyer, 39 P.3d 1139, 1148 (Colo. 2001); Nevius v. Smith, 279 P. 44 (Colo. 1929). Colorado and Utah base their approach upon the realization that stream flow depends on runoff. Landowners may still acquire water rights in diffused surface waters so long as they comply with state appropriation law.

## B. RAINWATER CATCHMENT

Rainwater catchment is a mechanism by which rainwater is collected, either actively or passively, and then made available for various uses. Active rainwater catchment involves a cistern or other artificial structure that gathers rain and diverts the stored water to gardens, lawns, or indoor uses. Frequently, landowners use active catchment to supplement residential uses of water. Passive rainwater catchment usually involves using the contours of the earth to collect the rain for irrigation or groundwater recharge. Troy L. Payne & Janet Neuman, *Remembering Rain*, 37 Envtl. L. 105 (2007).

States that follow the prior appropriation doctrine have struggled with how to handle rainwater harvesting. Aastha Madaan & Alf W. Brandt, *Western States Recognize Rainwater Capture for Water Supply*, ABA Water Res. Committee Newsl., Feb. 2013, at 12. If water is being collected at the source, there may be less available for downstream appropriators. Some states, like Colorado, have passed statutes that require a permit to harvest rainwater for non-residential use or storage beyond 110 gallons. Col. Rev. Stat. Ann. § 37–90–105(f). Permits limit the amount, use, and location of rainwater that can be appropriated. Permits are not required for small residential rainwater barrels with a combined storage capacity of 110 gallons or less. Colo. Rev. Stat. Ann. § 37–96.5–103.

Some states adopt a more neutral approach to rainwater catchment. Utah, for example, allows the harvest of rainwater so long as there is no injury to downstream appropriators. Wrathall v. Johnson, 40 P.2d 755, 766 (Utah 1935). Utah does not require a permit, but those who harvest rainwater must register with the state engineer. Utah Code Ann. § 73–3–1.5(5)(a). California does not require a permit for the collection of rooftop rainwater. Cal. Water Code § 10574.

Other arid states encourage, or even mandate, rainwater catchment. Arizona accomplishes this through city-level ordinances for xeriscaping and rainwater harvesting. *See, e.g.,* Tucson Unified

Development Code § 7.6.6.E.2. California encourages homeowners to build new rainwater capture systems by excluding the value of those permanent improvements from their property tax assessments (effective until 1/1/2029). Cal. Rev. & Tax. Code § 74.8; California SBOE Letter to Assessor 2018/062. Texas does not charge any sales tax on purchased items used for capturing and storing rainwater, which can include collection surfaces, filtration and purification equipment, gutters and downspouts, rain barrels, roof washers and flush diverters, and screens and filters. Tex. Tax Code § 151.355; Texas Tax Policy News (May 2017).

New Mexico similarly encourages rainwater capture, but with the condition that any rainwater catchment should not reduce the amount of runoff that would have occurred from the site in its natural pre-development state. Rainwater Harvesting, N.M. Office of the State Eng'r, https://www.ose.state.nm.us/WUC/wuc_rainHarvesting.php (visited Oct. 1, 2020). Some cities in New Mexico have adopted ordinances that require rainwater harvesting for large residential and commercial development. Santa Fe Code § 14–8.4.

Even wetter states and cities promote rainwater catchment as a strategy to reduce stormwater entering and overwhelming combined sewer systems. New York City offers a property tax abatement for eligible buildings with "green roofs" that have vegetation that can absorb rainwater. N.Y. Real Prop. Tax Law § 499–bbb (sunsetting June 30, 2027).

Rainwater harvesting may seem like a relatively new innovation, but ancient societies relied extensively on active and passive collection systems for both domestic and agricultural purposes. *See Payne, supra,* at 114, 121. Today, climate change, drought, and overdevelopment are stimulating increased interest in rainwater harvesting and other conservation techniques, old and new.

# CHAPTER SEVEN
# NAVIGABLE WATERS

Use of navigable waterways has played an important role in the exploration, settlement, and economic development of North America. Lewis and Clark's exploration of the Louisiana Purchase lands relied partly on river transport, as did the early westward movement of settlers. Before the advent of railroads and modern motorized transport, waterways provided the most feasible means of shipping freight. Large cities grew on the banks of the nation's rivers, nourished by these natural arteries of transportation and trade. Accordingly, there was strong federal interest in assuring the free flow of commerce along navigable waterways.

The federal government continues to play a significant role in water resources management through its primacy in matters concerning navigation, water development projects, public lands management, regulation of water quality, and protection of endangered species. As the federal role in water resources management has grown, so too have tensions between state and federal sovereignty. Conflicts tend to be especially acute in the western states because of water scarcity and the concentration of federal lands there.

Waters within state boundaries are generally allocated according to state and local laws absent some preemptive exercise of congressional power. In California Oregon Power Co. v. Beaver Portland Cement Co., 295 U.S. 142 (1935), the Supreme Court held that persons taking title to public lands take only those water rights perfected according to state law because estates in land and water were severed by the 1877 Desert Land Act, 43 U.S.C. § 321. Nevertheless, federal authority is paramount when Congress chooses to exercise a constitutionally based power that requires water. The sources of federal authority include the commerce power (and its subsidiary the navigation power), the property power, and the treaty power. Even the defense power has been invoked to uphold the federal government's construction of a hydroelectric dam that provided power to munitions plants. Ashwander v. Tennessee Valley Auth., 297 U.S. 288 (1936). The question is rarely whether power *exists*, but rather whether Congress *intended* to exercise its power to displace state law.

Several constitutional provisions, plus the equal footing doctrine, operate as constraints on federal power over navigable waters. The Tenth and Eleventh Amendments protect the states' reserved powers and their sovereign immunity from certain lawsuits, while the Fifth Amendment requires due process and just compensation for the taking of property for public use. The equal footing doctrine places new states on equal footing with the original thirteen colonies, and gives them sovereign and proprietary interests in submerged lands underlying navigable waters. Pollard's Lessee v. Hagan, 44 U.S. (3 How.) 212 (1845).

The preemptive federal power to reserve waters from appropriation in order to carry out the purposes designated for public lands is discussed in Chapter Eight. This chapter is concerned with other uses of federal power pertaining to navigable waters.

## I. CONTEXT COUNTS IN DETERMINING NAVIGABILITY

Historically, navigation has had tremendous commercial importance throughout history. In dividing sovereign prerogatives between the states and the national government, the Constitution gives commerce power to the U.S. Congress. U.S. Const. art. I § 8, cl. 3. In Gibbons v. Ogden, 22 U.S. 1 (1824), the Supreme Court held that a state grant to Robert Fulton of an exclusive right to operate steamships on New York waterways was repugnant to the commerce clause. Chief Justice Marshall declared, "All America understands, and has uniformly understood, the word 'commerce' to comprehend navigation." *Id.* at 190. *See* Kaiser Aetna v. United States, 444 U.S. 164 (1979) ("It has long been settled that Congress has extensive authority over this Nation's water under the Commerce Clause.").

Courts have generally accepted explicit congressional findings that a statutory provision is necessary for navigation as conclusive evidence that the provision is within the commerce power. *See, e.g.*, United States v. Chandler-Dunbar Water Power Co., 229 U.S. 53 (1913); United States v. Twin City Power Co., 350 U.S. 222 (1956). In an early case, the United States sought to enjoin a private irrigation project from diverting water from a non-navigable tributary of a river because the diversions threatened the navigability of the river's mainstem. The Supreme Court held that the navigation power extended to tributaries of navigable rivers, upholding a federal statute that prohibited obstructions to the "navigable capacity" of United States waters. United States v. Rio Grande Dam & Irr. Co., 174 U.S. 690, 708 (1899). The Court has even upheld federal projects that arguably interfere with navigability as proper exercises of the commerce power. *See* Arizona v. California, 283 U.S. 423 (1931) (rejecting Arizona's contention that the recital of navigation as the purpose of the Boulder Canyon Project Act, which authorized extensive damming and consumption of the Colorado River, was a subterfuge). In addition, the Court upheld flood control projects on non-navigable tributaries as within the purview of the commerce clause. Oklahoma ex rel. Phillips v. Guy F. Atkinson Co., 313 U.S. 508 (1941). However, in United States v. Gerlach Live Stock Co., 339 U.S. 725 (1950), the Court did not accept Congress's declaration in the Flood Control Acts of 1937 and 1940 that the comprehensive multi-purpose Central Valley Project was "for the purposes of improving navigation. . . ." Nevertheless, the Court found authority for the project under the constitutional power to spend for the general welfare. *Id.* at 738 (citing U.S. Const. art. I, § 8, cl. 1).

Beyond the commerce clause power, issues often arise as to which definition of "navigability" applies to a particular situation. It is critical to consider the context of the dispute to determine whether the waterbody in question is "navigable" in fact and in law. These topics are covered in detail in the following sections of this chapter, but a snapshot of the legal landscape is provided here.

The federal test of navigability for admiralty jurisdiction—the body of law that governs maritime disputes—was first articulated by the Supreme Court in The Daniel Ball, 77 U.S. 557, 563 (1871): "Those rivers must be regarded as public navigable rivers in law which are navigable in fact. And they are navigable in fact when they are used, or are susceptible of being used, in their ordinary condition, as highways for commerce, over which trade and travel are or may be conducted in the customary modes of trade and travel on water." While the issue in *The Daniel Ball* involved admiralty, the Court subsequently adopted the same test for determining ownership of submerged lands beneath rivers and lakes. *See, e.g.*, United States v. Utah, 283 U.S. 64, 76 (1931); PPL Montana v. Montana, 565 U.S. 576, 592 (2012).

A narrower test has emerged to determine whether the federal government must compensate a private property owner for taking an interest in a waterbody or submerged lands. This doctrine, known as the navigational servitude, recognizes the public's paramount interest in the flows of "great navigable streams," and makes private rights subordinate on such streams. However, only those waterbodies that are capable "of being used as a continuous highway for the purpose of navigation in interstate commerce" in their natural condition are subject to the non-compensation rule of the navigational servitude. *Kaiser-Aetna*, 444 U.S. at 178.

Several modern statutes define navigability much more broadly. For example, the Federal Power Act defines navigable waters as those waterbodies that are suitable "for use for the transportation of persons or property in interstate or foreign commerce." 16 U.S.C. § 796(8). The Clean Water Act (CWA) casts an even broader net by defining navigable waters as "waters of the United States, including the territorial seas." 33 U.S.C. § 1362(7). A waterway does not need to be navigable in fact by commercial or recreational vessels to be covered by the CWA. U.S. v. Riverside Bayview Homes, 474 U.S. 121 (1985). Even some wetlands adjacent to navigable rivers and lakes may be included, although most intermittent flows of water are not. Sackett v. Env't Prot. Agency, 598 U.S. 651, 676 (2023). For details on the CWA's definition of "navigable waters," see *supra* Section VI and Chapter 6.D.2.

In addition to the myriad definitions found at the federal level, states apply their own definitions of navigability for purposes such as the public trust doctrine and public recreational access and use. These topics are covered in Sections II.B–C of this chapter.

## II. NAVIGABILITY FOR TITLE

Determining title to submerged lands is one of the most important uses of the term "navigability." Whether a waterway is navigable for title turns on whether it is "navigable in fact." The Daniel Ball, 77 U.S. 557, 563 (1870). It is not necessary that the waterway is actually used for navigation at a given time; if the stream once was navigable, navigability for title is not defeated by subsequent disuse. Utah v. United States, 403 U.S. 9 (1971); United States v. Appalachian Elec. Power Co., 311 U.S. 377, 407 (1940). If the waterbody is navigable when a state enters the Union, under the Equal Footing Doctrine, title to the submerged lands passes to the state. PPL Montana v. Montana, 565 U.S. 576 (2012). From that point forward, states have leeway to adopt a state law definition of "navigability" to determine ownership, public access rights, and the application of the public trust doctrine.

## A. FEDERAL DEFINITION OF NAVIGABILITY FOR TITLE

Under English common law, people possess the right to navigate, hunt, and fish on certain public waterways. Submerged lands that were susceptible to these uses were held by the Crown, subject to public rights. Unlike other lands held by the Crown, these lands could not be used or conveyed by the monarch contrary to public rights. Because of the nature of the public's uses of the waterways, these restrictions were held to apply to all lands affected by the ebb and flow of the tide. Although tidal influence may have adequately described the waterways that were most important to the public in the island kingdom of England, it fell short in the United States, where large navigable rivers go far inland, well beyond the point where they are affected by the tides. Consequently, the U.S. Supreme Court expanded federal jurisdiction and title beyond the "ebb and flow" test in favor of looking also at the navigable character of the river or lake. The Propeller Genesee Chief v. Fitzhugh, 53 U.S. 443 (1851).

Generally speaking, if a stream or lake was navigable under the federal test (explained in detail below), title to the bed passed to the state upon its admission to the Union. Litigation over title of submerged lands has arisen when both the federal government and a state claim title, or between grantees when both sovereigns have attempted to transfer the same land. *See* Alaska v. U.S., 545 U.S. 75 (2005) (finding that Congress retained title to submerged lands underlying the waters of Glacier Bay National Park in the Alaska Statehood Act). In some cases, disputes arise over oil and other valuable resources found in the submerged lands. *See, e.g.*, Boone v. Kingsbury, 273 P. 797 (Cal. 1928); Phillips Petroleum Co. v. Mississippi, 484 U.S. 469 (1988); PPL Montana v. Montana, 565 U.S. 576 (2012).

The navigability for title doctrine granted new states title to ribbons of land through large expanses of federal public lands. The original thirteen states inherited their sovereignty from foreign nations, principally England. Because the Crown held title to the beds and waters in all waters affected by the tide, the Crown's rights passed to the original thirteen states as England's successors. Upon formation of the United States, the states ceded control of the waters flowing in navigable rivers and granted the national government the power to regulate interstate and foreign commerce. Because commerce was then primarily waterborne, the commerce clause was understood to establish federal control of navigable waterways. Thus, control of the *flow* was necessarily surrendered to the federal government, but the states retained title to the *beds*, subject to the federal government's "navigational servitude"—or right to keep waterways open to navigation. As such, the state's title to the beds comes by operation of the Constitution and not as a conveyance from Congress. Idaho v. Coeur d'Alene Tribe, 521 U.S. 261 (1997).

In Pollard v. Hagan, 44 U.S. (3 How.) 212, 216 (1845), the Supreme Court held that states acquired title to noncoastal tidelands upon admission into the Union. Prior to admission, tidelands were held in trust by the federal government for the people of future states. Later, the Court held that *coastal* tidelands remained in federal ownership. United States v. California, 332 U.S. 19 (1947). Congress responded by passing the Submerged Lands Act, which turned over control of tidelands to the states. 43 U.S.C. § 1311.

The definition and rules for deciding whether a waterway is navigable are matters of federal common law. Hughes v. Washington, 389 U.S. 290 (1967). The federal test of navigability for title is whether the waterbody was "navigable in fact;" meaning the waterway must have been susceptible to being used as an "avenue of commerce" in its ordinary condition at the time of statehood. The Daniel Ball, 77 U.S. 557 (1870). The Great Salt Lake was found to meet the test based on evidence that a few small boats used the lake for trade at the time Utah became a state. Utah v. United States, 403 U.S. 9 (1971). In contrast, upper Missouri River segments that included waterfalls and other obstructions that had to be portaged by canoes at the time of statehood were not "navigable in fact." PPL Montana v. Montana, 565 U.S. 576, 597–99 (2012). *See* N. Carolina v. Alcoa Power Generating, Inc., 853 F.3d 140 (4th Cir. 2017), *cert. denied,* 583 U.S. 1115 (2018) (finding that a 45-mile segment characterized by shoals containing waterfalls, ledges, and boulders was not navigable at statehood).

In addition to lands beneath navigable waters, the federal government also conveyed to new states the beds of non-coastal, non-navigable waters that were influenced by the tides. Phillips Petroleum Co. v. Mississippi, 484 U.S. 469 (1988). These were former Crown lands too, but since they were not navigable, the federal government did not assume admiralty jurisdiction or a navigational servitude over them. *Id.* at 476. They remained, nevertheless, subject to the public trust for non-navigation purposes. Thus, the Supreme Court held that the beds of non-coastal tidelands were held in trust by the United States until a state was formed, at which point they passed to the new state. *Id.* at 484. *See* Section II.C below (The Public Trust Doctrine).

Submerged land extending from the water to the mean high water line belongs to the state. (This line is the shoreline "established by the fluctuations of water and indicated by physical characteristics such as a clear, natural line impressed on the bank. . .", *see* 33 C.F.R. § 329.11(a)(1)). Along a navigable watercourse, riparian property ownership extends from the uplands to this line. The mean high-water line also delineates the area in which the federal navigational servitude may operate to destroy private property interests that interfere with navigation without paying compensation. *See* Section III.B below.

In Alaska, state ownership of submerged lands underlying navigable waters has led to unique challenges regarding access to waterways and adjacent federal public lands. In Sturgeon v. Frost, 587 U.S. 28 (2019), the Supreme Court interpreted the Alaska Native Interest Lands Conservation Act (ANILCA), 16 U.S.C. § 3103, to preclude the National Park Service's regulation of hovercraft on navigable waters within the Yukon-Charley National Preserve. It reasoned that, under the statute, lands (including water) owned by the State of Alaska are not "subject to the regulations applicable solely to public lands" within a National Preserve. *Id.* at 39–40 (citing 16 U.S.C. § 3103(c)).

As for the beds of non-navigable waters, title usually passed from the federal government to riparian landowners. However, some states took title to the lands beneath certain non-navigable waters that had not been conveyed to private parties at the time of statehood. *See* Shortell v. Des Moines Electric Co., 172 N.W. 649 (Iowa 1919); Angelo v. R.R. Comm'n, 217 N.W. 570 (Wis. 1928).

### B. STATE DEFINITIONS OF NAVIGABILITY FOR TITLE

The U.S. Supreme Court has recognized that states may allocate navigable waters within their borders, riparian lands, and state-owned submerged lands according to state law. PPL Montana, LLC v. Montana, 565 U.S. 576, 591 (2012); Arkansas v. Tennessee, 246 U.S. 158, 176 (1918). With some exceptions, "it is left to the States to determine the rights of riparian owners in the beds of navigable streams which, under federal law, belong to the State." Bonelli Cattle Co. v. Arizona, 414 U.S. 313, 319 (1973), *overruled on other grounds,* Oregon v. Corvallis Sand & Gravel Co., 429 U.S. 363 (1977). Thus, states may adopt restrictions on conveyances of private or state-owned beds of waterways by common law or by statute. These restrictions, and commensurate public use rights, are often based on a state definition of navigability.

States vary considerably in the tests they use to delineate public versus private title to the beds and banks of waterbodies within their boundaries. *See* Reed D. Benson, *Public Ownership, Public Rights: Recreational Stream Access Decisions in the Mountain West,* 23 Wyo. L. Rev. 73, 74 (2023); Robin Kundis Craig, *Navigability and its Consequences: State Title, Mineral Rights, and the Public Trust Doctrine,* 60 RMMLF-INST 7–1 (2014). Some states recognize both the navigable-in-fact test and the ebb and flow test in asserting state title to submerged lands. Others use a floatability or "saw log" definition, asking whether a stream would allow passage of valuables such as logs on their way to the mill. *See, e.g.,* Kamm v. Normand, 91 P. 448, 449 (Or. 1907); State ex rel. Medlock v. South Carolina Coastal Comm'n, 346 S.E.2d 716, 719 (S.C. 1986); Michigan Citizens for Water Conservation v. Nestle

Waters N. Am. Inc., 709 N.W.2d 174, 219 (Mich. App. 2005), *aff'd in relevant part,* 737 N.W.2d 447 (2007).

Several states have adopted expansive definitions of navigability that are directly related to the stream's capacity for recreation—the "pleasure boat," People v. Mack, 97 Cal. Rptr. 448 (Ct. App. 1971), or "recreational use," Arkansas v. McIlroy, 595 S.W.2d 659 (Ark. 1980); Parks v. Cooper, 676 N.W.2d 823 (S.D. 2004). In these states, a waterway that is useful for canoes, rafts, or the like, is considered navigable and subject to public use. Property rights of riparian landowners are qualified to the extent necessary to allow such public use rights.

Some state legislatures have delineated ownership and public interests in waterways by statute. Mississippi, for example, declared all waterways with at least 100 cubic feet per second mean annual flows to be "public waterways," with the stream and bed subject to "the right of free transport" and to fishing and water sports. Miss. Code. Ann. § 51–1–4(1). However, small waters and man-made ponds are susceptible of private ownership and cannot be taken without just compensation. Ryals v. Pigott, 580 So.2d 1140 (Miss. 1990), *cert. denied,* 502 U.S. 940 (1991). A Georgia statute extends the rights of riparian landowners on navigable streams to the streams' low-water mark, and defines "navigable" as being "capable of transporting boats loaded with freight in the regular course of trade." Ga. Code Ann. § 44–8–5. By comparison, the Arizona legislature has empowered a special commission to determine whether a watercourse is non-navigable; when it does, that determination constitutes relinquishment of the state's interest in the bed of the watercourse. Ariz. Rev. Stat. Ann. § 37–1130.

## C. THE PUBLIC TRUST DOCTRINE

Following the tradition in the English common law and Roman law before that, United States courts recognized that navigable waters and the submerged land under those waters are held for the common benefit. The Daniel Ball, 77 U.S. 557, 563 (1871). Thus, when state governments granted private rights to submerged land, they did so subject to conditions designed to protect the public's interest in these resources—the so-called public trust doctrine. Arnold v. Mundy, 6 N.J.L. 1, 13 (1821); Commonwealth v. Alger, 61 Mass. 53, 94 (1851).

Under the equal footing doctrine, which places new states on equal footing with the original thirteen colonies, states hold navigable waters and the land underneath them as an attribute of state sovereignty, subject to public purposes. Pollard's Lessee v. Hagan, 44 U.S. 212 (1845); Shively v. Bowlby, 152 U.S. 1, 49–50 (1894). In comparison to ordinary real property, navigable waters and their underlying soils are especially valuable for public purposes, and as such these public trust resources cannot be freely transferred to private ownership. THOMPSON, LESHY, ABRAMS, AND ZELLMER, LEGAL CONTROL OF WATER RESOURCES 617–654 (7th ed. West 2025).

The 1892 case of Illinois Central Railroad v. Illinois, 146 U.S. 387 (1892), is considered the seminal case on the public trust doctrine. The case involved a conflict between a railroad and the state of Illinois over title to nearly all of the submerged Lake Michigan lands in the Chicago harbor. In holding that Illinois did not have the authority to dispose of the lakebed to a private party, the U.S. Supreme Court articulated the contours of the public trust as a servitude on private interests:

> The State holds the title to the lands under the navigable waters. . . . But it is a title different in character from that which the State holds in lands intended for sale. It is different from the title which the United States holds in the public lands which are open to preemption and sale. It is a title held in trust for the people of the State that they may enjoy the navigation of the waters, carry on commerce over them, and have liberty of fishing therein freed from the obstruction and interference of private parties.

*Id.* at 452.

*Illinois Central* did not specify whether the public trust doctrine rests primarily on state or federal law. However, in 2012, the Supreme Court stated that the public trust doctrine is "a matter of state law." PPL Montana, LLC v. Montana, 565 U.S. 576 (2012). The existence of a separate or parallel federal public trust doctrine is an open question. *See* Juliana v. United States, No. 6:15-CV-01517-AA, 2023 WL 9023339, at *21 (D. Or. Dec. 29, 2023) (allowing youth plaintiffs to seek declaratory judgment for alleged violations of a federal public trust doctrine in relation to the territorial sea); In re United States, 2024 WL 5102489 (9th Cir. May 1, 2024), *cert. denied sub nom.*

Juliana v. United States, 145 S. Ct. 1428 (2025) (dismissing plaintiffs' claims due to lack of standing).

In some jurisdictions, the public trust doctrine has been interpreted broadly in favor of public access. *See* Glass v. Goeckel, 703 N.W.2d 58 (Mich. 2005) (recognizing public's right to walk below the ordinary high water mark of Lake Huron as consistent with the traditional right of passage); Gunderson v. State, Indiana Dep't of Nat. Res., 90 N.E.3d 1171 (Ind. 2018), *cert. denied,* 586 U.S. 1184 (2019) (walking below the ordinary high water mark on the shore of Lake Michigan is a protected public use); Adobe Whitewater Club v. New Mexico Game Comm'n, 519 P.3d 46, 49 (N.M. 2022), *cert. denied,* 143 S.Ct. 980 (2023) (invalidating Game Commission regulations that allowed landowners to close public access to public waters flowing over private property because the right to recreate and fish also allows the public the right to touch privately owned beds below public waters).

Other jurisdictions have interpreted the public's rights narrowly by limiting the doctrine's reach to the specific purposes listed in *Illinois Central*—fishing, commerce, and navigation. Bell v. Town of Wells, 557 A.2d 168 (Me. 1989); Ross v. Acadian Seaplants, Ltd., 206 A.3d 283, 290 (Me. 2019) (harvesting living rockweed is neither "fishing" nor "navigation," even when those terms are interpreted in a "sympathetically broad and generous" way; rockweed attached to land in the intertidal zone belongs to the upland property owner). However, courts are sometimes willing to revisit these narrow holdings.

In McGarvey v. Whittredge, 28 A.3d 620, 636 (Me. 2011), the court found that the public has the right to walk across intertidal lands to reach the ocean to go scuba diving, even if diving could not be "shoehorned" into the definition of "navigation," because the activity constituted "a reasonable balance between private ownership of the intertidal lands and the public's use of those lands." *Id.*

Colorado courts have been especially restrictive, having repeatedly rejected any notion of a public trust in water resources. In People v. Emmert, 597 P.2d 1025, 1027 (1979), the state Supreme Court recognized various policy-oriented reasons to allow public use of waterways but refused to upset the existing common law rule that land underlying non-navigable streams is subject to private ownership. Likewise, in State v. Hill, 530 P.3d 632 (2023), the court rejected a claim brought by an avid fly-fisherman who had been chased off a segment of the Arkansas River by riparian owners. Mr. Hill argued that he had a right to wade along the riverbed because the River was navigable at the time of statehood and therefore subject to the public trust doctrine. The court dismissed his claim for lack of standing. *Id.* at 636.

Public access aside, litigants have sometimes asserted that the public trust doctrine covers far more than navigable waters, and far more than mere access. In Marks v. Whitney, 491 P.2d 374, 380 (Cal. 1971), the court stated that the doctrine could be expanded to encompass changing public needs, such as preservation of tidelands in their natural state.

Subsequently, in National Audubon Society v. Superior Court (Mono Lake), 658 P.2d 709 (Cal. 1983), the court applied the doctrine to limit diversions from non-navigable tributary streams where the diversions were causing ecological harm. For details, see *supra* Chapter 3.V.B.3 and 3.VI.A.5.

Courts have split on whether the public trust doctrine applies to groundwater. A few have said no. *See, e.g.,* Rhode Island v. Atl. Richfield Co., 357 F. Supp. 3d 129, 144 (D.R.I. 2018). In White Bear Lake Restoration Ass'n v. Dep't of Nat. Res., 928 N.W.2d 351, 367 (Minn. App. 2019), a Minnesota court rejected an attempt to include groundwater, even though groundwater pumping impacted surface waters. The Minnesota Supreme Court affirmed, but on other grounds. Instead of distinguishing between groundwater and surface water, it reasoned that the judiciary ought not extend the common law into an area governed by comprehensive permitting measures. White Bear Lake Restoration Ass'n v. Dep't of Nat. Res., 946 N.W.2d 373 (2020).

By contrast, California, Alaska, and a few other states have applied the public trust doctrine to groundwater pumping if pumping adversely affects surface waters. *See, e.g.,* Williams Alaska Petroleum, Inc. v. State, 529 P.3d 1160, 1187 (Alaska 2023), *cert. denied,* 144 S. Ct. 555 (2024); Env't L. Found. v. State Water Res. Control Bd., 237 Cal. Rptr. 3d 393, 409 (2018) (holding that the Sustainable Groundwater Management Act (SGMA), Cal. Water Code §§ 10720 *et seq.*, did not abrogate the state's public trust duty to consider the impact of groundwater pumping on navigable waters); Clean Wisconsin v. Wisconsin Dep't of Nat. Res., 961 N.W.2d 611, 619 (Wisc. 2021) (finding that the state has broad authority to consider the environmental impacts of proposed high capacity wells).

Hawaii applies the public trust doctrine to *all* waters, including groundwater. In re Water Use Permit Applications (Waiahole), 9 P.3d 409, 445 (Haw. 2000). State and local permitting authorities must use a high level of scrutiny when they examine proposals for private use of springs and other public resources. *See* Kauai Springs, Inc. v. Plan. Comm'n of Cnty. of Kauai, 324 P.3d 951, 985 (Haw. 2014).

Some state legislatures have adopted constitutional environmental rights, which may be seen as encompassing public trust resources and values. *See, e.g.*, Held v. State, 560 P.3d 1235 (Mont. 2024) (holding that Montana's constitutional guarantee of "the right to a clean and healthful environment" encompasses the public trust doctrine and includes a stable climate system); Yaw v. Delaware River Basin Comm'n, 49 F.4th 302 (3d Cir. 2022) (upholding a ban on high-volume hydraulic fracturing ("fracking") under the public trust and the Pennsylvania constitution).

In some circumstances, a state may be allowed to transfer public trust resources, particularly where such transfers further a value within the scope of the trust or where developing trust lands or waters does not substantially impair the public's interest. *See* Eldridge v. Cowell, 4 Cal. 80, 87 (1854) (filling of San Francisco Bay upheld because development allowed for a deep water port); Caminiti v. Boyle, 732 P.2d 989 (Wash. 1987) (en banc) (in dicta, stating that private recreational docks constructed on public trust lands were acceptable because they promoted public trust objectives); Chelan Basin Conservancy v. GBI Holding Co., 413 P.3d 549, 555 (Wash. 2018) (finding that the state may dispose of tidelands and shorelands subject to the "paramount right of navigation and the fishery"); Min. Cnty. v. Lyon Cnty., 473 P.3d 418 (Nev. 2020) (finding that Nevada's statutory water scheme satisfies the requirements for transferring public trust property by limiting permits to those based on beneficial use and by prohibiting transfers that would be detrimental to the public interest).

Despite instances where the courts have held that trust property may be transferred, there is a strong presumption against such transfers, which requires that the legislature's intent be clearly expressed. *See* People v. Calif. Fish Co., 138 P. 79, 86, 88 (Cal. 1913); CWC Fisheries, Inc. v. Bunker, 755 P.2d 1115, 1118–21 (Alaska 1988); Coastal Petr. v. American Cyanamid, 492 So.2d 339, 344 (Fla. 1986).

Some states have sought to legislatively exempt certain bodies of water, or even the entire state, from the public trust doctrine. However, most courts have held that state legislatures do not have plenary authority to abolish the public trust doctrine. *See* Brusco Towboat Co. v. State ex rel. State Land Bd., 589 P.2d 712, 718 (Or. 1978); San Carlos Apache Tribe v. Superior Court ex rel. Cnty. of Maricopa, 972 P.2d 179, 215 (Ariz. 1999) (en banc); Lawrence v.

Clark Cnty., 254 P.3d 606, 612 (Nev. 2011). In Idaho, the state legislature recognized the public trust doctrine with regard to the beds of navigable waterways, but expressly prohibited the application of the doctrine to the appropriation or use of water. Idaho Code Ann. § 58–1203(2)(b). For commentary, see Erin Ryan, *From Mono Lake to the Atmospheric Trust: Navigating the Public and Private Interests in Public Trust Resource Commons*, 10 Geo. Wash. J. Energy & Envtl. L. 39, 57 (2019).

Utah provides an interesting example of the interplay between courts and legislatures. In Conaster v. Johnson, 194 P.3d 897 (Utah 2008), the court determined that the public held an easement to touch the beds of all Utah waterways for recreational or other lawful purposes. In response, the legislature adopted the Public Waters Access Act, which limits recreational access to navigable waters and water bodies situated on public property. Utah Code Ann. § 73–29–103. Streams that are useful for commerce (e.g., log-floating) are considered navigable for purposes of public access. Utah Stream Access Coal. v. Orange St. Dev., 416 P.3d 553, 560 (Utah 2017). If the streambed is privately owned, however, the public has a right to float, to fish, and to portage around obstructions, but cannot wade in the streambed without obtaining the landowner's permission. Utah Stream Access Coal. v. VR Acquisitions, LLC, 531 P.3d 195, 216 (Utah 2023).

Details about the application of the public trust doctrine to prior appropriation water rights can be found in Chapter 3.V.B.3.

## III. NAVIGATIONAL SERVITUDE

The "navigational servitude" is a concept that allows the federal government, in certain circumstances, to affect private property without paying compensation. Although the Fifth Amendment to the Constitution prohibits the taking of private property for a public use without just compensation, when the government destroys or removes privately-owned structures in or near navigable waterways for navigational purposes, it is not required to compensate the owners.

### A. BASIS OF THE NAVIGATIONAL SERVITUDE

Historically, navigation was an important public right. In England, any rights that had been granted by the Crown to utilize the beds of certain waters were subordinate to the public right of free and unhindered passage of vessels for navigation; interference with the public right created a nuisance subject to abatement. A similar concept authorizes the United States government to control and protect the navigable capacity of waterways through the commerce clause of the Constitution, in some cases without compensating affected property owners.

Some decisions have attempted to justify the non-compensation rule, known as the navigational servitude, on a "notice" theory. Since investments in navigable waterways are made with knowledge of the paramount importance of navigation, investors can have no reasonable expectation of compensation for removal or destruction of a structure that obstructs travel on a navigable waterway. *See, e.g.*, Boone v. United States, 944 F.2d 1489, 1495 (9th Cir. 1991); U.S. v. Kansas City Life Ins. Co., 339 U.S. 799, 808 (1950). *See also* Pellegrini v. United States, 132 Fed. Cl. 64, 71 (2017) ("The government's exercise of power within the navigational servitude 'is not an invasion of any private property right in such lands. . .' ") (citing United States v. Chicago, Milwaukee, St. Paul & Pac. R.R., 312 U.S. 592, 596–97 (1941)). Other courts have alluded to the servitude as a facet of the government's public trust duties to protect navigation and fisheries. Martin v. Lessee of Waddell, 41 U.S. (16 Pet.) 367, 413 (1842); Phillips Petroleum Co. v. Mississippi, 484 U.S. 469, 483 n.12 (1988). *See also* Nw. Louisiana Fish & Game Pres. Comm'n v. United States, 574 F.3d 1386, 1390 (Fed. Cir. 2009) ("The servitude is derived from the principle that all navigable waters . . . are considered public property.").

## B. EXTENT OF THE NAVIGATIONAL SERVITUDE

The application of the navigational servitude depends on the location of the affected property, the type of property rights involved, and the purpose of the government action. Ordinarily, the navigational servitude applies only to property located on, and property rights in, navigable streams. Takings of property on non-navigable tributaries must be compensated. U.S. v. Kansas City Life Insurance Co., 339 U.S. 799 (1950). However, claims for compensation can be defeated if Congress expressly states that its purpose is the improvement of navigation and there is a reasonable relation to navigation.

On a waterway subject to the navigational servitude, the servitude extends to the ordinary high water mark of the stream. Non-compensability applies to the streambed (including all land under the stream up to the ordinary high water mark) and structures within the stream.

### 1. Obstructions to Navigation

The earliest cases applying the navigational servitude concerned removal of obstructions to navigation. The first case to reach the Supreme Court involved the condemnation of a toll-collecting franchise on the Monongahela River. Monongahela Navigation Co. v. United States, 148 U.S. 312 (1893). The Court found that the government action was compensable because the locks and dam had been constructed at the "implied invitation" of Congress. *Id.* at 334. *Monongahela* has been distinguished in later decisions as an estoppel case. *See, e.g.,* United States v. Rands, 389 U.S. 121, 126 (1967).

Subsequent cases have held that obstructions to navigation are subject to the servitude. For instance, in Union Bridge Co. v. United States, 204 U.S. 364 (1907), the government successfully utilized the 1899 Rivers and Harbors Act, 33 U.S.C. § 403, to force modifications of a bridge on the Allegheny River. Finding the loss non-compensable, the Court justified the servitude on a notice theory: the company built the bridge with the knowledge that the federal government might someday assert its navigation power.

### 2. Damage to Property in Navigable Waterways

An early case, United States v. Lynah, 188 U.S. 445 (1903), held that flood damage to the land between a stream's low and high water marks caused by a federal dam was compensable. The decision, had it stood, might have given landowners on navigable streams a right to have the water level maintained in its natural or historic condition. *Lynah* was overruled, however, by United States v. Chicago, Milwaukee, St. Paul & Pac. R.R., 312 U.S. 592 (1941), which held that the servitude extends to land on a navigable stream up to the ordinary high water mark—an average of high water marks over all seasons.

Everything below the ordinary high water mark within a navigable waterway is subject to the navigational servitude. Thus, compensation has been denied for private oyster beds destroyed by dredging in Great South Bay, New York. Lewis Blue Point Oyster Cultivation Co. v. Briggs, 229 U.S. 82 (1913). *See also* Avenal v. United States, 100 F.3d 933 (Fed. Cir. 1996) (dismissing a takings claim by oyster lessees because they had no compensable interest in the salinity of water adversely affected by a freshwater diversion project).

### 3. Projects on Navigable Streams Causing Damage to Property Rights on Non-Navigable Tributaries

When water backs up behind a dam on a navigable stream, causing flooding or other damage to property on a non-navigable tributary, the damage is compensable unless Congress expressly invokes the navigation power to protect the navigable capacity of the river. In United States v. Cress, 243 U.S. 316 (1917), a government dam on a navigable mainstem raised the water level in tributaries, flooded lands along the tributaries, and destroyed the water power potential of a mill located on a tributary. The Supreme Court held that the injuries were compensable. *Id.* at 327.

The *Cress* rule has been criticized because it makes the compensability of property turn upon its location: taking of property on a non-navigable tributary is compensable, while an identical injury on a navigable stream is non-compensable. Yet the Court reaffirmed the *Cress* rule, awarding compensation in a case in which farmland became saturated because a dam on the Mississippi River caused an adjacent non-navigable tributary to flood. United States v. Kansas City Life Ins. Co., 339 U.S. 799 (1950).

By contrast, in United States v. Willow River Power Co., 324 U.S. 499 (1945), a dam on a navigable river raised water levels in both the mainstem and a tributary. This destroyed the waterpower value of a diversion through an artificial channel from a tributary into the mainstem. The Court denied compensation, finding that the affected property right was in the mainstem, not in the tributary as in *Cress. Id.* at 510.

When flooding on a tributary is caused by a dam on the tributary, Congress can avoid compensation only if it invokes its power to protect the navigable capacity of the mainstem. In United States v. Grand River Dam Auth., 363 U.S. 229, 230 (1960), the Grand River Dam Authority (GRDA) was tasked by the Oklahoma legislature to develop hydroelectric power on the Grand River, a non-navigable tributary to the Arkansas River. Three dams were planned in pursuit of this goal, with the Fort Gibson site being the furthest downstream. The federal government, as part of a comprehensive plan for the basin, constructed a dam at the site for flood control purposes. The GRDA asserted a "taking" of its right to develop electric power at the Fort Gibson site. The Court rejected the claim, stating that "[w]hen the United States appropriates the flow either of a navigable or a nonnavigable stream pursuant to its superior power under the Commerce Clause, it is exercising established prerogatives and is beholden to no one." *Id.* at 233. Federal use of the dam, however, did not destroy the state's rights in the dam for purposes of hydropower—the state's interest merely became inferior to federal usage for flood control. *Id. See* Wagoner Cnty. Rural Water Dist. No. 2 v. Grand River Dam Auth., 241 P.3d 1132 (Okla. Civ. App. 2010), *cert. denied,* 562 U.S. 1200 (2011) ("The fact that one interest may be superior to another does not extinguish the inferior interest; it merely establishes the priority of the superior use.").

### 4. Waters Rendered Navigable by Private Effort or by Flooding

If waters formerly non-navigable are rendered navigable by private activity, the government must pay compensation if it seeks to assure public access to the newly navigable waterway. In Kaiser Aetna v. United States, 444 U.S. 164 (1979), a developer deepened a pond and converted it into a marina by opening a channel to the ocean. The Army Corps of Engineers sought a public right of access to the marina in exchange for the issuance of a federal permit. The Supreme Court found that the navigational servitude did not apply to the pond because, prior to its improvement, the pond was incapable of being used as a highway for the purpose of navigation in interstate commerce. Its maximum depth at high tide was only two feet, it was separated from the adjacent bay and the ocean by a natural barrier beach, and its principal commercial value was limited to fishing. Moreover, the pond had always been considered private property under Hawaiian law. Although present navigability was sufficient to invoke federal regulatory power (*i.e.,* to prevent activities from interfering with navigation or to require federal permits for development), payment of just compensation was required to obtain public access. *Id.* at 179–80. A companion case, Vaughn v. Vermilion Corp., 444 U.S. 206 (1979), applied *Kaiser Aetna* to deny the servitude to a system of human-made canals in Louisiana that connected the Gulf of Mexico with an inland waterway.

Whether an altered waterbody qualifies as "navigable" may be a material question of fact that precludes summary judgment. *See* Pellegrini v. United States, 132 Fed. Cl. 64 (2017) (holding that the extent to which properties fell below the mean high-water mark was an issue of fact that precluded summary judgment on landowners' claim that dredging caused their seawall and docks to collapse).

In an interesting twist on the navigational servitude, Parm v. Shumate, 513 F.3d 135, 143 (5th Cir. 2007), *cert. denied,* 555 U.S. 813 (2008), found that fishermen did not have a right to hunt and fish over private riparian lands temporarily flooded by the Mississippi River both because the servitude does not apply to waterways that become navigable due to flooding and because the servitude does not encompass recreational fishing. The court in *Parm* also noted that Louisiana law limits public use to navigation and reserves to landowners the right to prohibit fishermen's entry on their land. *Id.* at 145. *See* Newbold v. Kinder Morgan SNG Operator, L.L.C., 65 F.4th 175, 179 (5th Cir.), *cert. denied,* 144 S. Ct. 186 (2023) ("The navigational servitude does not burden land that is only submerged when the river floods.").

## C. MEASURE OF DAMAGES FOR CONDEMNATION

The taking of uplands (lands above the ordinary high-water mark) is compensable even if they are located on a navigable stream. However, private rights that depend on the flow of a navigable stream, such as waterpower value, site value, and consumptive use of water, are subject to the navigational servitude and are non-compensable.

### 1. Value of Water Power

In United States v. Chandler-Dunbar Water Power Co., 229 U.S. 53 (1913), the United States condemned both a power plant located in St. Mary's River and the adjacent uplands to preserve the river's navigability. Although there was no dispute that compensation must be paid for the uplands, the Supreme Court found the taking of the waterpower value attributable to rapids in the stream non-compensable, both because the servitude allowed removal of structures from the river and also because the claimed water power right turned on unimpeded streamflow. *Id.* at 73–74. The Court dismissed as "inconceivable" the idea that rights to the flow of running water in a navigable stream are capable of private ownership subject to compensation. *Id.* at 69.

### 2. Site Value

Land adjacent to a waterway may be more valuable because of its usefulness as a hydroelectric power site, a recreational area, or a port or marina. When riparian lands above the ordinary high-water mark are condemned as part of a federal project, the question arises whether the condemnation award should include the site value. United States v. Twin City Power Co., 350 U.S. 222 (1956), involved land along the navigable Savannah River acquired by a power company as a possible reservoir site. The power site value was approximately seven times the agricultural value of the land. The Court held that the increment of value attributable to the land's location on the stream was inherent in the flow of the stream and thus non-compensable. *Id.* at 226 (citing *Chandler-Dunbar*).

The decision in *Twin City Power Co.* does not modify the physical reach of the servitude as including only that part of the streambed below the high-water mark. It does, however, exclude from compensability the portion of the value of uplands attributable to the streamflow. Although uplands are clearly compensable, their value may only include suitability for non-riparian purposes such as agriculture or mining.

United States v. Rands, 389 U.S. 121 (1967), reaffirmed this principle. Rands owned land along the Columbia River, and the state held an option to buy the land for use as a port site. The land, which was about five times more valuable as a port site than for the next most valuable uses (sand, gravel, and agriculture), was taken by the United States as part of a comprehensive plan for development of the Columbia River. The Court held that special values, such as port site value arising from access to a navigable waterway, are subject to the navigational servitude, thus denying any compensation attributable to such values. In addition, the Court held that the increased value of the land remaining in Rands' ownership due to its new riparian location was a benefit to be deducted from the amount of any compensable harm. *Id.* at 126.

The rule of *Rands* may have harsh results, as illustrated in an example provided by the late Dean Trelease. Suppose a tract of land is worth $10,000 regardless of proximity to water, but location on the waterfront adds a value of $5,000 to the portion of land on the water. If the half of the tract on the water is condemned and flooded, the award is limited to the nonriparian value ($5,000). But value is added to the remaining land because it is now on the waterfront ($5,000) and this value will be deducted from the award. Consequently, the owner receives no compensation for the flooding of the lost land.

Because of the effect of the *Rands* rule, pressure was brought to bear on Congress to expand compensability for condemned lands. In 1970, Congress passed § 111 of the Rivers and Harbors Act, 33 U.S.C. § 595(a), which provides that the compensation for land taken for a navigation improvement project is the fair market value of the property in its highest and best use, which may be based upon access to or utilization of navigable waters. Thus, an owner can recover waterfront value of land taken, but the amount of actual recovery still must be reduced by the enhanced value of uplands now located on the water. In Trelease's hypothetical above, § 111 would give the landowner $10,000 for the flooded land (port site value included), but $5,000 would be deducted for appreciation of the remaining land for a net compensation of $5,000. Section 111 also limits compensability for depreciation of remaining (uncondemned) land that results from loss of access to navigable waters.

The courts have also limited the *Rands* rule by allowing compensation if flowage easements are taken. A flowage easement is an interest in land that allows the holder to flood the land of another. In United States v. Virginia Elec. & Power Co., 365 U.S. 624 (1961), a company planned to construct a reservoir for hydropower purposes and bought a flowage easement to allow it to flood the land. The United States then decided to build a project on the same site. The company conceded that potential hydropower value was non-compensable but argued that the easement had other value not dependent upon streamflow. The Court agreed, reasoning that the holder of a flowage easement has the right to destroy, by flooding, the value of the subservient fee. The fee owner, before sacrificing the use of the land for agriculture, timber, or grazing, would charge the easement holder the value of those uses. Thus, the easement has "a marketability roughly commensurate with the marketability of the subservient fee." *Id.* at 630. The Court limited the award by discounting the easement's value to reflect the possibility of its non-exercise since a fee owner would sell a flowage easement for less if the holder of the easement were unlikely to flood the land. The fact that the government had decided to build the project, however, was not to be included in the calculation of the "probability of the easement's exercise." *Id.* at 632, n.5.

Government-caused flooding that exceeds the scope of a flowage easement may trigger a takings claim, as discussed below in Section V.C.

### 3. Water Rights Created Under State Law

Federal power may come into conflict with state-created water rights in a number of ways. Two basic types of issues arise: whether the federal government has authority to affect or displace state water rights, and, if so, whether the water rights holder is entitled to compensation. (Takings claims related to water rights but arising in other contexts are covered in Chapters 3, 4, 5, and 10 of this book.)

The Commerce Clause, the Treaty Clause, the Property Clause, and the spending power provide authority for the United States to regulate water use to carry out federal purposes. The primary question for a court is whether Congress intended to override, or preempt, state law. California v. U.S., 438 U.S. 645 (1978). In United States v. Rio Grande Dam & Irrig. Co., 174 U.S. 690 (1899), the Supreme Court sustained the federal government's regulatory power to prevent the exercise of state-created water rights in order to carry out federal legislation protecting the navigable capacity of streams. Congress may also authorize officials to distribute water from a federal project without regard to priorities established under state law. Arizona v. California, 373 U.S. 546 (1963).

When a federal project makes it necessary to appropriate or destroy a state-created water right, compensation must be paid unless the purpose of the project is for navigation, in which case the rights are subject to the navigational servitude. In United States v. Gerlach Live Stock Co., 339 U.S. 725 (1950), farmers in California's Central Valley irrigated their grasslands with the seasonal overflow of the

Sacramento River. As part of the massive Central Valley Project, the government constructed Friant Dam, which eliminated the river's seasonal flooding and deprived downstream landowners of the overflow. The government contended that the loss was non-compensable since Congress had authorized the project for the control of navigation. The Court found that the project was a reclamation project, not a navigation project, despite a general congressional declaration that the entire project was to improve navigation. *Id.* at 739. Because the 1902 Reclamation Act expressed an intention that the federal government comply with state law in acquiring property for such projects, 43 U.S.C. §§ 383, 421, the water rights were held to be compensable.

## IV. HYDROPOWER

Hydroelectric power is a significant source of non-carbon-based, renewable energy. Hydroelectric generation typically uses the energy of a river's flow, plus gravity, to produce electricity. The federal government has been involved in hydropower projects for over a century, beginning with the exercise of its authority to prevent obstructions to navigation and evolving into a more extensive role through the Federal Power Act of 1920. Through this Act and other statutes, the federal government has also taken steps to address the adverse effects of hydropower dams on fish and wildlife.

## A. FEDERAL POWER ACT

The Federal Power Act of 1920 established a comprehensive national policy for hydroelectric power development. 16 U.S.C. §§ 791a *et seq*. The Act was the result of years of effort by conservationists, who had sought federal legislation to ensure nationwide waterpower planning. The Act's purposes are to reconcile conflicting uses (*e.g.*, navigation, irrigation, recreation, wildlife preservation, flood control, and hydropower), develop "the long idle water power resources of the nation," and "avoid unconstitutional invasion of the jurisdiction of the states." First Iowa Hydro-Elec. Co-op. v. Fed. Power Comm'n, 328 U.S. 152, 171 (1946).

The Federal Power Commission, now the Federal Energy Regulatory Commission (FERC), an independent agency within the Department of Energy, administers the Act. 16 U.S.C. § 792. FERC has authority to license private hydropower facilities and to regulate interstate sale and transmission of electricity. 16 U.S.C. § 797. It may also issue permits for the use of surplus water or waterpower from government dams. 16 U.S.C. § 797(e).

In the absence of an existing, pre-1920 right-of-way, the Act requires that a license be obtained from FERC for hydroelectric facilities, including "dams, water conduits, reservoirs, powerhouses, or other works incidental thereto," that cross, adjoin, or are located in navigable waters, public lands, or federal reservations. 16 U.S.C. § 817. A waterway is navigable under the Act if "(1) it *presently* is being used or is suitable for use, or (2) it has been used or was suitable for use in the *past,* or (3) it could be made suitable for use in the *future* by reasonable improvements." Turlock Irr. Dist. v. F.E.R.C., 786 F.3d 18, 26 (D.C. Cir. 2015) (applying 16 U.S.C. § 796(8)) (emphasis in original). Once it is found to be navigable, a waterway remains so for the purpose of licensure. *Id.* at 28.

Facilities on non-navigable waters require licenses if FERC finds the "interests of interstate or foreign commerce would be affected" by the proposed project. 16 U.S.C. § 817. Citing this language, courts have upheld broad extensions of FERC's licensing jurisdiction. In Federal Power Commission v. Union Elec. Co., 381 U.S. 90, 110 (1965), a power company proposed to build a "pumped-storage" facility, in which water is pumped to a high reservoir, stored, and then released to generate power during periods of peak demand. The Supreme Court sustained a decision to require a license because the power would be transmitted across state lines. The Court added that, if the project was not properly operated, the flows of the navigable portion of the river downstream could be affected. *Id.* at 93, n.5. *See also* North Carolina v. FERC, 3 F.4th 655, 665 (4th Cir. 2021) (upholding FERC's jurisdiction over a dam on a non-navigable tributary of a navigable river; although the dam had not been operated for over a decade, the proposed use of the dam in interstate commerce triggered licensing requirements).

In addition to addressing navigational and public power concerns, FERC also requires owners of high-hazard dams to prepare and maintain a dam safety program. If the owner refuses, FERC may revoke the license. 16 U.S.C. § 823b. In 2018, FERC revoked a license for a facility in Michigan. The licensee failed to address inadequate spillway capacity, and the State of Michigan assumed regulatory authority over the dams. Two years later, during a heavy rainstorm, the dams failed, flooding the surrounding communities. Kristin Taylor et. al., Agency and Legislative Oversight As Problem Feedback: The Case of the Mid-Michigan Dam Failures, 68 Wayne L. Rev. 31, 44–45 (2022). No lives were lost, but the incident triggered federal and state investigations, and the former dam owner was found liable for $120 million in damages to fisheries and property. Michigan Dep't of Env't. v. Mueller, No. 1:20-CV-528, 2023 WL 9848689 (W.D. Mich. Nov. 27, 2023).

Despite its wide-ranging authority, FERC has declined to exercise jurisdiction in certain situations, even where power generation has a substantial effect on navigable waters and interstate commerce. The Supreme Court upheld its refusal to regulate several huge coal-fired power plants that would use large quantities of cooling water from the Colorado River and would transmit power throughout the Southwest. Chemehuevi Tribe v. Federal Power Comm'n, 420 U.S. 395 (1975). It found that the plants were not "project works" requiring a license under the Act, nor did they use "surplus water" from a federal dam. *Id.* at 412–13. The Court reasoned that Congress only intended to license hydroelectric power plants, not plants that burn fossil fuels to make steam for power generation. *Id.* at 405.

Hydroelectric licenses are issued for a period not exceeding fifty years. 16 U.S.C. § 799. *See* Duke Energy Carolinas v. Fed. Energy Regulatory Comm'n, 883 F.3d 923 (D.C. Cir. 2018) (affirming FERC's decision to limit a license renewal to forty years instead of fifty). FERC must give a preference to license applications by states and municipalities so long as their applications are "equally well adapted" as competing applications to serve the public interest in the water resources of the region. W. Minnesota Mun. Power Agency v. Fed. Energy Regulatory Comm'n, 806 F.3d 588 (D.C. Cir. 2015) (citing 16 U.S.C. § 800(a)).

Upon expiration, FERC may relicense existing projects, but must examine them "completely anew" to ensure that they will continue to meet the requirements of federal law. City of Tacoma v. FERC, 460 F.3d 53, 74 (D.C. Cir. 2006). In *City of Tacoma,* FERC imposed a number of conditions to protect the environment, to restore fish populations, and to mitigate a project's effect on the Skokomish Tribe's reservation. The City claimed that these conditions made license renewal economically infeasible and that it had no choice but to shut its project down; thus, FERC had effectively decommissioned its project. Although the Act directs FERC to grant licenses "upon reasonable terms," the court held that Congress gave FERC the power to shut down projects by imposing reasonable and necessary conditions that cause the licensee to reject the license. *Id.* (citing 16 U.S.C. § 808(a)(1)).

In some cases, FERC's relicensing conditions have resulted in the removal of dams that no longer meet the FPA's requirements. A notable example involves four hydroelectric dams that had blocked salmon runs for many decades on 420 miles of the Klamath River. A complex deal involving the dams' owner, Indian tribes, the states of California and Oregon, local irrigation districts, and numerous federal agencies led to the dams' removal in 2024. Charles V. Stern and Pervaze A. Sheikh, Klamath River Dam Removal and Restoration (Cong. Res. Service 2024).

FERC also has the authority to refuse to relicense the original licensee, and to instead recommend that the federal government take over a hydropower project for "public purposes," upon payment of the licensee's net investment. 16 U.S.C. § 800(c). Although a state may wish to step into the shoes of the federal government, "Congress authorized federal recapture for *federal use*, not subsequent transfer to state entities." North Carolina v. Fed. Energy Regulatory Comm'n, 913 F.3d 148, 151 (D.C. Cir. 2019) (emphasis supplied). During the application period, however, a state may seek licensure by filing its own competing application. *Id.*

## B. CONFLICT WITH STATE LAW

Dams can dramatically affect the flow of streams, disrupting state water allocation. Although conflicts usually involve state-sanctioned water rights, state laws for the protection of fish habitat and the environment may also be affected. This is especially evident in states such as Oregon and Washington, where large dams obstruct spawning and migration of salmon and other anadromous fish.

The Federal Power Act has two provisions that appear to shield state law from federal encroachment. Section 9(b) requires license applicants to submit satisfactory evidence of compliance with state laws concerning hydropower development. 16 U.S.C. § 802(b). Also, in Section 27, Congress included a typical savings clause:

> Nothing contained in this chapter shall be construed as affecting or intending to affect or in any way to interfere with the laws of the respective states relating to the control, appropriation, use, or distribution of water used in irrigation or for municipal or other uses, or any vested right acquired therein.

*Id.* § 821. Both sections seem to preserve state law, but judicial interpretation has limited their sweep.

In First Iowa Hydro-Electric Co-op. v. Federal Power Comm'n, 328 U.S. 152, 180–81 (1946), the Supreme Court held that § 9(b) does not give states a veto power over federal projects. The Commission had granted a license to a hydropower co-operative to construct a dam on an Iowa River tributary. The Court found that where compliance with both state and federal permit requirements appeared impossible, subjecting the project to state law would frustrate the Act's purpose of comprehensive nationwide planning. According to the Court, § 9(b) is merely informational; if the Commission is satisfied with the degree of state law compliance, a state permit need not be obtained. *Id.* at 178.

The *First Iowa* rule was extended in California v. FERC, 495 U.S. 490 (1990), when California attempted to impose higher minimum flow requirements on a hydroelectric project than compelled by the FERC license. Unlike *First Iowa,* where the issue was whether a state could effectively *deny* a permit to the project, the question was whether a state could determine the *conditions* on which water could be used by the project. The Supreme Court found that § 27 added nothing to the § 9(b) requirement of state law compliance as interpreted in *First Iowa. Id.* at 498. The Court distinguished its contrary interpretation of a different statutory provision with nearly identical language, Section 8 of the Reclamation Act, 43 U.S.C. § 383, which authorizes state-imposed conditions on water use permits for federal Bureau of Reclamation projects. *Id.* at 504. *See* California v. United States, 438 U.S. 645 (1978). In *California v. FERC,* the Court found that the Federal Power Act "envisioned a considerably broader and more active federal oversight role in hydropower development than did the Reclamation Act" in financing and building water projects. 495 U.S. at 492. Thus, § 27 is a general provision that cannot override the preemptive effect of specific provisions or the overall purpose of the Federal Power Act. *See* Otwell v. Alabama Power Co., 747 F.3d 1275, 1284 (11th Cir. 2014) (holding that state-recognized rights to enjoy recreational uses on a lake did not allow riparian owners to veto the operation of a FERC-licensed project).

Where a federal statute delegates responsibility for environmental protection to a state, however, FERC's exclusive authority may be qualified. The Clean Water Act § 401, 33 U.S.C. § 1341, is a key example. Section 401 requires that, before a federal permit or license is granted, the federal agency must obtain a certification that state water quality standards will not be violated by the permitted activity. The Supreme Court has upheld a state's imposition of minimum streamflow requirements deemed necessary to satisfy water quality standards as a condition of certification for a FERC license. PUD No. 1 of Jefferson Cnty. v. Washington Dep't of Ecology, 511 U.S. 700 (1994); S.D. Warren Co. v. Maine Bd. of Envtl. Protection, 547 U.S. 370 (2006). States that fail to act on a certification request within a year are deemed to have waived their right to require certification. 33 U.S.C. § 1341(a)(1). *See* Hoopa Valley Tribe v. Fed. Energy Regulatory Comm'n, 913 F.3d 1099, 1104 (D.C. Cir.), *cert. denied*, 589 U.S. 1117 (2019) (noting that, absent this limitation, states could usurp FERC's control over federal licensing by simply "shelving water quality certifications"). But courts may demand relatively conclusive evidence of waiver, given that "States' rights and responsibilities to ensure compliance with their own water-quality standards are too important to be . . . easily stripped away." North Carolina v. FERC, 3 F.4th 655, 676 (4th Cir. 2021).

A hydropower license endows the licensee with certain preemptive powers of the federal government. In City of Tacoma v. Taxpayers of Tacoma, 357 U.S. 320 (1958), the city applied for a

FERC license to build a dam on a tributary of the Columbia River. The State of Washington opposed the project because the reservoir behind the dam would flood a state fish hatchery and state law forbade municipalities from condemning state property. Nonetheless, the Commission granted the license. The Supreme Court held that the license delegated federal eminent domain power to the city to condemn state property. *Id.* at 340. However, compensation must be paid if state-created rights are taken by eminent domain. Portland General Elec. Co. v. Federal Power Comm'n, 328 F.2d 165 (9th Cir. 1964); Scenic Hudson Preservation Conference v. Federal Power Comm'n, 453 F.2d 463 (2d Cir. 1971).

## C. PROTECTION FOR FISH AND WILDLIFE

Hydroelectric facilities significantly disrupt fish habitat and migration patterns. Columbia River harvests of salmon are now only a small fraction of their size 100 years ago, in large part because of the construction of hydropower dams. Such facilities obstruct spawning migration, alter water temperatures, and change the water's chemical composition, thereby harming fish and other species.

Under the Federal Power Act, prior to issuing a license, FERC must find that the proposed project is "best adapted to a comprehensive plan" for water development, navigation, water power, "and for other beneficial public uses, including recreational purposes." 16 U.S.C. § 803(a). *Compare* National Wildlife Fed'n v. Federal Energy Regulatory Comm'n, 801 F.2d 1505 (9th Cir. 1986) (finding that

FERC's refusal to develop a comprehensive plan for the Salmon River Basin was not supported by the record), *with* Brady v. FERC, 416 F.3d 1, 9–10 (D.C. Cir. 2005) (holding that FERC had authority to approve a marina proposal even though the state agency had not yet completed a comprehensive shoreline management plan).

To help ensure protection of state interests in fish and wildlife, the Act requires coordination among the agency undertaking or permitting a project, the U.S. Fish and Wildlife Service, and relevant state fish and wildlife agencies before construction of a project. 16 U.S.C. § 662(a). In addition, the 1986 amendments to the Act expressly direct FERC to "give equal consideration" to a project's effects on environmental quality, recreational opportunities, and fish and wildlife. 16 U.S.C. § 797(e). This provision also requires FERC to accept conditions that the Secretaries of Interior or Agriculture deem necessary for the protection and utilization of public lands and other reservations of the United States, including lands held in trust for Indians, when issuing licenses upon any part of those public lands or reservations. Escondido Mut. Water Co. v. La Jolla Band of Mission Indians, 466 U.S. 765 (1984). *See* Keating v. FERC, 114 F.3d 1265 (D.C. Cir. 1997) (upholding conditions imposed by the Forest Service on a proposed project when the conditions were reasonably related to protecting forest resources).

FERC may revoke a utility's license if the licensee refuses to construct fishways or undertake other mitigating measures pursuant to the terms of the license. E. Hydroelectric Corp. v. Fed. Energy Regulatory Comm'n, 887 F.3d 1197 (11th Cir. 2018). Before issuing a revocation order, however, FERC must "take[ ] into consideration the nature and seriousness of the violation and the efforts of the licensee to remedy the violation." 16 U.S.C. § 823b(b).

FERC orders will be overturned if they are arbitrary and capricious. In City of Centralia, Wash. v. FERC, 213 F.3d 742 (D.C. Cir. 2000), the court remanded a FERC order requiring an applicant to conduct a $300,000 study to determine if the impacts of its facility on anadromous fish necessitated the construction of a $1,000,000 tailrace barrier. The court found that FERC had failed to balance energy and environmental values, and had marshaled no meaningful evidence that the facility was harmful to fish. Under the circumstances, requiring an expensive and inconclusive study "borders on the absurd." *Id.* at 750.

Several other federal environmental statutes require consideration of fish and wildlife values in projects constructed or licensed by the federal government. The Fish and Wildlife Coordination Act (FWCA), 16 U.S.C. §§ 661–666c, demands "equal consideration" for wildlife conservation in water resource development programs. Washington State Dep't of Fisheries v. FERC, 801 F.2d 1516, 1519 (9th Cir. 1986). In practice, it is extremely difficult to balance the values of the multiple purposes of water projects on one hand and fish and wildlife values on the other. However, if FERC fails to consider fishery impacts before issuing a license under the FPA, it fails to give fish "equal consideration" under the FWCA. Confederated Tribes & Bands of the Yakima Indian Nation v. FERC, 746 F.2d 466 (9th Cir. 1984), *cert. denied,* 471 U.S. 1116 (1985).

When Indian tribes have treaty fishing rights on a river, interference with instream flows by diversion, impoundment, or pollution that damages fish habitat may reduce the ability of tribes to take a meaningful share of fish. *See* Skokomish Indian Tribe v. United States, 410 F.3d 506, 512 (9th Cir. 2005) (finding that a treaty may provide rights of action for equitable relief but not monetary damages against non-parties such as licensees), *cert. denied,* 546 U.S. 1090 (2006). The federal government may be liable in damages for failing to protect treaty rights. U.S. v. Mitchell, 463 U.S. 206 (1983). Moreover, section 4(e) of the Federal Power Act requires the U.S. Department of Interior to develop license conditions to protect the purposes and uses of Indian reservations. *See* City of Tacoma v. FERC, 460 F.3d 53 (D.C. Cir. 2006) (citing 16 U.S.C. § 797(e)).

The National Environmental Policy Act (NEPA), 42 U.S.C. § 4332(2)(C), requires preparation of an environmental impact statement (EIS) identifying the environmental consequences of any proposal for a major federal action that may significantly affect the human environment. Major federal actions include licensing and permitting decisions, which means that NEPA plays a significant role in hydropower operations and many other types of actions with a federal nexus. NEPA ensures that decisionmakers are aware of the environmental effects of their actions as well as the existence of any reasonable, less destructive alternatives, but it does not require the agency to choose the most environmentally friendly outcome. Seven County Infrastructure Coal. v. Eagle County, 605 U.S. 168 (2025) (quoting Robertson v. Methow Valley Citizens Council, 490 U.S. 332 (1989)); LaFlamme v. FERC, 852 F.2d 389, 398 (9th Cir. 1988).

Hotly contested cases arise over the scope and depth of an agency's NEPA analysis, especially regarding whether indirect or cumulative effects are likely to be significant. In *Seven County Infrastructure Coal.*, 145 S.Ct. at 1515, the Court acknowledged that "indirect effects can sometimes fall within NEPA . . . even if those effects might extend outside the geographical territory of the project or might materialize later in time—for example, run-off into a river that flows many miles from the project and affects fish populations elsewhere, or emissions that travel downwind and predictably pollute other areas." But it refused to require the agency to consider the environmental effects of separate projects that "break[ ] the chain of proximate causation between the project at hand [a railroad line connecting rural oil fields with a national freight rail network] and the environmental effects of the separate project [oil extraction and refining]." *Id.* at 1516.

The *Seven Counties* opinion emphasized the need to give deference to an agency's assessment of significant environmental effects and alternatives, which turn on "fact-dependent, context-specific, and policy-laden choices about the depth and breadth of its inquiry. . ." *Id.* at 1513. Such choices should be upheld under "a broad zone of reasonableness." *Id.* Judicial deference will not be forthcoming if an agency relies on baseless or biased data. In Am. Rivers v. Fed. Energy Regulatory Comm'n, 895 F.3d 32, 54 (D.C. Cir. 2018), the court found that FERC's relicensing order for Alabama Power's Coosa River projects was arbitrary and capricious under NEPA where FERC had relied heavily on a flawed biological opinion prepared pursuant to the Endangered Species Act (ESA), and had given insufficient attention to past actions that were perpetuating the river's heavily damaged ecosystem.

Of all of the statutory provisions that protect fish and wildlife, the ESA is the most powerful. Section 9 of the ESA prohibits the "take" of any listed species, including habitat destruction that foreseeably harms the species, by any person, including federal, state, and private actors. 16 U.S.C. § 1538; 50 CFR § 17.3. *See* Babbitt v. Sweet Home Chapter, 515 U.S. 687 (1995) (upholding FWS's definition of harm to include habitat modification that kills or injures listed species). Dam operations that foreseeably cause injury to listed fish or other species may result in liability for a "take" of the species. *See* San Luis Obispo Coastkeeper v. Santa Maria Valley Water Conservation Dist., 49 F.4th 1242 (9th Cir. 2022), *cert. denied* (2023). It can be difficult to prove proximate cause, however, if numerous variables contribute to the harm. In Aransas Project v. Shaw, 775 F.3d 641 (5th Cir. 2014), for example, the court held that a state agency did not take endangered cranes by allowing irrigators to deplete flows that had supported food sources and riparian habitat because the states' licenses did not proximately cause harm. However, in Bear Warriors United, Inc. v. Lambert, 778 F.Supp.3d 1242 (M.D. Fla. 2025), the court found that the State's wastewater regulations constituted a foreseeable take of endangered manatees by allowing discharges of pollutants that caused algae blooms and seagrass destruction.

In addition to section 9, section 7 of the ESA requires each federal agency to "insure that any action authorized, funded, or carried out by [the] agency . . . is not likely to jeopardize the continued existence of any endangered species or threatened species." 16 U.S.C. § 1536(a)(2). Agency "action" includes "all activities or programs of any kind authorized, funded, or carried out, in whole or in part, by Federal agencies. . ." 50 CFR § 402.02. If an agency determines that a proposed action "may affect" a listed species or its critical habitat, the agency must engage in consultation to avoid jeopardy to the species. 50 C.F.R. § 402.14(a). *See* TVA v. Hill, 437 U.S. 153 (1978) (finding that Tellico Dam would jeopardize an endangered snail darter and enjoining its completion); Nat'l Wildlife Fed'n v. Nat'l Marine Fisheries Serv., 886 F.3d 803 (9th Cir. 2018) (enjoining Columbia River Power System operations because they jeopardized listed salmonids).

In rare cases where an agency has no discretion, however, consultation is not required. Nat'l Ass'n of Home Builders v. Defs. of Wildlife, 551 U.S. 644, 673 (2007). One of these rare examples is WildEarth

Guardians v. U.S. Army Corps of Eng'rs, 947 F.3d 635 (10th Cir. 2020), where the Corps was not compelled to consult because the statutes governing its operation of certain dams focused solely on flood control, with no discretion to protect listed species. More typical is San Luis Obispo Coastkeeper v. Santa Maria Valley Conserv. Dist., 49 F.4th 1242 (9th Cir. 2022), *cert. denied,* 144 S.Ct. 74 (2023), where the multi-purpose statute governing Bureau of Reclamation actions provided sufficient discretion to consult and to avoid jeopardy to species.

Both NEPA and the ESA reach far beyond hydropower, and these statutes are addressed in other sections of this book, e.g., *infra* Chapter 10.VI. To conclude this section, one final statute with special relevance to hydropower should be mentioned. Although not really an environmental statute, the Pacific Northwest Electric Power Planning and Conservation Act ("Northwest Power Act"), 16 U.S.C. § 839, is a comprehensive act for allocating supplies and mitigating impacts of federally produced hydropower. The Act contains significant requirements for preserving and restoring anadromous fisheries in the Pacific Northwest, the region hardest hit by the impacts of hydropower facilities. Under the Act, a regional council develops a plan for protection, mitigation, and enhancement of fish and wildlife. Furthermore, managers of federal power facilities are required to afford "equitable treatment" to fish and wildlife, ensuring that their operations do not subordinate fish and wildlife to other project objectives. 16 U.S.C. § 839b. The Council's plans must be "tak[en] into account at each relevant stage" of FERC proceedings. *Id.*; National Wildlife Fed'n v. Federal Energy Regulatory Comm'n, 801 F.2d 1505 (9th Cir. 1986). For an assessment of the Northwest Power Act's impact, see Michael C. Blumm et. al., *A Half-Century of Pacific Salmon Saving Efforts: A Primer on Law, Policy, and Biology*, 64 Nat. Res. J. 137, 202 (2024).

## V. FLOOD CONTROL

Historically, the federal interest in water development was closely tied to maintaining navigation. However, federal interests in flood control expanded significantly during the twentieth century. Today, there are numerous legislative provisions focused on flood control. The Army Corps of Engineers is most frequently at the heart of flood-related disputes, as it is the entity often tasked with carrying out federal flood control legislation.

### A. THE RIVERS AND HARBORS ACT

The Rivers and Harbors Act of 1899 gave the Corps authority to carry out projects to prevent obstructions to navigation and to promote federal navigational interests. 33 U.S.C. §§ 401–418. For years, the Corps focused primarily on navigation and did little under the Act in terms of flood control, in part because Congress stipulated that no federal money could be used to protect land from flooding or for any purpose other than navigation. Even so, the Corps constructed miles of levees along the Mississippi River not only to constrict and improve the navigational channel but also to provide incidental flood control benefits. Today, the Corps has undertaken extensive transportation improvements as well as flood control on mainstems and tributaries of navigable waters.

## B. THE FLOOD CONTROL ACTS

A series of catastrophic floods throughout the early twentieth century prompted Congress to supplement the Rivers and Harbors Act of 1899 with legislation specifically aimed at flood control. The Flood Control Acts, enacted between 1917 and 1965, expanded federal power on navigable rivers for purposes of flood control. For a detailed history and assessment, *see* Christine A. Klein & Sandra B. Zellmer, MISSISSIPPI RIVER TRAGEDIES: A CENTURY OF UNNATURAL DISASTERS (NYU Press 2014).

Although state and local governments often derive extensive economic benefits from federal flood control projects, they have not always embraced the influx of federal infrastructure. For example, the Denison Dam and Reservoir project on the Red River in Texas and Oklahoma inundated both state and private lands. Oklahoma sued, alleging that it would be injured by the project due to the loss of 100,000 acres. Oklahoma ex rel Phillips v. Guy F. Atkinson Co., 313 U.S. 508, 511 (1941). The Supreme Court ruled that the project was a proper exercise of Congress' commerce power, specifically citing the history of flooding in the river basin: "Floods pay no respect to state lines. Their effective control in the Mississippi valley has become increasingly a subject of national concern in recognition of the fact that single states are impotent to cope with them effectively." *Id.* at 521–22. The Court additionally found that the commerce power was by no means limited to maintaining navigability. "There is no constitutional reason why Congress cannot under the commerce clause treat the watersheds as key to flood control on navigable streams and their tributaries." *Id.* at 525.

The Flood Control Act of 1917 was the first federal enactment that explicitly appropriated money for river improvements other than navigation. Pub. L. No. 64–367, 39 Stat. 948 (1917). Congress allocated $45 million for flood control work between the mouth of the Ohio and the mouth of the Mississippi. The project was supervised by the Mississippi River Commission, an entity comprised of Corps officials, a representative of the U.S. Geological Survey, and a few civilian members. Local institutions were required to secure the necessary rights-of-way for levees and to contribute half of the cost of levee construction. The 1917 Act also authorized the Corps to implement the Sacramento River Flood Control Project, in partnership with the state of California. Federal-state levees and other projects were aimed at controlling Central Valley and San Joaquin River floods, largely to protect the populated centers of Sacramento and Stockton. Alf W. Brandt & Andrea P. Clark, *Preparing for Extreme Floods: California's New Flood Plan*, 27 Nat. Res. & Env't 45 (2012). In 1953, the federal government transferred responsibility for the Sacramento River Flood Control Project to the state. *Id. See* Cal. Water Code § 8533 (Sacramento and San Joaquin Rivers).

In 1928, after a devastating flood killed hundreds of people and caused over $200 million in property damage (about $2 billion in 2000 dollars) in the lower Mississippi River Basin, Congress "passed a veritable deluge of Flood Control Acts." Christine Klein & Sandra Zellmer, *Mississippi River Stories: Lessons from a Century of Unnatural Disasters*, 60 SMU L. Rev. 1471, 1485 (2007). The 1928 Act declared that the government would take responsibility for the Mississippi River through the construction of more levees, spillways, and reservoirs, but it also immunized the federal government from any liability "of any kind . . . for any damage from or by floods or flood waters at any place." 33 U.S.C. § 702c.

Each subsequent enactment added another layer to the complicated assortment of authorities for the construction and maintenance of flood control devices. Importantly, the 1936 Flood Control Act delegates broad discretion to the Corps to construct any flood control project it chooses (so long as Congress appropriates the necessary funds) whenever "benefits to whomsoever they may accrue are in excess of the estimated costs." 33 U.S.C. § 701a.

The Flood Control Act of 1944, ch. 665, 58 Stat. 887 (codified as amended in scattered sections of 16, 33, and 43 U.S.C.), authorized the addition of five huge mainstem dams on the Missouri River. The Corps was given control over these dams for flood control and navigation purposes, while the Bureau of Reclamation was charged with promoting irrigation through projects primarily on the tributaries. As is the case with other rivers under its management, the Corps must adopt a Master Water Control Manual to outline management strategies and lay out a hierarchy of river management goals. Earlier versions of the Missouri River Manual specifically prioritized flood control over other functions, but recent versions attempt to balance flood control, navigation, irrigation, water supply, hydroelectric power, recreation, and wildlife. Sandra Zellmer, *Mudslinging on the Missouri: Can Endangered Species Survive The Clean Water Act?*, 16 Drake J. Agric. L. 89, 94 (2011).

In addition to the Flood Control Acts, periodic Water Resources Development Acts (WRDAs) often include flood control and related projects. The WRDA of 1986 authorized the construction or modification of a variety of flood control and navigation projects, along with a number of projects intended to protect coastal concerns, recreation, and fisheries. Pub. L. No. 99–662, 100 Stat. at 4109, 4111. Similarly, the WRDA of 1990 included projects for navigation and flood control as well as storm water management. Pub. L. No. 101–640, 104 Stat. 4604, 4605–11. Congress typically considers proposed WRDA's biennially, but the timing of enactment varies, with WRDA-type legislation enacted in 2000, 2007, 2014, 2016, 2018, 2020, 2022, and 2024. CRS, *Water Resources Development Acts: Primer*, IF11322 (2025).

Under these statutes and other enactments, the Corps has carried out its flood control duties with a vengeance by constructing dams, reservoirs, and levees on rivers throughout the nation. In return, population centers and farmers along the river gained a heightened perception of safety and developed ever-more land in floodplain and coastal areas. The federal government is not always able to hold back the flood waters, though, and the extreme weather events and rising sea levels associated with climate change are likely to make floodplain and coastal properties more vulnerable in the future. A series of devastating hurricanes has demonstrated this point in dramatic fashion. *See, e.g.,* St. Bernard Par. Gov't v. United States, 887 F.3d 1354 (Fed. Cir. 2018), *cert. denied,* 586 U.S. 1069 (2019) (holding that the Corps' failure to maintain the Mississippi River-Gulf Outlet could not be the basis for liability to landowners affected by Hurricane Katrina).

## C. FIFTH AMENDMENT TAKINGS CLAIMS

Landowners who suffer losses when dams are overwhelmed or levees fail may allege that the government should pay for a "taking" of inundated land. *St. Bernard Par. Gov't,* 887 F.3d at 1358. The Supreme Court allowed a takings claim to proceed in Arkansas Game and Fish Comm'n v. U.S., 568 U.S. 23 (2012). There, the Corps deviated from its Water Control Manual for a dam on the Black River by extending flooding, at the request of local farmers, into a state wildlife management area during the area's peak timber growing season. The Court held that " 'where real estate is actually invaded by superinduced additions of water, earth, sand, or other material . . . so as to effectually destroy or impair its usefulness, it is a taking . . . ,' " where the damage is foreseeable and severe, albeit temporary. *Id.* at 32 (citation omitted).

Compensation will not be required if the federal project did not increase the danger of floods "to which respondent's land had always been subject." U.S. v. Sponenbarger, 308 U.S. 256, 265 (1939). Likewise, where the project conferred more benefit than harm to a particular property, the "relative benefits" doctrine will bar recovery. *Id.*; Alford v. U.S., 961 F.3d 1380, 1386 (2020). In Big Oak Farms, Inc. v. United States, 131 Fed. Cl. 45, 54 (2017), the court held that plaintiffs whose land was located in a floodway had the burden of showing that the Corps' activation of a floodway caused more flooding than what would have occurred absent the flood control project, but that the Corps had the burden to show that the relative benefits received by landowners "on the whole" offset the damages they suffered. However, in Ideker Farms, Inc. v. United States, 71 F.4th 964, 986 (Fed. Cir. 2023), the court rejected the Corps' "relative benefits" defense where risk-reducing government actions (dams and levees) preceded risk-increasing government actions (flow alterations for ESA and other purposes). Subsequently, the court awarded compensation to farmers whose properties on the Missouri River flooded for the taking of a *de facto* permanent flowage easement by the Corps. *Id.* at 974, 990.

If landowners cannot lodge a viable takings claim, they may attempt to proceed with tort claims. *See Bernard Par. Gov't,* 887 F.3d at 1362 (holding that the Corps' failure to properly manage the Mississippi

River Gulf Outlet channel cannot be the basis of takings liability; rather, "Plaintiffs' sole remedy for these inactions, if any, lies in tort"). However, the Flood Control Act immunizes the government from tort liability arising from damages caused by flood control measures. Big Oak Farms, Inc. v. United States, 105 Fed. Cl. 48, 53 (2012) (citing 33 U.S.C. § 702c). *See* Central Green Co. v. United States, 531 U.S. 425, 437 (2001) (stating that § 702c immunity attaches to a release of flood waters but not to irrigation waters); In re Katrina Canal Breaches Litigation, 696 F.3d 436 (5th Cir. 2012) (finding that the Corps was immune from flood damages caused by breached levees, but it was not immune for damages caused by the MRGO navigational channel).

## VI. ECOLOGICAL CONCERNS AND ENVIRONMENTAL LEGISLATION

Navigation, hydropower, and flood control measures are often at odds with environmental goals. Dams, reservoirs, levees, and channelization have radically changed the function, processes, and structure of riparian ecosystems. Klein & Zellmer, *Mississippi River Stories,* 60 SMU L. Rev. at 1508–10; Dave Owen & Colin Apse, *Trading Dams*, 48 U.C. Davis L. Rev. 1043, 1057–61 (2015); Blumm et. al., *A Half-Century of Pacific Salmon Saving Efforts,* 64 Nat. Res. J. at 170-198.

Valuable sediment deposits, which fertilized land during flooding and sustained sandbars, islands, and other natural formations in and beside the rivers, have been trapped behind dams and levees or moved too rapidly through channelized river corridors to serve their ecological purposes or to provide ecosystem services. Sandra Zellmer & Lance Gunderson, *Why Resilience May Not Always Be a Good Thing: Lessons in Ecosystem Restoration from Glen Canyon and the Everglades,* 87 Neb. L. Rev. 893, 906–07, 913–19, 924 (2009). Additionally, dams disrupt the life cycles of migrating fish. *See* Nat'l Wildlife Fed'n v. Nat'l Marine Fisheries Serv., 886 F.3d 803, 820 (9th Cir. 2018) (describing irreparable harms to salmonids caused by the Columbia River Power System dams). In Marsh v. Oregon Natural Res. Council, 490 U.S. 360 (1989), the Corps sought to construct a flood control dam on Elk Creek in the Rogue River Basin. The Oregon Natural Resources Council (ONRC) argued that the Corps' NEPA analysis had not taken into consideration possible "worse case scenarios" following an internal report that cited concerns about the fish population of Elk Creek, and had failed to consider the cumulative effect of three dam projects in the basin. The Court rejected ONRC's argument that a supplemental EIS was necessary to account for the new information, and found that the Corps had conducted a "reasoned evaluation" of impacts to fish. *Id.* at 385.

Several federal environmental statutes address the ecological problems posed by dams and other water development projects. NEPA, the ESA, and other important enactments, including Clean Water Act (CWA) § 401, are addressed *supra* Section IV.B-C. Other sections of the CWA related to water quality and, by extension, riparian ecology and water-dependent species, are discussed here.

The CWA expresses an overarching goal "to restore and maintain the chemical, physical, and biological integrity of the Nation's waters." 33 U.S.C. § 1251(a). The Act also includes an interim goal of achieving "water quality which provides for the protection and propagation of fish, shellfish, and wildlife." *Id.*

To achieve these goals, the CWA regulates discharges of pollutants, including soil and nutrients like phosphorous and nitrogen, from point sources through various permit programs. 33 U.S.C. §§ 1342, 1344. However, the U.S. Environmental Protection Agency (EPA) and several courts have found that dams and water transfers are not point sources. *See* Nat'l Wildlife Fed'n v. Gorsuch, 693 F.2d 156 (D.C. Cir. 1982); Nat'l Wildlife Fed'n v. Consumers Power Co., 862 F.2d 580 (6th Cir. 1988); Catskill Mountains Chapter of Trout Unlimited v. EPA, 846 F.3d 492, 503 (2d Cir. 2017), *cert. denied,* 583 U.S. 1155 (2018); S. Side Quarry v. Louisville & Jefferson Cnty. Metro. Sewer Dist., 28 F.4th 684, 699 (6th Cir. 2022) (citing 40 C.F.R. § 122.3(i)). By contrast, pollutants that enter navigable waters after traveling through groundwater may be from a point source if time, distance, and other factors indicate that the entry is the "functional equivalent" of a direct discharge into navigable waters. Cty. of Maui v. Hawaii Wildlife Fund, 590 U.S. 165 (2020). The inquiry is highly fact-specific. *See* Stone v. High Mountain Mining Co., LLC, 89 F.4th 1246 (10th Cir. 2024) (holding that the district court erred in concluding that pollutants that entered groundwater and then a stream through a mine's unlined settling ponds were point sources, and remanding for consideration of additional factors "[i]n light of the complex topography" of the area).

Under the CWA, navigable waters are defined as "waters of the United States, including the territorial seas." 33 U.S.C. § 1362(7). There has been a great deal of judicial and regulatory wrangling over the scope of "waters of the United States" (WOTUS) in recent years. In Sackett v. Env't Prot. Agency, 598 U.S. 651 (2023), the Supreme Court struck down a regulation that included "[i]ntrastate lakes and ponds, streams, or wetlands that either have a continuous surface connection to categorically included waters or have a significant nexus to interstate or traditional navigable waters." *Id.* at 679 (citing 88 Fed. Reg. 3143). Instead, the Court held that only waters that have "geographic[al] features that are described in ordinary parlance as 'streams, oceans, rivers, and lakes'" can be included, plus adjacent wetlands that are "indistinguishable" from those bodies of water due to a continuous surface connection. *Id.* at 671, 676.

The CWA also requires states to develop water quality standards. 33 U.S.C. § 1313(a)–(c). Water quality standards include designated uses of water bodies, numeric or narrative criteria as necessary to protect those uses, and the prevention of degradation of the current condition of water bodies within the state. States submit their water quality standards to EPA for review and approval. Water bodies that fail to meet approved water quality standards must be identified as impaired, and total maximum daily loads (TMDLs) and pollutant management plans must be adopted. 33 U.S.C. § 1313(d). *See* Columbia Riverkeeper v. Wheeler, 944 F.3d 1204 (9th Cir. 2019) (finding that EPA violated the CWA by failing to issue a TMDL for rivers in which salmon and trout had been adversely affected by warm temperatures). Water quality standards that fail to promote riparian ecology or to protect the conservation needs of aquatic species may violate the CWA and possibly the ESA. Zellmer, *Mudslinging on the Missouri,* 16 Drake J. Agric. L. at 102.

In addition to the CWA and the ESA, the Wild and Scenic Rivers Act (WSRA) preserves the "outstandingly remarkable" values (ORVs) of designated river segments by protecting the rivers and their banks from the adverse effects of dams, hydroelectric projects, roads, and other activities. 16 U.S.C. § 1271. ORVs may include "scenic, recreational, geologic, fish and wildlife, historic, cultural, or other similar values." 16 U.S.C. § 1271. *See* Simmons v. Smith, 888 F.3d 994, 997 (8th Cir. 2018) (affirming the agency's determination of WSRA boundaries for the Niobrara Valley, which "possesses a 'profusion of habitats and animal species' that are an 'outstanding example of Great Plains biological diversity,' . . . and 'potential critical habitat[s] for several threatened or endangered species.' ").

Although the WSRA does not prohibit any and all development, *see* Rivers Unlimited v. U.S. Dep't of Transp., 533 F. Supp. 2d 1 (D.D.C. 2008) (upholding a determination to construct a bridge over the Little Miami River), designated river segments are to be preserved in free-flowing conditions and managed to protect and enhance their ORVs for the benefit and enjoyment of present and future generations. 16 U.S.C. § 1281(a). The "protect and enhance" directive imposes some constraints on the managing agency, but it provides much discretion. *Compare* Friends of Yosemite Valley v. Kempthorne, 520 F.3d 1024, 1035 (9th Cir. 2008) (the Park Service's management plan for the Merced wild and scenic river failed to adopt a level of visitor use that would protect the river's ORVs), *with* Am. Whitewater v. Tidwell, 770 F.3d 1108, 1118 (4th Cir. 2014) (the Forest Service reasonably protected the "recreational value" ORV).

The Act places additional responsibilities on federal agencies with jurisdiction over "any lands which include, border upon, or are adjacent to" designated rivers "to take action" necessary to protect the river's ORVs, especially with respect to timber harvest and road construction. 16 U.S.C. § 1283(a). Idaho Rivers United v. Hudson, 173 F. Supp. 3d 1027, 1032 (D. Idaho 2016) (the Forest Service's failure to consider whether Idaho's use of a forest road along the Selway River for logging on adjacent state lands violated § 1283(a)).

Another key provision of the Act forbids FERC from licensing "any dam, water conduit, reservoir, powerhouse, transmission line or other project works under the Federal Power Act on or directly affecting any [designated] river. . . ." 16 U.S.C. § 1278(a). The Act also prohibits all other federal agencies from assisting in the construction of any water resources project that would have a direct and adverse effect on a designated river. 16 U.S.C. § 1278(a). *See* Sierra

Club N. Star Chapter v. Pena, 1 F. Supp. 2d 971 (D. Minn. 1998) (upholding a determination that a proposed bridge would adversely affect the St. Croix River's ORVs and enjoining federal agencies from assisting in the bridge's construction); Sierra Club N. Star Chapter v. LaHood, 693 F. Supp. 2d 958 (D. Minn. 2010) (issuing a permanent injunction against the bridge).

In addition, the Act requires that each wild and scenic river segment be "administered in such manner as to protect and enhance the values which caused it to be included in said system. . . ." 16 U.S.C. § 1281(a). *See Idaho Rivers United,* 173 F. Supp. 3d at 1032 (the Forest Service's failure to consider whether the use of a logging road was consistent with a designated river's values was arbitrary). Activities that detract from the river's values, such as grazing, may be allowed to continue if they "do not substantially interfere with public use and enjoyment of these values." Oregon Wild v. U.S. Forest Serv., 193 F. Supp. 3d 1156, 1173 (D. Or. 2016) (citing 16 U.S.C. § 1281(a)).

By the time the Act reached its 50th Anniversary, Congress had designated 226 rivers and 13,391 river miles as wild, scenic, or recreational. Michael C. Blumm & Max M. Yoklic, *The Wild and Scenic Rivers Act at 50: Overlooked Watershed Protection*, 9 Mich. J. Envtl. & Admin. L. 1, 5 (2019). Going forward, implementation of its goals will necessitate more effective coordination between management agencies and other stakeholders in the river corridor, plus heightened attention to the eligibility of rivers that need restoration measures (such as dam removal) and to the "overlooked WSRA command that managing agencies protect and enhance the water quality of designated segments." *Id.* at 59 (citing 16 U.S.C. §§ 1281(a) and 1283(a)).

# CHAPTER EIGHT

# FEDERAL AND INDIAN WATER RIGHTS

## I. RESERVED RIGHTS DOCTRINE

The reserved water rights doctrine provides that the federal government reserves sufficient water for lands set aside for particular purposes, including Indian reservations, National Parks, and other public land designations. When the federal government reserves land, it may make an express reservation of water for that land. If the language of the land designation is silent, a reservation of water to carry out the purposes of the designation may be implied.

The doctrine encompasses two lines of case law—one dealing with reserved rights on Indian lands and the other addressing reserved rights for other federal purposes. In either case, reserved water rights are defined by federal rather than state law.

State-based water rights in the western United States are based on the priority of when water is first put to a beneficial use. By contrast, reserved rights hold priority dates no later than the date of the reservation, even if those claims have not been previously recognized or enforced under state priority systems. These federal rights, once established, may be senior to existing state-based water rights. Moreover, principles of state law, such as diversion, beneficial use, and forfeiture, do not apply to reserved rights.

Despite their basis in federal law, reserved rights may be quantified in state general stream adjudications under the waiver of sovereign immunity in the McCarran Amendment, 43 U.S.C. § 666. Regardless of the forum, some of the most controversial issues arise at the interface of state and federal law, where quantification, adjudication, and administration of water rights decrees are at stake.

## A. ORIGIN OF THE DOCTRINE— *WINTERS V. UNITED STATES*

In Winters v. United States, 207 U.S. 564 (1908), the Supreme Court considered a conflict that arose between the tribes of the Fort Belknap Reservation in Montana and nearby non-Indian landholders. In 1888, the indigenous tribes entered into a treaty with the United States in which they ceded a great deal of territory and retained a relatively small reservation. Although not explicit in the treaty, the purposes of the reservation lands implied a water right. As settler-colonizers began to occupy the ceded land, they used water from the Milk River for irrigation, perfecting their water rights under Montana state law with a diversion point upstream from the Fort Belknap Reservation. A short time later, the tribes began diverting water for irrigation. The United States, as trustee for the tribes, brought suit to protect the tribal water rights.

The Court held that, although the non-Indian irrigators had established rights under state law, the Tribes held a prior water right beginning at least with the date of the reservation. Because the reserved lands were arid, and because the government's policy—expressed in the 1888 treaty—was to encourage the indigenous population to become (in the now quite offensive language used by the Court) a "pastoral and civilized people," the Court found it inconceivable that the parties to the treaty would have agreed to the land cession without reserving enough water to make the lands useful for that purpose. *Id.* at 576. Although the treaty was silent on the subject, the court found that water rights existed by *necessary implication* to accomplish its stated purposes. The Court applied the established canons of construction that ambiguities in an agreement with tribal nations should be resolved in favor of the Tribe and as the Tribe would have understood the agreement. *Id.*

Once asserted, and more importantly adjudicated, Indian reserved rights may impact the quantity of water available for non-Indian water rights established under state law with a later priority date. Often, the priority dates for tribal claims predate many of the state law-based claims. Moreover, Indian reserved rights cannot be extinguished except by express language, even after the reservation is terminated and the land sold off, so long as there is a continuing purpose to be served. As a result, the presence of unadjudicated Indian reserved rights creates a tension for water resources management. To address this tension, many states initiated comprehensive general stream adjudications, where tribal water rights claims are addressed through litigation or negotiated settlements between the tribe, federal government, and the state, among others (discussed in Section IV of this chapter).

## B. APPLICATION TO FEDERAL NON-INDIAN RESERVATIONS—*ARIZONA V. CALIFORNIA*

Beginning in 1955 with Federal Power Comm'n v. Oregon, 349 U.S. 435 (1955) (Pelton Dam), the Supreme Court foreshadowed its view that the federal government, through its regulatory function under the Commerce Clause and its proprietary function under the Property clause, retained some authority over water on public lands after statehood when those lands were reserved for specific federal purposes. In *Pelton Dam*, the Court held that a *reservation* of federal public land for particular purposes (unlike public lands available for homesteading or other activities) removed water sources on that land from appropriation pursuant to state law. *Id.* at 444. In Arizona v. California, 373 U.S. 546 (1963), the Court explicitly extended the reserved rights doctrine to federal lands reserved for non-Indian purposes. In this context, Congress or the Executive has the power to reserve water from appropriation when it sets aside federal lands so long as water is necessary to carry out the purposes of the reservation.

Following *Arizona v. California*, the Supreme Court continued to recognize the implied reservation of water for federal lands as necessary to fulfill the purposes of the land reservation. For example, the Court upheld the government's claim to the amount of water in a cavern at Devil's Hole National

Monument required to preserve the habitat of the pupfish, a prehistoric species mentioned in the proclamation setting aside the monument. Cappaert v. United States, 426 U.S. 128 (1976). The quantity of water reserved, however, is limited to the amount necessary for the reservation's specific purposes. United States v. New Mexico, 438 U.S. 696 (1978). *See* Section III.D of this chapter. No Supreme Court decision has questioned the existence of federal authority to reserve water. Rather, the persistent question is whether Congress intended to exercise its powers and, if so, the quantity reserved.

## C. BASIS FOR THE EXERCISE OF FEDERAL AUTHORITY

The reserved water rights doctrine is closely tied to the history and settlement of the western United States. Prior to statehood, the federal government held land pursuant to treaties, purchases, and conquest. From 1866–1877, a series of federal statutes authorized public land to be "patented" into private ownership and ultimately made subject to the jurisdiction of newly formed states. The territorial governments and soon-to-be-formed state governments, at around the same time, were recognizing and applying prior appropriation principles among miners and settlers. *See supra* Chapter Three (Prior Appropriation). Through federal statutes that allowed for land disposition, including the Mining Act of 1866 and the Desert Land Act of 1877, among others, Congress began to recognize these appropriative rights. *See* Basey v. Gallagher, 87 U.S. 670 (1875); California Oregon

Power v. Portland Beaver Cement, 295 U.S. 142 (1935). Until the Supreme Court's decision in *California Oregon Power*, however, there were questions about whether federal land patents included some kind of water right for the private patentees. The Court concluded the 1877 Desert Land Act had "effected a severance of all waters upon the public domain, not theretofore appropriated, from the land itself" and recognized private water rights established under state law. 295 U.S. at 158, 164. With this decision, the Court established that the allocation of water rights to private parties was a matter of state law, and that a federal patent carried no right to water under federal law.

While *California Oregon Power* made clear the federal government was not in the business of allocating private water rights, the Court also articulated several important exceptions where federal law would continue to apply, including securing water needed to carry out purposes on federal land and water needed to protect navigational interests. These exceptions are rooted in the federal Constitution under the Property Clause, Article IV § 3; the Commerce Clause and the Indian Commerce Clause, Article I § 8; the Treaty Power, Article II § 2; and the Supremacy Clause, Article VI cl. 2.

With regard to management of federal property, Congress has authority to reserve water for use on public lands under the Property Clause, which allows it "to dispose of and make all needful Rules and Regulations respecting the Territory or other Property belonging to the United States." The

Navigation Power, based in Article I § 8 of the Commerce Clause, also provides federal authority to protect the public's interest in water. In United States v. Rio Grande Dam & Irrigation Co., 174 U.S. 690 (1899), the Court upheld the ability of Congress to regulate the flow of a non-navigable stream that affected the navigable capacity of navigable waters. It stated, in dictum, that a state "cannot by its legislation destroy the right of the United States, as owner of lands bordering on a stream, to the continued flow of its waters; so far at least as may be necessary for the beneficial uses of the government property." *Id.* at 703.

In addition to treaties and other agreements with the federal government, reserved water rights for Indian tribes may also be based on aboriginal rights. *See* Makah Indian Tribe v. Quileute Indian Tribe, 873 F.3d 1157, 1166 (9th Cir. 2017) ("Absent a clear written indication, courts are reluctant to conclude that a tribe has forfeited previously held rights."). A leading example can be found in the Northwest treaties, which guarantee a right to fish at usual and accustomed grounds or locations. United States v. Adair, 723 F. 2d 1394, 1417–18 (9th Cir. 1983). *See* United States v. Winans, 198 U.S. 371 (1905); Amy K. Kelley, ed., *Reserved Water Rights,* 2 Waters and Water Rights § 37.01(b) (2025).

## D. RELATIONSHIP TO STATE WATER LAW

### 1. Prior Appropriation Jurisdictions

As discussed above, the 1877 Desert Land Act was interpreted in *California Oregon Power v. Beaver Portland Cement* as confirming that private rights on federal land are established according to state law. Notwithstanding the role of the states in allocating private rights, the Court also established that the federal government retained the power to reserve water to protect federal property. These federal rights create conflict within the states because they operate under federal, not state, law.

For example, a federal reserved right is not subject to abandonment or forfeiture for non-use. *Winters*, 208 U.S. at 577; Colville Confederated Tribes v. Walton (Walton II), 647 F.2d 42 (9th Cir. 1981). Additionally, a federal reserved right is not required to satisfy the state's definition of beneficial use. The beneficial use exception is especially controversial where the federal need for water is for instream or non-consumptive uses that are not protected under state law. *See* Cappaert v. United States, 426 U.S. 128 (1976); United States v. New Mexico, 438 U.S. 700 (1978); High Country Citizens' Alliance v. Norton, 448 F.Supp.2d 1235 (D. Colo. 2006).

While all water rights are exercised based on a priority date, the reserved rights doctrine uses the date of the reservation, not the date of diversion for beneficial use. This raises concerns among state administrators and holders of state water rights because federal reserved rights often remain unused for many years and exist in uncertain quantities. Unquantified or unused reserved rights create a cloud on active water users and potentially disrupt a state's water rights system. With regard to tribal rights, a tribe can assert a right with a very senior priority date or even "time immemorial"—a time in prehistory. These reserved rights hold priority dates before most state-based rights were established. United States v. Adair, 723 F.2d 1394 (9th Cir. 1983).

Lastly, state law cannot interfere with federal property rights or defeat federal purposes. Only Congress can relinquish water interests held by the United States. *High Country Citizens' Alliance*, 448 F.Supp.2d at 1248. Because the doctrine is based on federal law, any conflicting state law is preempted under the Supremacy Clause. *See* U.S. Const. Art. VI, cl. 2; California v. United States, 438 U.S. 645 (1978).

### 2. Riparian Jurisdictions

*Winters* and other reserved rights cases arose in jurisdictions that follow the doctrine of prior appropriation, which uses priority to allocate water rights. Under riparian water law, no special significance attaches to the order in which water use begins. *See supra* Chapter Two (Riparian Rights). Generally, every landowner bordering a stream has a right to use a reasonable quantity of water. In times of shortage, available supplies are shared by all riparian users. If the federal government must share the burden of shortage equally with other users, there is no assurance that federal purposes can be satisfied.

The courts have not decided how the concept of reserved rights applies in a riparian jurisdiction. However, a Virginia state court addressed the issue and questioned whether reserved rights would be necessary in a riparian jurisdiction where all reasonable uses of riparian owners are protected. Mattaponi Indian Tribe v. Commonwealth, 72 Va. Cir. 444 (2007). However, the court recognized that, unlike the reserved rights doctrine, "riparian law does not guarantee a riparian owner sufficient water for a particular purpose." *Id.* at 457–58.

Three other developments are notable, though none are dispositive. First, reserved rights were asserted by the Seminole Tribe in Florida and by the Chickasaw and Choctaw in Oklahoma, but the issues were resolved in a settlement agreement. *See* Pub.L. 100–228, § 2, Dec. 31, 1987 (codified at 25 U.S.C. § 1772). Second, in Penobscot Nation v. Frey, 3 F.4th 484, 492 (1st Cir. 2021), the court held that a reservation in Maine that included "solely. . . islands" within a river did not include surrounding waters or submerged lands. Finally, the Ninth Circuit Court of Appeals recognized reserved rights to groundwater for a tribe in California. Agua Caliente Band of Cahuilla Indians v. Coachella Valley Water Dist., 849 F.3d 1262 (9th Cir.), *cert. denied,* 538 U.S. 996 (2017). The court reasoned that appurtenant groundwater was necessary to achieve the purpose of a reservation that lacked adequate surface water. One may make an analogy to reserved rights for adjacent lands in riparian jurisdictions, because California applies a riparian-like rule of correlative, reasonable use to groundwater.

In any event, riparian rights, like prior appropriation rights, are premised on state law, while reserved rights depend on the intent of Congress (and the tribes in the case of Indian reserved rights). If there is evidence of intent to reserve water for a federal purpose, it should preempt state law to the contrary. Judith V. Royster, *Winters in the East: Tribal Reserved Rights to Water in Riparian States*, 25 Wm. & Mary Envtl. L. & Pol'y Rev. 168, 197–201 (2000).

## II. FEDERAL WATER RIGHTS FOR INDIAN LANDS AND PURPOSES

Federal law recognizes three categories of aboriginal or Indian water rights: (1) those based on the reservation of land, referred to as "Winters" or reserved rights; (2) preexisting rights recognized in a treaty, referred to as "Winans" rights; and (3) those based on Pueblo title to lands and the Treaty of Guadalupe Hidalgo.

### A. DETERMINING PURPOSES FOR WATER RIGHTS—*WINTERS, WINANS,* AND PUEBLO WATER RIGHTS

Indian reserved rights arise under federal law through treaties, statutes, agreements, and executive orders. Like all federal rights, the Supremacy Clause protects Indian reserved rights from interference by conflicting state law. The purpose associated with the water right can have a tremendous impact on the quantity of water needed to accomplish that purpose.

Reserved water rights to support aboriginal practices are referred to as *Winans* rights and are most often associated with treaty reservations. Typically, tribes ceded vast portions of land to the United States in these treaties in exchange for recognition of certain pre-existing, aboriginal activities that usually involve non-consumptive use of water. United States v. Adair, 723 F.2d 1394 (9th Cir. 1983); State ex rel. Greely v. Confederated Salish and Kootenai Tribes of the Flathead Reservation, 712 P.2d 754 (Mont. 1985). For Pacific Northwest tribes included in the Stevens' Treaties, the ability to fish at usual and accustomed fishing grounds provides the basis for a reserved water right to accomplish this purpose. United States v. Winans, 198 U.S. 371 (1905); Washington v. Washington State Commercial Passenger Fishing Vessel Ass'n, 443 U.S. 658 (1979). *Winans* rights can include water sufficient to support hunting, fishing, and trapping rights, as well as water sufficient to support productive habitat. U.S. v. Adair (Adair III), 187 F.Supp.2d 1273 (D. Or. 2002) (vacated on other grounds). *See* In re Coeur d'Alene-Spokane River Basin Adjudication, 448 P.3d 322 (2019) (holding that the purpose of the tribe's reservation was to provide a homeland, which includes the aboriginal consumptive uses for domestic needs and agriculture and nonconsumptive uses for hunting (wildlife habitat), fishing (fish habitat), plant gathering, and cultural activities).

Reserved water rights established through the reservation of ceded aboriginal lands are known as "Winters" rights. The federal government's purpose in setting aside this land was typically to encourage indigenous peoples to become farmers who would need water to accomplish this purpose. Arizona v. California, 373 U.S. 546 (1963). However, it also intended to create a homeland for the tribes. *See* In re General Adjudication of the Gila River System, 35 P.3d 68 (Ariz. 2001); *Agua Caliente Band of Cahuilla Indians,* 849 F.3d at 1271.

Pueblo rights differ from *Winans* and *Winters* rights primarily because Pueblo communities own the underlying land in fee (as opposed to being held in trust by the federal government), and their water rights derive from Spanish and Mexican law. When the United States signed the Treaty of Guadalupe Hidalgo to obtain much of the Southwest, it expressly recognized pre-existing property titles, including water rights. Treaty of Guadalupe Hidalgo, Art. VIII, 9 Stat. 922 (1848). *See* N.M. ex rel. Reynolds v. Aamodt, 618 F. Supp. 993 (D.N.M. 1985); State ex rel. Martinez v. Kerr McGee, 898 P.2d 1256 (N.M. App. 1995). In United States v. Abouselman, 976 F.3d 1146 (10th Cir. 2020), the court recognized that the Pueblos' pre-existing aboriginal water rights were not extinguished by the imposition of Spanish authority. Subsequently, on remand, the district court held that the Pueblos' aboriginal water rights had not been extinguished by various federal statutes, either. United States v. Abousleman, 695 F. Supp. 3d 1277 (D.N.M. 2023).

## B. QUANTIFYING RESERVED WATER RIGHTS

### 1. *Winters* Rights—Practicably Irrigable Acreage (PIA Standard)

*Winters* rights are associated with the reservation of land for Indian people for agrarian purposes. In *Arizona v. California*, the Supreme Court articulated the "PIA standard" as the measure of the *Winters* reserved right. 373 U.S. at 600. This standard grants the amount of water needed to irrigate all of the *practicably irrigable acreage* (PIA) of the reservation.

The PIA standard was also used to establish a quantity associated with what some may deem non-agricultural purposes. The Court adopted it over the objection of the Colorado Basin states, who urged a standard based on the tribes' reasonably foreseeable needs or based on equitable apportionment of available water. *Id.* at 601.

In a case involving the Wind River Reservation, the Wyoming Supreme Court established a two-part test for lands subject to the PIA standard: (1) the land must be capable of sustained irrigation, and (2) the land must be irrigable at a reasonable cost. In re General Adjudication of All Rights to Use Water in the Big Horn System (Big Horn I), 753 P.2d 76 (Wyo. 1988). The U.S. Supreme Court granted certiorari and the PIA test was affirmed, without opinion, by an evenly divided court. Wyoming v. United States, 492 U.S. 406 (1989).

In *Big Horn*, the Wyoming court also limited the purpose of the reservation to purely agricultural needs, notwithstanding several references to a "permanent homeland" in the treaty in question. 753 P.2d at 96. It refused to recognize reserved rights for fisheries, mining, industrial, or wildlife purposes. The U.S. Supreme Court did not review this portion of the decision, and the United States and tribes continue to assert other purposes in other cases.

After the *Big Horn* decision, courts have taken different approaches to quantifying *Winters* rights. The Arizona Supreme Court found that the PIA method should not be the sole method for determining the amount of water necessary for a tribe, and established a "feasibility test" plus a non-exclusive list of factors to be considered when evaluating reserved rights claims. In re General Adjudication of the Gila River System, 35 P.3d 68, 78–79 (Ariz. 2001). These factors include the tribe's culture, history, natural resources, and present and future population. Idaho reached a similar result in In Re Coeur d'Alene-Spokane River Basin Adjudication, 448 P.3d 322 (Idaho 2019). For additional cases, *see* 1 Cohen's Handbook of Federal Indian Law § 21.03 (2025).

### 2. *Winans* Rights—Needs-Based Standards for Non-Irrigation Rights

*Winans* rights are based on particular and often non-consumptive uses of water that are protected through treaties or reservation documents. This doctrine recognizes that Indian reservations are established by a grant of rights *from* the tribe, not a grant of rights *to* the tribe. United States v. Winans, 198 U.S. 371, 381 (1905).

For example, a treaty right to take fish in common with non-Indians has been interpreted to entitle the tribes to a maximum of 50 percent of the harvest of salmon each year. *See* Washington v. Washington State Commercial Passenger Fishing Vessel Ass'n, 443 U.S. 658, 686 (1979) (providing that "the central principle here must be that Indian treaty rights to a natural resource that once was thoroughly and exclusively exploited by the Indians secures so much as, but not more than, is necessary to provide the Indians with a livelihood—that is to say a moderate living"). The Klamath Tribe's treaty rights ensure a quantity of water sufficient to support hunting and fishing. United States v. Adair, 723 F.2d 1394 (9th Cir. 1983), *cert. denied,* 467 U.S. 1252 (1984). The Ninth Circuit has also recognized the Colville Tribe's right to re-establish a fishery to replace the one lost to dam construction. Colville Confederated Tribes v. Walton (Colville I), 647 F.2d 42 (9th Cir. 1981).

A tribe's nonconsumptive reserved rights have a "time immemorial" priority date because the tribe's retained rights were not created by a treaty; rather, the treaty confirmed the continued existence of aboriginal rights. *Adair,* 723 F.2d at 1414; *In re Coeur d'Alene-Spokane River Basin Adjudication,* 448 P.3d at 557.

### 3. Pueblo Rights—Looking to Historic Uses

Pueblo rights are a unique feature of water law. As noted above, Pueblo water rights generally derive from Spanish and Mexican land grants and law. In addition to land grants, many Pueblos also possess other lands and waters reserved by executive order or by Congress. Richard W. Hughes, Pueblo Indian Water Rights: Charting the Unknown, 57 Nat. Resources J. 219, 222 (2017).

The Winters standard has not been applied to Pueblo water rights derived from land grants. *See* New Mexico v. Aamodt, 537 F.2d 1102, 1111 (10th Cir. 1976) ("[t]he recognized fee title of the Pueblos is logically inconsistent with the concept of a reserved right"). For those Pueblo water rights, adjudicating courts have looked at "historically irrigable acreage" or an estimated average of the water used to irrigate between the signing of the 1848 Treaty of Guadalupe Hidalgo and the 1923 Pueblo Lands Act. State ex rel. Reynolds v. Aamodt, 618 F. Supp. 993, 996 (D.N.M. 1985); State ex rel. Martinez v. Kerr McGee, 898 P.2d 1256, 1264–65 (N.M. App 1995). However, lands reserved by the United States for Pueblo use after 1848 may have Winters rights that would be treated much like the federal reserved water rights of other tribes. *Aamodt,* 537 F.2d at 1010.

## C. CHANGE IN USE ON-RESERVATION

Once Indian reserved water rights are quantified, they may be put to uses other than those for which they were quantified. For example, the Indian reservations along the Colorado River are entitled to certain quantities of water based upon their irrigable acreage. But the tribes may apply the water allocated to them to non-agricultural purposes, including domestic, commercial, and industrial uses. *See* Arizona v. California (Arizona II), 439 U.S. 419 (1979) (recognizing that, once rights were established, they could be utilized or disposed of for the benefit of the Indians as relevant law would allow). *See also* United States v. Washington, 375 F.Supp.2d 1050 (W.D. Wash. 2005); Colville Confederated Tribes v. Walton (Walton II), 647 F.2d 42 (9th Cir. 1981); *Agua Caliente Band of Cahuilla Indians,* 849 F.3d at 1270. Modern courts recognize that "allocations should not be limited to only an amount of water sufficient to support the pastoral life often contemplated in the nineteenth century, but rather, calculated to provide the tribes with water in quantities sufficient to promote survival and the success of the reservations." State ex rel. State Eng'r v. United States, 425 P.3d 723, 734 (N.M. App. 2018).

Wyoming appears to be the outlier on this issue. A divided decision of the Wyoming court in a later phase of the *Big Horn* case held that rights quantified based on practicably irrigable acreage could not be changed to instream flow uses for fish without complying with Wyoming state law procedures for changes of use. In re General Adjudication of All Rights to Use Water in Big Horn River System (Big Horn III), 835 P.2d 273 (Wyo. 1992). The decision was not appealed, and there was no majority opinion for the court explaining the rationale.

## D. USES OUTSIDE THE RESERVATION—TRANSFER OF INDIAN WATER RIGHTS

Transfers of Indian water rights can provide substantial economic returns, support the tribes' right to make full use of their reserved water, and more broadly, promote tribal self-sufficiency. However, as appurtenant interests in real property, federal reserved rights are likely subject to the restraints on alienation established by the Indian Non-Intercourse Act. 25 U.S.C § 177. Although the Act prohibits any "purchase, grant, lease, or other conveyance of lands, or of any title or claim thereto" without federal consent, most authorities agree that the Act applies to the marketing of water rights. 1 Cohen's Handbook of Federal Indian Law § 21.03(7)(c) (2025); David H. Getches, *Management and Marketing of Indian Water: From Conflict to Pragmatism*, 58 U. Colo. L. Rev. 515, 545 (1988). *See* In re General Adjudication of the Big Horn System, 753 P.2d 76 (Wyo. 1988) (refusing to separate reserved water rights from reservation lands).

Absent federal legislative permission, tribes probably cannot sell, lease, or exchange their water rights. However, if water rights are considered "lands" under the Non-Intercourse Act, they may also be covered by 25 U.S.C. § 415, which allows tribal "lands" to be leased for certain purposes. Cohen, *supra*, § 21.03(7)(c). That said, Congress has not yet given any blanket approval to water leasing or other marketing arrangements, *id.*, which is likely why negotiators of tribal water settlements strive to address these issues explicitly in their agreements.

Indeed, nearly all water rights settlements approved by Congress have given specific authorization for transfer or lease of water rights off-reservation. *See, e.g.*, Public Law 109–410, 120 Stat. 2762 (2006) (authorizing Assiniboine and Sioux Tribes to enter into leases); Public Law 106–382, 114 Stat. 1454 (implementing provisions of the Fort Peck/ Montana Compact of 1985 that allow leasing of Indian water rights); Montana Water Rights Protection Act, Pub. L. No. 116–260 (2020) (codified at Mont. Code Ann. § 85–20–1901) (ratifying a compact with the Confederated Salish and Kootenai Tribes that authorizes 99-year leases). Such leases provide financial benefits to tribes and enable non-Indians to make efficient use of water resources not immediately needed by the tribes. National Water Commission, Water Policies for the Future—Final Report to the President and to the Congress of the United States, 51–61 (1973).

## E. WATER RIGHTS FOR INDIVIDUAL INDIAN ALLOTMENTS

The General Allotment Act of 1887, known as the "Dawes Act," fostered a policy of dividing up tribal lands into individual holdings. Act of Feb.8, 1887, 24 Stat. 388, ch. 119 (codified as amended in scattered sections of 25 U.S.C.). The purpose was to convert tribes from nomadic ways to agricultural pursuits; it was thought the most efficacious way to do this was to give each individual tribal member a parcel to farm. This devastating policy continued for nearly fifty years until the passage of the Indian Reorganization Act of 1934. 25 U.S.C. § 461. Section

7 of the Act empowered the Secretary of Interior to promulgate regulations to "secure a just and equal distribution" of irrigation water among reservation Indians. 25 U.S.C. § 381. *See* Colville Confederated Tribes v. Walton (Walton III), 752 F.2d 397 (9th Cir. 1985); United States v. Adair, 723 F.2d 1394 (9th Cir. 1983), *cert. denied,* 467 U.S. 1252 (1984). This provision merely confirmed that allottees have a right to use some share of tribal water rights. United States v. Powers, 305 U.S. 527 (1939).

Many of the lands that were distributed through allotment were conveyed to non-Indian owners. Under the rule developed in litigation with the Colville Confederated Tribes, see, e.g., *Walton III*, 752 F.2d at 401–402, a non-Indian purchaser of an allotment obtains a right to use a share of the tribe's reserved water with a priority date as of the creation of the reservation provided there has been reasonable diligence in putting the water to use.

These so-called "Walton" rights have been criticized as giving allotment purchasers an advantage over their neighbors whose lands were homesteaded; they obtain rights superior to most other private water users. This can disrupt state law water allocation schemes, provide an incentive to transfer tribal lands to non-tribal members, and divest tribes of their reserved water rights in a piecemeal fashion without congressional authorization. *See* David H. Getches, *Water Rights on Indian Allotments,* 26 S.D. L. Rev. 405 (1981). Nonetheless, the Wyoming Supreme Court and others have followed the *Walton* rule in considering claims of non-Indian allottees holding water rights. In re General Adjudication of All Rights to Use Water in the Big Horn River System, 899 P.2d 848 (Wyo. 1995); State ex rel. Greely v. Confederated Salish & Kootenai Tribes, 712 P.2d 754 (Mont. 1985). *See* In re Yakima River Drainage Basin, 296 P.3d 835 (Wash. 2013) (resolving Yakama Nation Indian, allottee, and non-Indian water rights in the long-running "Acquavella" adjudication).

If tribes reacquire former reservation lands, the water rights associated with those lands are maintained, including a priority date of the time of the reservation, unless the lands were ceded "surplus" lands. Cohen, *supra*, at § 21.30(8)(c). Both the Ninth Circuit and the Wyoming Supreme Court have held that lands formerly part of a reservation, lost through allotment and then reacquired in trust, have *Winters* rights. United States v. Anderson, 736 F.2d 1358 (9th Cir. 1984); In re General Adjudication of All Rights to Use Water In the Big Horn River System, 753 P.2d 76 (Wyo. 1988).

If tribes reacquire lands that were deemed "surplus" under the General Allotment Act, those lands have reserved rights, but courts have split on the priority date that will attach at reacquisition. The Ninth Circuit has held that the priority date is the date of reacquisition. *Anderson*, 736 F.2d at 1363. The Wyoming Supreme Court held that the water rights have the original reservation priority date. In re Big Horn (Big Horn II), 753 P.2d 76 (Wyo. 1988).

## F. WATERS SUBJECT TO RESERVATION

Reserved rights can be established for any water that is unappropriated at the time of the federal reservation. Winters v. United States, 207 U.S. 564 (1908); Arizona v. California, 373 U.S. 546 (1963). Questions arise as to whether water is available for appropriation and whether the water sources must be within the reservation's boundaries for a reserved right to exist. A reservation is not necessarily deprived of the benefit of reserved rights simply because there are no water sources within its boundaries or because those located there are inadequate for reservation purposes. Thus, in *Arizona v. California*, the Supreme Court upheld an allocation of water from the Colorado River to the Cocopah Reservation some two miles away; water from the river had been delivered to the reservation by an irrigation canal for several years before the decision. *Id.* at 596–98. Judicial references to federal water rights being "appurtenant" to reserved lands most likely refer not to some physical attachment of water to land, but to the legal doctrine that attaches water rights to land to the extent necessary to fulfill reservation purposes. *See* Katie John v. United States, 720 F.3d 1214 (9th Cir. 2013) (reserved rights are not limited to water within the borders of a federal reservation), *cert. denied*, 572 U.S. 1042 (2014); In re Coeur d'Alene-Spokane River Basin Adjudication, 448 P.3d 322 (Idaho 2019) (reserved rights include protection of upstream fish habitat).

In addition to the question of off-reservation water, important questions exist regarding the reservation of groundwater. Several courts have recognized that Indian reserved rights include groundwater. Confederated Salish and Kootenai Tribes of the Flathead Reservation v. Stults, 59 P.3d 1093 (Mont. 2002); *In re Coeur d'Alene-Spokane River Basin Adjudication,* 448 P.3d at 350; Agua Caliente Band of Cahuilla Indians v. Coachella Valley Water Dist., 849 F.3d 1262 (9th Cir.), *cert. denied,* 538 U.S. 996 (2017). These cases and others related to non-Indian reserved rights are discussed below in Section III.F.

## III. FEDERAL RIGHTS FOR OTHER (NON-INDIAN) RESERVATIONS OF LAND

In the *Pelton Dam* case in 1955 and in *Arizona v. California* in 1963, the Supreme Court recognized that the reserved water rights doctrine, thought by some to be a principle of Indian law, applied to non-Indian federal reserved lands. Federal Power Comm'n v. Oregon (Pelton Dam), 349 U.S. 435 (1955); Arizona v. California, 373 U.S. 546 (1963). In *Pelton Dam,* the Court upheld an implied reserved water right for a power site withdrawal. In Arizona v. California, 373 U.S. 546 (1963), the Court applied the doctrine to a national recreation area, a national forest, and two wildlife refuges. The application of the doctrine to non-Indian federal lands is now firmly established.

### A. EXPRESS V. IMPLIED RIGHTS

The federal government exercises its power to reserve water whenever it sets aside land for purposes that require water. The land and appurtenant water rights can be set aside by an act of Congress, a treaty, or an executive order. *Arizona v. California,* 373 U.S. at 598; Parravano v. Babbitt, 70 F.3d 539 (9th Cir. 1995).

Given the uncertainty, time, controversy, and cost associated with litigating reserved rights, Congress and the Executive have increasingly been explicit about reserved rights in new public land reserves. John D. Leshy, *Water Rights for New Federal Land Conservation Programs: A Turn-Of-The-Century Evaluation,* 4 U. Denv. Water L. Rev. 271, 278 (2001). *See* Jeffrey C. Fereday & Christopher H. Meyer, *What is the Federal Reserved Water Rights Doctrine, Really?*, 52 Idaho L. Rev. 341, 351 (2016) (opining that Congress will never create another federal reserve without explicitly claiming or denying a federal water right). Examples include the Calif. Desert Protection Act of 1994, Pub. L. No, 103–433, 108 Stat. 4471; Great Sand Dunes National Park and Preserve Act of 2000, Pub. L. 106–530, 114 Stat. 2527; Agua Fria Proclamation No. 7263 65 Fed. Reg. 2817, 2818 (2000); Cascade Siskiyou Proclamation No. 7318, 65 Fed. Reg. 37247, 37250 (2000).

As with federal Indian reservations, a reserved right can be *implied* for federal public lands if the reservation document is silent as to water rights. *See, e.g.,* Winters v. United States, 207 U.S. 564 (1908); United States v. Powers, 305 U.S. 527 (1939); Arizona v. California, 373 U.S. 546 (1963); Cappaert v. United States, 426 U.S. 128 (1976); United States v. New Mexico, 438 U.S. 696 (1978). Implied reserved water rights are based on an examination of the intent in reserving the federal land. "Intent is inferred if the previously unappropriated waters are necessary to accomplish the purposes for which the reservation was created." *Cappaert*, 426 U.S. at 139.

## B. PRIORITY DATE

Reserved water rights have a priority date based on the date of the reservation. Cappaert v. United States, 426 U.S. 128 (1976). Reservations that have lands added at a later date for similar or additional purposes may have more than one priority date. See United States v. Denver, 656 P.2d 1 (1982) (recognizing that Rocky Mountain National Park has multiple priority dates—1897, when the area was set aside as a national forest, and 1915 and 1930, when the area was established as a national park). In Arizona v. California, 373 U.S. 546 (1963), the Supreme Court followed the relation back doctrine in setting the priority date of reserved water rights as the date the lands were withdrawn rather than the date of the final decision to designate those lands for particular purposes.

## C. DETERMINING THE PURPOSES OF THE RESERVATION

### 1. Quantity

The quantity of water subject to federal reserved rights for non-Indian federal lands is limited to the quantity necessary to fulfill the purposes of the reservation. The amount may change over time as needs change, provided it remains within the original purposes for establishing a reservation. The Supreme

Court held that the government impliedly reserved "only that amount of water necessary to fulfill the purpose of the reservation, no more." Cappaert v. United States, 426 U.S. 128, 141 (1976). In United States v. New Mexico, 438 U.S. 696, 700, 702 (1978), the Court further limited the quantity that could be reserved to the water necessary to fulfill the "specific" or "very purposes" for which the land was reserved, not secondary purposes.

## 2. Specific Purposes of the Reservation

In *New Mexico*, the Court found that, at the time of the Forest Service Organic Act of 1897, Congress had two specific purposes for establishing national forests: timber production and watershed protection. 438 U.S. at 714–715 (citing 16 U.S.C. § 473). The Act did not refer to fish and wildlife or stock watering purposes. The Court contrasted the Organic Act with legislation expressing concern for wildlife as a specific purpose (such as the National Park Service Act of 1916, 54 U.S.C. 100101). Subsequent legislation, such as the 1960 Multiple-Use Sustained-Yield Act, broadened the mandates for national forests to include wildlife, recreation, and range, but did not change the specific purposes of the forest reservations and did not reserve any additional water for secondary purposes. *Id.* at 714–15. *See* United States v. City and County of Denver, 656 P.2d 1 (Colo. 1982); United States v. City of Challis, 988 P.2d 1199 (Idaho 1998).

The *New Mexico* opinion is often cited as distinguishing between primary and secondary purposes. The only mention of primary purposes, however, comes near the end of the opinion in a footnote. 438 U.S. at 717 n.23. The opinion seems to turn rather on the notion of specific or principal purposes of the reservation as opposed to secondary or attendant uses of water. *See id.* at 700, 702–05, 707, 711–12, 715–16 ("specific purposes"; "very purposes"; "principal purposes"; "direct purpose"). Similarly, in *Cappaert,* 426 U.S. at 139, the Court referred to "the purposes" of a monument in finding that a reserved water right was implied.

### 3. Securing Water for Secondary Uses Under State Law

In *United States v. New Mexico*, the Supreme Court stated that the federal government must turn to state law to fulfill "secondary purposes" that were outside or beyond the specific purposes of the reservation. The federal government can and does hold rights under state law. *See, e.g.,* 60 Fed. Reg. 9894, 9937 (1995) (stating that BLM will assert rights under state law for livestock grazing on public land). In some instances, Congress may explicitly direct the federal government to acquire rights under state law. *See, e.g.,* Great Sand Dunes National Park and Preserve Act of 2000, Pub. Law 106–530, 114 Stat. 2527, 16 U.S.C. § 410hhh.

Often, questions of ownership, control, subordination, and enforcement of federal rights established under state law make state-based water rights much less attractive for the federal government. Adell L. Amos, *The Use of State*

*Instream Flow Laws for Federal Lands: Respecting State Control While Meeting Federal Purposes,* 36 Envtl. L. 1287, 1249 (2006). States, however, cannot restrict the federal government's ability to secure state-based water rights or regulate those rights if those restrictions frustrate a federal purpose. In California v. United States, 438 U.S. 645 (1978), the Supreme Court held that the state could condition use of water rights acquired by the United States for a federal reclamation project, but any conditions that conflicted with congressional directives on how the project was to operate would be invalid. For details on reclamation law, see Chapter 10.V.2.

Applications by the federal government to appropriate water under state law are considered on an equal basis with applications by private parties. State v. Morros, 766 P.2d 263 (Nev. 1988). However, difficult issues arise if state law fails to recognize the kind of right the federal government needs to protect federal purposes. This tension often emerges in the context of instream flow rights. Several western state courts have recognized federal rights for instream flow. *See, e.g., id.*; DeKay v. U.S. Fish and Wildlife Serv., 524 N.W.2d 855 (S.D. 1994); Phelps Dodge Corp. v. Arizona Dep't of Water Res., 118 P.3d 1110 (Ariz. App. 2005).

In states where riparian rights are recognized, the federal government, as a riparian landowner, may have water rights under state law. After the Supreme Court's decision in *U.S. v. New Mexico*, the Forest Service sought and secured recognition of riparian rights under California law to protect wildlife resources in the Plumas National Forest. In re Water of the Hallett Creek Stream System, 749 P.2d 324, *cert. denied*, 488 U.S. 824 (Cal. 1988). The court noted, however, that these riparian rights were subject to state administrative control and could be restricted, like any other riparian right, when a conflict arose. *Id.* at 337.

### 4. Other Regulatory Authority to Secure Water—Federal Regulatory Rights

Another outgrowth of the Supreme Court's decision in *U.S. v. New Mexico* was the emergence of efforts to utilize various federal regulatory authorities to protect water resources on federal reservations. Three categories of these "federal regulatory rights" exist. A. Dan Tarlock & Jason Robison, *Federal Regulatory Water Rights,* L. of Water Rights & Resources § 9:22 (2025).

The first category of federal regulatory rights emerges from the federal government's authority to own, manage, and protect federal public lands and to carry out congressionally-mandated purposes. The federal government possesses the authority to assert non-reserved federal rights to carry out congressional purposes on federal lands. 6 Op. Off. Legal Counsel 328 (1982); *see* Great Sand Dunes National Park and Preserve Act of 2000, Pub. L. No. 106–530, § 9(b)(2)(B) (directing the federal government to secure a federal water right to protect the Dunes ecosystem using state processes).

The second category involves using general regulatory authority to manage public lands in a manner that protects environmental values. For example, the Forest Service and the Bureau of Land Management have broad authority to regulate activities on federal land, including placing conditions on rights-of-ways to protect resources. 43 U.S.C. §§ 1761(a)(1), 1765(a). The Ninth Circuit has upheld the Forest Service's authority to impose bypass flow restrictions to protect fish and wildlife habitat as a condition of an irrigation ditch's right-of-way permit. County of Okanogan v. National Marine Fisheries Services, 347 F.3d 1081 (9th Cir. 2003). *See also* Trout Unlimited v. U.S. Dept. of Agriculture, 320 F.Supp.2d 1090 (D. Colo. 2004) (upholding authority to impose bypass flows), appeal dismissed, 441 F.3d 1214 (10th Cir. 2006).

The third category of federal regulatory rights involves the mandates of regulatory statutes that do not involve the management of federal lands, such as the Clean Water Act, the Endangered Species Act, and the Federal Power Act. 33 U.S.C. §§ 1251–1387; 16 U.S.C. §§ 1531–43; 16 U.S.C. §§ 792–825. Water may be needed to satisfy the requirements of these statutes—achieving water quality standards, protecting endangered species, or complying with terms of a hydropower license. The courts have generally upheld the exercise of this type of authority despite implications for water rights and state water management authority. *See, e.g.,* Riverside Irrig. Dist. v. Andrews, 758 F.2d 508 (10th Cir. 1985); United States v. Glenn-Colusa Irrig. Dist., 788 F. Supp. 1126 (E.D. Cal. 1992). *See also* Bear Warriors United, Inc. v. Lambert, 778 F.Supp.3d 1242 (M.D. Fla. 2025) (issuing an injunction against the Florida

Department of Environmental Protection (FDEP) where pollutants discharged under its wastewater regulations caused ongoing harm to manatees in violation of the ESA, despite FDEP's implementation of a water quality action plan). "In sum, Congress in these statutes mandated a dominant federal role that seems inconsistent with much deference, even if the national interests in clean water or species protection incidentally infringe on state water allocation authority." Reed D. Benson, *Deflating the Deference Myth: National Interests vs. State Authority Under Federal Laws Affecting Water Use*, 2006 Utah L. Rev. 241, 310 (2006).

## D. APPLICATION TO SPECIFIC CATEGORIES OF FEDERAL LAND

Under *Cappaert v. United States* and *U.S. v. New Mexico*, determining reserved water rights—and the quantities subject to protection—requires careful consideration of the specific purposes of each federal land reservation. These purposes are quite varied for different types of federal reservations.

### 1. National Forests

In United States v. New Mexico, 438 U.S. 696 (1978), the Supreme Court assessed the government's claims of reserved rights for instream flows for a national forest established in 1899. Instream flows, the government argued, were needed for wildlife, recreation, aesthetics, and stock watering. The stated purposes of the 1897 Organic Act were "to improve and protect the forest within the boundaries, or for the purpose of securing favorable conditions of water flows, and to furnish a continuous supply of timber. . . ." *Id.* at 706. In a 5–4 opinion, the Court read the 1897 Act narrowly, stating that it only recognized two purposes: "Congress intended that water would be reserved only where necessary to preserve the timber or to secure favorable water flows for private and public uses under state law." *Id.* at 717. The Court noted that the Multiple-Use Sustained-Yield Act of 1960 expanded the purposes of national forests to outdoor recreation, range, watershed, and fish and wildlife, but held that these purposes were secondary and thus outside the scope of the reserved rights. *Id.* at 715. However, the Court clarified that the United States could secure rights for so-called "secondary uses" under state law (see *supra* Section C.III.3).

## 2. National Parks and National Monuments

Reserved water rights for National Parks derive from the 1916 Organic Act, which aims to conserve unimpaired "the scenery and the natural and historic objects and the wild life therein." 54 U.S.C. § 10101(a). It also specifically mentions the inclusion of land and water within the National Park System. 54 U.S.C. § 100501.

In *United States v. New Mexico,* 438 U.S. at 708, the Court contrasted the broad coverage of this Act with the narrower coverage of the Forest Service's Organic Act. Under this precedent, the National Park Service has been relatively successful in securing water for park purposes. Cappaert v. United States,

426 U.S. 128 (1976); High Country Citizens' Alliance v. Norton, 448 F.Supp.2d 1235 (D. Colo. 2006). *Cf.* United States v. Denver, 656 P.2d 1 (Colo. 1982) (narrowly construing the purposes of Dinosaur National Monument, but broadly construing Rocky Mountain National Park purposes).

In addition to National Park units, the Park Service also manages numerous National Monuments. National Monuments are generally created by the President pursuant to the Antiquities Act of 1906, 54 U.S.C. § 320301. Reserved water rights may be asserted for the purposes of protecting a monument's historic or scientific significance. *See Cappaert*, 426 U.S. 128 (affirming reserved rights for Devil's Hole Monument); *U.S. v. Denver*, 656 P.2d at 28–29 (finding no reserved rights for recreation at Dinosaur Monument, but recognizing that there may be reserved rights for fish habitats of historic and scientific interest). Several National Monument declarations have included explicit statements about reserved water rights. *See, e.g.*, Rio Grande Del Norte National Monument, 78 Fed. Reg. 18,783 (2013) (disclaiming any reserved rights to water); Grand Staircase-Escalante National Monument, 61 Fed. Reg. 50,223 (1996) ("This proclamation does not reserve water as a matter of Federal law").

### 3. National Wildlife Refuges

Wildlife refuges are managed by the U.S. Fish and Wildlife Service (FWS) and are often established through Executive Order. 16 U.S.C. § 668dd. Federal reserved water rights turn on the particular language of the various Orders. *See* Arizona v. California, 373 U.S. 546 (1963) (recognizing a reserved water right for Havasu Lake National Wildlife Refuge); United States v. Alaska, 423 F.2d 764 (9th Cir. 1970) (recognizing a reserved water right for Kenai National Moose Range).

The United States has asserted successful *Winters* claims for lands acquired for national wildlife refuges in the Klamath River (Oregon) and Pecos River (New Mexico) adjudications. *See* Pac. Coast Fed'n of Fishermen's Ass'ns v. U.S. Bureau of Reclamation, 138 F. Supp. 2d 1228 (N.D. Cal. 2001); Bureau of Reclamation, Pecos River Channel Restoration at the Bitter Lake National Wildlife Refuge Env'l Assessment 3–8 (2009). In Audubon of Kansas, Inc. v. United States Dep't of Interior, 67 F.4th 1093 (10th Cir. 2023), however, an attempt to compel the FWS to enforce its senior water right for the Quivira Wildlife Refuge was dismissed on jurisdictional grounds.

The state courts have been reluctant to recognize reserved rights for national wildlife refuges. The Deer Flat National Wildlife Refuge experienced a devastating loss in United States v. State, 23 P.3d 117 (Idaho 2001), as amended (May 1, 2001), when the court rejected a federal reserved water rights claim to protect the islands of the Deer Flat National Wildlife Refuge. The court construed the doctrine narrowly in finding that the purpose of the Refuge was to protect migratory birds from hunters, not to provide riparian habitat. *Id.* at 126.

In contrast to litigation, settlement agreements have shown promise. *See, e.g.*, Mont. Code Ann. § 85–20–701 (recognizing reserved rights for the Benton Lake and Black Coulee National Wildlife Refuges). Alternatively, where reserved rights are in doubt, federal agencies have had some success when they utilize state law to secure water rights for wildlife refuges. For example, in United States v. Alpine Reservoir Co., 341 F.3d 1172 (9th Cir. 2003), the court upheld the Nevada State Engineer's transfer of irrigation rights to the Stillwater National Wildlife Refuge for wetland restoration.

## 4. Wild and Scenic Rivers

Unlike other federal designations, Wild and Scenic Rivers are not tied to federal lands. The Wild and Scenic Rivers Act creates an express reserved water right to free flowing water necessary to sustain the "outstandingly remarkable scenic, recreational, geologic, fish and wildlife, historic, cultural, or other similar values" for which a Wild and Scenic section is designated. 16 U.S.C. § 1271. This provision applies wherever the designated section may be located. *See* Potlatch Corp. v. United States, 12 P.3d 1256, 1258 (Idaho 2000) (upholding a reserved right for Wild and Scenic segments throughout the Snake River Basin but limiting it to the minimum amount necessary to accomplish the purposes). *See also* New Mexico ex rel. State Eng'r v. Aragon, 2004 WL 7338079 *2 (D.N.M. Mar. 16, 2004) (finding reserved rights for a designated segment of the Rio Chama).

### 5. National Recreational Areas

National Recreation areas are managed by various agencies and are typically subject to heavy recreational use. Federal reserved water rights were recognized for the Lake Mead National Recreation Area in Arizona v. California, 373 U.S. 546, 601 (1963). Results in other cases have been mixed. *See Potlatch Corp.*, 12 P.3d at 1268–69 (recognizing an express reserved right for Hells Canyon National Recreational Area); Idaho v. United States, 12 P.3d 1284 (Idaho 2000) (rejecting reserved rights for the Sawtooth National Recreation Area, finding that its purposes did not require water).

### 6. Wilderness Areas

Wilderness Areas are established under the Wilderness Act and managed by various agencies. The purpose of the Wilderness Act is to preserve the "untrammeled" wilderness character of designated areas. 16 U.S.C. § 1131(a). The Act also recognizes "the public purposes of recreational, scenic, scientific, educational, conservation, and historical use" of wilderness areas. 16 U.S.C. § 1133(b).

In some instances, Congress has expressly reserved water rights for wilderness areas. *See* California Desert Protection Act, 108 Stat. 4471, 4498 (1994); Washington Park Wilderness Act, PL 100–668 102 Stat. 3961 (1998); Arizona Desert Wilderness Act, Pub. L. No. 101–628, 104 Stat. 4469 (1990). In other cases, Congress has disclaimed reserved rights for wilderness areas, usually to alleviate irrigators' concerns and facilitate passage.

Colorado Canyons National Conservation Area and Black Ridge Canyons Wilderness Act, Pub. L. No. 106–353, 114 Stat. 1374, 1378, § 6(*l*)(2) (2000).

The issue of implied reserved water rights in federally designated wilderness remains largely unsettled. The first court to confront the question held that reserved water rights are created when a wilderness area is established. Sierra Club v. Block, 622 F. Supp. 842 (D. Colo. 1985). However, the decision was vacated on appeal because the issue was not "ripe." Sierra Club v. Yeutter, 911 F.2d 1405, 1414 (10th Cir. 1990). In a subsequent case, a Colorado District Court confirmed that the primary purposes of the Wilderness Act include water necessary for the protection of wildlife, fish, and other preservation-oriented uses. *High Country Citizens' Alliance*, 448 F. Supp. 2d at 1247. Although *Yuetter* and *High Country* recognized that there was a reserved right for wilderness, the Idaho Supreme Court has gone back and forth on this issue, eventually reversing a politically unpopular decision that had reserved all unappropriated waters within the bounds of wilderness areas. Potlatch Corp. v. United States, 12 P.3d 1260 (Idaho 2000). For analysis, *see* Sandra Zellmer, *Wilderness, Water, and Climate Change*, 42 Env't. L. 313, 357–60 (2012).

### 7. Bureau of Land Management (BLM): Specified and Unspecified Public Lands

Unlike other federal lands, BLM lands are generally not reserved for particular purposes to which water rights attach. Even the Federal Land

Policy and Management Act of 1976, which outlines specific purposes for BLM lands, was held to reserve no express or implied water rights on its own. Sierra Club v. Watt, 659 F.2d 203 (D.C.Cir. 1981). In some cases, however, certain BLM lands may have reserved rights based on specific establishment provisions. *See, e.g.,* Bureau of Land Mgmt. v. Barthelmess Ranch Corp., 386 P.3d 952 (Mont. 2016) (recognizing a reserved right to pothole lakes for stockwatering purposes).

However, the BLM administers a handful of National Monuments for which water may be reserved to protect specific historic or scientific purposes of the Monuments. Additionally, the National Landscape Conservation System Act included in the 2009 Omnibus Public Lands Act names the BLM as an administrator over certain conservation areas, wilderness study areas, Wild and Scenic rivers, and a National Monument. Pub. L. No. 111–11, § 2002(a); 123 Stat. 991. These areas may have reserved rights to fulfill specific purposes.

### 8. Military Lands

Water is essential to run a military base, whether for consumption, power generation, or other military purposes. Unlike other federally reserved lands, very little litigation has been brought involving military bases, although a few federal cases have addressed the issue in tangential ways. In Nevada, the federal court found that state law did not govern groundwater pumping on a naval base. Nevada ex rel. Shamberger v. United States, 165 F. Supp. 600

(D. Nev. 1958). *See* United States v. District Ct. for Water Div., 401 U.S. 527 (1971) (implying reserved right for petroleum and shale oil reserves). The State of Nevada recognized groundwater rights for Nellis Air Force Base for national defense purposes. *See* Michael J. Cianci Jr. et al, *The New National Defense Water Right—An Alternative to Federal Reserved Water Rights for Military Installations*, 48 A.F. L Rev. 159 (2000). By contrast, the State of Idaho rejected a reserved water rights claim for the Mountain Home Air Force base. In re Snake River Basin Adjudication, Case No. 39576, Subcases 61–11783 (Idaho Dist. Ct. April 6, 2001).

## E. WATER SUBJECT TO RESERVATION

The courts have not provided a definitive answer on whether reserved rights may be claimed for water outside the boundaries of the reservation. However, in United States v. Cappaert, 426 U.S. 128 (1976), the Supreme Court recognized a reserved right that impacted shared groundwater resources, some of which occurred outside the reservation boundary. The Court upheld an injunction against groundwater pumping by an irrigator who had perfected water rights under state law after the establishment of a nearby national monument. The purpose of the monument—preservation of the desert pupfish—would have been jeopardized by continued groundwater pumping. The Supreme Court held that "the United States can protect its water from subsequent diversion, whether the diversion is of surface or groundwater." *Id.* at 143.

The issue has come up most frequently in cases involving Indian reserved rights. The Ninth Circuit has recognized reserved rights to appurtenant groundwater for the Agua Caliente Band of Cahuilla Indians, where surface water within the reservation was lacking for most of the year. Agua Caliente Band of Cahuilla Indians v. Coachella Valley Water Dist., 849 F.3d 1262 (9th Cir.), *cert. denied,* 583 U.S. 996 (2017). It made no difference that the Band had not used groundwater in the past; its rights were not lost through nonuse. *Id.* at 1272.

State courts have generally agreed that reserved water rights can include groundwater. *See* In re Coeur d'Alene-Spokane River Basin Adjudication, 448 P.3d 322 (Idaho 2019) (tribes' reserved rights include groundwater); In re General Adjudication of All Rights to Use Water in the Gila River System & Source, 989 P.2d 739 (Ariz. 1999) (similar); Confederated Salish & Kootenai Tribes v. Stults, 59 P.3d 1093, 1098 (Mont. 2002) (finding "no distinction between surface water and groundwater" where "those rights are necessary to the purpose of an Indian reservation").

A Colorado water court ruled that reserved rights include water "on, under, or touching the reserved lands," but on appeal, the state Supreme Court declined to address this issue. United States v. Denver, 656 P.2d 1, 31–33 (Colo. 1982). A few years later, the Colorado Supreme Court held that public water holes leased initially for oil development and subsequently withdrawn under Public Water Reserve No. 107 may have their entire yield reserved for public purposes. Park Ctr. Water Dist. v. United States, 781 P.2d 90, 96–97 (Colo. 1989).

Once again, Wyoming appears to be an outlier on this issue. Although, like other jurisdictions, the court recognized that "[t]he logic which supports a reservation of surface water to fulfill the purpose of the reservation also supports reservation of groundwater," it refused to include groundwater due to an absence of precedent at that time. In re General Adjudication of All Rights to Use Water in the Big Horn River System, 753 P.2d 76, 99–100 (Wyo. 1988).

## IV. ADJUDICATION AND ENFORCEMENT OF RESERVED RIGHTS

Ideally, in a prior appropriation system, the priority dates and quantities of everyone's rights are known, so that the water basin can be efficiently and effectively administered. This information, together with information on annual and seasonal flows, enables water rights holders to predict how much water may be diverted. In reality, the kind of perfect information about water rights, priority dates, precise quantities put to beneficial use, and other details are rarely known, even without the added dynamics of federal reserved water rights. Incorporating reserved rights into state water law schemes presents unique challenges. First, the rights impliedly reserved are not quantified unless there has been an adjudication. Second, historically, holders of reserved rights, the United States and Indian tribes, were immune from suit by virtue of their sovereign status, frustrating state efforts to adjudicate their rights or to regulate their use. Third, if the reserved rights claims are substantial and hold an early priority but are not quantified, there is a high degree of uncertainty for all junior water rights holders. Fourth, even when reserved rights are recognized through state or federal proceedings, administration and enforcement may be complicated.

There have been several attempts to address these complexities. First, with the McCarran Amendment in 1952, 43 U.S.C. § 666, Congress waived sovereign immunity such that the United States must assert reserved rights claims in a state general stream adjudication. Second, the U.S. continues to have the option of asserting reserved rights claims in federal court, particularly if there is no general stream adjudication pending in the state. However, the Colorado River abstention doctrine, discussed below, urges federal courts to abstain from deciding the quantity if the state has a pending proceeding. Third, federal entities can participate in the state system, as a matter of comity, to try to protect federal rights. Finally, the trend toward negotiated settlements that are often enacted as congressional legislation provides a non-litigation mechanism for quantifying federal reserved water right claims.

## A. QUANTIFICATION BY ADJUDICATION

Until recently, the most common method of quantification was by adjudication in federal or state court. With the passage of the McCarran Amendment in 1952, 43 U.S.C. § 666, Congress waived sovereign immunity and consented to be joined in state suits determining the water rights of all users on a system. Dugan v. Rank, 372 U.S. 609 (1963). While the McCarran Amendment allowed federal water rights to be determined in state court, it did not remove jurisdiction over those claims from federal courts, and federal law still defines the scope and quantity of the water right. With the McCarren Amendment, Congress created a system of concurrent state and federal court jurisdiction. The Supreme Court eventually articulated an abstention doctrine, known as Colorado River abstention, to address the appropriate relationship between state and federal courts when exercising this concurrent jurisdiction. Colorado River Water Conservation District v. United States, 424 U.S. 800 (1976).

### 1. Joinder of the United States in State Court Actions—McCarran Amendment

Because the United States may not be sued without its consent, Congress must waive immunity for a particular action or a general class of cases. The United States has waived its sovereign immunity for certain water rights cases through the McCarran Amendment, 43 U.S.C. § 666. The statute specifically consents to joinder of:

> the United States as a defendant in any suit (1) for the adjudication of rights to the use of water of a river system or other source, or (2) for the administration of such rights, where it appears that the United States is the owner of or is in the process of acquiring water rights by appropriation under State law, by purchase, by

exchange, or otherwise, and the United States is a necessary party to such suit.

Thus, when the state initiates a proceeding, typically a comprehensive general stream adjudication, to determine the relative rights of private parties throughout a stream system, the United States has consented to jurisdiction over reserved rights claims. United States v. District Ct. in & for Cty. of Eagle, 401 U.S. 520 (1971). The Amendment's language refers only to federal "rights by appropriation under State law, by purchase, by exchange, or otherwise," but the *Eagle County* Court found that the word "otherwise" included reserved rights. *See* Justin Huber & Sandra Zellmer, *The Shallows Where Federal Reserved Water Rights Founder: State Court Derogation of the Winters Doctrine,* 16 U. Denv. Water L. Rev. 261, 289 (2013) (critiquing state court adjudication of federally reserved rights).

This language has been interpreted to include tribal reserved rights claims as well. Colorado River Water Conservation District v. United States (Akin Case), 424 U.S. 800 (1976); Arizona v. San Carlos Apache Tribe, 463 U.S. 545 (1983). In the *Akin* case, the Supreme Court ruled that tribal reserved rights are covered by the Amendment because, "bearing in mind the ubiquitous nature of Indian water rights in the Southwest, it is clear that a construction of the Amendment excluding those rights from its coverage would enervate the Amendment's objective." 424 U.S. at 811. The Court has recognized that the McCarran Amendment does not waive the immunity of a tribe.

Therefore, tribes may bring their own suits to adjudicate water rights.

The McCarran Amendment authorizes joinder of the United States only in a comprehensive adjudication of water rights. This includes ongoing proceedings in Colorado's water courts, *United States v. District Ct. in & for Cty. of Eagle*, 401 U.S. 520, and even comprehensive proceedings that are adjudicative in nature and are overseen by the courts. United States v. Oregon, 44 F.3d 758 (9th Cir. 1994). However, it does not subject the government to state court jurisdiction in private suits to decide priorities between the United States and a particular claimant. Dugan v. Rank, 372 U.S. 609 (1963).

When the government is joined, it must adhere to state procedural requirements. *See* United States v. Bell, 724 P.2d 631 (Colo. 1986) (failure to claim a water source specifically precludes later filing for priority dates). But the Supreme Court has made clear that the Amendment's reach is jurisdictional only. It does not change the federal substantive law of reserved rights. Arizona v. San Carlos Apache Tribe, 463 U.S. 545 (1983); Cappaert v. United States, 426 U.S. 128 (1976). Moreover, the Amendment does not allow a state court to collect statutorily required filing fees from the United States. United States v. Idaho, 508 U.S. 1 (1993).

Once the issues have been litigated, the doctrine of res judicata, or claim preclusion, bars the parties and those in privity with them from re-litigating issues that were conclusively determined. Nevada v. United

States, 463 U.S. 110 (1983); Montana v. United States, 440 U.S. 147 (1979).

## 2. Reserved Rights Claims in Federal Court

Federal court jurisdiction exists if the United States initiates suit. *See* 28 U.S.C. § 1345 (setting forth original jurisdiction in federal district courts for all civil actions, suits, or proceedings commenced by the United States). The federal courts have concurrent jurisdiction with state courts pursuant to the McCarran Amendment's waiver of sovereign immunity. However, a federal court may dismiss a federally initiated claim without prejudice for reasons of "wise judicial administration." *See* Colorado River Water Conservation District v. United States (Akin Case), 424 U.S. 800, 818–20 (1976). In *Akin*, comprehensive state proceedings concerning the stream system in question had been ongoing, and some 1000 other parties were already before the state court. By contrast, nothing had yet occurred in federal court. Under those unique facts, the Court found that the federal policy evinced by the Amendment—avoiding duplicative, piecemeal adjudication of water rights in a river system—warranted dismissal of the federal suit. *Id.* at 819.

The Supreme Court provided additional guidance on the relationship between state and federal courts in Arizona v. San Carlos Apache, 463 U.S. 545 (1983). While emphasizing that federal courts possessed concurrent jurisdiction, the Court observed that concurrent proceedings could spawn an "unseemly and destructive race to see which forum can resolve the same issue first." *Id.* at 567. Citing the McCarran Amendment's policies, the expertise and administrative machinery available to state courts, the infancy of the federal lawsuit, and the judicial bias against piecemeal litigation, the Court found that the federal district court had properly deferred to pending state proceedings. *Id.* at 569–570.

After *San Carlos*, the lower courts have been divided on when the federal court should abstain in light of an ongoing state proceeding. *See* United States v. Adair, 723 F.2d 1394 (9th Cir. 1983), *cert. denied,* 467 U.S. 1252 (1984) (upholding the federal court's decision to proceed on the existence of tribal claims in Oregon but deferring to state proceedings for quantification); *cf.* Salt River Pima-Maricopa Indian Community v. United States, 12 Indian L. Rep. 3009 (D. Ariz. 1985) (refusing to retain jurisdiction in federal court except with regard to certain exclusion of Indian lands); United States v. Bluewater-Toltec Irrig. Dist., 580 F.2d 1095 (D.C. Cir. 1974) (recognizing concurrent jurisdiction but abstaining from state court proceeding). The resolution of jurisdiction between federal and state courts in water rights litigation is highly fact-specific.

### 3. Duty to Assert Reserved Rights Claims

Often, non-governmental entities, or tribes in the case of Indian reserved rights, have significant interests in the federal government robustly defending and prosecuting its reserved rights claims. With regard to Indian reserved rights, the United States is the trustee for those rights, but the U.S.

Attorney General has the discretion, as the entity that represents the U.S. on tribal interests, to determine when to assert these rights. 25 U.S.C. §§ 2, 9. In Pyramid Lake Paiute Tribe v. Morton, 354 F. Supp. 252 (D.D.C. 1972), *rev'd on other grounds*, 499 F.2d 1095 (D.C.Cir. 1974), the court held that the United States had abused its discretion in failing to claim and protect an Indian tribe's reserved rights. However, in Arizona v. Navajo Nation, 599 U.S. 555 (2023), the Supreme Court found that an 1868 treaty with the Navajo lacked explicit language regarding any duty to obtain water on behalf of the Navajo; thus, the United States could not be compelled to quantify the Navajo's rights or to construct necessary infrastructure to secure water. *Id.* at 566–68. The decision has fomented a great deal of commentary, including Jason Anthony Robison, *Relational River: Arizona v. Navajo Nation & the Colorado,* 72 UCLA L. Rev. 116 (2025).

With regard to non-Indian federal reserved rights, most attempts to compel the government to claim reserved rights have been unsuccessful. *See, e.g.*, Sierra Club v. Yeutter, 911 F.2d 1405 (10th Cir. 1990); Audubon of Kansas, Inc. v. United States Dep't of Interior, 67 F.4th 1093 (10th Cir. 2023). Some cases have been dismissed on jurisdictional grounds. In Sierra Club v. Andrus, 487 F. Supp. 443 (D.C. Cir. 1980), the Sierra Club alleged that the United States was not effectively prosecuting its reserved water rights in Utah. The D.C. Circuit dismissed the case on ripeness grounds, but stated in dicta that, "in the event of a real and immediate water supply threat to the scenic, natural, historic or biotic resource values . . . the Secretary must take appropriate action." Nonetheless, in *Audubon,* the court found that the plaintiffs had failed to assert a viable claim to compel agency action unlawfully withheld under the Administrative Procedure Act (APA) and refused to require the U.S. Fish & Wildlife Service to enforce its senior water right despite degradation of wildlife habitat. 67 F.4th at 1110–11 (citing 5 U.S.C. § 706(1)).

By contrast, plaintiffs lodged a successful claim in High Country Citizens Alliance v. Norton, 448 F. Supp. 2d 1235 (D. Colo. 2006). There, the court held that the Park Service's relinquishment of a senior right for the Black Canyon of the Gunnison was "nonsensical" and an abuse of discretion. *Id.* at 1253.

## B. NEGOTIATED SETTLEMENTS

Another means of quantifying reserved rights is by negotiated agreement. In the face of lengthy and costly adjudication proceedings and the potential impact of unquantified time-immemorial (or early priority date) rights, negotiated settlements began to emerge as an option to addressing reserved water rights claims. These settlements can be costly and time-consuming because, regardless of the format—adjudication or settlement—the complexities of bringing all the appropriate parties and determining the quantity of water rights are immense.

There is considerable variation in the form of these negotiated agreements—from the Reserved Water Rights Compact Commission in Montana, to stipulated settlement agreements as part of an ongoing McCarran adjudication, to settlement facilitated through the Secretary's Indian Water Rights Office at the Department of the Interior.

The federal government's guidance for conducting Indian water rights settlements provides a starting point for parties seeking to explore settlement options. Robert T. Anderson, *Indian Water Rights, Practical Reasoning, and Negotiated Settlements,* 98 Cal. L. Rev. 1133, 1157 (2010) (citing 55 Fed. Reg. 9223 (1990)). Settlements typically not only quantify Indian rights, but also provide funds (federal plus state cost sharing) or water sources (often from a new or existing federal project) to enable tribes to use water without infringing on established non-Indian uses. Many settlements allow for limited marketing of water on and off the reservation. Some provide development funds to the tribes. In addition, a settlement may deal with matters like efficient use, conservation, environmental concerns, and interstate compact obligations. *See id.;* Celene Hawkins, *Beyond Quantification: Implementing and Sustaining Tribal Water Settlements,* 16 U. Denv. Water L. Rev. 229 (2013).

Once the terms are agreed upon, most agreements are ratified and often funded by Congress. As of November 2024, 39 Indian water rights settlements had been federally approved, with total estimated costs around $8.5 billion. Congressional Research Service, *Indian Water Rights Settlements* 1 (2024), at https://fas.org/sgp/crs/misc/R44148.pdf.

# CHAPTER NINE

# INTERSTATE AND INTERNATIONAL ALLOCATION

Because state and international political boundaries generally do not align with the boundaries of watersheds, unique approaches are often required to manage water and resolve disputes. Traditional exercises of state police power or national sovereignty may be inadequate to manage transboundary waters. As the demand for water within shared basins intensifies, the need for interstate and international planning increases, as does the need for a reliable method of resolving disputes over the allocation, depletion, and pollution of transboundary waters.

The first three sections of this chapter illustrate how interstate disputes are resolved by judicial allocation (interstate litigation), compacts (interstate agreements), and legislation (congressional apportionment). Section IV addresses constitutional constraints on state efforts to prevent water exports. Finally, Section V turns to international water treaties, conventions, and disputes.

## I. INTERSTATE ADJUDICATION

### A. LITIGATION BETWEEN PRIVATE PARTIES

A typical interstate suit between private parties involves a downstream plaintiff alleging harm from diversions of an upstream defendant in another state. Some cases involve upstream pollution. The court in which the suit is brought must have jurisdiction over both the parties and the subject matter.

### 1. Personal Jurisdiction

Personal jurisdiction is usually obtained by personal service upon the defendant within the defendant's state of residence. Long-arm statutes, however, have removed the necessity of bringing suit in the defendant's state. 4 Wright and Miller, Fed. Prac. & Proc. Civ. § 1068 (4th ed. 2020 update).

### 2. Subject Matter Jurisdiction

Private parties generally bring suit in the state courts of the defendant's or plaintiff's state. Action may be brought in federal court if the suit meets the requirements of subject matter jurisdiction (*i.e.*, diversity of citizenship and amount in controversy, or a federal question).

The ability of a court in one state to adjudicate water use in another was not always well settled. An early view held that an action to establish water rights was in the nature of a quiet title action over real property; thus, the suit must be brought in the state where the real property is situated. Conant v. Deep Creek & Curlew Valley Irr. Co., 66 P. 188 (Utah 1901). Subsequent opinions adopted the more liberal view that once a court obtains personal jurisdiction over a nonresident *party*, the decree need not operate directly upon the *property*; the court can enforce its decree by using the coercive effect of its contempt power. The Ninth Circuit employed this theory in

Brooks v. United States, 119 F.2d 636 (9th Cir. 1941). *Brooks* involved the water rights of Arizona and New Mexico users on the Gila River. Defendants had submitted to jurisdiction in Arizona, and the court was held to have exclusive jurisdiction to adjudicate the matter, although the rights of water users in the adjoining state had to be considered.

Problems of jurisdiction are magnified in a general stream adjudication, where all affected users must be joined. If the United States has water rights on the stream, it too must be joined. The McCarran Amendment waives sovereign immunity and consents to state court jurisdiction to adjudicate federal water rights in general stream adjudications. 43 U.S.C. § 666. To invoke the McCarran Amendment, plaintiffs must demonstrate that the contested matter is "a comprehensive adjudication of all water rights" of the basin in that particular state. Frenchman Cambridge Irr. Dist. v. Heineman, 974 F. Supp. 2d 1264, 1280 (D. Neb. 2013).

### 3. Applicable Law

Where individual water users in one state attempt to prevent interference with interstate waters by individual water users in another state, substantial differences in state laws can make it difficult to determine rights. For instance, if a downstream state follows riparian law and an upstream state follows appropriation law, can an individual in the downstream state insist on reasonable flows, thereby defeating the established uses of upstream appropriators? However, it is theoretically simpler to integrate the priorities of water users on a stream that crosses state lines when both are appropriation states. In an early case, the Supreme Court presumed that disputes among such users would be resolved by priority, as if no state boundary existed. Bean v. Morris, 221 U.S. 485 (1911). The decision did not limit either state in how it defines or regulates rights to waters within its boundaries (absent federal legislation or an interstate adjudication). The idea that Congress conveyed public lands into private hands upon the condition that waters would be allocated by prior appropriation without regard to state lines is arguable, but not widely accepted. *See, e.g.*, Howell v. Johnson, 89 F. 556 (C.C.Mont. 1898).

Basic differences in state water laws, as well as jurisdictional and enforcement problems, led states to pursue litigation in which they represent their citizens collectively in their *parens patriae* capacity to protect the health, safety, and welfare of the citizenry. *See, e.g.*, Kansas v. Colorado, 206 U.S. 46, 117 (1907). This type of litigation allows for more comprehensive solutions, but is limited to major interstate rivers and lakes where there are multiple interested parties rather than litigation among individuals on small streams with few competing users, as in Bean v. Morris, 221 U.S. 485 (1911).

### 4. *Parens Patriae* Suits

When one state sues private parties in another state in its role as *parens patriae* to prevent harm to its own citizens, the Supreme Court has original, but not exclusive, jurisdiction; concurrent jurisdiction also exists in federal district courts. 28 U.S.C. § 1251(b)(3).

States have standing to sue in *parens patriae* capacity under certain limited conditions. The state must have an interest independent of its citizens, so the suit is not merely an attempt to act on behalf of individuals, and a substantial portion of the state's inhabitants must be adversely affected. Massachusetts v. EPA, 549 U.S. 497, 519 (2007); Georgia v. Tenn. Copper Co., 206 U.S. 230 (1907). In disputes over water, this usually requires that the downstream state be substantially affected by actions in an upstream state. Kansas v. Colorado, 206 U.S. 46 (1907).

A state suing in *parens patriae* is deemed to represent all its citizens, and each citizen is bound by the decree. Thus, private suits are often foreclosed once the state's rights are adjudicated. *Parens patriae* actions are further limited by the Eleventh Amendment of the U.S. Constitution, which states that the judicial power of the United States shall not be construed to extend to any suit brought by citizens of one state against another state. This prevents a state from invoking the Supreme Court's original jurisdiction in a suit against another state if the plaintiff state is seeking a remedy for individual citizens (*e.g.*, money damages) that are prohibited in a suit brought directly by the individuals. *See id.*; New Hampshire v. Louisiana, 108 U.S. 76 (1883); North Dakota v. Minnesota, 263 U.S. 365 (1923).

### 5. Enforcement

Decrees in private interstate suits can raise difficult enforcement problems, particularly when continuing supervision is required. For instance, in Lindsey v. McClure, 136 F.2d 65 (10th Cir. 1943), the court invalidated the New Mexico State Engineer's attempt to forbid a company from taking water from a New Mexico dam for use in Colorado. The court stated that the proper enforcement mechanism was by judicial procedure, not by order of the state engineer. In Bean v. Morris, 221 U.S. 485 (1911), however, the Supreme Court upheld a federal court's enforcement of priorities across state lines where both states followed the prior appropriation doctrine.

## B. LITIGATION BETWEEN STATES

### 1. Original Jurisdiction of the Supreme Court

The Supreme Court has original jurisdiction in all cases in which a state is a party. U.S. Const. art. 3, § 2, cl. 2; 28 U.S.C. § 1251(a)(1). In suits between states, the Supreme Court serves as a trial court. Procedurally, the action begins when a state files a complaint and typically moves to hearings on motions to dismiss on jurisdictional or other grounds. If the complaint survives the motions, the respondent state files an answer. The Court often appoints a special master to hear and evaluate evidence, prepare findings of fact and conclusions of law, and recommend a decree, which the Court is free to follow or disregard.

The decree in an adjudication between states is binding on all claimants to the water in question, whether or not they were parties to the suit, because private users have no rights in excess of the state's share of the stream under the doctrine of *parens patriae*. Kansas v. Colorado, 206 U.S. 46 (1907). In addition, Compact obligations are enforceable on private parties, even if the Compact was entered after the date of the right holders' decree. Hill v. State, 894 N.W. 2d 208 (Neb. 2017). A decree in such a suit has *res judicata* (claim preclusion) effect. Alaska Sport Fishing Ass'n v. Exxon Corp., 34 F.3d 769 (9th Cir. 1994). Private intervenors are not permitted unless they can show a compelling interest different than the interests generally held by citizens of the state parties. South Carolina v. North Carolina, 558 U.S. 256 (2010).

## 2. Justiciability

Article III of the U.S. Constitution confines federal court jurisdiction to "cases or controversies." Even if a court has both personal and subject matter jurisdiction, it may decline to adjudicate cases that are not "justiciable"—that is, in a form suited to judicial resolution. Nebraska v. Wyoming, 325 U.S. 589 (1945). A suit may be rendered non-justiciable if it is moot, collusive, not ripe, or a "political question" that implicates executive or legislative authority.

The issue of justiciability often arises in water cases as a ripeness problem (*i.e.*, there is no present "harm" to a downstream state claiming excessive use upstream, leading courts to find no case or controversy). In such cases, the allocation of water rights for future development cannot be adjudicated. Further, the Supreme Court has refused to issue declaratory decrees in interstate water disputes. Arizona v. California, 283 U.S. 423 (1931).

The Supreme Court's reluctance to hear water allocation disputes is due to several reasons, including the vague standards of apportionment, the need for continuing supervision and the Court's disinclination to play the role of referee, the daunting nature of technical data involved, and the Court's lack of expertise. This reluctance can perpetuate inequitable or uneven development on interstate streams by hindering investment financing or congressional authorization of water development projects.

### 3. Sources of Law: The Doctrine of Equitable Apportionment

The Supreme Court has developed a body of federal common law to resolve disputes over the allocation of interstate rivers. The Supreme Court has also found that interstate groundwater aquifers can be subject to equitable apportionment. State of Mississippi v. Tennessee, 595 U.S. 15 (2021). Federal common law is applied in a narrow class of cases where there is a significant federal interest that will not be effectuated by the application of state law or by federal statutes. As such, federal courts play a unique role in shaping the rules of decision in cases involving state boundaries or shared resources, like interstate waters.

If Congress has spoken directly on the issue, the courts will defer to statutory law rather than apply common law. In the rare instances where Congress has entered the realm of interstate water allocation, it displaces the federal common law. *See, e.g.,* Arizona v. California, 373 U.S. 546 (1963). For most disputes between states over interstate allocations, however, the Supreme Court has developed a comprehensive federal common law doctrine known as "equitable apportionment," announced in Kansas v. Colorado, 206 U.S. 46 (1907). A basic tenet of the doctrine is that "equality of right," not equality of amounts apportioned, should govern. "Equality of right" means that the states stand "on the same level," or "on an equal plane . . . in point of power and right, under our constitutional system." Wyoming v. Colorado, 259 U.S. 419, 465 (1922).

The Court is not bound by the laws of the individual states. Thus, where strict application of riparian law would have prevented New York, an upstream state, from diverting water for use in New York City, the Court denied downstream New Jersey's request for an injunction. Instead, it sought to balance equities to achieve an equitable apportionment. New Jersey v. New York, 283 U.S. 336 (1931).

In a dispute between two prior appropriation states, the Court has applied the prior appropriation doctrine as the method of equitable apportionment. Wyoming v. Colorado, 259 U.S. 419 (1922). Application of the prior appropriation doctrine is qualified, however, in that the allocation must be equitable. Factors that might justify deviation from strict priority include:

(1) Physical and climatic conditions;

(2) Consumptive use of water in the several sections of the river;

(3) Character and rate of return flows;

(4) Extent of established uses and economies built on them;

(5) Availability of storage water;

(6) Practical effect of wasteful uses on downstream areas; and

(7) Damage to upstream areas compared to the benefits to downstream areas if upstream uses are curtailed.

Nebraska v. Wyoming, 325 U.S. 589, 618 (1945).

In Colorado v. New Mexico, 459 U.S. 176 (1982), the Court refused to apply strict priorities between two prior appropriation states where the effect would have been to protect wasteful downstream uses in New Mexico at the expense of newer, more efficient uses in Colorado. But in Colorado v. New Mexico II, 467 U.S. 310 (1984), the Court declined to allocate water to junior users in Colorado to the detriment of the inefficient appropriators in New Mexico because Colorado lacked a concrete, long-term plan for future water use.

Environmental considerations may be considered when determining whether to follow strict priorities in an interstate apportionment. In Nebraska v. Wyoming, 515 U.S. 1 (1995), the Court allowed Nebraska to amend its pleadings to allege injury both to downstream wildlife habitat and to downstream irrigators. In Florida v. Georgia, 592 U.S. 443 (2021), the Court examined whether diminished streamflows harmed Florida's oyster beds, fish, mussels, and vegetation, ultimately finding that Florida failed to prove their claims by clear and convincing evidence.

The Supreme Court occasionally deviates from strict priority among appropriators in prior appropriation states by use of the "mass allocation" approach. *See* Wyoming v. Colorado, 259 U.S. 419 (1922), *modified*, 260 U.S. 1 (1922), *vacated*, 353 U.S. 953 (1957). Since the Court is reluctant to intervene in intrastate allocations, it awards each state a quantity of water to be distributed through the state's own water rights system. However, the Court may hold that certain diversions are within one state's share of the allocation, that a state may have a stated quantity of water, or that a state may have a percentage of the flow, regardless of the mix of individual priorities within the state.

Even when the Court takes jurisdiction over a water rights dispute, it suggests that interstate compacts can lead to superior solutions. Sporhase v. Nebraska ex rel. Douglas, 458 U.S. 941 (1982) (citing Colorado v. Kansas, 320 U.S. 383 (1943)).

## II. INTERSTATE COMPACTS

Interstate compacts effectuate a variety of objectives by mutual agreement of two or more states. Compacts relating to interstate waters are formed to allocate water between the states, but also to address issues involving storage, flood control, pollution control, and comprehensive basin planning (principally by joint federal-state compacts). Although the first interstate water allocation compact was adopted in the arid West in response to a dispute over the Colorado River, compacts have also been used to settle conflicts in the East and the South (notable examples include the Delaware, Potomac, Great Lakes St. Lawrence River Compact and Susquehanna River Compacts). Compacts have an advantage over adjudication in that compacts avoid the justiciability problems encountered when the stream system in question is not yet over-appropriated. A compact allows parties to allocate unappropriated water, thus making a present appropriation for future use. The ability to make such determinations in advance is crucial to long-range water planning and can allow for creative approaches. For examples the Great Lakes Compact sets a common decision-making standard for in basin uses of water, establishes shared data collection, creates a body to adjudicate, and prohibits all diversions out of the basin that don't meet limited exception standards.

## A. CONSTITUTIONAL AUTHORITY

The basis for negotiating interstate compacts is found in Article I, § 10, clause 3 of the Constitution, which states:

> No state shall, without the consent of Congress . . . enter into any agreement or compact with another state, or with a foreign power. . . .

The compact clause impliedly recognizes state power to negotiate and enter into agreements subject to congressional consent. Compacts "adapt[ ] to our Union of sovereign States the age-old treaty making power of independent sovereign nations." Hinderlider v. La Plata River & Cherry Creek Ditch Co., 304 U.S. 92, 104 (1938).

Typically, compact formation involves four steps. First, Congress authorizes the negotiation of the compact, typically providing for a federal representative to attend the negotiations. Then, the compact is negotiated. Next, the affected state legislatures approve the compact. Finally, Congress must consent to the compact.

Congressional consent is necessary for the compact to be a permissible agreement instead of a constitutionally prohibited "treaty, alliance, or confederation." Exactly what kind of interstate agreement requires congressional consent is the subject of considerable debate. One view is that consent is required only for agreements that alter the political power of states, potentially upsetting the political balance of the union. Virginia v. Tennessee, 148 U.S. 503 (1893). Others contend that consent is required for all interstate compacts, based on an implication in State ex rel. Dyer v. Sims, 341 U.S. 22, 27 (1951), stating that congressional consent was required for a water sanitation compact, "as for all compacts." Nevertheless, there is general agreement that compacts allocating interstate waters require congressional consent.

## B. ADMINISTRATION AND ENFORCEMENT OF COMPACTS

Compacts often require the creation of an administrative agency, known as a "compact commission," that makes compact implementation rules and collects information on physical circumstances (*e.g.*, rate of river flow) to determine whether and to what extent certain provisions of the compact are applicable. Compact commissions are usually comprised of members appointed by the governors of the party states and a federal member, who either has no vote or only a tie-breaking vote.

A state found in violation of a compact may be required to pay damages in cash rather than increased future water deliveries. Texas v. New Mexico, 482 U.S. 124 (1987); Kansas v. Colorado, 533 U.S. 1 (2001). In Kansas v. Nebraska, 574 U.S. 445 (2015), the Court required Nebraska to pay $1.8 million in disgorgement, in addition to $3.7 million in damages to Kansas, under the Republican River Compact. The Court found disgorgement an appropriate remedy because it would "remind[ ] Nebraska of its legal obligations, deter[ ] future violations, and promote[ ] the Compact's successful administration." *Id.* at 1057.

## C. LEGAL EFFECT OF COMPACTS

### 1. Limitations on Private Water Users

Just like equitable apportionments by the Supreme Court, apportionments by compact are binding upon the citizens of the compacting states, whether or not individual citizens were parties to the negotiations. In Hinderlider v. La Plata River & Cherry Creek Ditch Co., 304 U.S. 92 (1938), New Mexico and Colorado agreed to divide the flow of the La Plata River equally, so each state received the full flow of the river every other day. The plaintiff, a senior appropriator, sought to enjoin the rotation scheme as a violation of rights established under state law. The Court denied relief, stating that a state cannot confer water right decrees that exceed the state's share of water. It also held that there was no compensable taking of vested property rights or violation of due process because the plaintiff had ample opportunity to object during negotiations, and there was no evidence of inequity or bad faith in the negotiations, nor a defect in the compact's formation. *Id.* at 108. *See* Hill v. State, 894 N.W.2d 208 (Neb. 2017) (citing *Hinderlider*). *See also* Baley v. United States, 942 F.3d 1312 (Fed. Cir. 2019), *cert. denied,* 141 S. Ct. 133 (2020) (denying irrigators' takings claims where the government supplied water to superior tribal treaty rights and endangered fish species).

### 2. Effect of Congressional Ratification

Uncertainty exists over the extent to which Congress is bound by its ratification of compact terms. While it cannot modify the terms of an agreement between states, Congress can condition its ratification upon an agreement by the states to modify the compact. Congress also retains the power to override a compact provision by explicit legislation. Once ratified, a compact has the same effect as federal law and can preempt any inconsistent state laws. *See infra* Section IV.

## D. INTERPRETATION OF COMPACTS

The Supreme Court is the final arbiter of the meaning of compacts. Although one guidepost is the Court's standard of equitable apportionment, the Court's ultimate mission is to determine the parties' intent. Montana v. Wyoming, 563 U.S. 368 (2011). In Oklahoma v. New Mexico, 501 U.S. 221 (1991), the Court probed extrinsic evidence of the history of Canadian River Compact negotiations to interpret ambiguous terms consistently with the probable intent of the parties.

The Pecos River Compact provided that New Mexico would deliver water to Texas based on "the 1947 conditions" of the river, with those conditions being defined in a document that used incorrect data. The compact commission, with even representation from the two states, deadlocked on whether to follow the document or base the allocation on actual river conditions. The special master recommended restructuring the commission to resolve the matter, but the Court found that doing so would alter the compact's terms. Instead, it ordered the special master to resolve the matter using accurate data, which the Court believed was the parties' intention. Texas v. New Mexico, 462 U.S. 554 (1983). The river master's determinations are generally upheld absent clear error. *See* Texas v. New Mexico, 592 U.S. 518 (2020) (upholding a decision that New Mexico was entitled to delivery credit for water that evaporated while being stored in New Mexico at Texas's request).

Whether lower federal courts have jurisdiction to interpret compacts turns on whether the dispute is a federal question (*i.e.*, "arises under the Constitution, laws, or treaties of the United States"). Although courts have found federal question jurisdiction to interpret compact provisions, *see* League to Save Lake Tahoe v. Tahoe Reg'l Planning Agency, 507 F.2d 517 (9th Cir. 1974), the suit may be barred by other jurisdictional impediments, such as sovereign immunity or lack of standing. Frenchman Cambridge Irr. Dist. v. Heineman, 974 F. Supp. 2d 1264 (D. Neb. 2013).

## III. LEGISLATIVE ALLOCATION

The Colorado River is the sole example of a legislative allocation of interstate waters. In Arizona v. California, 373 U.S. 546 (1963), the Court held that Congress intended to divide the waters of the river among the lower basin states in passing the Boulder Canyon Project Act of 1928. With this holding, the Court recognized Congress's authority to act when the other apportionment mechanisms (compacts and judicial allocation) have failed, are unavailable, or are not used.

What made the situation so compelling that Congress ultimately stepped in? Of the lower basin states, California experienced rapid early economic growth and a large population influx. Water was used extensively for irrigation, especially in the Imperial Valley. Arizona experienced relatively gradual expansion, but it anticipated future growth. Most of Arizona's historic uses were met by pumping groundwater, as geographical obstacles and a lack of diversion facilities limited its access to the Colorado River. When Arizona's water tables declined from groundwater mining, it became clear that preserving Arizona's economy required the waters of the Colorado. The parties developed an elaborate diversion and transportation project, known as the Central Arizona Project, to bring Colorado River water to the most populated parts of the state.

In 1922, a compact commission agreed to allocate the Colorado's annual flow approximately equally between the upper basin states (Colorado, New Mexico, Utah, and Wyoming) and the lower basin states (Arizona, California, and Nevada). At the time, the annual flow was assumed to be over 15 million acre-feet (MAF); we now know that it varies dramatically, from a low of 4.4 MAF to a high of about 24 MAF, which makes compact implementation challenging.

A long-standing dispute between Arizona and California over their respective shares in the 7.5 MAF allocated to the lower basin stalled the compact's ratification. Arizona feared the compact would solidify California's claim to most of the water and refused to ratify it. Weary of the impasse, Congress enacted the Boulder Canyon Project Act in 1928, authorizing the construction of Hoover Dam and other storage reservoirs on the Colorado. The Act was contingent upon the acceptance of the compact arrangement by at least six of the seven states—Arizona opposed it. California also had to agree to limit its allocation to 4.4 MAF plus half of any lower-basin surplus. The legislation further authorized a separate lower basin compact that would allocate 2.8 MAF to Arizona and 300,000 AF to Nevada. No such compact was negotiated.

After several attempts to stop the construction of the Hoover Dam failed in the Supreme Court, Arizona sued for an equitable apportionment of the waters of the lower Colorado. The suit was dismissed because the United States, an indispensable party, refused to be joined. Arizona v. California, 298 U.S. 558 (1936). The U.S. later consented to suit, and after a three-year trial before a special master, the Supreme Court, approving most aspects of the master's report, held:

(1) Congress may, under its navigation and general welfare powers, apportion interstate streams by legislation.

(2) By enacting the Boulder Canyon Project Act, Congress exercised this power by "apportioning" 4.4 MAF to California and by specifying Arizona's and Nevada's shares through the authorization of a lower

basin compact. Furthermore, Congress delegated to the Secretary of the Interior the power to contract for storage and delivery of project waters, and the Secretary then executed contracts reflecting the authorized shares.

(3) Federal law controls both the interstate and intrastate distribution of project waters, preempting state water law. (Note the contrast to the mass allocation approach, which leaves intrastate allocation to state law.) The Secretary is empowered to allocate waters in times of shortage by any reasonable method, although "present perfected rights" must be satisfied.

(4) Water from Arizona's tributaries (1.75 MAF) is not part of the allocation to be shared with California but is available to Arizona in addition to its allocation of 2.8 MAF of mainstem water.

Arizona v. California, 373 U.S. 546 (1963). The Court's inclination to find that federal power to allocate water between states existed and was exercised in the Boulder Canyon Project Act likely reflects the Court's preference for congressional allocations of interstate waters over judicial allocations that require complex litigation.

A series of large dams and reservoirs were built under the authority of the Boulder Canyon Project Act and subsequent legislation. After many years, the Central Arizona Project was built, placating

Arizona's concerns. 43 U.S.C. § 1521. However, as a condition of the authorizing legislation, Arizona had to agree to subordinate its share of the Colorado River to California's entitlement.

Subsequently, California's demands outstripped its legal entitlement. The Secretary of the Interior deferred to the seven basin states to negotiate rules for facilities operations and address shortages and surpluses, particularly as it became apparent that historical flows and cyclical shortages frustrated water users' expectations for fulfillment across the Colorado basin. With rare exceptions, the Secretary adopted rules reflecting the agreements. These agreements aimed to optimize use of the river's water, with provisions for conservation, sharing shortages, redefining "surplus," and allowing water marketing. In 2003, California began implementing a complicated Quantification Settlement Agreement to bring its use of Colorado River water within the limits of the Compact. In re Quantification Settlement Agreement Cases, 134 Cal. Rptr. 3d 274 (2011), *cert. denied,* 568 U.S. 902 (2012).

Meanwhile, Arizona created a "water bank" to store its currently unneeded allocation of Colorado River water in aquifers for future use. In 2004, Arizona agreed to store 1.25 MAF of its share for Nevada to use in times of shortage. Nevada agreed to pay $400 million for storage and delivery costs, and the two states agreed to a maximum recovery rate of 40,000 acre-feet per year until the bank reserves are fully exhausted. Simply put, the deal allows Arizona to store surplus Colorado River water in its aquifers, which Nevada can then withdraw from Lake Mead, reducing Arizona's consumption from the Central Arizona Project. Robert Glennon and Jacob Kavkewitz, *A "Smashing Victory": Was Arizona v. California a Victory for the State of Arizona?*, 4 Ariz. J. Envtl. L. & Pol'y 1, 35 (2013). The Colorado River continues to be in a state of flux and the source of considerable attention, controversy, and innovation as decreased water availability, increased demand and the impacts of climate change affect the entire basin.

## IV. STATE RESTRICTIONS ON WATER EXPORT

The Commerce Clause of the U.S. Constitution, Art. I, § 8, cl. 3, empowers Congress to regulate commerce with foreign nations, Indian tribes, and among the states. The Constitution does not explicitly limit states from burdening commerce, but courts have found "negative implications" from the grant of commerce power to Congress. This doctrine, known as the Dormant Commerce Clause, forbids states from discriminating against or unreasonably burdening interstate commerce. The doctrine aims to prevent protectionism and promote free trade.

When evaluating state legislation for potential conflict with the Commerce Clause, courts first consider whether the statute facially discriminates against nonresidents. "Discriminatory" in this context means differential treatment of in-state and out-of-state economic interests. Facially discriminatory provisions motivated by economic protectionism are subject to a "virtually *per se* rule of invalidity," which can only be overcome by a showing that there is no other means to advance an important local purpose. United Haulers Ass'n, Inc. v. Oneida-Herkimer Solid Waste Mgmt. Auth., 550 U.S. 330, 337 (2007). If the statute is not facially discriminatory but imposes incidental burdens on interstate commerce, it will be upheld unless "the burden imposed on such commerce is clearly excessive in relation to the putative local benefits." Pike v. Bruce Church, Inc., 397 U.S. 137, 142 (1970). This balancing test considers: (1) whether a legitimate state interest is present; (2) if so, whether the state interest outweighs any competing national interest; and (3) whether less burdensome alternatives are available to accomplish the state's purpose.

In Sporhase v. Nebraska ex rel. Douglas, 458 U.S. 941 (1982), the Supreme Court found a Nebraska statute that restricted groundwater exports to only those states that gave it reciprocal privileges facially unconstitutional. The *Sporhase* opinion reviewed two earlier decisions: Hudson Cnty. Water Co. v. McCarter, 209 U.S. 349 (1908), which held that New Jersey could prohibit the interstate transfer of surface water, and City of Altus v. Carr, 255 F. Supp. 828 (W.D. Tex. 1966), which struck down a Texas law that prohibited the export of groundwater, finding it is an article of commerce under Texas groundwater law. The *Sporhase* Court held that groundwater in the interstate Ogallala aquifer, which irrigates agriculture that is exported to global markets, is an article of commerce subject to the Commerce Clause.

The Court recognized, however, that a state may have a legitimate interest in granting "in times of severe shortage . . . a limited preference for its own citizens"; thus "[a] demonstrably arid State conceivably might be able to marshal evidence to establish a close means-end relationship between even a total ban on the exportation of water and a purpose to conserve and preserve water." *Id.* at 958. However, states have had little success in utilizing this caveat since. *See* El Paso v. Reynolds, 597 F. Supp. 694 (D.N.M. 1984) (finding that provisions that gave priority to New Mexico citizens during severe water shortages unlawfully discriminated against interstate commerce).

Although states cannot unilaterally impose protectionist measures, Congress has authorized export restrictions on several occasions, including the Great Lakes-St. Lawrence River Basin Compact, Pub. L. No. 110–342 § 4.11, 122 Stat. 3740 (2008), which prohibits diversions outside of the Basin. In Tarrant Reg'l Water Dist. v. Herrmann, 569 U.S. 614 (2013), Texas claimed that the Red River Compact allowed it to cross state lines to divert a portion of Oklahoma's allocated water, and that Oklahoma's attempt to stop Texas violated the Dormant Commerce Clause. Oklahoma law requires out-of-state diversions to be approved by the Oklahoma Water Resources Board, prohibits permit issuance when the proposed diversion would prevent Oklahoma from meeting its interstate compact obligations, and requires that water be "developed to the maximum extent feasible for the benefit of Oklahoma so that out-of-state downstream users will not acquire vested rights therein to the detriment of the citizens of [Oklahoma]." *Id.* at 625. The Supreme Court found that the Compact did not create cross-border rights as Texas claimed, and that Congress insulated the states from Dormant Commerce Clause challenges for decisions within the compact's purview by consenting to the compact. *Id.* at 640.

## V. INTERNATIONAL ALLOCATIONS

Transboundary surface waters and aquifers are of vital importance to the countries and people who share them. Over time, upstream nations have sought to control waters originating in their territory. However, the historic doctrine of "absolute territorial sovereignty" gave way to the practical necessity of amicably dealing with neighboring nations. Today, more flexible doctrines of limited territorial sovereignty and equitable apportionment generally govern the resolution of international water disputes, most often through treaties.

The United States is party to several water treaties with Canada, including the 1909 Boundary Waters Treaty, the Niagara River Water Diversion Treaty, the Saint Lawrence Treaty, and the Columbia River Treaty. Treaties with Mexico include the 1906 Irrigation Convention and the 1944 Treaty concerning the Colorado and other rivers.

### A. SUPREMACY OF TREATIES OVER STATE WATER LAW

Article I, Section 8 of the U.S. Constitution gives Congress the power to regulate foreign commerce.

Additionally, Article II, Section 2 grants the President the power to enter into treaties with the advice and consent of the Senate.

Article VI, Section 2 provides for the supremacy of treaties and other federal laws. Once the federal government enters into a treaty with another nation, the treaty is the "Supreme Law of the Land" with preemptive strength over state law. Zschernig v. Miller, 389 U.S. 429, 441 (1968). Thus, treaties affect the manner and extent to which state-defined rights may be exercised. For example, in Sanitary Dist. of Chicago v. United States, 266 U.S. 405 (1925), the Supreme Court enjoined the City of Chicago from diverting water out of Lake Michigan because the diversions lowered the lake level and were in excess of amounts allowed under the 1909 Boundary Waters Treaty with Canada.

## B. NOTABLE INTERNATIONAL TREATIES

### 1. Mexico

The 1944 Treaty for the "Utilization of Waters of the Colorado and Tijuana Rivers and of the Rio Grande," 59 Stat. 1219, was an effort to end years of disagreement between the United States and Mexico over the waters of rivers shared by the two countries. Among other things, it established the U.S.-Mexico International Boundary and Water Commission (IBWC) to administer the treaty and resolve disputes. The commission oversees water allocations and projects related to flood control, hydroelectric power, and water quality. The Commission's decisions are recorded in the form of Minutes. Once approved by both governments, Minutes enter into force as binding obligations. For a comprehensive list of Minutes and their text, *see* IBWC, https://www.ibwc.gov/minutes/.

Management of the Colorado River proved to be the most troublesome issue addressed by the treaty. The United States, as the upstream nation, initially relied on the "Harmon Doctrine," which is based on a theory of absolute territorial sovereignty. However, pressures from Mexico to receive a share of water from the river grew as uses in Mexico increased.

The 1922 Colorado River Compact required the seven compact states to contribute equally to any future water delivery obligation to Mexico. The 1944 treaty between the two countries allocated to Mexico a guaranteed annual flow of 1.5 MAF of Colorado River water, to be reduced in the event of a serious drought in the U.S. Negotiations were concluded in haste, and several troublesome ambiguities were glossed over. Most notably, the treaty said nothing about water quality. Later, upstream development increased water consumption and spurred the construction of large dams and storage reservoirs, which reduced water in the river and increased evaporation from reservoirs, resulting in greater concentrations of salinity. Irrigators magnified the problem by returning water with high concentrations of dissolved solids.

In 1961, the Wellton-Mohawk Irrigation District in Arizona began pumping saline drainage water and releasing it into the Colorado River, just north of the

Mexico border. Mexico protested, and the U.S. and Mexico subsequently reached a series of interim agreements under which the U.S. consented to undertake salinity abatement measures. The final agreement, Minute 242, limits the increase of the River's salinity below Imperial Dam, located on the California/Arizona border. The U.S. implemented several abatement projects, including bypassing the Wellton-Mohawk return flows, building projects that intercept natural and human-made sources of salt, and constructing a large desalination plant. Additionally, in 1979, Minute 261 expanded IBWC's authority over water quality in the border region.

However, many water problems between the U.S. and Mexico remain unsettled. For instance, there is no system for dividing transboundary groundwater. As unregulated pumping continues, border cities such as El Paso and Juarez find themselves competing for dwindling supplies. The two nations developed cooperative plans to share scientific information and study the shared aquifers.

Environmental concerns are a key focus of U.S.-Mexico relations, as the once-flourishing Colorado River Delta is now only a fraction of its historic size. In 2012, Minute 319 recognized the benefits of providing water for the delta ecosystem. It allocated thousands of acre-feet for a seasonal pulse flow, along with a $21 million contribution from the U.S. to Mexico for infrastructure and environmental projects. Minute 319 was strengthened in 2017 by Minute 323, which contains more durable provisions for environmental flows and funding to restore the delta. Surabhi Karambelkar and Andrea K. Gerlak, *Collaborative Governance and Stakeholder Participation in the Colorado River Basin: An Examination of Patterns of Inclusion and Exclusion*, 60 Nat. Res. J. 1, 20 (2020).

### 2. Canada

The Boundary Waters Treaty of 1909, 36 Stat. 2448, revolutionized international relations between the United States and Canada. The treaty established the International Joint Commission, which has the power to resolve water disputes over shared resources between the two countries. Additionally, the Commission must approve any new project that would raise the water levels on either side of the international boundary.

The Columbia River Treaty resolved issues concerning storage responsibilities and Canada's right to receive benefits from U.S. water storage in Canada. Large-scale storage was most feasible in Canada, but Canada had no incentive to build it. The U.S. initially offered to pay Canada compensation for any damages caused by flooding behind the U.S. dams. However, Canada sought a share of the far more valuable downstream benefits the U.S. received from storage: increased hydroelectric power and protection from floods.

After much debate, in 1964, the two nations agreed in the Columbia River Treaty to share economic benefits equally. The treaty specifies that Canada provides 15.5 MAF of storage, the U.S. operates dams to obtain maximum benefits from the Canadian storage, and the U.S. may (for a price) demand storage releases in emergencies despite Canadian hydropower needs. In addition, Canada agreed not to divert water from the Columbia River away from the U.S. and into the Fraser River for power production in Canada. The Treaty allows either country to terminate the Treaty in 2024 if it gives notice to the other in 2014; neither did. The U.S. and Canada continue to negotiate updates to the Treaty to address future needs for flood control, power generation, and the interests of tribal and First Nations communities, as well as improve ecosystem integrity for salmon and other species. Matthew J. McKinney et. al., *A Sacred Responsibility: Governing the Use of Water and Related Resources in the International Columbia Basin Through the Prism of Tribes and First Nations,* 37 Pub. Land & Res. L. Rev. 157, 247–49 (2016).

The boundary waters of the Great Lakes have also been subject to negotiations over water quality and quantity. In 1978, the Canadian provinces and the Great Lakes states entered into several water quality agreements, which Congress subsequently ratified. https://www.ijc.org/en/what/glwqa-ijc. In 2005, the eight Great Lakes states ratified the Great Lakes-St. Lawrence River Basin Water Resources Compact, to which Congress consented. The Provinces of Ontario and Quebec have agreed to participate through a binding agreement, and not a treaty. The Compact and Agreement cover surface and groundwater and establish decision-making standards for withdrawals and consumptive uses. Importantly, it provides that withdrawals and consumptive uses may not cause "significant individual or cumulative adverse impacts to the quantity or quality of the Waters and Water Dependent Natural Resources and the applicable Source Watershed," and must comply with all applicable laws and international agreements. Pub. L. No. 110–342 § 4.11, 122 Stat. 3740. For updates, see Great Lakes-St. Lawrence River Basin Water Resources Council, https://www.glslcompactcouncil.org/water-diversions.

### 3. International Court of Justice and International Treaties

The International Court of Justice (ICJ) hears international disputes and has the authority to interpret treaties under the general principles of international law. Its jurisdiction has rarely been invoked, however, as it only has jurisdiction in cases where states consent or submit to jurisdiction. ICJ Statute, art. 36, June 26, 1945, 59 Stat. 1055, 1060, 33 U.N.T.S. 993. The decisions of the ICJ have no binding force except between the parties and in respect to the case brought before it. *Id.* art. 59. The ICJ has issued several important decisions on water allocation though none of those decisions involve U.S. waters.

The United States initially accepted the ICJ's general compulsory jurisdiction; it later withdrew its consent in 1985 after the ICJ issued an unfavorable decision following U.S. military intervention in Nicaragua. As a result, the U.S. recognizes ICJ jurisdiction only on a case-by-case basis or in specific treaties. *See* Medellin v. Texas, 552 U.S. 491, 500

(2008) (citing Letter from U.S. Dept. of State (Oct. 7, 1985), *reprinted in* 24 I.L.M. 1742 (1985)). This stance effectively limits the United States' potential liability, but also undermines the effectiveness of the ICJ and erodes faith in the rule of law. Jean Galbraith, *Rejoining Treaties,* 106 Va. L. Rev. 73, 118–19 (2020).

# CHAPTER TEN

# WATER INSTITUTIONS AND EQUITY

While much of the study of water law focuses on the rights of individuals who obtain their water directly from surface or groundwater, most domestic and commercial users, as well as a significant number of agricultural users, receive their water through public, quasi-public, or private water institutions. These range in size from small, local water delivery companies to large federal and state agencies. Examples include the Metropolitan Water District in Los Angeles, California; the Southern Nevada Water Authority, headquartered in Las Vegas, Nevada; and the for-profit American Water, headquartered in New Jersey, with offices in 15 states. One or more agencies may be involved in the process of getting water from its source to the end user's tap, encompassing water collection or extraction, transportation, storage, treatment, and distribution. Dave Owen, *Water and Taxes,* 50 U.C. Davis L. Rev. 1559, 1568 (2017).

Water organizations come in many different forms, and much of the private practice of water law involves representing these entities. Understanding their legal authorities, which can include the authority to condemn land and water, tax local property, and issue tax-exempt bonds to fund operations and infrastructure, is essential. Moreover, when an individual is part of a water organization, the individual typically does not hold the water rights. Rather, the water entity holds and manages the water right on behalf of, or in service to, those who are part of the organization.

By eliminating the need to construct their own access and water delivery systems, water organizations reduce the cost and risk of such development. Organizations can consolidate water supplies from multiple sources or water rights, thereby reducing the risk associated with relying solely on a single source. Organizations can also take advantage of special legal powers associated with their formation under state or federal laws.

Private water companies outnumber public water companies, but public systems are much larger in terms of the volume of water delivered and the number of people serviced. Most private water companies are investor-owned; a few are cooperatives or "mutuals" owned by the water users. Some water companies are considered public utilities and are regulated as such by a state agency. Elizabeth Burleson, *Distribution and Storage Organizations,* 2 Waters and Water Rights § 25.01 (Kelley, ed., 2020). There are almost 3, 300 water cooperatives in the U.S., mostly operating smaller systems for their rural and suburban consumer-members." Melissa Scanlan, Prosperity in the Fossil-Free Economy: Cooperatives and the Design of Sustainable Businesses, Chapter 10 (Yale University Press 2021).

Municipalities and local governments sometimes struggle to afford the cost of maintaining public facilities, making transfers to private suppliers seem attractive. *See* Craig Anthony Arnold, *Privatization of Public Water Services: The States' Role in Ensuring Public Accountability*, 32 Pepp. L. Rev. 561 (2005) (examining implications of state laws authorizing public entities to contract with private firms to provide water services). However, private companies or districts receive criticism for overcharging, favoring some users over others, and failing to reinvest in infrastructure. "In the United States, one investigation showed private water corporations charged consumers 59% more for water service than local government utilities." Scanlan, infra.

Whether the provider is public or private, the failure to invest in infrastructure can lead to dire public health crises, with the burdens disproportionately impacting poor and minority populations. Flint, Michigan, is a stark example. The majority of Flint's residents are African American, and nearly 50 percent live below the poverty line. In 2014, officials decided to save money by switching from the Detroit Water and Sewerage Department to the Karegnondi Water Authority, and by drawing water from the Flint River, with tragic consequences. E. coli, coliform bacteria, and alarmingly high levels of lead began to flow through Flint's taps, causing a state of emergency to be declared. The city has since been required to replace thousands of lead pipes with funding from the state, provide funding for comprehensive tap water testing, and offer health programs to help residents deal with the residual effects of the tainted water.

Researchers trace the origins of the crisis to "contemporary mismanagement, political disenfranchisement, and the region's long history of structural inequality." *See* Andrew R. Highsmith, *A Poisonous Harvest: Race, Inequality, and the Long History of the Flint Water Crisis,* 18 J. L. Society 121 (2018). Flint is not an isolated incident. There is a "growing body of evidence . . . that communities of color suffer disproportionately from water hazards." Martha F. Davis, *Let Justice Roll Down: A Case Study of the Legal Infrastructure for Water Equality and Affordability,* 23 Geo. J. on Poverty L. & Pol'y 355, 365 (2016). The lack of adequate, safe water supplies has also plagued Native American communities. Lack of access to water likely contributed to the spread of COVID-19 among the Navajo Nation by making handwashing and sanitation more difficult, and by exposing people to the virus while seeking water. Kate Harrison Belz, *How COVID-19 Spurred an Urgent and Lasting Response to the Navajo Nation's Water Crisis,* Hopkins-Bloomberg Public Health (Fall 2020). Access to safe drinking water is essential to environmental justice and is recognized as a fundamental human right. Office of the High Commissioner on Human Rights No. 15 (2003), at https://www.refworld.org/pdfid/4538838d11.pdf.

## I. WATER ORGANIZATIONS IN HISTORY

Historically, in the southwestern United States, Pueblo communities and Spanish colonial settlements distributed water through small acequias, some of which are still operational today. *See* JUAN ESTEVAN ARELLANO, ENDURING ACEQUIAS: WISDOM OF THE LAND, KNOWLEDGE OF THE WATER

(2014). The early acequia communities used communal ditches to irrigate their lands, providing models for cooperative irrigation efforts.

The Mormon pioneers were the earliest settlers to adopt and utilize cooperative methods; their strong social organization facilitated successful irrigated agriculture in the arid Utah Territory. These early enterprises evolved into a variety of public and private organizations created to deliver water. Gregory J. Hobbs, Jr., *The Role of Climate in Shaping Western Water Institutions,* 7 U. Denv. Water L. Rev. 1, 13 (2003).

Those who occupied federal public lands settled near streams where water was readily accessible for use in mining and agriculture. But as development expanded, the construction and maintenance costs of delivering water to land that lacked reliable water supplies posed a substantial obstacle. Water users first began building ditches to distribute irrigation water, but the growing number of farmers soon exhausted the supply of easily irrigable lands. Users unable to pay the cost of building their own ditches formed cooperatives to carry water over considerable distances. Often, they would construct a main canal with lateral ditches to distribute water to several farmers. They also built storage facilities to ensure water availability during times of limited supply and high demand. *Id.* at 20.

In the early 1900s, federal and state governments initiated major projects to store and transport large quantities of water, sometimes over thousands of miles, to develop the agricultural sector and provide municipal and industrial water for growing cities in the arid West.

These various water organizations are formed under state or federal law. In eastern states, where riparian rights prevailed, it was necessary to pass special laws granting authority to companies and municipalities to take water for use on non-riparian lands. In the West, both the federal and state governments adopted laws that facilitated the creation of organizations to deliver water to users and mitigate the risks associated with development. Today, about 50% of the water used for irrigation in the western United States is controlled and delivered by one form of water organization or another.

## II. STATE WATER ORGANIZATIONS

Under state law, there are five broad categories of water organizations: (1) regulatory bodies; (2) municipal water suppliers; (3) private suppliers; (4) irrigation districts; and (5) state-owned and operated water projects.

### A. REGULATORY STRUCTURE AT THE STATE LEVEL

State regulatory bodies are responsible for administering water laws, including permitting requirements for withdrawals, setting rates, planning water supply, maintaining water quality, and implementing conservation initiatives. These entities include state natural resources districts, state engineer offices, water resources departments, and local groundwater management districts. It is common for the water allocation function and the water quality function to be separated into different agencies, creating potential challenges for managing two fundamental aspects of water resources. In each state, the exact names and jurisdictional scope of the agencies may differ. The key to understanding the dynamics of water allocation and management within any given state often lies in mapping the inter-relationships of the state agencies. Three examples, from Colorado, Nebraska and Oregon are provided below.

The Colorado Water Quality Control Commission promulgates water quality standards under the Colorado Water Quality Control Act and assists in administering pollution control measures. The Colorado Division of Water Resources, also known as the Office of the State Engineer, administers water rights, represents Colorado in interstate compact proceedings, monitors stream flows and water use, approves the construction and repair of dams, and maintains databases of Colorado water information. The Colorado Water Conservation Board engages in joint federal-state water projects, water use planning and is involved in financing irrigation projects. The Ground Water Commission determines rights and regulates water use in designated groundwater basins. For details, *see* Gregory J. Hobbs, Jr., *Colorado Water Law: An Historical Overview*, 1 U. Denv. Water L. Rev. 1 (1997).

Nebraska's unique system splits governance responsibilities among the state Department of Natural Resources, which oversees appropriation permits for surface water uses; the state Department of Environmental Quality, which handles water pollution issues; and local natural resources districts (NRDs), which are responsible for groundwater management. Neb. Rev. Stat. § 46–703. In cases of over- or fully appropriated river basins, NRDs and the state develop integrated management plans to coordinate surface water and groundwater management. Neb. Rev. Stat. § 46–715. NRDs are authorized to levy certain taxes and to issue bonds to carry out their functions; however, they may not levy property taxes for state-wide purposes. Kiplinger v. Nebraska Dept. of Nat. Res., 803 N.W.2d 28 (Neb. 2011); Garey v. Nebraska Dept. of Nat. Res., 759 N.W.2d 919 (Neb. 2009).

The Oregon Department of Environmental Quality regulates water quality through various state programs and fulfills the state's obligations under the Clean Water Act. The Water Resources Commission, appointed by the Governor, regulates water quantity by setting policies, adopting rules, and delegating authority to the Water Resources Department. The Commission develops "basin programs"—place-specific strategies for managing water resources within a river basin. In each basin program, the Commission may "classify" allowable beneficial uses, detail preferences for future water use, and even withdraw streams and aquifers from appropriation if necessary to conserve the state's water resources. Or. Rev. Stat § 536.340(1), Or. Rev. Stat. § 536.410(1). With its delegated authorities, the Water Resources Department directly administers and enforces surface and ground water rights.

## B. MUNICIPAL WATER COMPANIES AND PUBLIC UTILITIES

Water utilities can be private companies or public organizations with the authority to divert, store, and distribute water to customers through constructed infrastructure and facilities. Nearly every state statutorily defines private and public water companies as "public utilities," authorizing them to provide a public service. Private companies may be corporations, partnerships, or sole proprietorships.

The water organization itself typically holds the water rights and sells the use of water to the end user. Thus, a consumer owns no water right as such, but has rights defined under state public utility law. Many states consider water to be publicly owned or held in trust by the State, so a company's fees cover water treatment and delivery, as well as facility maintenance. In exchange for an exclusive franchise or monopoly to serve an area, these utilities are subject to regulation by a state commission or board. Typical regulations require the delivery of water to all consumers within a defined service area, non-discrimination among consumers, and the submission of major transactions (*e.g.*, sale of assets, mergers, dissolutions, or acquisitions) for approval to the relevant commission or board. The most significant form of control is rate regulation. As with other types of utilities (*e.g.*, electricity and gas), rates are typically fixed to allow a reasonable profit. One benefit of public ownership is that no profit is included in the rate. In California, Proposition 218 limits rates to "the proportional cost of the service attributable to the parcel." Cal. Const. art. 13D, § 6(b)(3).

Unlike other utilities, such as electricity, natural gas, and telephone services, municipal water supply continues to be run primarily by public agencies, usually a city or municipality. Most states recognize the authority of cities to distribute water to their residents. A municipality that serves its citizens may be considered a public utility subject to regulation; however, some states exempt municipal water suppliers from public utility regulation. *See* Fla. Stat. § 367.022(2) (exempting water systems owned, operated, managed, or controlled by governmental authorities from regulation by the Public Service Commission); Bd. of County Comm'rs of Arapahoe County v. Denver Bd. of Water Comm'rs, 718 P.2d 235 (Colo. 1986) (a city is a public utility, but is statutorily exempt from Public Utilities Commission regulation); Moongate Water Co., Inc. v. City of Las Cruces, 302 P.3d 405 (N.M. 2013) (small municipalities are not subject to the Public Utilities Act).

Additionally, state statutes or constitutions often authorize municipalities to circumvent certain restraints in water law to carry out their water service responsibilities. For example, in prior appropriation jurisdictions, municipalities may be able to appropriate water in ways and for purposes not available to other users. *See* Thornton v. Farmers Reservoir & Irr. Co., 575 P.2d 382 (Colo. 1978) (state legislation could not limit city's constitutional powers by restricting condemnation of water rights to those needed for 15 years in the future). Cities can secure a water right to meet reasonably anticipated future needs, even if they cannot yet demonstrate a beneficial use for it, despite otherwise applicable laws against speculative uses. United Water and Sanitation Dist. by and through the United Water Acq. Project Water Activity Enter. v. Burlington Ditch Reservoir and Land Co., 476 P.3d 341 (Colo. 2020) Also, municipalities may not be held to the same presumptions of non-use of their water rights. City of Helena v. Community of Rimini, 397 P.3d 1 (Mont. 2017) (upholding Mont. Code Ann. § 85–2–227, which created a presumption of non-abandonment for municipal water rights).

Likewise, riparian states may allow municipalities (which are not riparians) to obtain and use rights to water on non-riparian lands. To obtain these rights, however, the municipalities will likely have to use their power of condemnation and compensate the affected riparians. *See* Schroeder v. City of New York, 371 U.S. 208 (1962) (noting that New York law gave the city power to condemn riparian rights, but finding that posting notices on trees in the general vicinity of plaintiff's property and publication in small newspapers many miles away did not constitute adequate notice required by due process). Most states allow cities to exercise their eminent domain power outside city borders to acquire needed water. *See* Matter of Vill. of Poland, 637 N.Y.S.2d 575 (N.Y. App. Div. 1996) (finding that the village had express statutory authority to condemn a parcel required for water supply even though the parcel was located mostly outside the village's boundaries).

A city can deny or withhold water service on grounds reasonably related to public health and safety. Dateline Builders, Inc. v. City of Santa Rosa, 194 Cal. Rptr. 258 (Ct. App. 1983) (city's denial of sewage service to a developer because development exceeded general growth plan was lawful); Swanson v. Marin Mun. Water Dist., 128 Cal. Rptr. 485 (Ct. App. 1976) (water district properly exercised its discretion to deny services to a new customer in anticipation of a future water shortage, but it may not limit the number of new customers solely to limit development). However, refusal to serve must not be arbitrary or malicious. County of Del Norte v. City of Crescent City, 84 Cal. Rptr. 2d 179 (Ct. App. 1999) (city's refusal to extend service outside of municipal boundaries was reasonable given financial and system capacity concerns).

Municipalities do not have a duty to serve consumers outside their boundaries, even if they have available water to do so. Fulghum v. Town of Selma, 76 S.E.2d 368 (N.C. 1953). But if they regularly do so, the majority rule provides that serving outsiders must be done on reasonable and nondiscriminatory terms. City of Texarkana v. Wiggins, 246 S.W.2d 622 (Tex. 1952); Platt v. Town of Torre, 949 P.2d 325 (Utah 1997). This does not mean that the same rates must be charged if, for example, the municipality incurs higher costs in delivering services to the area in question, provided that charging differential rates is reasonable.

Courts have split when the municipality's primary goal in denying service is to limit local development.

In some cases, development moratoria pending the municipality's good faith efforts to expand service capacity have been upheld. *See, e.g.*, *Swanson*, 128 Cal. Rptr. at 493; Kaplan v. Clear Lake City Water Auth., 794 F.2d 1059 (5th Cir. 1986). Other courts have ruled that communities may not use water connection moratoria simply to slow growth. *See, e.g.*, In re Centex Homes, LLC, 985 A.2d 649 (N.J. Super. App. Div. 2009); Robinson v. City of Boulder, 547 P.2d 228 (Colo. 1976), *overruled on other grounds*, Bd. of County Com'rs of Arapahoe County v. Denver Bd. of Water Com'rs, 718 P.2d 235 (Colo. 1986). For discussion, see *infra* Section VII.

Landowners sometimes argue that the denial of service, which leaves land with no economic value, is a regulatory taking of property compensable under the Fifth Amendment. *See, e.g.*, Lockary v. Kayfetz, 917 F.2d 1150 (9th Cir. 1990). Such a finding would depend on rather difficult proof that the plaintiff's land has no economically viable use without the water service, not that there is a mere reduction in property value. *Id.* at 1155. However, *Lockary* was a test case, and the plaintiffs ultimately dropped the suit. By the same token, the denial of a service provider's abstract right to serve a community (not actual service) is not compensable as a taking. Moongate Water Co., Inc. v. City of Las Cruces, 302 P.3d 405 (N.M. 2013).

Some states authorize the creation of special districts, variously named, to address problems related to procuring a water supply. *See* Nadav Shoked, *Quasi-Cities*, 93 B.U. L. Rev. 1971, 1986

(2013) (describing the growth and implications of special districts). Special districts are similar to "irrigation districts" that develop, transport, and distribute water to water companies, municipalities, and large consumers. Colorado uses "water and sanitation districts" as vehicles for providing water and sewage infrastructure for housing developments. *See* Colo. Rev. Stat. Title 32 (authorizing special districts); United Water & Sanitation Dist. v. Burlington Ditch Reservoir & Land Co., 476 P.3d 341 (2020) (assessing a district's applications for conditional storage for residential development). California passed enabling legislation for the creation of special districts, known as municipal water districts and replenishment districts. Cal. Water Code § 20200. These districts manage imported surface waters and local groundwater resources by administering rights determined in basin-wide adjudications, limiting pumping to safe annual yield rates, importing supplies, and preventing saltwater intrusion. Texas utilizes special districts to manage groundwater in areas of extreme scarcity, such as the Edwards Aquifer. League of United Latin Am. Citizens v. Edwards Aquifer Auth., 937 F.3d 457 (5th Cir. 2019), *cert. denied,* 140 S. Ct. 2717 (2020).

## III. PRIVATE AND QUASI-PUBLIC WATER SUPPLIERS AUTHORIZED BY STATE LAW

The three major types of private and quasi-public water suppliers are covered in this Section: for-profit carrier ditch companies, mutual ditch companies, and irrigation districts. *See* Eagle Creek Irr. Co., Inc. v. A.C. & C.E. Invs., Inc., 447 P.3d 915 (Idaho 2019).

## A. CARRIER DITCH COMPANIES

Private, for-profit companies, known as carrier ditch companies, achieved early popularity during the settlement of the West. As people settled farther from water sources, profit-seeking investors created carrier ditch companies to finance the construction of irrigation works to deliver water to individual users. The relationship between the water user and the carrier ditch company is contractual. The company typically holds the legal interest in the appropriation and, in turn, carries the water for sale to consumers who have contracted with the company. As with other types of appropriators, if the company fails to ensure continued beneficial use of the water, it could lose its appropriation. City of Westminster v. Broomfield, 769 P.2d 490 (Colo. 1989).

Nearly all carrier ditch companies failed due to infeasibility, often resulting from poor financial planning, engineering errors, or because projected uses did not materialize. Fearful that these companies would take advantage of their natural monopoly and charge excessive fees, some farmers opted for "free" groundwater or chose to dry-land farm rather than pay for water delivery. Although a few carrier ditch companies still operate in Texas, California, and Colorado, many investors recouped some of their money by selling their interests to entities that reorganized as irrigation districts or non-profit mutual ditch companies. *See, e.g.,* Glenn-

Colusa Irr. Dist. v. Paulson, 242 P. 494 (Cal. App. 3d Dist. 1925).

## B. MUTUAL DITCH COMPANIES AND IRRIGATION COMPANIES

Mutual ditches are distinct from carrier ditches in that the shareholders of mutual ditch companies are the sole owners of both the ditch and the diversion works, and they share the costs of operation without profit. In contrast, carrier ditches are entitled to reasonable returns on their investments, in addition to their costs. Left Hand Ditch Co. v. Hill, 933 P.2d 1, 3 (Colo. 1997).

Some mutual ditch companies were formed to contract with the federal government for reclamation project water. *See* Reed D. Benson, *Whose Water Is It? Private Rights and Public Authority over Reclamation Project Water,* 16 Va. Envtl. L.J. 363, 403 (1997) (describing interests of entities with reclamation contracts). The organizational structure gained popularity when western states (Arizona, Colorado, New Mexico, Utah, and Wyoming) exempted ditches, canals, and the associated works owned by mutuals from state property taxation. The Internal Revenue Code also exempts many mutual companies from income taxes. 26 U.S.C. § 501(c)(12)(A).

Mutual companies exist to serve their shareholders, essentially acting as a cooperative venture. Some states regulate them as public utilities, but most do not, as they are nonprofit corporations or associations owned by the water users themselves, theoretically making regulation less necessary.

Typically, irrigators who want to jointly construct ditches to deliver water to their fields organize a non-profit company if allowed under state law. These non-profit companies generally are not permitted to sell water to anyone but their own shareholders, nor are they required to do so. Water rights of a mutual company are typically held by the shareholders, whose quantity of rights are evidenced by shares of stock. *See* East Jordan Irr. Co. v. Morgan, 860 P.2d 310 (Utah 1993); Jacobucci v. District Court, 541 P.2d 667 (Colo. 1975). Bylaws usually restrict the shareholders from asserting and changing their water rights through the company. *East Jordan Irrig. Co.*, 860 P.2d at 321–322.

As early as the 1860s, state laws authorized the formation of irrigation companies. These companies were formed in several ways, including: by holders of water rights who transferred their rights to the newly formed companies in exchange for stock; by joint owners of a ditch who traded their interests for stock, expanded the facilities, and sold stock to others; by land developers who conveyed a share of stock along with each acre sold; and by local water users after for-profit companies serving the area declared bankruptcy.

A number of these quasi-private companies were formed under the 1894 Carey Act, 43 U.S.C. § 641, which awarded one million acres of arid federal lands to any western state that would irrigate and settle the land. Often, this goal could be accomplished by encouraging the formation of companies to build irrigation works. The state then sold the land to individuals who bought shares in a mutual ditch or irrigation company. Like carrier companies, many Carey Act corporations failed because they could not repay capital costs, and some reorganized as irrigation districts. For an assessment of Carey Act corporations in Idaho, *see* John A. Rosholt, *The Carey Act,* 53 Advocate (Idaho) 24, 26 (2010). *See also* Curry v. Pondera County Canal & Reservoir Co., 370 P.3d 440 (Mont. 2016) (dispute involving quantity of a water right for an irrigation company developed under the Carey Land Act).

### 1. Financing

Irrigation and mutual ditch companies secure revenue almost exclusively from water users (*i.e.,* by user fees and stock assessments), but some issue bonds secured by irrigation works or shareholders' lands. Assessments of stock (to pay operating costs and bond amortization) may be enforced by withholding water for non-payment. Henderson v. Kirby Ditch Co., 373 P.2d 591 (Wyo. 1962). Shares are not subject to securities laws because they represent a contractual arrangement among shareholders for the distribution and use of jointly owned water, rather than a medium of investment in an entity organized for profit. *See* Salt Lake City Corp. v. Cahoon Irrigation Co., 879 P.2d 248 (Utah 1994). *See also* Southam v. S. Despain Ditch Co., 337 P.3d 236 (Utah 2014) (rejecting challenges to a mutual company's restrictions on the transfer of shares).

## 2. Ownership of Rights

Companies typically issue shares of stock that represent the quantum of the shareholder's right to receive water. There is no obligation to serve members of the public in the service area who are not shareholders. Thayer v. California Dev. Co., 128 P. 21 (Cal. 1912). However, the district must treat all water users within the district equitably. *See* Abatti v. Imperial Irrigation Dist., 266 Cal. Rptr. 3d 26 (Cal. App. 4th Dist. 2020) (district's adoption of an apportionment prioritization order allowing non-agricultural users to receive water before agricultural users and imposing fewer usage limits on non-agricultural users violated its statutory duties).

The company holds the water rights and represents its users against other appropriators; however, each shareholder is a beneficial owner of their water rights. *Abatti*, 266 Cal. Rptr. 3d at 50; High Plains A & M, LLC v. So. Colorado Water Conservancy Dist., 120 P.3d 710 (Colo. 2005). *See* Fort Vannoy Irr. Dist. v. Water Res. Com'n, 188 P.3d 277 (Or. 2008) (stating that the district holds ownership interests in trust for its landowner-members).

## 3. Transfers

Holding water rights as shares of a ditch company stock facilitates transfers among the company's shareholders. Barton H. Thompson, Jr., *Institutional Perspectives on Water Policy and Markets*, 81 Cal. L. Rev. 671, 736 (1993). Transfers of the right to the delivery of water may be accomplished by transferring the stock certificate and recording the transfer on the company's books. Moreover, stock in mutual companies is commonly considered appurtenant to (and thus passes with) the land described on the face of the stock certificate. *See, e.g.*, Locke v. Yorba Irr. Co., 217 P.2d 425 (Cal. 1950). In some small companies, no paper shares exist because rights simply pass with the land. However, contrary presumptions may be imposed by statute. For example, Utah statutes provide that irrigation company stock does not pass with the land without an express declaration by the transferor that the stock is appurtenant. Zundel v. Ramsdell, 553 P.3d 1075 (Utah App. 2024), *cert. denied*, 564 P.3d 956 (Utah 2025) (citing U.C.A. § 73–1–10 to –11).

To protect the company against making uneconomical water deliveries to distant users, shares may be made inseverable appurtenant to land, or transfers may be subject to approval under provisions in the articles of incorporation or bylaws. The company itself may restrict transferability, *e.g.*, by requiring the company's consent. Riverside Land Co. v. Jarvis, 163 P. 54 (Cal. 1917). California recognizes companies' right to prohibit transfers to another ditch or to lands not served by an irrigation district. Consolidated People's Ditch Co. v. Foothill Ditch Co., 269 P. 915 (Cal. 1928); Bull Field, LLC., v. Merced Irrigation Dist., 301 Cal. Rptr. 3d 662 (Cal. App. 2d Dist. 2022). Although Colorado allows transfers if the transferor continues to bear a proper share of maintenance costs, Wadsworth Ditch Co. v. Brown, 88 P. 1060 (Colo. 1907), a bylaw limitation on changing the place of use to lands within a single county has been upheld. Fort Lyon Canal Co. v. Catlin Canal Co., 642 P.2d 501 (Colo. 1982). If a change in the place or type of use results in harm to others, the transfer may be restricted. City of Boulder v. Boulder and Left Hand Ditch Co., 557 P.2d 1182 (Colo. 1976). Transfers from agricultural shareholders to urban interests have also been restricted. *See* Mark Squillace, *Water Transfers for a Changing Climate,* 53 Nat. Res. J. 55, 108 (2013) (noting that "most ditch companies' water rights were granted strictly for agricultural use over a relatively small geographic area that may not include significant urban centers," and advocating for reform to allow excess distribution capacity to be made available to third parties).

### 4. Priorities

As a rule, no priorities exist among shareholders in the same water supply, so each receives a proportionate share when supplies are insufficient for all users. In other words, the rights of mutual ditch company shareholders are contingent upon the amount of water available and the number of shareholders entitled to use the water. Great Western Sugar Co. v. Jackson Lake Reservoir & Irr. Co., 681 P.2d 484 (Colo. 1984). This is true among shareholders of the same class. However, if users convey water rights to a mutual company with different priority dates, the company can issue different classes of stock related to these priorities, each with its own burdens and privileges, including priority in a water distribution schedule. Thus, a holder of shares evidencing a high priority may be assessed at a higher rate because the high priority confers greater benefits. Robinson v. Booth-Orchard Grove Ditch Co., 31 P.2d 487 (Colo. 1934). *But see* Abatti v. Imperial Irrigation Dist., 52 Cal. App. 5th 236, Cal. Rptr. 3d 26 (2020) (finding that an order prioritizing non-agricultural users over agricultural users violated the district's statutory duty to treat all water users equitably under Cal. Water Code § 22252).

### 5. Regulation

If incorporated, mutual ditch and water companies are subject to general state statutes applicable to private business organizations. Colo. Rev. Stat. Ann. § 7–42–101; N.D. Cent. Code § 61–13–02; Wyo. Stat. Ann. § 17–12–101. Some states incorporate mutual ditch companies under special statutes relating to nonprofit corporations. Utah Code Ann. § 16–6a–202; Okla. Stat. Ann. tit. 18 § 863.

A mutual ditch or irrigation company may be, but is not always, treated as a public utility subject to regulation. Public utility status may be triggered if water is provided to users other than shareholders. *See, e.g.*, Yucaipa Water Co. No. 1 v. Pub. Utils. Comm'n, 357 P.2d 295 (Cal. 1960).

## IV. QUASI-PUBLIC IRRIGATION DISTRICTS

Irrigation districts, as compared to private business organizations described above, are formed under special provisions of state law and enjoy a governmental or quasi-governmental status, yet most have a certain degree of legal autonomy that exempts them from taxation and public accountability. They are somewhat akin to local government entities but are governed by an elected board of directors that distributes water within a geographical boundary. Some perform additional functions, such as electric power generation, drainage, and flood control. Together with mutual companies, irrigation districts distribute about half of all water used in the West, giving them significant economic power and political influence. Squillace, *Water Transfers, supra,* at 65.

Irrigation districts exist under several names, including conservancy district, reclamation district, water control district, and fresh water supply district. Although they have many different organizational forms and powers, the distribution of irrigation water is common to each. As John Leshy stated, the form of these districts is "rather like snowflakes, each with its own unique form designed to meet the needs and interests of each region and its water users." Special Water Districts—The Historical Background, chapter in Special Water Districts: Challenges for the Future, Nat. Res. Law Center, U. Colo., 11, 23 (1983).

## A. FORMATION OF DISTRICTS

Beginning with California's Wright Act in 1887, all western states passed laws authorizing the formation of irrigation districts. The statutes define the organizational form, powers, and purposes of the districts. Typically, they provide for formation upon petition of local landowners or electors. Sometimes, a state court can act upon a petition after a hearing; however, an election is often required. Some types of districts may be formed by an act of the legislature without voter or landowner consent.

Reluctant property owners can be compelled to participate in a district project for the benefit of the area when the project is feasible only with full participation. Once enough voters have elected to form a district, everyone within the district's jurisdiction is subject to its authority, including its powers of taxation and eminent domain. In Fallbrook Irr. Dist. v. Bradley, 164 U.S. 112 (1896), the Supreme Court concluded that irrigation is a "public use" and thus the state can use its powers of taxation and eminent domain to bring water to the land. Since this decision, objecting landowners have been uniformly unsuccessful in challenging the formation of districts. *See, e.g.*, People ex rel. Rogers v. Letford, 79 P.2d 274 (Colo. 1938) (inclusion and taxation of non-irrigable lands with an adequate water supply and within incorporated cities did not violate due process); Crouse v. Pioneer Irr. Dist., 719 N.W.2d 722 (Neb. 2006) (the district was not required to exclude land when landowners failed to show that it was non-irrigable).

## B. BENEFITS OF DISTRICTS

Legislatures motivate communities to form irrigation districts by granting districts the benefits of governmental status, such as tax exemptions, the ability to raise capital by selling tax-exempt bonds, and the power to levy assessments against property within district boundaries. Irrigation districts may also enjoy governmental immunity from suit. *See* Love v. Harlem Irr. Dist., 802 P.2d 611 (Mont. 1990); Krenning v. Heart Mountain Irr. Dist., 200 P.3d 774 (Wyo. 2009). However, where a district is formed for a governmental purpose, such as irrigation supply, and then engages in other economic activities, it may lose status. 26 U.S.C. §§ 115, 501(c)(12). *Cf.* Hohokam Irr. & Drainage Dist. v. Arizona Pub. Serv. Co., 64 P.3d 836 (Ariz. 2003) (irrigation district could sell electricity purchased on the wholesale market because revenues reduced the cost of providing water to the district's member-farmers).

The formation of an irrigation district also facilitates participation in federal reclamation projects. John D. Leshy, *Irrigation Districts in a Changing West-An Overview*, 1982 Ariz. St. L.J. 345. The federal reclamation program began around the turn of the century. It subsidizes water projects benefiting much of the irrigated agriculture in the western United States. *See infra* Section VI.B. Initially, the government intended to operate the projects directly; however, a 1922 statute authorized contracts with irrigation districts to manage, operate, and maintain federal projects, as well as distribute water from them. 43 U.S.C. § 511. The districts usually must agree to repay project costs directly attributable to irrigation benefits, which is accomplished by imposing assessments and user charges.

## C. OWNERSHIP OF WATER RIGHTS

Irrigation districts, not their constituents, typically own the water rights they exercise. Their users' rights are essentially contractual. Fort Vannoy Irr. Dist. v. Water Res. Comm'n, 188 P.3d 277 (Ore. 2008); Eagle Creek Irrigation Co. v. A.C. & C.E. Investments, 447 P.3d 915 (Idaho 2019). However, federal or state statutes may characterize the ownership interests differently. *See* Bryant v. Yellen, 447 U.S. 352 (1980) (by requiring satisfaction of "present perfected rights," the Boulder Canyon Project Act preserved individual users' rights under state law).

## D. ELECTION OF BOARDS

Board members of irrigation districts are usually elected, though some states have different types of districts that provide for the appointment of members (*e.g.*, "conservancy districts"). The right to vote in a district election may be granted to each elector, each landowner, or weighted according to the amount of acreage owned. Irrigation district voting is not subject to the one-person, one-vote principle of the Equal Protection Clause. Ball v. James, 451 U.S. 355 (1981).

In *Ball*, a multipurpose district limited voting privileges to landowners and allowed one vote per acre of owned land. The plaintiffs, who each owned less than one acre of land, alleged that the district's broad powers (to condemn property and sell tax-exempt bonds) and non-irrigation purposes (providing hydroelectric power to metropolitan

Phoenix) affected non-landowning voters sufficiently to require that they be given voting rights. The Court disagreed, following the rule of Salyer Land Co. v. Tulare Lake Basin Water Storage Dist., 410 U.S. 719 (1973), that certain districts may limit the voting franchise to landowners. The Court in *Ball* found the voting scheme constitutional because it had a "reasonable relationship" to its statutory objective. Therefore, the district could rationally limit the vote to landowners and weigh the votes depending on acreage, as this reflected the risks each landowner could incur. As a result, a few large landowners can exert significant influence over decision-making in certain districts.

*Ball* and *Salyer* have been distinguished in cases where the nature of a water district is not directly linked with land ownership. Where the decisions of a district can substantially affect non-landowner residents, laws disenfranchising the non-landowner residents by denying them a vote in district elections may be constitutionally suspect. *See* Bjornestad v. Hulse, 281 Cal. Rptr. 548 (Cal. App. 3d Dist. 1991) (examining constitutional concerns raised by non-landowner residents who paid for a district's provision of water and sanitation services); League of United Latin Am. Citizens v. Edwards Aquifer Auth., 937 F.3d 457 (5th Cir. 2019) (upholding an apportionment plan for the Edwards Aquifer Authority as rationally related to different water interests in agricultural, spring-flow, and urban counties), *cert. denied,* 140 S. Ct. 2717 (2020).

## E. FINANCIAL ASPECTS

Irrigation districts may be empowered to raise revenue by assessing property, imposing taxes, charging users for water, and marketing other services. *See* Hohokam Irr. & Drainage Dist., 64 P.3d at 842 (Ariz. 2003) (irrigation district may sell electricity to defray costs of providing water). The state law that authorizes the district's creation specifies which of these powers the district can utilize. For instance, Colorado "conservancy districts" may tax all lands within their boundaries, but "irrigation districts" are limited to taxing irrigable lands. It is not necessary that taxes be in proportion to the benefits received. Millis v. Bd. of Cnty. Comm'rs of Larimer County, 626 P.2d 652 (Colo. 1981).

State law may allow assessments to be levied on all land in a district based on the value of the land or land classifications (*e.g.*, tract size or type of soil). Some districts impose a flat assessment for each acre. In addition to taxes and assessments, user fees are sometimes charged for water actually used.

Bonds may be issued for purposes authorized by statute, including securing indebtedness and financing district operations. Judith Basin Land Co. v. Fergus Cnty., Mont., 50 F.2d 792 (9th Cir. 1931); Sullivan v. Blakesley, 246 P. 918 (Wyo. 1926). In fact, this governmental authority stimulated the formation of most early districts.

## F. FUNCTIONS

Irrigation districts began as relatively simple organizations whose sole purpose was to deliver irrigation water; however, many districts today provide additional services, including hydroelectric power generation, operation of recreation facilities, drainage, flood control, sanitation, and municipal and industrial water supply. The Salt River Project Agricultural Improvement and Power District, serving metropolitan Phoenix, Arizona, is an example. *Ball,* 451 U.S. 355; City of Mesa v. Salt River Project Agr. Imp. & Power Dist., 373 P.2d 722 (Ariz. 1962). This district derives ninety-eight percent of its total revenue from power sales. Naturally, multiple purposes complicate administration and may lead to conflicts among different constituencies. *See, e.g.,* SolarCity Corp. v. Salt River Project Agric. Improvement & Power Dist., 859 F.3d 720 (9th Cir. 2017) (addressing solar company's complaint that new fees imposed by the Project would dissuade consumers from installing solar energy systems, in violation of antitrust laws). Irrigation users may feel, with some justification, that their interests are subordinated in disregard of the original legislative purpose for creating irrigation districts.

Although irrigation districts are commonly referred to as political subdivisions of state governments, *id.* at 723, they have both public and private attributes. Their public character grants them tax-exempt status, the power to tax, and freedom from regulatory agency interference, while their private character affords them entrepreneurial flexibility and a degree of independence from electors. In *Ball, supra,* the Supreme Court recognized that the Salt River Project Agricultural Improvement and Power District was both a "governmental entity" and a "business enterprise" in its dealings with power consumers. As the federal government's willingness to finance costly reclamation projects declines and the functions of irrigation districts move farther from their original purposes, state legislatures may reappraise the place of the districts in political and economic life.

## V. STATE OWNED AND OPERATED WATER PROJECTS

Though playing a much smaller role than the federal government, a few states engage in acquiring and distributing water supplies. The California State Water Project (SWP), in particular, plays a significant role in providing water for municipal, industrial, and agricultural uses. After being approved in 1959, the SWP developed extensive pumping and power plants, reservoirs, lakes, storage tanks, canals, tunnels, and pipelines to deliver water to 29 water suppliers and over 23 million people. Today, the SWP bills itself as the nation's largest publicly built and operated water and power delivery system. California Dept. of Water Resources, *State Water Project* (2020), https://water.ca.gov/Programs/State-Water-Project. *See* Marc Reisner, Cadillac Desert: The American West and Its Disappearing Water (1993).

Unlike the subsidies and tax revenues required by most federal projects, state projects are mostly financed by water payments and revenue bonds. Close coordination between a state and federal project is sometimes necessary. The SWP shares some facilities with the federal Central Valley Project (CVP), and water can be interchanged between SWP and CVP canals to meet peak demands. *See, e.g.* Nat. Resources Def. Council v. Haaland, 102 F.4th 1045 (9th Cir. 2024), (upholding the U.S. Fish and Wildlife Service's biological opinion on CVP's and SWP's impacts on federally listed smelt); United States v. State Water Res. Control Bd., Cal. Rptr. 161 (Cal. App. 1st Dist. 1986) (assessing water quality implications of appropriation permits for various units of CV and SWP).

## VI. FEDERAL ORGANIZATIONS

Two agencies dominate the playing field of federal institutional water law: the U.S. Army Corps of Engineers (USACE) and the Department of Interior's Bureau of Reclamation. As federal actors, the decision making processes of both agencies must satisfy all applicable law, including, most notably, the National Environmental Policy Act (NEPA), 42 U.S.C. § 4332, and the Endangered Species Act (ESA) 16 U.S.C. §§ 1536, 1538. These environmental provisions are increasingly important to the procedures and outcomes of both agencies. This section, however, focuses on provisions directly related to the authorizing legislation for these federal organizations and the allocation of water resources within the projects managed by these agencies.

## A. ARMY CORPS OF ENGINEERS

The USACE has broad congressional authority to investigate, construct, and operate water projects as part of its mission to maintain America's infrastructure in and around navigable waters. An array of federal statutes provides the USACE with significant operational discretion regarding navigational concerns and flood control. *See, e.g.*, Rivers and Harbors Act of 1899, 33 U.S.C. §§ 401, 403, 540; Water Resources Development Act, 33 U.S.C. § 1962; Flood Control Act, 33 U.S.C. §§ 701a, 2309a. Each individual USACE project also has numerous specific authorizations that provide further details on the project's purposes and scope. *See, e.g.*, Flood Control Act of 1936 § 5 (authorizing bank protection); Flood Control Act of 1938 § 2, 33 U.S.C. § 701–1(b) (approving comprehensive plan for flood control and navigation); Flood Control Act of 1944 § 7, 33 U.S.C. § 709 (specifying project operations).

The USACE is responsible for employing both engineering and economic principles to promote navigation, control floods, provide recreational opportunities, protect water quality, and store water supplies. *See* 33 U.S.C. § 701a (stating the "Federal Government should improve or participate in the improvement of navigable waters or their tributaries, including watersheds thereof, for flood-control purposes if the benefits to whomsoever they may accrue are in excess of the estimated costs"). The USACE's role as a water supplier is featured in equitable apportionment litigation between Florida,

Georgia, and Alabama. Florida v. Georgia, 585 U.S. 803 (2018) (citing River and Harbors Act of 1945, 59 Stat. 17).

The USACE also plays a large part in providing hydroelectric power and numerous other water development activities. Additionally, the USACE conducts a research and development program dedicated to water resources. USACE Institute for Water Resources, *Mission*, https://www.iwr.usace.army.mil/About/Mission-and-Vision/ (visited August 23, 2020).

In fulfilling its duty to regulate and protect the Nation's water resources, balanced with the need for sustainable development, the USACE evaluates Clean Water Act § 404 permits and determines whether to allow activities that result in dredging or placement of fill materials in the nation's waters and wetlands. 33 U.S.C. § 1344(a); *see infra* Chapter 6.II.D.2. Permits may be denied if the project is not water-dependent, and the U.S. Environmental Protection Agency may veto them if they "will have an unacceptable adverse effect on municipal water supplies, shellfish beds and fishery areas (including spawning and breeding areas), wildlife, or recreational areas." *Id.* § 1344(c). Once a valid permit has been issued, USACE enforces its terms and imposes penalties for non-compliance. *Id.* §§ 1319, 1344(n).

## B. BUREAU OF RECLAMATION

To facilitate westward expansion, Congress passed the Reclamation Act of 1902, 43 U.S.C. §§ 371 *et seq.*, authorizing the federal government to construct irrigation projects to provide more reliable sources of water. Farmers who utilized the irrigated land were expected to pay off the government's debt, interest-free, over a period of years. 43 U.S.C. §§ 461, 485h(e). Subsidized by general tax revenues, the Bureau of Reclamation embarked on an ambitious program of water development throughout the 17 western states, constructing hundreds of dams and power plants, as well as miles of canals.

Although it was successful in fostering westward expansion, the reclamation program has, in most areas, not recovered the full cost of development. *See* San Luis Unit Food Producers v. United States, 772 F. Supp. 2d 1210 (E.D. Cal. 2011) (rejecting an argument that the Bureau violated its statutory duties by failing to collect water revenues because statutes did not instruct it to recoup costs in any particular time or amount per annum), *aff'd,* 709 F.3d 798 (9th Cir. 2013). Water users within Bureau projects continue to repay the capital investments, but often at subsidized or reduced rates. The Bureau contracts with local water districts and charges them for operating and maintenance costs to cover the initial costs of its original water development. However, these contracts often do not generate sufficient funds to cover the cost of project development. 43 U.S.C. §§ 390aa *et seq.*

Like the USACE, each reclamation project has specific authorizing legislation that builds upon the foundation of the Reclamation Act of 1902 and sets forth specific direction for that particular project.

*See, e.g.,* Boulder Canyon Project Act of 1928, 43 U.S.C. § 617 *et seq.*; Central Valley Project Improvement Act (CVPIA), 106 Stat. 4706 (1992). In many specific legislative enactments in the mid-to-late 1900s, Congress mandated purposes beyond the storage and delivery of irrigation water. For example, the CVPIA Act mandates changes in management practices of California's Central Valley Project to protect, restore, and enhance fish and wildlife habitat. In addition, water rights settlements with Indian tribes may alter irrigation deliveries from federal reclamation projects. *See* Ak-Chin Indian Cmty. v. Cent. Arizona Water Conservancy Dist., 378 F. Supp. 3d 797 (D. Ariz.), *appeal dismissed*, 2019 WL 5874374 (9th Cir. 2019) (holding that the Ak-Chin Water Rights Act required a water district to deliver additional Central Arizona Project (CAP) water to the Ak-Chin tribe).

Except when state law directly conflicts with a provision of the federal reclamation law, Section 8 of the Reclamation Act, 43 U.S.C. § 383, requires federal compliance with state water law. California v. United States, 438 U.S. 645 (1978); San Luis & Delta-Mendota Water Auth. v. Haugrud, 848 F.3d 1216 (9th Cir. 2017). State law generally governs disputes between federal reclamation interests and state-sanctioned water rights, provided there is no conflict with federal law. Teas v. New Mexico, 602 U.S. 943 (2024); Wild Fish Conservancy v. Jewell, 730 F.3d 791 (9th Cir. 2013); In re Application of Denver By Bd. of Water Comm'rs, 935 F.2d 1143 (10th Cir. 1991).

Conflicts between state water law and federal law often arise when applying the Endangered Species Act (ESA) to Reclamation projects. *See, e.g.*, Natural Res. Def. Council v. Houston, 146 F.3d 1118 (9th Cir. 1998); Klamath Water Users Protective Ass'n v. Patterson, 204 F.3d 1206 (9th Cir. 1999). One major issue is whether ongoing operations of Reclamation dams trigger ESA Section 7 consultation and no-jeopardy requirements, with courts providing mixed results. *See, e.g.*, Rio Grande Silvery Minnow v. Bureau of Reclamation, 601 F.3d 1096 (10th Cir. 2010); Nat'l Wildlife Fed'n v. Nat'l Marine Fisheries Serv., 524 F.3d 917 (9th Cir. 2008). For discussion, see Reed D. Benson, *Ongoing Actions, Ongoing Issues: Trying Again to Free Federal Dams from the ESA*, 49 Envtl. L. Rep. News & Analysis 11019 (2019).

Another example of the tension between state and federal law comes from the Central Valley Project in California, where Reclamation is required to operate its facilities in conformity with California water law, based on Section 8 of the Reclamation Act. *See San Luis & Delta-Mendota Water Auth.*, 848 F.3d at 1235 (holding that the Bureau could release water from a CVP dam to protect downstream fish without seeking permission to change its state water rights permits, since California law required the Bureau to allow sufficient water to pass by the dam to maintain fisheries). Whether Reclamation can renew water supply contracts when the delivery of the water is alleged to threaten the existence of the threatened delta smelt and thus violate the ESA has been the subject of protracted litigation. *See, e.g.*, Nat. Res.

Def. Council v. Jewell, 749 F. 3d 776 (9th Cir.), *cert. denied*, 574 U.S. 1011 (2014); Nat. Res. Def. Council v. Haaland, 102 F.4th 1045 (9th Cir. 2024).

As these ESA and fisheries cases illustrate, significant controversy surrounds the environmental degradation caused by reclamation projects. The Bureau proclaims that its mission "is to manage, develop, and protect water and related resources in an environmentally and economically sound manner in the interest of the American public." Bureau of Reclamation, *Mission Statement* (last updated Feb. 12, 2025), https://www.usbr.gov/main/about/mission.html. The Bureau tries to address environmental concerns, as well as dwindling water supplies and increasing demands, through water conservation, recycling and reuse initiatives, and operational changes. *See* Reed D. Benson, *Environmental Issues in the Allocation and Management of Western Interstate Rivers,* 24 Ind. Int'l & Comp. L. Rev. 183 (2014). Invariably, however, dams and related infrastructure alter the natural flow regime of rivers, impact water temperature and dissolved oxygen levels, increase salinity, and allow contaminants to enter waterbodies, thereby jeopardizing fish and other aquatic and riparian species. Benson, *Ongoing Actions, supra,* at 11024.

Irrigators whose water deliveries are curtailed to protect at-risk species have asserted Fifth Amendment takings claims, with mixed results. *See* Tulare Lake Basin Water Storage Dist. v. United States, 49 Fed. Cl. 313 (2001); Casitas Municipal Water District v. United States, 543 F.3d 1276 (Fed.

Cir. 2008) (holding that the government's diversion of reclamation water to a fish ladder was a physical taking), *on remand,* 102 Fed. Cl. 443 (2011) (dismissing suit on ripeness grounds); United Water Cons. Dist. V. United States, 133 F.4th 1050 (Fed. Cir. 2025) (letter restricting water diversion characterized as a regulatory, as opposed to a physical taking and dismissed for lack of ripeness because district could still obtain an incidental take permit). In Baley v. United States, 942 F.3d 1312 (Fed. Cir. 2019), *cert. denied,* 141 S. Ct. 133 (2020), the court found that it was not necessary to determine whether a physical taking analysis should be applied to the dispute, because the claimants were junior to Indian tribes who held superior reserved water rights for fisheries and other purposes.

## VII. THE INTERFACE OF WATER ORGANIZATIONS AND LAND USE PLANNING ORGANIZATIONS

Historically, land use planners did not consider water scarcity a barrier to urban growth. As a practical matter, however, access to clean, reliable water supplies is a limiting factor, not just in the arid West but also in the more populous areas of the East. Developers have traditionally incorporated the cost of new roads, utilities, schools, and other infrastructure into their decisions; it only makes sense that water supplies should be factored into those decisions as well. Some states have started to incorporate the reality of water scarcity into their development plans. Several enacted "assured water supply" laws, essentially requiring developers to show that an adequate water supply exists for new communities before receiving approval for such expansion.

Arizona's program mandates that, in areas where water is being overdrafted, developers must obtain a certificate of assured water supply from the Director of Water Resources. The Arizona legislature defined "assured water supply" as "sufficient ground water, surface water, or effluent that will be continuously available to satisfy the water needs of a proposed use for at least one hundred years." Ariz. Rev. Stat. § 45–576.07(A); *see infra* Chapter 5.II.D.4.

In the 1990s, California passed a law requiring developers to show a sufficient water supply for their projects. Developers found ways around the legislation, so in 2001, the law was strengthened to require a Water Supply Assessment for developments of 500 or more residential units (or the equivalent) to prove that the project would have sufficient water for at least twenty years. Cal. Gov. Code § 66473.7. The law also restricts local cities and counties from issuing construction permits to developers unless sufficient water is available.

Some states require land use planners and water agencies to assess expected water demand and supply as a condition for approving municipal water permits or permit extensions, thereby better integrating water and land-use planning. This encourages local land-use entities to update their plans to account for new development and population increases, and to connect that data to available water supplies. *See, e.g.,* Or. Admin. R. 690–086–0010 *et seq*. (Water Management and Conservation Plans in Oregon); Oregon Dept. of Land Conservation and Dev., *Oregon's Statewide Planning Goals and Guidelines*, https://www.oregon.gov/lcd/op/pages/goals.aspx (visited August 23, 2020) (describing Statewide Planning Goals, including Goal 5—Assessing groundwater and other natural resources, and Goal 11—Public Facilities, which include water systems).

Some water districts adopted moratoria, stopping the supply of water for new development altogether. The districts' authority to do so has been upheld when water is limited. *See* Figaro v. City of Bellingham, 194 Wash. App. 1043 (2016); Bldg. Indus. Ass'n v. Marin Mun. Water Dist., 1 Cal. Rptr. 2d 625 (Cal. App. 1st Dist. 1991); Swanson v. Marin Mun. Water Dist., 128 Cal. Rptr. 485 (Cal. App. 1st Dist. 1976) (district's moratorium on new service and denial of landowner's request for pipeline extension to furnish his property with water was not unreasonable and did not invade plaintiff's constitutional rights where district's consumption was already exceeding its net safe water yield).

# INDEX

**References are to Pages**

---